Political Scandal

Political Scandal

POWER AND VISIBILITY IN
THE MEDIA AGE

JOHN B. THOMPSON

Polity

First published in 2000 by Polity Press
in association with Blackwell Publishers Ltd

Editorial office:
Polity Press
65 Bridge Street
Cambridge CB2 1UR, UK

Marketing and production:	*Published in the USA by*
Blackwell Publishers Ltd	Blackwell Publishers Inc.
108 Cowley Road	350 Main Street
Oxford OX4 1JF, UK	Malden, MA 02148, USA

ISBN 0-7456-2549-5
ISBN 0-7456-2550-9 (pbk)

A catalogue record for this book is available from the British Library.

Library of Congress Cataloging-in-Publication Data

Thompson, John B. (John Brookshire)
Political scandal : power and visibility in the media age / John B. Thompson.
p.   cm.
Includes index.
ISBN 0-7456-2549-5 – ISBN 0-7456-2550-9 (pbk.)
1. Scandals in mass media.   2. Mass media – Political aspects.   I. Title.
P96.S29.T49   2000
306.2 – dc21

00-037469

Typeset in 10.5 on 12.5 pt Plantin
by Best-set Typesetter Ltd., Hong Kong
Printed in Great Britain by TJ International, Padstow, Cornwall

This book is printed on acid-free paper.

Contents

Illustrations

Preface

In a long-running saga that veered at times into farce, Bill Clinton reminded us that scandal has become an occupational hazard of life in the public domain. Who would have imagined that, as the twentieth century drew to a close, the fate of the President of the most powerful nation in the world could be seriously thought by some to depend on whether a stain on a young woman's cocktail dress bore the traces of the President's semen? Despite the huge resources that are poured into government PR organizations today, and despite the fact that politicians and other public figures know very well that their activities will be subjected to intense media scrutiny, scandal has lost none of its capacity to disrupt the flow of events, to derail the most well-constructed plans and, from time to time, to destroy the reputations and careers of the individuals engulfed by it. Like some obstreperous child who refuses to play by the rules, scandal is an ever-present threat to those who have staked their careers on gaining power and achieving success in the games of public life.

Why have scandals acquired such salience in the public life of modern societies? Are they merely an expression of a general decline in moral standards, a weakening of our commitment to the moral codes which – or so it might seem – governed people's behaviour in the past? Or perhaps the profusion of scandals in recent years has more to do with the unscrupulous activities of journalists and others who make their living in the media and off the media, and who have found that disclosing the private lives of public figures can be a rich source of profit. Undoubtedly scandal pays, and those who have most to gain by fuelling scandal in the public domain have little reason to refrain from cashing in when the opportunity presents itself.

But we would misunderstand the nature of scandal and its consequences for social and political life if we interpreted it solely as an expression of moral decline or as a product of unscrupulous journalism. As I shall try to show in the following pages, the salience of scandals today is linked to a broader set of transformations which have shaped the modern world and which have, among other things, altered the very nature of public life. Thanks to the development of communication media, politicians and other public figures are much more visible today than they were in the past; today it is much more difficult for them to throw a veil of secrecy around activities or events which they would prefer to keep out of the public eye. The rise of scandal as a significant feature of public life is symptomatic of this broader transformation in the nature and extent of visibility which has characterized the development of modern societies. This is not to say that all scandals are shaped by the new forms of visibility which characterize modern societies: on the contrary, scandal is a pervasive and ordinary feature of social life, and conversations are commonly spiced with the little scandals of everyday life. But scandal would not have acquired the salience it has in the public domain today, and would not be such a critical factor in determining the course of political events and the fate of politicians and other public figures, were it not for the fact that scandal has become interwoven with the transformations which have shaped the modern world.

This book is a contribution to the understanding of scandal and its consequences for social and political life. It is not intended to be a general survey of the many scandals which pepper the history of modern societies, nor is it meant to be an in-depth account of the circumstances surrounding the most recent exemplifications of the genre; my concerns are more analytical than descriptive, more thematic than encyclopaedic, and my interest in the phenomenon of political scandal arose long before the forty-second President of the United States found himself in deep water with a White House intern. This book was not written as a moralizing complaint about the culture of political scandal which seems to have grown up around us, nor was it conceived as a polemical attack against those who have sought to turn scandalmongering into a way of life; I shall not sidestep the moral and practical issues raised by political scandal, but I shall try to avoid a sweeping and vituperative approach. My principal aim in this book is to develop an analytical account of political scandal and to outline a social theory of its conditions and consequences. If I take scandal more seriously than some might deem appropriate, this is because I believe that, beyond all the hype, scandal is an important social phenomenon which can have serious consequences, both for the lives and careers of the individuals involved in them and for the institutions of which those individuals are part. And I shall try to show that the significance of scandal is rooted in the characteristics of a world where visibility has been transformed by the media and where power and reputation go hand in hand. Scandal matters because, in our modern mediated world, it touches on real sources of power.

J. B. T., Cambridge, January 2000

Acknowledgements

I owe a substantial debt to numerous friends and colleagues with whom I have discussed the issues addressed in this book, and who have provided me with many helpful pointers and suggestions. I am especially grateful to Peter Burke, Anthony Giddens, David Held and Michael Schudson, who took the time to read an earlier draft of the text and gave me detailed and incisive comments; I have done my best to take account of their remarks, but any shortcomings in the final product are of course my sole responsibility. The University of Cambridge and Jesus College, Cambridge have been generous in granting me leave, without which it would have taken me much longer to write this book; I am grateful for their support. I should also like to thank Vanessa Parker for her help in preparing the text; Thelma Gilbert and Jackie Newman for their help in clearing permissions; Ann Bone for her typically meticulous copy-editing; and the many people at Polity and Blackwell – including Sandra Byatt, Gill Motley, Sue Pope, Serena Temperley, Kathryn Murphy, Leanda Shrimpton and Pam Thomas – who have helped to steer this book through the production process.

The author and publishers gratefully acknowledge the following for permission to reproduce copyright material.

Text

CBS News Archives, New York, for the extract from 'Steve Kroft interview with Bill and Hillary Clinton, 26 January 1982', as shown on *60 Minutes*.

The Free Press, a Division of Simon & Schuster Inc., for the extract from Stanley I. Kutler, *Abuse of Power: The New Nixon Tapes.* Copyright (c) 1997 by Stanley I. Kutler.

The Mirror, Syndications, for the extract 'John Profumo's letter to Christine Keeler', *Sunday Pictorial,* 9 June 1963.

New York Times, for the extract from 'Conversation between Nixon and Dean', 21 March 1973.

Illustrations

The British Library, shelfmark 108a (6); The Guardian, the Syndics of Cambridge University Library and Sportsphoto Ltd (14); © Hulton-Getty (8); Mary Evans Picture Library (1, 2); National Archives (18); National Security Archive, microfiche collection item 2614, p. 5 (20); Press Association / Topham (7); Press Association (10); Princeton University Library (3); Punch and the Syndics of Cambridge University Library (13); the Syndics of Cambridge University Library (4); the Syndics of Cambridge University Library for a print from *Complete Works of William Hogarth*, Richard Griffin and Company, London (5); Times Newspapers Ltd and the Syndics of Cambridge University Library (9); courtesy of the Washington Post (11, 12, 17, 19).

Introduction

'Domestic treachery, systematic and long-continued deception, the whole squalid apparatus of letters written with the intent of misleading, houses taken under false names, disguises and aliases, secret visits, and sudden flights make up a story of dull and ignoble infidelity . . . The popular standard of morality may not be too exalted, but even the least prudish draw the line for public men above the level of a scandalous exposure like this, and cynically observe that, when the man of loose life is found out he must take the consequences.'[1] Such was the judgement of *The Times* commenting more than a century ago on the well publicized affair of Mr Charles Parnell and Mrs Katharine O'Shea, an affair which eventually culminated in a successful divorce action brought by Captain William O'Shea on grounds of adultery. The affair might have generated relatively little interest in the press had it not been for the fact that Mr Parnell was a prominent political figure at the time. Heralded as the 'uncrowned King of Ireland', Parnell was the Member of Parliament (MP) for Cork and the charismatic leader of the Irish parliamentary party at Westminster; he was also a fervent advocate of Irish home rule, a cause to which Gladstone's Liberal Party had lent its support but which the Tories, among others, opposed. It was in this sensitive political context, where Parnell was a key power-broker at Westminster and a pivotal figure in the complex negotiations concerning the future of Anglo-Irish relations, that the affair with Katharine O'Shea suddenly burst into public view.

Charles Parnell had met Katharine O'Shea in the summer of 1880, shortly after Captain O'Shea had been elected as MP for County Clare. Captain O'Shea spent much time abroad on business, while Mrs O'Shea lived with their three children at their home, Wonersh Lodge, near Eltham in Kent. In the early 1880s Parnell became a regular visitor at Wonersh Lodge, where he frequently stayed over-night; rumours began to circulate about a possible affair, but specu-lation was curtailed by firm and repeated denials. Between 1882 and 1884 Mrs O'Shea gave birth to three daughters which Captain O'Shea apparently believed to be his own, but which were almost certainly fathered by Parnell. In May 1886 the suspicions of an affair were fuelled by the public disclosure of the fact that Parnell was effectively residing at Wonersh Lodge. Under the headline 'Mr. Parnell's suburban retreat', the *Pall Mall Gazette* reported rather dis-creetly (it was a small article on an inside page) that the MP for Cork had been involved in a collision with a market gardener's cart shortly after midnight on a Friday evening. 'During the sitting of parliament', the *Gazette* continued, 'the hon. Member for Cork usually takes up his residence at Eltham, a suburban village in the south-east of London.'[2] Discretion notwithstanding, the implications of this para-graph were perfectly clear. The article caught the attention of Captain O'Shea who, angered and no doubt embarrassed by this public comment, fired off a letter to his wife, demanding an explanation. She responded by feigning ignorance ('I have not the slightest idea what it means, unless, indeed, it is meant to get a rise out of you'), but by now their relationship was on a downward spiral. In 1889 Mrs O'Shea sold Wonersh Lodge and moved to Brighton, where she rented a house with Parnell. Captain O'Shea became increasingly estranged from his wife and on 24 December 1889 he filed for divorce, naming Charles Parnell as co-respondent.

When the trial opened on 15 November 1890, it was the focus of intense interest and was widely reported in the press. Parnell flatly denied the charge of adultery. Mrs O'Shea similarly denied the charge and filed a counter-petition, alleging that her husband had been guilty of cruelty and neglect and that he himself had commit-ted adultery (including adultery with her sister, Mrs Anna Steele); she also alleged that he had connived in her own adultery, a claim which was curiously inconsistent with her denial that she had been unfaithful. But neither Mrs O'Shea nor Parnell turned up to defend the action. Captain O'Shea's counsel, on the other hand, produced a string of letters and called witnesses – including former servants whose testimonies were reported in detail in the press – which seemed to establish a pattern of infidelity and deceit that had

1 Charles Stewart Parnell

2 Katharine O'Shea

lasted for several years. One witness, a certain Caroline Pethers who described herself as 'a professed cook', described an occasion towards the end of 1883 when Captain O'Shea had arrived unexpectedly at the door of a house in Brighton which was being rented by the O'Sheas.[3] Parnell was upstairs in the drawing room with Mrs O'Shea when the Captain arrived, but ten minutes later Parnell appeared at the front door and rang the bell, requesting to see Captain O'Shea. When asked how Mr Parnell could have managed to appear at the front door so soon after being in the upstairs drawing room, the cook explained that there were two rope fire-escapes from the window which enabled him to exit unnoticed – an observation which caused a minor sensation and gave rise to much scathing criticism in the press.

As expected, the jury found in favour of the plaintiff and granted the divorce. In the days and weeks following the trial, the press was filled with speculation about Parnell's political future. His political opponents called for his resignation and some of his erstwhile allies – including Gladstone, who feared that the divorce case would unsettle the alliance between the Irish parliamentary party and the Liberals and jeopardize the cause of home rule – urged him to retire at least temporarily from public life. Parnell's critics claimed that he no longer had the moral authority to lead a party, that he could no longer be trusted and that he had lost the respect of honourable men. Parnell refused to stand down and launched a counter-attack, issuing a manifesto which, among other things, denounced Gladstone for trying to influence the Irish parliamentary party in its choice of leader. But the tide was turning against Parnell; the alliance with the Liberals was collapsing and his position as leader of the Irish parliamentary party was becoming increasingly precarious. In December 1890, after lengthy and heated debates, the party split into two factions, one supporting Parnell and the other opposed to him. In the following months Parnell took the struggle to Ireland, where he campaigned in several by-elections, often amid angry and raucous scenes. But by now the Catholic hierarchy was also speaking out against Parnell, which greatly weakened his position in the countryside, and in each case the by-election was lost to the anti-Parnellite candidate. In June 1891 Parnell married Katharine O'Shea, but their marriage was not to last for long. Addressing a crowd in the rain in County Galway in late September 1891, Parnell caught a severe chill and died of rheumatic fever several days later, at the age of forty-five.[4]

This sorry tale of a lofty career undone by scandal has, at the end of the twentieth century, a wearisomely familiar ring. John Profumo, Jeremy Thorpe, Cecil Parkinson, Richard Nixon, Edward Kennedy, Gary Hart, Bill Clinton: these are but a few of the more recent names in a long list of public figures, many now forgotten, whose lives and careers have been indelibly marked by the scandals that unfolded around them. In our post-Profumo, post-Watergate age, we could be forgiven for thinking that political scandals are a curiosity of the late twentieth century, but the most cursory glance at the long and ignoble history of scandal would quickly dispel this impression. It could be said with some justification that, in the late twentieth century, scandal has assumed a significance in public life which out-weighs the significance it had for previous generations, for reasons we shall try to understand. But scandal was not our invention.

Despite the long history of scandal and the profusion of scan-dalous disclosures of various kinds in the public domain today, there is a dearth of serious scholarly literature on the subject. There are various anthologies which offer informative but rather light-hearted tours of a terrain strewn with the damaged reputations of politicians and other public figures;[5] and there are numerous books and arti-cles, written both by journalists and by participants who have varying degrees of insider knowledge, which retell the stories of particular scandals from different points of view. However, there are relatively few studies which seek to examine, in a more analytical fashion, the nature of scandals and the social conditions which shape their emer-gence, development and consequences.[6] Why this neglect?

No doubt scandal is viewed by many academic commentators as a subject too frivolous to warrant serious scholarly attention. Scandal should be left to the tabloid journalists and the gossip columnists; a subject so trivial – or so they might claim – does not deserve the attention of serious scholars. Others may be less dismissive, but feel nonetheless that to study scandal is to become preoccupied with the inessential. Scandal is the froth of social and political life, whipped up by unscrupulous journalists and media organizations who know how to use the sexual indiscretions of the powerful to make a quick buck. Worse still, it is a froth that obscures what really matters in social and political life, diverting public attention away from issues of real importance: unemployment, poverty, famine and civil wars in distant places are hardly mentioned in the daily press, while the sexual antics of a junior minister make front-page news.

This suspicion of scandal is understandable, but if we wish to make sense of the prominence that scandals have come to assume in the public life of modern societies then we must put these prejudgements aside. We must analyse scandal as a social phenomenon in its own right and try to understand its distinctive characteristics, without allowing our view of this phenomenon to be predetermined by a belief in its insignificance or by a sense of despair about the quality of public debate. The study of scandal may raise important questions concerning the role of the media in shaping public debate – for example, questions concerning the interests and priorities of journalists and media organizations, or concerning the legitimate scope for the journalistic investigation of the private lives of individuals who are in the public eye. But to refuse to take the phenomenon of scandal seriously on the grounds that it is a distraction from the issues that really matter (and one, moreover, whose effects on public debate can only be baneful) would be very short-sighted indeed.

In this book I shall take a different view. Rather than treating scandal as a topic too frivolous for the serious scholar or too inconsequential for the serious analyst of current affairs, I shall regard the prominence of scandal in the public life of modern societies as an issue of some significance – a puzzling issue which demands more analysis and exploration than one might at first think, and a revealing issue in terms of what it tells us about the kind of world in which we live today. I shall try to show that, if we want to understand the rise of political scandal and its prevalence today, then we must view it in relation to some of the broad social transformations which have shaped the modern world. We can understand the current prevalence of scandal only if we see that this phenomenon, which might seem so ephemeral and superficial to the impatient observer, is rooted in a series of developments which have a long history and which have had a deep and enduring impact on social and political life. Foremost among these developments is the changing nature of communication media, which have transformed the nature of visibility and altered the relations between public and private life. Scandal has become such a prominent feature of public life in modern societies primarily because the individuals who walk on the public stage are much more visible than they ever were in the past, and because their capacity to draw a line between their public persona and their private life is much more limited. In this modern age of mediated visibility, scandal is a risk that constantly threatens to engulf individuals whose lives have become the focus of public attention.

But political scandal also tells us something about the nature of power and its fragility, about the ways in which power is exercised in our societies, about the kinds of resources on which it is based and about the speed and the suddenness with which it can be lost. Political scandals can be, and often are, terrible personal tragedies for the individuals who are caught up in them; their lives may be thrown into chaos and their careers may be disrupted or even destroyed. But political scandals are not only personal tragedies: they are also social struggles which are fought out in the symbolic realm, in the to and fro of claims and counter-claims, of revelations, allegations and denials. They are struggles which have their own protagonists, each pursuing their own strategies in an unfolding sequence of events which often outpace the individuals involved and which, thanks to the media, are made available on a public stage for countless others to watch or listen to or read about. And they are struggles in which part of what is at stake are the very resources upon which power to some extent depends. Those who hold or aspire to positions of political power know very well that scandal is dangerous, that it can thwart their plans and bring their careers to an abrupt end. But scandal can also undermine their capacity to command the respect and support of others and it can have a deeply corrosive impact on the forms of social trust which underpin cooperative social relations.

In this book I shall try to develop an account of political scandal which, while attending to the specificity of particular cases and cultures, brings out the broader social and political significance of this phenomenon. I shall try to analyse the characteristics of political scandal with some degree of precision, to develop a framework for studying political scandal and to outline a social theory of scandal and its consequences. I shall also try to retrace the historical rise of political scandal, to examine the development of political scandals in different social and national contexts and to explain why political scandal has come to assume such significance in our societies today. The reader will find many specific scandals discussed in this volume, from Parnell to Profumo, from Watergate to Whitewater to the Clinton–Lewinsky affair. But this book is not a compendium of political scandals, nor does it seek to be comprehensive in its scope and coverage. My aim is to offer a systematic analysis of the phenomenon of political scandal, to relate this phenomenon to broader features of modern societies and to reflect on its implications for the nature and the quality of our public life. I shall draw on a wide range of materials, including newspaper articles and televised broadcasts, the reports of special commissions and committees of inquiry, the biographies and autobiographies of individuals whose lives were affected by scandal and the writings of journalists, political commentators, historians and other chroniclers of the past. I shall try to bring some order and clarity of thought to what is a very complex and muddy domain, to develop new ways of thinking about a phenomenon with which we are all very familiar but about which we understand very little, and to help us to see why political scandal has become, despite the efforts of our governments and their increasingly numerous spin doctors, a pervasive and ineluctable feature of our public life.

The first three chapters are concerned with the nature of scandal and its relation to the media. I begin by analysing the concept of scandal and differentiating it from related concepts, such as gossip, rumour and corruption (chapter 1). I then attempt to reconstruct the historical rise of scandal as a mediated event (chapter 2). I try to show that, while the word 'scandal' and its cognates were frequently used in pamphlets and other printed materials from the sixteenth century on, it was only in the late eighteenth and nineteenth centuries that a distinctive type of scandal event – what I call 'mediated scandal' – began to emerge. This development was linked to certain broader social transformations, including the changing economic bases of the media industries and the rise of journalism as a profession. In chapter 3, I focus on this distinctive type of event, mediated scandal, and analyse its principal characteristics.

This conceptual and historical analysis provides the basis upon which I begin, in chapter 4, to examine in detail the phenomenon of political scandal. I develop an account of power and of the political field which enables us to understand why scandal matters in politics, and why the consequences of scandal can be so devastating for those who hold or aspire to positions of political power. I also try to explain why political scandals have become increasingly prevalent in countries such as Britain and the United States in recent decades. I argue that the growing prevalence of political scandal is linked to certain changes in the media and in the culture and practice of journalism, but it is also linked to certain broad changes in the social context of politics. The social transformations of the postwar period have gradually weakened the 'ideological politics' of the traditional class-based parties, with their strongly opposed belief systems and their sharp contrasts between left and right, and have created the conditions for a growing emphasis on what I shall call the 'politics of trust'. With the weakening of the forms of reassurance once provided by the long-standing social affiliations of political parties, many people look increasingly to the credibility and trustworthiness of political leaders or aspiring leaders, to their character (or lack of it), as a means of assessing their suitability or otherwise for office. And in these circumstances, scandal assumes a newly potent and self-reinforcing role as a 'credibility test'.

In chapters 5, 6 and 7, I develop an analytical framework for studying political scandal and put it to work in reconstructing the development of political scandals in Britain and the United States. I distinguish between three basic types of political scandal – sex scandals, financial scandals and what I call 'power scandals' – and devote a chapter to each. Guided by this analytical framework and by the account of scandal developed in earlier chapters, I look back at some of the earlier scandals, like the Marconi affair in Britain and the Teapot Dome scandal in the United States, which were significant in their time but which have now largely faded from the collective memory; I examine some of the great scandals of more recent decades, such as Profumo and Watergate, which have helped to shape the political cultures of our time; and I analyse some of the scandals which have dominated the headlines in recent years, like the cash-for-questions scandal in Britain and the various scandals which have dogged the Presidency of Bill Clinton. While attending to the very specific and often labyrinthine details of these events, I also try to show that they generally display the characteristics of scandals as mediated events and that they form part of distinctive political cultures of scandal.

In the final chapter I stand back from the detail and offer a more reflective view on political scandal and its consequences for social and political life. I consider various theories of scandal – some drawn from the relatively limited literature on the topic, others invented as more-or-less plausible possibilities – and I try to show why they won't suffice. I then develop an alternative account – what I call simply a social theory of scandal – which treats scandals as struggles for symbolic power and which highlights the connections between scandal, reputation and trust. In the conclusion I address some questions of a more normative kind about how we should assess the contribution that scandals have made, and are likely to make, to the quality of our public life.

I should add one important qualification. Most of my examples will be drawn from the Anglo-American world – and, for the most part, from the relatively recent political history of Britain and the United States. However, this restriction is not meant to imply that scandal is a recent phenomenon (it isn't), that all scandals are political (they aren't), or that Anglo-Saxons have a peculiar propensity for scandal (they don't). One of the striking things about scandal is its omnipresence: from Japan to Brazil, from Italy to Argentina, scandal is a phenomenon that features prominently in the public domain. Of course, different national cultures of scandal have different characteristics; sex scandals typically play a much less significant role in French or Italian political life than they do in Britain, for example, while political scandals in France and Italy have been concerned primarily with corruption and the abuse of power.[7] But there are relatively few countries where scandal in some form has not become a significant feature of contemporary political life. So the fact that my examples are drawn primarily from the Anglo-American world should not be construed as a comment on the political geography of scandal. And if my account of scandal and its consequences is sound, then it should help us to understand not only the scandals which have occurred in the Anglo-American world, but also those which have loomed large in the public domain elsewhere.

1

What is Scandal?

Today we take the notion of scandal for granted. 'Scandal' is a word that appears frequently in the press and slips effortlessly from the lips, and yet, like many of the words we use, its origins are obscure and its meaning is hard to pin down. How many of the journalists who are so quick to proclaim a scandal could, if asked, provide a definition of 'scandal' or delineate the characteristics of the phenomenon whose existence they are claiming to unveil? How many of the readers or viewers who are bombarded with an incessant flow of scandalous revelations could, if asked, explain what makes an event a 'scandal', or what distinguishes revelations which are 'scandalous' from those which are not?

In fact, the concept of scandal is much more complicated than it might at first seem. This is a concept with a long and complex history, in the course of which some connotations have been preserved and others discarded. It is a concept which conveys much more than it clearly articulates and which, when one begins to unravel the layers of meaning, reveals some unusual traits. In this chapter I shall retrace this history and begin to analyse some of the characteristics of this much used but seldom studied notion.

The Concept of Scandal

The word 'scandal' and its cognates became increasingly common in European languages from the sixteenth century on, but the word has a much longer history which can be traced back to Greek, Latin and early Judaeo-Christian thought. In terms of its etymological origins, the word probably derives from the Indo-Germanic root *skand-*, meaning to spring or leap. Early Greek derivatives, such as the word *skandalon*, were used in a figurative way to signify a trap, an obstacle or a 'cause of moral stumbling'.[1] The word was first used in a religious context in the Septuagint, the Greek version of the Old Testament. The idea of a trap or an obstacle was an integral feature of the theological vision of the Old Testament. It helped to explain how a people indissolubly linked to God, to *Yahweh*, could nonetheless begin to doubt Him and to lose their way: such doubt stemmed from an obstacle, a stumbling block placed along the path, which was intended to test people and to see how they would react.[2] This idea was expressed in the Septuagint by the word *skandalon*.

The notion of a trap or obstacle became part of Judaism and of early Christian thought, but it was gradually prised apart from the idea of a test of faith. Christian theology placed more emphasis on individual culpability; if individuals stumble and lose their way, if they commit sinful acts, this may stem from their own inner weakness and fallibility. Moreover, with the development of the Latin word *scandalum* and its diffusion into Romance languages, the religious connotation was gradually attenuated and supplemented by other senses. Hence the word *escandre* in Old French (eleventh century); this was derived from *scandalum* and meant both 'scandal' and 'calumny'. Hence also the Old French word *esclandre*, from which the English word *slander* was derived.

The word 'scandal' first appeared in English in the sixteenth century. Similar words appeared in other Romance languages at roughly the same time (in Spanish, *escándalo*; Portuguese, *escandalo*; Italian, *scandalo*). 'Scandal' was derived from Latin, and probably from the French word *scandale*, which had been introduced to convey the strict sense of the ecclesiastical Latin term *scandalum*, as distinct from the senses that had been developed by *esclandre*. The early uses of 'scandal' in the sixteenth and seventeenth centuries were, broadly speaking, of two main types.[3] First, 'scandal' and its cognates were used in religious contexts to refer (Ia) to the conduct of a religious person which brought discredit to religion, or (Ib) to something that hindered religious faith or belief (as in Francis Bacon's phrase of 1625, 'Heresies and Schismes, are of all others, the greatest scandals'). The latter usage (Ib) retained the sense, derived from the original Greek, of scandal as a moral lapse or stumbling block.

The second type of usage was more secular in character and had to do with (IIa) actions or utterances which were scurrilous or defamatory, (IIb) actions, events or circumstances that were grossly discreditable, or (IIc) conduct which offended moral sentiments or the sense of decency. The use of 'scandal' to refer to actions and utterances which were defamatory attests to the fact that, in terms of their etymological origins, 'scandal' and 'slander' were very close. Both words were used to refer to damaging or defamatory imputations, but they differed in one important respect: the use of 'scandal' did not necessarily imply, whereas the use of 'slander' did, that the imputations made were false.

In using 'scandal' to refer to grossly discreditable actions, events or circumstances (IIb), or conduct which offended moral sentiments or the sense of decency (IIc), the word acquired an additional and important connotation. In its religious uses, 'scandal' involved a relation between an individual or individuals (believers or waverers) and a religious doctrine or system of belief. In the use of 'scandal' to refer to damaging or defamatory imputations, the word implied a relation between individuals (the individual whose words defamed another, and the individual who was defamed). But when 'scandal' was used to describe grossly discreditable actions, events or circumstances, or to describe conduct which offended moral sentiments or the sense of decency, a different kind of relation was implied – a relation between, on the one hand, an individual or humanly created event or circumstance and, on the other hand, a social collectivity whose moral sentiments were offended.[4] Scandal thus involved a transgression of moral codes which could be, but did not have to be, religious in character, and with reference to which the action or event was denounced.

It is the latter presuppositions which underlie the most common uses of the word 'scandal' today. While the word continues to have some use as a specialized religious term,[5] 'scandal' is used today primarily to describe a broader form of moral transgression, one which is no longer linked specifically to religious codes. What is a scandal in this modern sense of the term? As a working definition, we could say that *'scandal' refers to actions or events involving certain kinds of transgressions which become known to others and are sufficiently serious to elicit a public response.* To be more precise, I shall suggest that, in its current usage, 'scandal' refers primarily to actions, events or circumstances which have the following characteristics:

1   their occurrence or existence involves the transgression of certain values, norms or moral codes;

2   their occurrence or existence involves an element of secrecy or concealment, but they are known or strongly believed to exist by individuals other than those directly involved (I shall refer to these individuals as 'non-participants');

3   some non-participants disapprove of the actions or events and may be offended by the transgression;

4   some non-participants express their disapproval by publicly denouncing the actions or events;

5   the disclosure and condemnation of the actions or events may damage the reputation of the individuals responsible for them (although this is not always or necessarily the case, as we shall see).

Let us briefly examine each of these characteristics in turn.

(1) The most obvious aspect of scandal is that it involves actions or events which transgress or contravene certain values, norms or moral codes. Some form of transgression is a necessary condition of scandal: there would be no scandal without it. But the nature of the transgression is also important: not all transgressions are scandalous (or even potentially so). Some transgressions may be too minor to constitute a scandal, while others may be too serious. It is doubtful, for example, whether a minor traffic offence (such as a parking ticket) would form the basis for a scandal (although one could imagine circumstances in which a minor offence of this kind was part of the unfolding plot of a scandal); on the other hand, we would hesitate to describe an act of large-scale genocide, such as that involved in the Holocaust or in the massacre carried out by the Khmer Rouge, as a 'scandal', since the scale and the horror of these calamities are far in excess of the kind of offence we normally associate with this term. In the first case, 'scandal' seems too strong a word to use, in the second case it seems too weak. As Anthony King rightly remarks, 'scandals occupy a sort of middle ground of impropriety':[6] they involve transgressions which are sufficiently serious to elicit the disapproval of others but which fall short of the most heinous crimes. There is, of course, a good deal of greyness here; the kinds of transgressions that could be regarded as scandalous behaviour shade into trivial misconduct at one extreme and serious crime at the other. But it is part of the concept of scandal that it occupies this middle zone of moral impropriety and that the boundaries of this zone are ill-defined.

While scandal necessarily involves some form of transgression, it is obvious to the most casual observer that there is a great deal of diversity and cultural variability in the kinds of values, norms and moral codes which are relevant here: what counts as scandalous activity in one context – say, extramarital affairs among members of the political elite – may be regarded as quite acceptable (even normal) elsewhere. Values and norms have differing degrees of what we could call 'scandal sensitivity', depending on the social-historical context and the general moral and cultural climate of the time, and depending on the extent to which these values and norms matter to particular individuals or groups. The values or norms must have some degree of moral force or 'bindingness' for some individuals or groups. The disclosure of Parnell's relationship with Katharine O'Shea was particularly damaging for the man and his cause precisely because it occurred in the context of late Victorian Britain, when adultery was condemned by an influential moral purity lobby within Gladstone's Liberal Party, with which Parnell was temporarily allied in the pursuit of home rule, and by the Catholic Church, which remained a powerful force in Ireland.

Despite the evident diversity and variability in the kinds of values and norms which are relevant to scandal, there are nevertheless certain types of norm which are more scandal-sensitive than others. Norms and moral codes governing the conduct of sexual relations are particularly prone to scandal: to transgress these norms is, depending on the context and the specific circumstances of the individuals concerned, to run a serious risk of scandal. Norms governing financial transactions are also scandal-prone, especially when the transgressions involve serious fraud or corruption. A third type of scandal-sensitive norm is represented by the rules, conventions and procedures which govern the pursuit and exercise of political power. Scandals stemming from the transgression of this type of norm are probably most likely to occur in liberal democratic regimes, since these regimes place particular emphasis on a formal system of laws and other procedures which are intended to apply equally and in principle to all individuals.[7] Sex, money, power: it is little wonder that scandal has exerted, and no doubt will continue to exert, a degree of fascination for the popular imagination.[8]

Just as certain norms are more scandal-sensitive than others, so too some individuals are more likely to be confronted by scandal on the occasion of transgressing a norm. All citizens may be formally equal before the law, but not all transgressors are equal in the court of scandal. This differential susceptibility to scandal is linked in part to the degree of visibility of the individuals concerned: some individuals, by virtue of their positions, achievements or responsibilities, are much more visible than others, and therefore more vulnerable to scandal in the event of transgressing a norm. Moreover, individuals who, by virtue of their positions or affiliations, espouse or represent certain values or beliefs (such as those advocated by a religious organization or a political party) are especially vulnerable to scandal, since they run the risk that their private behaviour may be shown to be inconsistent with values or beliefs which they publicly espouse. Many scandals involve an element of hypocrisy – not just the transgression of norms, but the transgression of norms by individuals whose practice falls short of what they (or their organizations) preach for themselves and others. I shall describe this circumstance as 'Parkinson's predicament', in reference to the British Conservative MP and former party chairman who found himself in the uncomfortable position of leading a party committed to the defence of traditional family values at the very moment when his long-standing affair with his former secretary became public.[9]

I have suggested that the transgression of a value or norm can give rise to a scandal only if the value or norm has some degree of moral force or 'bindingness' for some of the individuals who become aware of its transgression. But this is not to say that these values or norms are likely to elicit general or widespread consensus in a particular social-historical context, nor is it to say that these values or norms are matters about which most people feel very strongly and with reference to which they organize their own lives. On the contrary, values and norms are often contested features of social life, adhered to by some individuals and groups and rejected (or simply ignored) by others. Hence scandals are often rather messy affairs, involving the alleged transgression of values and norms which are themselves subject to contestation. Moreover, values and norms are always embedded in relations of power; they structure social life in ways that permit certain kinds of activity and exclude or forbid others (or force them underground). In many cases, scandals are not just about actions which transgress certain values or norms: they are also about the cultivation or assertion of the values or norms themselves. Thus the making of a scandal is often associated with a broader process of 'moralization' through which certain values or norms are espoused and reaffirmed – with varying degrees of effectiveness and good faith – by those who denounce the action as scandalous.

Scandals are often messy affairs not only because values and norms are commonly contested, but also because, in the unfolding sequence of actions and utterances that constitute a particular scandal, a multiplicity of values and norms may be implicated. A specific transgression may lie at the origin of a particular scandal and may form the initial focus of attention, but the unfolding sequence of actions and events may shift the focus elsewhere, in such a way that the initial transgression is overshadowed by other concerns. Many scandals involve what I shall describe as 'second-order transgressions' where attention is shifted from the original offence to a series of subsequent actions which are aimed at concealing the offence. The attempt to cover up a transgression – a process that may involve deception, obstruction, false denials and straightforward lies – may become more important than the original transgression itself, giving rise to an intensifying cycle of claim and counter-claim that dwarfs the initial offence and fuels a scandal which escalates with every twist. It seems clear that second-order transgressions played a crucial role in the downfall of John Profumo, the British Secretary of State for War whose political career was destroyed by the scandal surrounding his affair with Christine Keeler. On 22 March 1963, amid much speculation in the press and at Westminster, Profumo made a personal statement in the House of Commons in which he explicitly denied that he had been involved with Christine Keeler ('There was no impropriety whatsoever in my acquaintanceship with Miss Keeler'), a denial that he was subsequently obliged to retract in his letter of resignation. The murky details of Profumo's affair with Christine Keeler were overshadowed by the clear-cut seriousness of this second-order transgression, a point brought out rather well in an anonymous rhyme:

> Oh what have you done, cried Christine,
> You've wrecked the whole party machine!
> To lie in the nude may be terribly rude,
> But to lie in the House is obscene.

Why do second-order transgressions become so important in the social dynamic of scandal? Partly because they may involve the violation of codes of behaviour which are regarded as *constitutive* of particular forms of life. Profumo's affair with Christine Keeler was an ill-judged action which seriously compromised his position as Minister of War (unfortunately for Profumo, Christine Keeler was sleeping with a Soviet naval attaché at the same time), but his position was ultimately undermined by the fact that he explicitly lied to his colleagues while making a personal statement in the House, thereby breaching the codes of behaviour which are constitutive of parliamentary life.[10] In some cases the codes of behaviour which are constitutive of forms of life are embodied in rules of law which govern the administration of justice. When second-order transgressions involve the violation (or suspected violation) of rules of law of this kind, the consequences may be particularly serious. That Watergate had such disastrous consequences for Nixon and his administration was due not so much to the discovery of the original break-in at the Democratic National Committee headquarters, but rather to the fact that, in the course of subsequent inquiries, it became increasingly clear that the White House was involved in a cover-up and that the President himself had sought to obstruct the FBI's investigation of the affair. Nixon was undone by a second-order transgression which, by obstructing the administration of justice, amounted to an impeachable offence.

(2) A second characteristic of scandal is that the actions or events typically involve a degree of concealment or secrecy, but they nevertheless become known by others, or are strongly believed by others to exist. Individuals who engage in activities which transgress some norm or code will commonly seek to conceal them from non-participants, or at least to prevent the activities from becoming generally known. But if knowledge of the transgression is restricted to those who are directly involved in it – if, for example, knowledge of an illicit affair is shared only by the two lovers, or knowledge of a bribe is restricted to the giver and the recipient – then a scandal will not and cannot arise. To become a scandal, an action or event must be known about by others, or strongly and plausibly believed by others to exist (in practice, most scandals involve a *mélange* of facts and more or less well founded suppositions). Unlike corruption and bribery, which can exist (and often do exist) when others do not know about them, scandal is always to some extent a 'public' affair.

Since non-participant knowledge is a necessary condition of scandal, scandals are often characterized by a *drama of concealment and disclosure*. Individuals involved in potentially scandalous activities may devote a great deal of effort to developing strategies of concealment, that is, methods of ensuring secrecy or of coping with unintended and unwanted revelations, since they know that the emergence of a scandal is dependent on the knowledge of others. On the other hand, when non-participants suspect the existence of potentially scandalous activities they may redouble their efforts to uncover the truth: the mere whiff of scandal is often sufficient to drive a scandal forward.

This enables us to see that scandal involves more than the actions and events which are, in any particular case, its principal focus, and more than the values and norms which these actions transgress. Scandal also involves (a) a degree of public knowledge of the actions or events, (b) a public of non-participants who know about them, and (c) a process of *making public* or *making visible* through which the actions or events become known by others. Activities that remain invisible to non-participants cannot, *ipso facto*, be scandalous. They can, at most, be potentially scandalous, and the transition from a potential to an actual scandal requires, among other things, a process of making public. This is one reason why communication media play a crucial role in many scandals, as we shall see. It is also one of the reasons why scandals often involve an element of deep embarrassment and shame on the part of the individuals whose actions lie at the centre of the unfolding drama, and who suddenly find that activities which were carried out in secrecy or privacy are suddenly opened up to the gaze of others.

(3) Scandal not only presupposes some degree of public knowledge: it also presupposes some degree of public disapproval. In order for a scandal to emerge, some non-participants must feel, on hearing or learning about it, that the transgression is (or was) a morally discreditable action. Non-participant knowledge of the action coincides or overlaps with disapproval of it; epistemic and evaluative judgements are fused together in the responses of some individuals who learn or hear about the transgression.

Undoubtedly there are some occasions when individuals not only disapprove of an action but are also offended or even shocked by it. The action may flout values or norms which are so fundamental to their sense of self and well-being that they are deeply upset – truly 'scandalized' – by it. But reactions of this kind are the exception rather than the rule, and they are probably increasingly rare in many Western societies today, as the pluralization of value systems and the weakening of some traditional norms have gradually attenuated their moral force. Today many scandals involve the transgression of values and norms which have become fairly routine features of social life. They are adhered to loosely (if at all) by most people, and may be adhered to more in principle than in practice. They are token values and nominal codes of behaviour to which many people pay lip service but which, when it comes to making key decisions, play a relatively marginal role in their lives. When scandals involve the transgression of token values and nominal codes of this kind, they have a certain formulaic character and a certain moral vacuousness. Genuine scandals they may be (and serious consequences they may have), but the values and norms whose transgression lies at the heart of these scandals may have little practically binding significance for most people. This is why some scandals can easily take on the appearance of a low-budget bedroom farce: few people are shocked or offended by what they hear, but many are mildly amused by the sight of a minister on stage with his pants down.

(4) For a scandal to arise, it is not sufficient for some individuals to disapprove of the actions or events: it is also necessary for some to *express* their disapproval to others. A transgression that became known to others but elicited no response from them would not give rise to a scandal, since scandal is shaped as much by the response of others as it is by the act of transgression itself. If no non-participants are sufficiently interested in or concerned about a transgression to express their concern to others, then a scandal will not arise. The phenomenon of scandal is constituted by both acts and speech-acts: by acts of transgression and by the speech-acts of others who respond to these acts with suitable forms of expression.

The responses of others thus have what we could call, following Austin, a performative role.[11] These responses do not merely describe a state of affairs – a scandal that exists independently of them: on the contrary, in uttering these responses individuals are performing actions which are partly constitutive of the state of affairs. The responses of others are integral to the scandal, not retrospective commentaries on it. In short: no responses, no scandal.

What forms of expression by non-participants are suitable for accomplishing this performative role? Although these forms can be extremely varied, there is one feature they share in common: they are all forms of what I shall call 'opprobrious discourse'. This is a kind of moralizing discourse which reproaches and rebukes, which scolds and condemns, which expresses disapproval of actions or individuals. It is discourse which carries the implication that the actions are shameful or disgraceful, and hence carries the implication that the actions bring shame, disgrace or discredit to the individual or individuals who performed them. It is a discourse which can stigmatize.

Opprobrious discourse can express differing degrees of reproach, from mild scolding and faint, even teasing disapproval to unrestrained moral outrage. It can also be expressed in different ways and contexts. But for a scandal to emerge, at least some of the opprobrious discourse of non-participants must assume the status of public speech-acts: that is, it must be uttered (or otherwise produced) in a way that can be heard (or otherwise received) by a plurality of others. If the opprobrious discourse exists only as a private communication between friends or acquaintances, uttered *sotto voce* and in confidence, then it may constitute gossip or rumour or some other form of privately articulated belief, but it will not constitute a scandal. Of course, gossip and rumour can fuel scandal, and many scandals are in fact preceded by rumours which circulate among interested parties, such as journalists and politicians, or simply among individuals who are in the know. But a scandal can arise only if the tacit agreement which keeps gossip and rumour at the level of a private communication among friends or acquaintances is broken and the revelations, together with some suitable forms of opprobrious discourse on the actions or events in question, are articulated in public – that is, in a manner which is to some extent 'open' and available for a plurality of others to see or hear or hear about.

Since scandal presupposes the public articulation of opprobrious discourse, it lends itself with particular ease to the use of communication media. Of course, opprobrious discourse can be articulated publicly without using the media (in a speech at a public meeting, for instance), and the use of communication media does not by itself ensure that the articulation of discourse will be public (a telephone conversation can remain private and confidential, provided that certain precautions are taken). Nevertheless, by using communication media such as printed materials (newspapers, magazines, pamphlets, etc.) or electronic media (from radio and television to the internet), individuals can express opprobrium in ways which, by virtue of the medium itself, endow the expressions with the status of public speech-acts: these are speech-acts which, thanks to the nature of the medium, circulate in a sphere which is no longer localized in time and space. These mediated speech-acts are not restricted to the spatial-temporal contexts within which the original transgressions took place but are available for many people – potentially millions of people – to see or hear or read. Mediated scandals, by their very nature, are not localized affairs. When a scandal breaks, it can spread quickly and uncontrollably, because the speech-acts and images which fuel the scandal can be transmitted across large distances instantaneously (or virtually so), and because the networks of communication are so ramified and complex that it is extremely difficult to contain damaging revelations.

(5) The final characteristic of scandal has to do with the reputations of the individuals involved. Since scandals involve the disclosure of hitherto covert activities which transgress some values or norms, and whose disclosure elicits opprobrious discourse of varying kinds, they may (and often do) seriously damage the reputations of the individuals whose actions lie at the centre of the scandal. I say 'may' advisedly: the damage or loss of reputation is neither a necessary feature nor an inevitable consequence of scandal (indeed, there are cases where individuals' reputations have been appreciably enhanced). But the damage or loss of reputation is a *risk* which is always present as a scandal erupts and unfolds. We could put it like this: scandal is a phenomenon where individuals' reputations are at stake. Of course, the threat to reputation is not the only issue at stake in many scandals. If the covert activities involve the contravention of legally binding norms or formally established procedures, the individuals may also face criminal prosecution and/or dismissal from their posts. In the most serious scandals (Watergate, the Iran-Contra affair, the corruption scandals in Italy, the Lockheed scandal in Japan, etc.) the revelations often result in an array of criminal prosecutions, sackings and broken careers; for the individuals involved, the marring of reputations is by no means their only concern. Nevertheless they know very well that, just beyond the legal wrangling, just above the fray and fury of courtroom proceedings and special congressional inquiries, lurks the question of reputation, of one's 'name' – that is, one's standing as a person of honesty, integrity and good character.

From this viewpoint one can understand why scandals are often characterized by what we could describe as 'struggles for "name"'. Knowing that their reputations are at stake, the individuals at the centre of a scandal may make a concerted effort to defend their reputations, or clear their names, by launching a counter-attack. They can do this in various ways. They can threaten legal action and, if necessary, seek to resolve the issues in a court of law. Whether this is a prudent strategy depends very much on the nature of the case and the strength of the evidence available to their opponents. Alternatively individuals can simply reject the allegations and deny that the transgressions took place, or deny that they were involved. But this too can be a risky strategy, since it can shift the focus of attention to the possibility of second-order transgressions which, if demonstrated, can be even more damaging for an individual's reputation than the disclosure of the original offence. A different strategy is to go for the moral high ground, to appeal to higher values in the name of which the original actions were carried out, in the hope of persuading others that the ends justified the means. This was the strategy used by Oliver North who, while admitting his involvement in the Iran-Contra affair, sought (not without some success) to redeem his reputation by showing that his illicit activities were justified – morally if not legally – by the resolute pursuit of a higher good (the defeat of the communist threat and the maintenance of US national security in a dangerous world). Another strategy sometimes used is the public confession, where individuals openly acknowledge their guilt in the hope that honesty in the face of adversity will elicit sympathy from others – the path followed, with varying degrees of straightforwardness and success, by the leader of the Liberal Democratic Party in Britain, Paddy Ashdown, when news broke of an affair with his former secretary,[12] by Prince Charles and Princess Diana when faced with allegations about their extramarital affairs, and by Clinton when faced with allegations about a long-standing affair with Gennifer Flowers.

In a later chapter I shall try to show that these struggles over reputation are not just a matter of honour and personal pride, for what is at stake in these struggles is, among other things, a certain form of power and the resources upon which it depends. Reputation is a kind of resource that individuals can accumulate, cultivate and protect. It is a valuable resource because it enables individuals to exercise what I call 'symbolic power', by which I mean the capacity to use symbolic forms to intervene in and influence the course of actions and events.[13] We all exercise symbolic power in our daily lives; we constantly use symbolic forms to influence others and to shape the course of events. Reputation is one of the resources that we can draw on in order to pursue our interests and aims in this way. It is a scarce resource that can take a long time and a great deal of effort to accumulate; it is also a fragile resource that can be quickly depleted, and that must be defended against incursions or events which threaten to diminish or destroy it. Scandals are events which threaten to do just that. The individuals who find themselves embroiled in scandal know very well that what is at stake is not just their pride but also their power, their capacity to draw on a reputation or good name in order to command the respect of others and to pursue their interests and aims.

On the basis of this analysis of the concept of scandal, we can distinguish, in a preliminary way, between two models of scandal. In the simplest case (figure 1.1), a concealed act of transgression is publicly disclosed or publicly alleged to have occurred, and the public disclosure and/or allegations elicit public expressions of disapproval. But in more complex cases (figure 1.2), the disclosures and allegations are met by denials and counter-allegations from the individuals involved, which in turn fuel further investigations and revelations and give rise to a series of second-order transgressions. In these more complex cases, the unfolding of the scandal becomes a cat-and-mouse game in which, with every denial, the stakes grow ever higher, and in which the second-order transgressions may come to assume much greater significance than the original offence.

In practice, most scandals are complex events which involve a variety of contingent factors and circumstances, and which rarely concur with the simple linear pattern of the first model. Some scandals may involve the public disclosure of concealed transgressions,

Figure 1.1 The basic ingredients of scandal

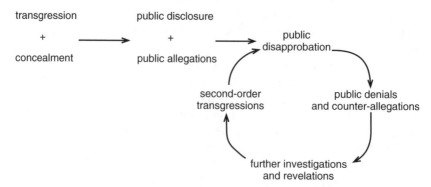

Figure 1.2 Some elements of more complex scandals

while others may be sparked off by public allegations about transgressions which may or may not have occurred. In most major scandals, disclosures and allegations of wrongdoing are met by denials and counter-allegations, thereby setting in motion the circular process highlighted by the second model. But even this more complex model is at best a rough approximation, and most actual scandals typically involve a variety of other elements and details which add greatly to their complexity. The unfolding of the scandal becomes a kind of narrative with multiple plots and subplots, many of which fizzle out but some of which may evolve into minor scandals of their own ('subscandals') or even into separate 'offshoot' scandals which are only tangentially related to the original scandal – in the way, for example, that the Clinton–Lewinsky scandal emerged out of quite separate investigations relating to the Paula Jones sexual harassment case and to a failed real estate deal in Arkansas. These are issues to which we shall return in later chapters.

Gossip, Rumour and Scandal

I mentioned that scandal is similar in some respects to gossip and rumour, and that scandals are often preceded by gossip and rumours which fuel them. But these concepts are not the same – how exactly do they differ?

Gossip is primarily a form of talk that takes place between friends or acquaintances. It is often small talk, idle chat, about other people who are not themselves party to the conversation, or about relatively trivial matters. The word is derived from the old English word *godsibb*, which was in use as early as the eleventh century.[14] In its original sense, a *godsibb* was a godparent, a person who had entered into a spiritual bond with another by acting as a sponsor at a baptism. Gradually the word was extended to apply to close friends and acquaintances, especially to a woman's female friends who were invited to be present at a birth. By the late sixteenth century, the word was used more generally to refer to a person (usually female) who engaged in light, idle talk; by the nineteenth century, the word was used to refer to idle talk itself.

To engage in gossip (as this word is used today) implies a degree of familiarity or intimacy between the interlocutors. One cannot gossip with a total stranger or with someone whom one regards as an enemy, since gossiping presupposes some shared knowledge about the subject matter and some degree of confidence and trust. To gossip is to confide in another; it involves treating the other as an insider, as someone who is sufficiently close to be interested in, and trusted with, informal talk of this kind. Hence gossip exists primarily within social networks of family relations, friends and acquaintances. Gossip is – to modify slightly the formulation of one commentator[15] – a form of communication that symbolizes intimacy.

Although the substance of gossip may be relatively trivial (as indicated by the phrase 'idle talk'), it does not follow that gossip is an insignificant or trivial phenomenon. On the contrary, gossiping is an activity through which social relationships are continuously reaffirmed or reworked, and through which bonds of trust are renewed or transformed. To gossip with others is to show that you regard them as sufficiently close, or sufficiently integral to a group, to engage in informal talk and, in some cases, to be trusted with confidential information or opinions (where the degree of confidentiality is generally calibrated to the degree of proximity: the closer someone is felt to be, the more likely it is that he or she will be trusted with confidential gossip). Gossip is also an activity through which the norms and values of groups can be reaffirmed without being explicitly asserted. For gossip often involves the telling of stories which have a moral edge, which highlight the lapses of others and thereby reaffirm the everyday moralities which others have failed to uphold. Moreover, by means of gossip, individuals can express their opinions about others with a degree of candour that would be difficult to sustain in a public setting, thereby enabling them to make judgements about others and to convey their views in a way that avoids the risks associated with open confrontation.[16]

Gossip is most commonly exchanged in contexts of face-to-face interaction, usually between two individuals and sometimes within small groups. But gossip can also be exchanged through mediated communication. This includes one-to-one forms of mediated communication – such as letter-writing and telephone conversations, which are popular settings for gossip – but it also includes forms of what are commonly called 'mass communication'. The gossip columns of magazines and newspapers constitute 'gossip' in a distinctive sense: they are written forms of 'small talk' about other people (usually media personalities) which presuppose and cultivate a certain kind of intimacy, what I call 'non-reciprocal intimacy at a distance'.[17] Gossip columns assume that their readers have an intimate relation with the personalities who are discussed in their columns. They treat their readers as 'insiders' who know a good deal about these personalities and who will be interested in further information and speculation about the changing fortunes of their lives. But this is a one-sided and non-reciprocal type of intimacy (readers know a good deal about these personalities but not vice versa); and the gossip is exchanged in a way which suspends any presumption of confidentiality, since the information is conveyed in a manner which makes it available for anyone to read. Gossip columns are purveyors of public secrets.

What is the relation between gossip and scandal? The notion of gossip is much more general than that of scandal: gossip is small talk which may or may not be true, which may be positive or negative in tone and which may be concerned with many different aspects of other people's lives. Scandal, on the other hand, involves a transgression of norms or values which is known by others and which elicits a public reproach. Gossip often remains at the level of private communication among friends or acquaintances; scandal can exist only when knowledge about a transgression is available to non-participants and negative judgements are articulated in public. Gossip can fuel scandal and provide a vehicle for the diffusion of information, but a scandal will exist only when certain additional conditions are met. Where gossip and scandal overlap most substantially is where gossip assumes a public character, as it does in gossip columns: here gossip can slide easily into scandal, precisely because the information is made available publicly and can be easily interlaced with opprobrious discourse.

Gossip is similar to rumour, although the word 'rumour' has a slightly different connotation. Derived from Old French, 'rumour' was initially used in English in the fourteenth century to describe a widespread report of a favourable nature.[18] Subsequently it was used more generally to refer to talk or hearsay which is not based on definite knowledge (as in 'rumour has it'). Gossip may or may not be true, but a rumour is always an unauthenticated report; a report which has been definitely confirmed or disconfirmed is, *ipso facto*, no longer a rumour.[19] Moreover, whereas gossip tends to be small talk about other people or relatively trivial matters, rumours can be about almost anything, including very serious issues, and they can have far-reaching consequences (for example, rumours about the state of health of a political leader or the stability of a financial institution). Rumours can be spread through face-to-face interaction or through mediated communication – and, given the nature of modern communication networks, they can spread very quickly.

Like gossip, rumour can fuel scandal by diffusing information (in this case, always uncorroborated) about the individuals or events which lie at the centre of a scandal or potential scandal. A scandal is often preceded by gossip and rumour; initially this may be restricted to people who are close to the individuals involved in the transgression, and strenuous efforts may be made to prevent the rumours from spreading. If the rumours are picked up by the media and conveyed either in the form of unconfirmed reports or innuendoes, then it becomes much more difficult to prevent a scandal from breaking out. The proliferation of rumours may reach a level at which it becomes difficult or impossible for an individual to ignore them, so that they may feel obliged to respond publicly, either by explicitly denying the rumours (and thereby running the risk of a second-order transgression) or by adopting some other strategy of defence.

Corruption, Bribery and Scandal

Today scandal is often associated with corruption and bribery, so much so that these concepts may now seem inextricably linked. But these concepts are, in fact, quite different, and the relations between them are complex and contingent. The word 'corruption' is derived from the Latin *corrumpere* and from Old French; it first appeared in English in the fourteenth century and was used to describe the disintegration, decomposition or spoiling of a body or substance.[20] This included not only the process of physical disintegration (as in the decomposition of a human body after death), but also the process of moral deterioration or decay. By the fifteenth century the word had also acquired the sense with which we commonly associate it today: the perversion or loss of integrity in the discharge of public duties by bribery or favour, especially by officials of the state or some other public institution.

Used in this present-day sense, the notion of corruption involves two key elements: (1) the infringement of rules, conventions or laws concerning the proper exercise of public duties for the purposes of private, pecuniary or personal gain; and (2) the perversion or undermining of the standards of integrity associated with public office.[21] These two elements are woven together in the notion of corruption, in a way that distinguishes it from related and partially overlapping concepts, such as bribery and nepotism. The making and accepting of bribes, for example, involves the exchange of inducements (often financial) which are intended to influence decisions or outcomes in favour of the giver. Bribery has a long history: the practice was common in the ancient world, as it is in many societies today.[22] We are now inclined to think of bribery as a particular form of corruption, but in fact only certain kinds of bribery are instances of corruption in the sense defined above. For to characterize an act of bribery as a form of corruption is to assume that the action involves a public official and that his or her behaviour represents a perversion of the standards of integrity to which the holders of public office are expected to adhere.

Corruption can give rise to scandal, and some of the most important and consequential scandals have been based on charges of corruption – such as the Teapot Dome scandal that rocked Warren Harding's presidential administration in the 1920s, the Lockheed scandal that undermined the political career of Japan's former prime minister Kakuei Tanaka in the 1970s and early 1980s, and the numerous financial scandals that have afflicted politics in Italy, Japan, South Korea, Germany, France, Spain, Brazil and many other countries in recent years. But not all scandals are corruption scandals, and not all instances of corruption give rise to scandals; corruption can (and often does) exist without becoming scandalous. So what makes the difference? What additional conditions must be fulfilled before corrupt activities can be constituted as scandalous?

In the first place, corrupt activities can become the focus of scandal only if they are known or strongly believed to exist by non-participants; in other words, corruption must be disclosed in order to become scandalous. If corrupt activities remain hidden from the view of others, if they are consigned to a shadowy existence in a world that is shielded from public scrutiny, then they will not and cannot become the focus of scandal. A scandal can arise if and only if the veil of secrecy is lifted and the corrupt activities become known to others or become the focus of a public investigation.

Some degree of non-participant knowledge is a necessary condition for corrupt activities to be constituted as scandalous, but it is not a sufficient condition. Corruption can be known or strongly believed to exist by others, and can even be quite widely known to exist, without giving rise to a scandal. What other conditions must be fulfilled? We have seen that corruption involves the infringement of rules, conventions or laws concerning the proper exercise of public duties: a scandal will arise only if the rules, conventions or laws have some degree of moral bindingness and only if the infringement is regarded by others as sufficiently serious and important to elicit a vigorous expression of disapproval. In some contexts, certain forms of corruption may be regarded as a quasi-legitimate way of conducting public affairs – a kind of 'honest graft' which, while gained in an illicit fashion, is nevertheless regarded as falling within the bounds of acceptable practice. In other contexts where corruption is widely condemned, a relatively minor offence – such as the acceptance of a modest gift – may not be regarded as sufficiently serious to give rise to a scandal. But the degree of moral censure associated with particular forms and instances of corruption will vary considerably from one social and historical context to another, and politicians may find that, in contexts where there is a high degree of sensitivity about corruption, even relatively minor offences can become a resignation issue.

The public articulation of opprobrious discourse is the final condition that must be fulfilled to turn corruption into scandal. A disclosure of corrupt activities that elicits no response, no publicly articulated condemnation or rebuke, will not give rise to a scandal. In circumstances where corruption is pervasive, is widely known to exist and is accepted as a quasi-legitimate way of conducting public affairs, the disclosure of a case of corruption may give rise to little more than a sigh of resigned indifference. The disclosure is a gauntlet thrown down but not yet taken up; whether the gauntlet will be taken up by others, and whether their rebukes will have sufficient resonance to trigger off a scandal and to keep it alive long enough to cause some damage, are questions whose answers will vary from case to case, depending on the nature of the corruption, on the kind of publicity generated by the media and on a range of other social and political circumstances. Most forms of corruption are never made public, and hence never exposed to the risk of scandal. But to engage in corruption and expect to survive in public life is to have either a generous faith in the mechanisms of secrecy or a confident sense of what one can get away with in the event that activities hitherto hidden are suddenly made visible to others.

2

The Rise of Mediated Scandal

Scandals are not new: scandalous events of various kinds have existed for many centuries. But with the development of modern societies, the nature, scale and consequences of scandals have changed in certain respects. And one way in which they have changed is that they have become increasingly bound up with mediated forms of communication. Scandals are no longer only local events which break out in contexts of face-to-face interaction, involving individuals who are largely known to one another as family, friends, neighbours, associates; 'localized scandals' of this kind continue to exist and are familiar to us all, but they are not the only form of scandal. A new form of scandal has emerged, what I shall call 'mediated scandals', the properties of which differ from those of localized scandals and the potential consequences of which are on an altogether different scale. Mediated scandals are not simply scandals which are reported by the media and exist independently of them: they are, in varying ways and to some extent, constituted by mediated forms of communication.

How did this connection between scandal and the media come about? What is it about scandal that lends itself to exposure in and through the media, and what is it about the media that facilitates the occurrence of scandal? There is, of course, an obvious affinity between scandal and the media which has been exploited by purveyors of the printed word since the age of pamphlets and broadsides: scandal sells. As commercial enterprises concerned with generating revenue through the commodification of symbolic forms, printing firms, publishers, newspapers and other media organizations have a financial interest in maintaining or increasing the sale of their products, and scandals provide vivid, racy stories that can help splendidly to achieve this aim. Moreover, with the professionalization of journalistic activity in the nineteenth century and the development of a tradition of investigative journalism, the disclosure of scandals and commentary on them has become an activity which concurs with the professional self-conceptions of some media personnel. The unveiling of the hidden secrets of power is seen by some journalists as a way of pursuing their calling as guardians of the public interest.

Considerations of this kind are important, but they are not the only factors that account for the affinity between scandal and the media. If we wish to understand this connection, we must see that the rise of mediated scandal is interwoven with a broader set of social transformations which have shaped the modern world, transformations which have, among other things, redefined the relations between public and private life and created new kinds of visibility and 'publicness' that simply did not exist before. By making actions and events visible in new ways, these transformations created the conditions under which a new form of scandal could emerge, a form detached from particular locales and made available for thousands, even millions, to observe.

In this chapter I shall briefly outline the social transformations which have shaped modern societies, focusing on the development of communication media and on the transformation of visibility brought about by it. This will enable me to introduce some concepts and ideas which will inform the analyses developed later in this chapter and in subsequent chapters. I shall then retrace the historical connection between scandal and mediated forms of communication. I shall try to show that, while the word 'scandal' was a relatively common feature of print culture in the sixteenth and seventeenth centuries, it was only in the late eighteenth and nineteenth centuries that the distinctive type of event which I describe as 'mediated scandal' began to emerge. Scandal is an ancient concept and mediated scandals are not new, but the distinctive circumstances which give rise to mediated scandals have not always been with us. Mediated scandal is, as we shall see, a largely modern phenomenon which is characteristic of the period that stretches from the late eighteenth century to the present day.

The Transformation of Visibility

The world in which we live today has been shaped by a range of institutional transformations which were set in motion in late medieval and early modern Europe.[1] Some of these transformations are well known and well documented, others less so. The transformations which are reasonably well documented are those concerned with the changing institutional forms of economic and political power. From roughly the eleventh century on, a new set of economic relations began to emerge in Europe, gradually replacing the predominantly agrarian economies of the early medieval period.[2] This new set of economic relations, involving the increased use of money and extended networks of exchange, developed into a distinctive system of commodity production and exchange which, by the end of the fifteenth century, had become well established in the major trading centres of Europe. The formation of the modern state, or 'nation-state', was also a lengthy historical process whose origins can be traced back to the late medieval period. Medieval Europe was characterized by a large number of political units of varying size and strength, from relatively small city-states and urban federations to larger and more powerful kingdoms and principalities. Gradually these multiple and varied forms of political power were replaced by a relatively small number of sovereign nation-states. This concentration of political power in the hands of nation-states was a process driven primarily by the need to build up the means of exercising coercive power – both the means for waging war against external rivals (armies, navies, weapons, ships, etc.) and the means for suppressing internal revolts and maintaining order within the territories over which political authorities claimed jurisdiction.[3] As the scale of military conflict increased, those states which could extract the resources to establish large standing armies and maintain them in a condition of war-readiness had a material advantage. They eventually became the key political units in an interlocking system of nation-states, each characterized by a centralized system of government and administration, each claiming sovereignty over a clearly defined territory, and each possessing the means to defend their claims by recourse to force if necessary.

These broad lines of economic and political change seem relatively clear; what is less clear is whether the development of modern societies has been characterized by institutional transformations in what might loosely be called the 'cultural' sphere. A great deal has been written about the changing role of religious institutions, about the expansion of secular systems of knowledge and learning, about the pluralization of value systems and the alleged decline of the significance of tradition in everyday life. Undoubtedly some of these changes are real and of considerable importance, but here I wish to focus on another development, or series of developments, which to some extent underlies them: namely, the developments associated with the invention and exploitation of new media of communication and information diffusion. The invention of the printing press was, of course, a key factor. Originally developed by Johann Gutenberg around 1440, the techniques of printing spread rapidly and, by the end of the fifteenth century, a flourishing book trade existed throughout Europe. In the early seventeenth century, regular journals of news began to appear in various European cities; these weekly news sheets (or 'corantos', as they were called at the time) were the precursors of the modern newspaper. By the early eighteenth century, a variety of daily and weekly newspapers were well established in most major European cities. The nineteenth century witnessed a major new invention in the sphere of communication: the discovery that electricity could be used for the purposes of transmitting information. The development of telegraph and telephone systems in the late nineteenth and early twentieth centuries – including the laying of underwater cables which spanned the globe – was one of the early consequences of this discovery. By the 1920s, the technology for transmitting messages via electromagnetic waves was sufficiently well advanced to permit the development of broadcasting on a commercial scale – initially radio and then, from the late 1940s on, television.

What were the implications of this massive growth of mediated forms of communication and information diffusion? In what ways did it affect people's lives? What impact did it have on the social organization of everyday life? In order to answer these questions, it is essential to see that the development of communication media involved the creation of new forms of action and interaction which differed in certain respects from the kinds of action and interaction that had existed previously. Prior to the development of printing in early modern Europe, and until quite recently in some other parts of the world, the exchange of information and symbolic content was a process that took place largely within the context of face-to-face interaction. In this type of interaction, the participants are immediately present to one another and share a common spatial-temporal reference system; in other words, the interaction takes place in a context of co-presence. Face-to-face interaction is also 'dialogical' in character, in the sense that it generally involves a two-way flow of information and communication: one individual speaks to another (or others), and the addressee can in turn respond (at least in principle) to the original speaker, and so on as the dialogue unfolds.

With the development of communication media, face-to-face interaction did not, of course, disappear, but it was supplemented by new forms of action and interaction which did not share its characteristics. These new forms of mediated interaction involved the use of a technical medium (paper, electrical wires, electromagnetic waves, etc.) which enabled information and symbolic content to be transmitted to individuals who did not share the same spatial-temporal locale. Hence the development of communication media involved a complex reordering of the spatial and temporal characteristics of social life. New forms of social exchange were created which did not share the spatial-temporal features of face-to-face interaction. Individuals could now interact with others who were located in distant spatial-temporal contexts; the interaction could be stretched across time and space (as, for example, with the exchange of letters that are physically transported from one place to another), or it could be stretched across space with a minimum degree of temporal delay (as with some forms of electronic communication).

There was another feature of some forms of mediated interaction which had important consequences for the social organization of everyday life. In the case of face-to-face interaction, the audience for a speaker's utterances is generally restricted to those individuals who are within hearing distance; the audience might consist of only one individual with whom the speaker is engaged in a dialogue, or it might consist of a plurality of others who have gathered together in a common locale to hear the speaker's words. However, in the case of mediated interaction, the audience is no longer restricted to those who are situated in the same spatial-temporal locale as the speaker. Moreover, in some forms of mediated interaction, such as those involving printed materials like books, newspapers and magazines or those involving the use of broadcasting, the scope of the audience is relatively open-ended, in the sense that the symbolic content conveyed through the interaction may be taken up by an indefinite range of potential recipients, located in a diverse array of spatial-temporal contexts.

I use the term 'mediated quasi-interaction' to describe this particular form of mediated interaction which is oriented towards an indefinite range of potential recipients. Whereas the kind of inter-action involved in writing a letter or using a telephone is oriented towards a specific other (and hence is, in this respect, relatively 'closed'), mediated quasi-interaction involves the production of symbolic materials which are made available to a plurality of potential recipients – it is, in other words, relatively 'open-ended'. Moreover, whereas the kind of interaction involved in writing a letter or using a telephone is generally dialogical in character, mediated quasi-interaction is predominantly 'monological', in the sense that the flow of symbolic content is largely one-way. The reader of a book or a newspaper is primarily the recipient of a symbolic form whose producer does not require (and generally does not receive) a direct and immediate response.

What were the consequences of the rise of mediated quasi-interaction as a significant form of social exchange in early modern and modern societies? One consequence was the transformation in the nature of what we could call 'publicness' – and, closely linked to this, a transformation of the ways in which individuals and events are made 'visible' to others. The distinction between the public and the private has a long history in Western social and political thought, a history which can be traced back to classical Greece and to the early development of Roman law. Here I shall not attempt to reconstruct this history or to disentangle the various meanings of these terms.[4] I shall focus instead on one sense of the distinction which is particularly relevant to the issues that concern us here. According to this sense, 'public' means 'open' or 'available to others'. What is public, in this sense, is what is visible or observable, what is performed in front of spectators, what is open for all or many to see or hear or hear about. What is private, by contrast, is what is hidden from view, what is said or done in secrecy or among a restricted circle of people. In this sense, the public–private dichotomy has to do with publicness versus privacy, with openness versus secrecy, with visibility versus invisibility. A public act is a visible act, performed openly so that anyone can see; a private act is invisible, an act performed secretly and behind closed doors.

Prior to the development of the media, the publicness of an individual or event (understood in the above sense) was linked to the sharing of a common locale. An event became a public event by being staged before a plurality of individuals who were physically present at its occurrence – in the manner, for instance, of a public execution in medieval Europe, performed before a group of spectators who had gathered together in the market square. I shall describe this as the 'traditional publicness of co-presence'. This traditional publicness drew on the richness of symbolic cues characteristic of face-to-face interaction. It was a publicness which involved sight as well as sound, visual appearance as well as the spoken word: the public event was a spectacle which, for those relatively few individuals who happened to be present at its occurrence, could be seen, heard, perhaps even felt in some way. Moreover, since the publicness of co-presence involves the gathering together of individuals in a common locale, it is potentially dialogical in character. The individuals who speak or perform on such an occasion do so before others who can in principle contribute to the event, whether by speaking or by displaying other kinds of spectator behaviour (booing, hissing, clapping, cheering, etc.), even if in practice they do not.

The development of the media created new forms of publicness which are quite different from the traditional publicness of co-presence. The key feature of these new forms is that, with the extension of availability made possible by the media, the publicness of individuals, actions or events is no longer linked to the sharing of a common locale. An action or event can be made public by being recorded and transmitted to others who are not physically present at the time and place of its occurrence. Actions or events can acquire a publicness – what I shall call 'mediated publicness' – which is independent of their capacity to be seen or heard directly by a plurality of co-present individuals. Of course, the emergence of these new forms of mediated publicness did not entirely displace the role of the traditional publicness of co-presence. The traditional form continues to play an important role in modern societies, as attested to by the continued presence of public meetings, mass demonstrations, political debates in the face-to-face settings of parliaments and other decision-making bodies, and so on. But as new media of communication became more pervasive, the new forms of publicness began to supplement, extend, transform and, in some cases, displace the traditional form of publicness.

We can briefly retrace some aspects of this process by considering a few episodes in the long and relatively neglected history of the relations between the changing forms of publicness and the exercise of political power. Prior to the development of print and other media, the publicness of political rulers was derived primarily from their physical appearance before others in contexts of co-presence. For the most part, these appearances could be restricted to the relatively closed circles of the assembly or the court: visibility required co-presence, and political rulers were generally visible only to those with whom they interacted routinely in the face-to-face settings of daily life. Their audiences consisted primarily of members of ruling elites or individuals who participated in the social life of the court.

There were occasions when rulers appeared before wider audiences comprising, among others, some of the subjects over whom they ruled. These occasions included major public events such as coronations, royal funerals and victory marches. The pomp and ceremony of such occasions enabled the ruler to maintain some distance from his subjects while enabling them temporarily to see and celebrate his existence in a context of co-presence. But for most individuals in ancient or medieval societies, the most powerful rulers were rarely if ever seen. Individuals who lived in rural areas or in the peripheral regions of an empire or kingdom would rarely have the opportunity to see the emperor or king in flesh and blood. Apart from royal progresses, which were transient and relatively infrequent, most public appearances of the monarch took place in the political centre – in the halls or courts of the palace or in the streets and squares of the capital city.[5]

With the development of print and other media, however, political rulers increasingly acquired a kind of publicness which was detached from their physical appearance before assembled audiences. Rulers used the new means of communication not only as a vehicle for promulgating official decrees, but also as a medium for fabricating a self-image which could be conveyed to others in distant locales. Monarchs in early modern Europe, such as Louis XIV of France or Philip IV of Spain, were well versed in the arts of image-making.[6] Their images were constructed and celebrated not only in traditional media, such as paint, bronze, stone and tapestry, but also in the newer media of print, including woodcuts, etchings, engravings, pamphlets and periodicals. Under the reign of Louis XIV, for example, periodicals like the *Gazette de France*, published twice a week, and the *Mercure Gallant*, published monthly, devoted regular space to the actions of the King.[7] While the monarchies of early modern Europe were mainly court-based societies in which rulers oriented their activities primarily towards elites who met in palaces and other specially designed milieux, nevertheless the images of monarchs and accounts of their activities were circulated well beyond these restricted circles through the medium of print. The circulation of these images and accounts rendered the activities of political rulers increasingly visible to a plurality of individuals who were not in a position to encounter these rulers (or other members of the political elite) in the course of their day-to-day lives. Gradually, the publicness of political rulers and others, the visibility of their actions, of their utterances and indeed of their selves, was prised apart from their appearance before others who were gathered together in the same spatial-temporal locale.

The development of electronic media – radio and above all television – represented in some ways the continuation of a process that had been set in motion by the advent of print, but in other respects it represented a new departure. As with print, electronic media created a kind of publicness which was severed from the sharing of a common locale, a publicness which, with the increasing availability of media products on a national and even international scale, impinged on the lives of a growing proportion of the population. But the kind of publicness created by electronic media was different in some respects from the publicness created by print. Electronic media enabled information and symbolic content to be transmitted over large distances with little or no delay. Hence electronic media created a kind of publicness which was characterized, at least in principle, by what we could call 'despatialized simultaneity': distant others could be visible in virtually the same time frame, could be heard at the very moment they spoke or seen at the very moment they acted, even though they did not share the same spatial locale as the individuals to whom they were visible. Moreover, the electronic media were characterized by a richness of symbolic cues which enabled some of the features of face-to-face interaction to be reproduced in these new media, even though the spatial properties of face-to-face interaction and mediated quasi-interaction were radically different. Radio enabled the oral quality of the human voice to be encoded and transmitted to distant others, while television allowed oral and visual cues to be recorded and relayed. With the advent of television, therefore, individuals are able to see persons, actions and events, as well as to hear the spoken word and other sounds, in a way that may be both simultaneous and despatialized. In the age of television, mediated publicness is increasingly defined by visibility in the narrow sense of vision (the capacity to be seen with the eyes), although this new field of vision is altogether different from the field of vision that individuals have in their day-to-day encounters with others.

The ways in which political leaders appeared before others was shaped by the changing forms of publicness created by the media. With the advent of radio, it was possible for political leaders to speak directly to thousands and even millions of others, in a way that allowed for a distinctive kind of intimacy – namely, non-reciprocal intimacy at a distance – which was quite different from the speaker–audience relations characteristic of mass gatherings. In the days before amplified sound, a speaker who wished to address a mass gathering had to project his or her voice with great force; speakers generally stood above the audience so they could be seen, and often used a fiery language which could elicit a collective response. But with the coming of radio, rhetorical aloofness gave way in part to mediated intimacy; the fiery oratory of the impassioned speech could be exchanged for the conversational intimacy of the fireside chat.[8] Add the visual richness of television and the stage is set for the flourishing of a new kind of intimacy in the public sphere. Now political leaders could address their subjects as if they were family or friends. And given the capacity of television to convey close-up images, individuals could scrutinize their leaders' actions and utterances – their facial expressions, personal appearance, mannerisms and body language, among other things – with the kind of close attention once reserved for those with whom one shared an intimate personal relationship.

The development of new communication media thus gave rise to a new kind of despatialized publicness which allowed for an intimate form of self-presentation freed from the constraints of co-presence. These were the conditions that facilitated the rise of what we could call 'the society of self-disclosure': a society in which it was possible and, indeed, increasingly common for political leaders and other individuals to appear before distant audiences and lay bare some aspect of their self or their personal life. The impersonal aloofness of most political leaders in the past was increasingly replaced by this new kind of mediated intimacy through which politicians could present themselves not just as leaders but as human beings, as ordinary individuals who could address their subjects as fellow citizens, selectively disclosing aspects of their lives and their character in a conversational or even confessional mode. What was lost in this process was some of the aura, the 'greatness', that surrounded political leaders and institutions in the past, an aura which was sustained in part by the aloofness of leaders and the distance they maintained from the individuals over whom they ruled.[9] What was gained was the capacity to speak directly to one's subjects, to appear before them as a flesh-and-blood human being with whom they could empathize and even sympathize, to address them not as one's subject but as one's friend. In short, political leaders acquired the capacity to present themselves as 'one of us'.

One consequence of the rise of the society of self-disclosure was that political leaders and other public figures could be, and were

likely to be, appraised increasingly in terms of their personal qualities as individuals, and not only in terms of their achievements in
public life. The more that political leaders and others sought to
present themselves through the media as ordinary individuals with
ordinary lives, the more likely it was that the audiences they
addressed would be inclined to assess them in terms of their *character* as individuals – their sincerity, their honesty, their integrity, their
trustworthiness. Hence, while the use of self-disclosure provided
political leaders and others with new ways of appealing to audiences
and seeking to win their support, it also carried new risks. By presenting themselves as ordinary individuals with their own values and
beliefs, with their own personal lives and commitments and with their
own reasons and motives for what they do, political leaders and
others were giving character and integrity ever greater salience in
public life. But character was an attribute by which they could just
as easily be hung.

Early Uses of 'Scandal' in the Media

The rise of scandal as a phenomenon of more than localized significance is a development which coincided with the emergence of print
and electronic media. These media created, as we have seen, a new
kind of publicness in the modern world, a kind of publicness which
endowed individuals, actions and events with much greater visibility
than they had had in the past. Thanks to the media, visibility was
severed from co-presence: it was increasingly possible for individuals,
actions and events to be seen, heard or heard about by others who
were located in distant contexts, far removed from the circumstances
in which the visible individuals were situated or in which the visible
actions occurred. This created new opportunities for individuals to
appear before others who were widely dispersed in space (and
perhaps also in time), providing them with a kind of visibility which
was inconceivable in earlier epochs, but it also created new risks.
Mediated visibility was a gift to those who were adept at using the
media to fashion their image or further their ends. But since the
media made visible whole arenas of action which were previously
hidden from view, and since they created a complex field of images
and information flows which were very difficult to control, mediated
visibility could also become a trap.

Political rulers in early modern Europe were well aware that print
was a powerful medium which could be used not only to promote

and enhance their image, but also to attack and undermine it. While the activities of monarchs were regularly described and celebrated in print, these rulers were also the target of pamphleteers and satirists who denounced them as vain, arrogant, unscrupulous, irreligious, incompetent and unjust. In France, for example, Louis XIV was commonly portrayed in the royal press as a war hero but he was lampooned by pamphleteers, who caricatured him as a battle-shy womanizer ('you flee wars but run after girls'[10]). Aspects of private life, which were generally avoided in the royal press, were often emphasized and parodied by the pamphleteers – Louis XIV's relationship with his mistresses, for example, and his second marriage to Madame de Maintenon, were openly and mirthfully discussed in pamphlets like *Les Conquêtes amoureuses du Grand Alcandre* (1685) and *The French King's Wedding* (1708), although these subjects were carefully avoided in the official media.[11] By the early eighteenth century a distinct genre of subversive political literature had emerged, comprising the *libelles* and the *chroniques scandaleuses*, which purported to recount the private lives of kings and courtiers and which presented them in an unflattering light.[12] These irreverent reports were often dressed up as authentic accounts of what happened behind the facade of power, with supposed excerpts from secret correspondence and private conversations. Volumes like the *Vie privée de Louis XV* and the *Anecdotes sur Mme la comtesse du Barry*, which allegedly recounted the exploits of a former prostitute who became the mistress of Louis XV and used her expertise in 'the most refined art of debauchery' to revive his ailing sex life, became bestsellers. Literature of this kind was formally forbidden in France in the seventeenth and eighteenth centuries, but it was extremely difficult for the authorities to suppress it. Printers and booksellers found countless ways to evade the censors, and texts banned in France were often printed in other territories (such as the Dutch Republic) and smuggled in by merchants and pedlars. Both authors and printers of polemical texts often remained anonymous or pseudonymous, and even places of publication were commonly disguised. Censorship stimulated a vigorous trade in contraband books.

In England the circulation of satirical pamphlets and broadsides was a common feature of the Elizabethan period. Much of this early pamphlet literature was sensationalist and moralistic in tone.[13] It often recounted strange or supernatural events, like cases of witchcraft, the sighting of monsters or the occurrence of freak weather conditions. But some of the Elizabethan pamphlets were also social satires, providing elaborate commentaries – often expressed in

3 The *libelliste*, from the frontispiece to *Le Gazetier cuirasse, ou anecdotes scandaleuses de la cour de France* by Charles Theveneau de Morande, 1771. The *libelliste* is portrayed as an armour-plated gazeteer who is firing his canons in all directions against the *ancien régime*.

allegorical form – on the vices and moral turpitude of the time. In this respect, the early pamphlet literature retained some of the moralistic concerns of the traditional spoken sermon (the theme of the seven deadly sins was a common preoccupation of the early pamphleteers), although these concerns were now expressed in print and grafted on to a literary genre which would acquire conventions of its own. The pamphlets and broadsides of the sixteenth century were thus a medium through which moral opprobrium could be (and commonly was) articulated publicly and circulated in a printed form.

The Elizabethan pamphlets often recounted the lives of rogues and vagabonds, but they seldom discussed and openly criticized the lives and actions of the powerful. A decree of the Star Chamber in 1586 established a comprehensive system of licensing and censorship which limited the number of printers in England and strictly controlled the publication of domestic news. When regular news sheets (or corantos) first began to appear in the early 1620s, attempts were made to suppress them and to ban the import of corantos published abroad. But as the crisis between Charles I and Parliament deepened, it became increasingly difficult for the Crown to enforce its control of the press, and in 1641 the Star Chamber was abolished. This was the beginning of a period of relatively uncontrolled and intensive publication of newspapers, newsbooks and pamphlets dealing with the events of the Civil War and the circumstances surrounding it.[14] The crisis stimulated a demand for up-to-date news of domestic political affairs, and the lapsing of strict controls on the press created an opportunity for publishers and printers to meet the growing demand. They responded not only by supplying regular news of domestic events, but also by producing pamphlets and newsbooks which became an integral part of the emerging conflict. Pamphlets and newsbooks appeared which aligned themselves with particular political factions and which explicitly attacked prominent political figures, including the King.

The autumn of 1641 thus marked the beginning of a 'pamphlet war' which became increasingly bitter and aggressive as the Civil War dragged on. Pamphlets and newsbooks were charged with fomenting sedition, poisoning the population and containing passages that were heretical, blasphemous, scurrilous and 'scandalous' in character. In August 1645, for instance, Marchamont Nedham – a prominent writer of the time and co-editor of the anti-royalist newsbook *Mercurius Britanicus* – launched an attack on the King which accused him of 'a guilty Conscience, bloody Hands, a Heart full of broken Vowes and Protestations' and which mocked his speech defect.[15] This

Numb. 92.

Mercurius Britanicus,
Communicating the affaires of great

BRITAINE:

For the better Information of the People.

From *Monday* the 28 ot *July,* to *Monday* the 4. of *August,* 1645.

WHere is King *Charles* ? What's become of him ? The ſtrange variety of opinions leaves nothing certain : for ſome ſay, when he ſaw the Storm comming after him as far as *Bridgwater,* he ran away to his *dearly beloved* in *Ireland* ; yes, they ſay he *ran away* out of his own *Kingdome* very *Majeſtically* : Others will have him erecting a new *Monarchy* in the Iſle of *Angleſey :* A third ſort there are which ſay he hath hid himſelfe. I will not now determine the matter, becauſe there is ſuch a deale of uncertainty ; and therefore (for the ſatisfaction of my Countrymen) it were beſt to ſend *Hue and Cry* after him.

Rumours concerning the King.

*If any man can bring any tale or tiding of a wilfull King, which hath gone aſtray theſe foure yeares from his Parliament, with a guilty Conſcience, bloody Hands, a Heart full of broken Vowes and Proteſtations : If theſe marks be not ſufficient, there is another in the * mouth ; for bid him ſpeak, and you will ſoon know him : Then give notice to* Britanicus, *and you ſhall be well paid for your paines :* So God ſave the Parliament.

Hue and a Cry after him.

* Bos in lingua.

But now I think on't (Reader) I know not what to ſay to him ; for I have been *telling* *him* *his* *owne* this good while, and yet no *amendment* at all : Nay, the dying *groanes* and

A Prince irrecoverably loſt.

Aaaaa   pangs

---

4 *Mercurius Britanicus*, no. 92, 28 July–4 August 1645. The first page of this anti-Charles number of Nedham's newsbook was condemned by the Lords as 'scandalous to the King's person'.

attack was condemned by the Lords as 'scandalous to the King's person'[16] and Nedham, together with the printer and licenser of *Britanicus*, was sentenced to prison; Nedham was released after a short period, having written, apparently under orders, a public apology.[17] In 1647 the Commons, concerned about the proliferation of royalist pamphlets critical of negotiations between parliamentary leaders and officers in the army and the King, drew up an ordinance to suppress 'scandalous and abusive' pamphlets.[18] Critical and satirical newsbooks nevertheless continued to appear, their authors sometimes using secret presses in order to evade government agents. The 1647 ordinance was followed by a much tougher Act of Parliament in September 1649 which effectively outlawed newsbooks and authorized the Stationers' Company to break into premises and search them for seditious and unlicensed pamphlets.

So the pamphlet wars of the 1640s saw the explicit use of 'scandalous' in relation to claims and counter-claims articulated in print. 'Scandalous' was being used in this context primarily to refer to damaging or defamatory allegations, rather than to describe moral transgressions which offend the sense of decency. But it was in this period – from roughly the time of the Elizabethan pamphleteers through to the end of the Civil War – that the concept of scandal gained prominence in English and was explicitly linked to the medium of print. The connection between scandal and the media thus owes its origins to the pamphlet culture of the late sixteenth and early seventeenth centuries, a culture in which 'scandalous' was used to characterize claims, allegations, accusations and portrayals articulated by the printed word.

The subsequent development of the relation between scandal and the media was shaped by changing forms of political regulation, changing conventions and practices of publication, changing media technologies and a gradual shift in the meaning of 'scandal' itself. By the end of the seventeenth century the system of licensing, which had been re-established in the aftermath of the Civil War, fell into abeyance and was followed by a spate of new periodical publications. Eighteenth-century England had a vibrant culture of print. The first daily newspaper in England, Samuel Buckley's *Daily Courant*, appeared in 1702 and was soon joined by others, such as the *Daily Post* in 1719 and the *Daily Journal* in 1724. A variety of more specialized periodicals appeared, including some – like the *Tatler*, the *Spectator*, Daniel Defoe's *Review* and Jonathan Swift's *Examiner* – which specialized in social and political commentary. By 1750 London had five well-established daily papers, six thrice-weeklies, five weeklies and numerous other periodicals, and there was a burgeoning provincial press. Newspapers and periodicals were distributed by networks of agents and hawkers, and papers were available in the inns and coffee houses which were common in London and other towns and cities in eighteenth-century England. The tradition of street literature also flourished, as broadsides, pamphlets and chapbooks were printed and sold in the streets by hawkers, pedlars and chapmen. Criticism of political leaders was common and occasionally fierce, and an increasingly wide readership was provided with an array of commentaries – some critical and sharply satirical, others broadly supportive – on the activities of government ministers and monarchs.

It was not uncommon for the periodical press of the eighteenth century to be attacked by government ministers and others for making scandalous allegations. As in the seventeenth century, 'scandalous' was used primarily in the sense of damaging or defamatory allegations which were potentially libellous or seditious. But in the eighteenth century, the political and intellectual context within which struggles of this kind took place was changing in important ways: the liberty of the press to express open criticism of government ministers and monarchs was increasingly proclaimed as a *right* that had to be defended in order to secure and protect the freedom of individuals from the restrictive and potentially oppressive actions of the state. Since the cessation of licensing in 1695, the main mechanisms used by the government to exercise some control over the media were the stamp duties, which imposed taxes on newspapers,[19] and stringent libel laws which, in the absence of prior restraint, provided a means of punishing individuals for publishing material judged to be dangerous or offensive. Eighteenth-century struggles over scandalous allegations in the printed media were thus interwoven with broader debates about the liberty of the press and its limits, in a context where the periodical press had, for the first time, become a central and assertive feature of political life.

Nothing illustrates this better than the controversy surrounding the publishing activities of John Wilkes. Elected as a Member of Parliament for Aylesbury in 1757, Wilkes became a fierce opponent of the governments of Lord Bute and George Grenville. In 1762 Wilkes founded a new weekly called the *North Briton*.[20] Espousing the liberty of the press, Wilkes used the *North Briton* as a platform from which to launch a series of sharp, vituperative attacks on Bute and Grenville among others. The government became increasingly impatient with the virulent tone of the criticism and began to scrutinize the paper for libel. *North Briton* No. 45 was the last straw. On 8 April 1763 Lord Bute resigned as prime minister, giving way to George Grenville, and on 19 April King George III closed the parliamentary session with a speech that reflected the political hue of Bute and Grenville. Incensed by the King's speech, Wilkes penned a scathing reply which implied that the impartiality of the Crown was being compromised by the willingness of the King to sanction 'the most odious measures'.[21] *North Briton* No. 45 was published on 23 April and, the following week, a warrant was issued for the arrest of the individuals responsible for the publication. Wilkes was arrested and committed to the Tower of London, where he was held for several days before being released on the grounds of parliamentary privilege.

Instilled with new vigour by his brief spell in the Tower, the audacious Wilkes established a printing press in his house in Great George Street and, among other things, reprinted the offending issue of the *North Briton*. Rather inadvisedly, he also used his press to publish a set of obscene verses called *An Essay on Woman* (mocking Pope's *Essay on Man*). When Parliament reconvened in November 1763, there was a move to expel Wilkes from the House of Commons for breach of privilege. The Lords condemned the *Essay* as 'a most scandalous, obscene, and impious libel', while the Commons passed a resolution declaring that *North Briton* No. 45 was 'a false, scandalous, and seditious libel, containing expressions of the most unexampled insolence and contumely towards his Majesty' and instructed that 'the said paper be burnt by the hands of the common hangman'.[22] Sensing that the tide was turning against him, Wilkes departed expeditiously for Paris, where he was to remain for several years. On 20 January 1764, the Commons carried a motion expelling Wilkes from the House, and on 21 February he was found guilty of libel in his absence.

Wilkes's political career was by no means finished. The fact that he had been punished for his outspoken criticism of the government and the King turned him into a popular hero. He returned to England in 1768, was imprisoned and fined and subsequently re-elected to Parliament, where his seat was denied until 1774, when he was finally allowed to return to the Commons as MP for Middlesex. Like many of the controversies involving charges of scandal in the eighteenth century, the Wilkes affair had less to do with the disclosure of actions which offended public morality than with the publication of allegations which were regarded as scurrilous and libellous, and which might be interpreted as a breach of public

5 'John Wilkes, Esq.', 1763. William Hogarth's famous portrait of the leering
Wilkes, whose *North Briton* No. 45 earned him the wrath of Parliament and
a brief spell in the Tower.

order. A figure whose activities were so closely associated with scandal could emerge as a popular hero precisely because, in the context of late eighteenth-century England, the suppression of his caustic, sometimes abusive and occasionally reckless publications could be interpreted in some quarters as an oppressive restriction on the liberty of the press.

The Emergence of Scandal as a Mediated Event

In the late eighteenth century and throughout the nineteenth century, the use of 'scandal' in relation to the media began to change, as the term was gradually prised apart from its close association with libel and sedition and increasingly applied to a range of phenomena which had certain distinctive properties. Already in the sixteenth and seventeenth centuries there were forms of popular literature, such as pamphlets and broadsides, which offered accounts – sometimes highly critical and satirical, as we have seen – of the lives and activities of the powerful. But in the late eighteenth century, this genre of printed material was adapted to the newspaper format and gradually endowed with a range of new characteristics. The first indications of this development were evident in the pages of a number of new daily papers established in London in the late eighteenth century such as the *Morning Post*, which devoted a good deal of space to recounting stories and anecdotes about prominent people of wealth and power.[23] But this emerging genre was given an altogether new significance by a series of fundamental changes which transformed the nature of the press in the course of the nineteenth century. Three changes were of particular importance.

First, there was the changing economic and technological basis of the press. The early newspapers of the seventeenth and eighteenth centuries were relatively small-scale commercial concerns, often run as family businesses. Print runs were relatively modest and prices relatively high, and the newspapers were aimed primarily at commercial, political and cultural elites. Even the *Morning Post*, which was oriented more towards entertainment than other papers, circulated primarily in London's fashionable West End. The early newspapers were financed through a mixture of sales revenue, advertising, subsidies provided by individuals or political parties, and fees charged to individuals, parties or governments for printing material on a regular or one-off basis. (In late eighteenth-century England it was common for newspapers to charge fees to political parties or individual politicians for printing their paragraphs – 'puffs', as the practice was known.) But technological developments in the early nineteenth century revolutionized the conditions of newspaper production, enabling large print runs to be produced at relatively low cost. At the same time, the growth of literacy created an expanding market for printed materials. From the 1830s on, the circulations of some established papers began to increase significantly and a variety of new papers, cheaply priced and aimed at a wider readership, began to appear. In England, the abolition of stamp duties and advertising taxes in the 1850s accelerated the trend. These were the origins of what is commonly known as 'the penny press'.

The new, cheap newspapers of the nineteenth century typically adopted a lighter and livelier style of presentation. Since they derived their revenue primarily through sales and advertising, they had a strong financial interest in expanding their circulation. They devoted considerable space to stories of crime, sexual violence, gambling and sport.[24] They commonly focused on individuals – the rich and powerful, of course, but also individuals from lower classes whose experiences were unusual in some way – and recounted aspects of their lives. They turned what would be described today as the 'human interest story' into a regularized feature of newspaper output. Indeed, one could even say, following Michael Schudson, that they 'invented' the modern concept of news, in the sense that they regarded 'the news' as something to be discovered through a process of inquiry and regarded everyday life as suitable subject matter for investigation.[25]

A second, closely related development was the changing relation between the press and political parties. In the seventeenth and eighteenth centuries, it was common for newspapers and other periodicals to have an explicit political orientation. Newspapers and periodicals were commonly owned by proprietors who had particular political affiliations, and some were subsidized by regular payments from political parties. But with the rise of cheap, mass circulation newspapers in the nineteenth century, the relation between the periodical press and partisan interests was altered in certain respects. The mass circulation newspapers relied less on financial support from political parties, and in some cases they explicitly proclaimed their political neutrality. They reported political news but they did not necessarily identify themselves with the advocacy of partisan interests. Many newspapers sought to distinguish more sharply between the reporting of news and the expression of opinion, restricting the latter to an editorial page. Of course, this broad trend towards the depoliticization of the press did not apply to all newspapers and periodicals; political papers and periodicals continued to exist and indeed to flourish, especially in Europe. Moreover, despite the attenuation of the link between political parties and the press, many newspapers and periodicals continued to align themselves with particular parties or factions, or to situate themselves in a particular region of the political spectrum.

A third important change was the emergence of journalism as a profession. The formation of the journalistic profession dates from the late nineteenth century.[26] Newspaper proprietors and editors relied increasingly on hired writers and reporters who were paid to gather news and write stories. As the corps of writers and reporters expanded, a professional ethos began to emerge which defined the principles of good journalistic practice. This ethos emphasized above all the duty to uncover and report the facts. But it also recognized the need to present the facts in the form of a story that would be lively, colourful and entertaining. Factuality and entertainment were the twin ideals of the emerging journalistic profession. But these ideals were not always wholly compatible, and they allowed for different emphases. Some newspapers placed more emphasis on the factual ideal and on the need to uncover the facts through a process of investigation, while others – especially those aimed at a large circulation – gave more emphasis to entertainment and story-telling.

The changes which transformed the press in the nineteenth century underlie the emergence and development of scandal as a mediated event. The modern phenomenon of mediated scandal – that is, of scandal as an event which involves the disclosure through the media of previously hidden and morally disreputable activities, the revelation of which sets in motion a sequence of further occurrences – was invented in the course of the late eighteenth and nineteenth centuries. The reorientation of the daily press, the invention of the modern concept of news as social facts that had to be uncovered or discovered, and the rise of the journalistic profession were among the key conditions which shaped the formation of scandal as a mediated event. In the sixteenth, seventeenth and early eighteenth centuries, 'scandal' and 'scandalous' had been used primarily to characterize publications and allegations that were regarded as libellous, seditious or obscene. From the late eighteenth century on, these terms would be used increasingly to describe a new and distinctive type of event which involved the disclosure through the media of previously hidden and morally discreditable activities.

By the late nineteenth century, this type of mediated scandal had become a relatively common feature of the political landscape. In

Britain there were a number of crusading editors – like W. T. Stead of the *Pall Mall Gazette*, Henry Labouchere of *Truth* and Ernest Parke of the *North London Press* – who were committed to combating social abuses and injustices, and who were not afraid to use their newspapers as vehicles to achieve their ends. In a context characterized by rapid social change and by growing unease about issues related to sexuality, such as prostitution and venereal disease, these editors played an important role in shaping the climate of public debate.[27]

W. T. Stead was a man of particular significance in this context.[28] The son of a Congregationalist minister, Stead was imbued with strong moral convictions. He began his career as a Sunday school teacher before joining the *Northern Echo* in 1871. In 1880 he moved to the *Pall Mall Gazette*, an influential liberal-leaning daily, of which he soon became the editor. His support was enlisted in the campaign against prostitution and the trafficking of young girls, which were highly controversial issues at the time. Stead undertook to use the *Gazette* as a means to mobilize public support for the Criminal Law Amendment Bill (which, among other things, proposed to raise the age of consent to sixteen and to ban the abduction of girls under eighteen for the purposes of sex).[29] He decided to set up a 'Special and Secret Commission of Inquiry' to investigate child prostitution, and took the highly unconventional step of purchasing a girl of thirteen, introducing her into a London brothel and then sending her abroad. Armed with this evidence, he ran a series of articles in the *Gazette* in July 1885 under the heading 'The maiden tribute of modern Babylon' in which he sought to expose the harsh realities of the child prostitution trade. Stead warned his readers that 'The story of an actual pilgrimage into a real hell is not pleasant reading, and it is not meant to be. It is, however, an authentic record of unimpeachable facts, "abominable, unutterable, and worse than fables yet have feigned or fear conceived." '[30] The articles recounted in graphic detail the story of the young girl who had been procured, using this as a device to expose the horrors of the prostitution trade. They also attacked the corruption of the police and the hypocrisy and immorality of the rich and powerful for turning a blind eye to a tragedy which they helped to create.

Stead's articles caused a sensation and contributed to the growing pressure on Parliament to pass the Criminal Law Amendment Bill, which became popularly known as 'Stead's Act' and which finally received the royal assent on 14 August 1885. Stead was subsequently convicted of abduction and imprisoned for three months, but his brazen exposé of the prostitution trade helped to define an emerging role for journalists as investigators[31] who could use the disclosure of hidden realities to intervene in public debate, and the *Gazette* continued to play a key role in the scandals which were prevalent in late nineteenth-century England.

Among these was a scandal that centred on a house in Cleveland Street, just off Tottenham Court Road in London's West End.[32] The house was a male brothel run by a man named Charles Hammond, who employed young boys to service his clientele. The scandal emerged from a routine police investigation of an unrelated incident. In early July 1889, a sum of money was stolen from a room in the Central Telegraph Office in the City of London. Suspicion fell on a fifteen-year-old telegraph messenger boy named Charles Swinscow, who was found to have more money in his pocket than might have been expected from the level of his wages. When questioned by the police, he admitted that he got the money by 'going to bed with gentlemen' in 19 Cleveland Street. He claimed that a fellow employee named Henry Newlove, who worked as a clerk in the GPO Secretary's office, had persuaded him to go to the house. Newlove was eventually arrested along with another man named George Veck, while Hammond fled to France.

When Newlove was arrested he complained that he was being forced to take the blame while men in high places were allowed to walk free, apparently claiming that Lord Arthur Somerset and the Earl of Euston regularly visited the house. These names were mentioned again when evidence was given against Newlove and Veck at the preliminary proceedings before the magistrate in Marlborough Street in August and September 1889. The connection with Lord Somerset and the Earl of Euston fuelled the interest of the press. When Newlove and Veck were tried at the Old Bailey in September, they pleaded guilty to charges of gross indecency and were sentenced to four and nine months' imprisonment respectively (relatively modest sentences for this offence at the time). The case took no more than half an hour. Many suspected that a deal had been struck: Newlove and Veck would be given light sentences and the case would quickly be closed, so as to avoid implicating others. Rumours were spreading that the house in Cleveland Street had counted among its clients not only Lord Somerset and the Earl of Euston, but also Prince Albert Victor (generally known as Prince Eddy), elder son of the Prince and Princess of Wales and second in line to the throne.

These rumours were turned into public allegations on 16 November 1889, when the *North London Press* – a small, radical paper concerned primarily with local government issues and with the

THE WEST-END SCANDALS.

COMMITTAL OF THE EDITOR OF THE "PRESS" FOR TRIAL.

A DEFENCE FUND OPENED.

Lord Euston emphatically denies the libellous statement, and explains the circumstances under which he once visited the house in Cleveland-street.

The editor of this paper has been committed to take his trial at the sessions of the Central Criminal Court, which open on Monday, 16 December. The proceedings were initiated last Saturday morning, when on the application of Mr. Lionel Hart, instructed by Messrs. Lewis & Lewis, Justice Field granted his fiat for the commencement of criminal proceedings against Mr. Ernest Parke, whose solicitor, Mr. Minton Slater, offered no opposition. At Bow-street Police Court the same afternoon, Mr. George Lewis obtained from Mr. Vaughan a warrant for

LORD EUSTON.

Mr. Parke's arrest, the Earl of Euston supporting the application by testifying to the truth of the affidavit he had made denying the libellous statements complained of. Sergeant Partridge was sent with the warrant to the *Star* office, but being by inadvertence informed that Mr. Parke had left, went to his place of residence at Clapham. Meanwhile, however, Mr. Parke heard of the issue of the warrant, and at once went to Bow-street

TO SURRENDER HIMSELF,

accompanied by gentlemen who offered bail to the amount of £1,500. The magistrate had, however, left, the hour being half-past five, and Detective-Inspector Conquest—who was in charge—had no authority to accept bail. The Chief Commissioner Mr. Monro was consulted, but finally at 10.30 Mr. Parke and his friends were informed that the ordinary course could not be departed from and he must be detained in the cells till Monday morning. Everything was done for his comfort that the police regulations

regarded as the disgrace and opprobrium of modern civilisation." The paragraph concluded by warning Mr. Matthews, the Home Secretary, that if he did not take action before Parliament met he would have a heavy reckoning to settle. Mr. Lewis continued that the accusation was a very atrocious one, and he should ask that the defendant be committed for trial. The circumstances, so far as Lord Euston was concerned, were these. He had never committed any crime of any sort or kind. That statement was

ABSOLUTELY WITHOUT ANY FOUNDATION

so far as he was concerned. He had never left the country, and there had been no warrant issued so far as he knew for his apprehension. If there was any warrant out, Lord Euston was present that day to be apprehended; but it was perfectly untrue that such a warrant had issued. All that he knew about the case was simply this. One evening at the end of May or the beginning of June Lord Euston was walking in Piccadilly at about 12 o'clock at night when a man put into his hand a card on which were the words "Poses Plas-

HAMMOND.

tiques.—Hammond, 19, Cleveland-street." About a week later

LORD EUSTON WENT TO THE HOUSE,

between 10.30 and 11 at night. A man opened the door to him and asked him for a sovereign, which Lord Euston gave him. Lord Euston asked about the poses plastiques, when the man made an indecent proposal to him, on which Lord Euston called him an infernal scoundrel, and threatened to knock him down if he did not at once allow him to leave the house. The door was then opened and Lord Euston at once left the house. That was all he knew of the matter.

Formal evidence was then given of the publication of the libel and of the connection of Mr. Parke with the paper, but Mr. Lockwood observed that the evidence was hardly necessary as the responsibility of the defendant was not disputed. The Earl of Euston was then examined by Mr. Lewis. He said—My name is Henry James, Earl of Euston. When in London I reside at

4, GROSVENOR-PLACE.

When not in London. I reside at Euston Lodge, Thetford, or Wakefield Lodge, Stoney Stratford, my father's place.

You have seen the copy of the paper of the 16th of November, *The North London Press?*—I have. I at once gave instructions for a criminal prosecution for libel in respect of the matter contained in

You say the statement was first made in the month of October?—Yes.
Have you made a statement at the Home Office about it?—No.
Or at the Treasury?—No.
Did you make no statement to any official?—None whatever.
Just wait and hear my question. You made no statement to any official at all either at the Treasury or the Home Office?—I have had no communication of any sort or kind either with the Treasury or the Home Office.
That you swear?—That I swear.
You said you first made your statement in October. That I take it meant to some friends?—Yes, privately.

IS LORD ARTHUR SOMERSET

a friend of yours?—I know him.
When did you see him last?—Last summer some time during the season. That is as near as I can remember. I was in London during May June, and July. I saw him in society. I was in the habit of meeting him constantly.
Did you meet him in society?—Yes.
You have not seen him since?—No.
Do you know where he is?—No.
Now just tell me with regard to this occurrence in May or June, you say you afterwards read the card. How long afterwards?—When I got home I think. I don't remember particularly. I think when I got home and took my coat off. I did not read it in the street. I just shoved it in my pocket and looked at it when I got home.
Just tell me what it was that was on the card; was it a printed or a lithographed card?—It was a lithographed card, but the words *poses plastiques* at the top were in writing.
Was the gentleman giving out these cards promiscuously, or

WERE YOU PARTICULARLY FAVOURED?

—Witness (laughing): I cannot tell you. He shoved one into my hand, and I put it in my pocket.
Was he giving them away to other people? —I really cannot tell you. I was walking along pretty smart home. I do not walk slowly as a rule.
Did you see him give a card to anyone else?— No. It was near 12 o'clock as I was walking home.
I suggest to you that you had not time to stop and read it?—Well (laughing), I did not stop to read it under a lamppost.

---

6 The *North London Press* announces the committal of its editor, Ernest Parke, to trial for libel. Parke was sued by the Earl of Euston for naming him in connection with the 'indescribably loathsome scandal in Cleveland-street'.

conditions of workers and the poor – published an article under the heading 'The West-End Scandals' in which it named Lord Somerset and the Earl of Euston in connection with the 'indescribably loathsome scandal in Cleveland-street' and suggested that these men had been allowed to slip away because 'their prosecution would disclose the fact that a far more distinguished and highly placed personage than themselves was inculpated in their disgusting crimes'.[33] Lord Euston instructed his solicitor to institute proceedings for libel against the editor of the *North London Press*, Ernest Parke. Called to the witness box, Euston admitted that he had been to 19 Cleveland Street, after being given, he claimed, a card advertising '*Poses plastiques*' (a term commonly used to describe girls posing nude), but he insisted that he left the house as soon as he discovered its true character and never returned. The defence relied heavily on the testimony of a male prostitute, John Saul, who claimed to have taken Lord Euston to Cleveland Street and described the incident in salacious detail, but the defence were unable to provide convincing corroborating evidence. Parke was found guilty of libel and sentenced to twelve months' imprisonment.

Lord Euston emerged from the scandal with his reputation largely intact. He was a prominent Freemason at the time and he went on to become Grand Master of the Mark Masons and was appointed an aide-de-camp by King Edward VII. Lord Somerset, on the other hand, never recovered. He fled the country in October 1889, shortly before a warrant was issued for his arrest (many were convinced that he had been tipped off), and he spent the remaining years of his life in exile in France, where he died in relative obscurity in 1926.

The Cleveland Street scandal was one of numerous scandals which featured in the press in late nineteenth-century England. Others included the controversy surrounding Oscar Wilde (who chose, unwisely as it happens, to initiate a libel action against the Marquess of Queensberry, an action which brought Wilde's homosexuality into the open and thereby sealed his fate), the fall of Sir Charles Dilke (a rising star of the Liberal Party whose political career was irrevocably damaged by the events surrounding a divorce action in which he was named as co-respondent) and, of course, the undoing of Charles Parnell. Many of these scandals involved sexuality – both heterosexuality and homosexuality – and, in this respect, they were shaped by the distinctive moral and legal climate of late Victorian England (a context in which acts of male homosexuality were illegal). But there were scandals involving allegations of fraud and corruption too, as we shall see in a later chapter. By the late nineteenth century, a distinctive type of event had become a common feature of social and political life. This type of event was the mediated scandal: that is, an event involving the disclosure through the media of activities that were previously hidden (or known only to a small circle of people), activities which are morally discreditable and which, on being made public in this way, may turn out to have damaging implications for the individuals concerned.

While the nineteenth century was the birthplace of mediated scandal, the twentieth century was to become its true home. Once this distinctive type of event had been invented, it would become a recognizable genre that some would seek actively to produce while others – especially those who were prominent in public life – would strive, with varying degrees of discretion and success, to avoid. But there were also several broader conditions which favoured its development. First, there was the growth and consolidation of the mass circulation press. By the early decades of the twentieth century, newspapers had become big businesses. Employing the common formula of low price, extensive advertising and mass circulation (sometimes described as the 'Northcliffe revolution', following Lord Northcliffe's success with the *Daily Mail* and the *Daily Mirror*), newspapers entered an ever intensifying struggle to define their positions *vis-à-vis* one another and to secure a larger (or at least financially viable) market share. One consequence of this struggle was the growing consolidation of newspapers into large conglomerates which controlled an increasing proportion of the market. Another consequence was the continued expansion of mass circulation newspapers which emphasized entertainment and story-telling, and which used strong headlines, vivid photos and popular styles of writing as ways of defining and strengthening their positions in an increasingly competitive field.

A second condition which favoured the development of mediated scandal was the rise of investigative journalism. The profession of journalism emerged, as we have seen, in the late nineteenth century, and its growth was accompanied by the gradual formation of a professional ethos which emphasized, among other things, the importance of uncovering and reporting the facts. Crusading editors in nineteenth-century England, like W. T. Stead, had shown how sustained inquiry on the part of the press could lead to startling stories which were capable of shaping public debate and influencing political processes. Journalistic exposés of this kind were also relatively common in late nineteenth-century America, where editors such as Joseph Pulitzer and E. W. Scripps had built up popular newspapers which commonly attacked corruption in government and abuses of corporate power. During the first decade of the twentieth century, the social criticism of the 'muckrakers' – a term used by Theodore Roosevelt in 1906 to describe journalists who, writing in magazines like *McClure's* and *Cosmopolitan*, sought to expose and condemn the social evils of the time[34] – became an integral part of the reform movement of the Progressive era. This kind of critical, investigative style of reporting, in which the search for hidden facts was combined with the idea that journalists had a moral responsibility to root out wrongdoing and expose social ills, gradually came to define part of the professional ethos of journalism. In the course of the twentieth century this emerging style of investigative journalism was shaped by the growing recognition that 'facts' were not simply there to be gathered and reported: facts could be concealed and manipulated (by governments and unscrupulous politicians among others), and even those facts which were less contestable often required a good deal of interpretation to make sense. The development of investigative journalism in the twentieth century was the outcome, to some extent, of the pursuit of the fact-finding ideal of the journalistic ethos in a cultural milieu which adopted a more sceptical attitude towards what is given.[35] Journalists became increasingly conscious of the fact that governments and others would seek actively to manage the news and to conceal material which might be damaging to them, and some journalists sought – with varying degrees of determination and success – to look beyond (and probe behind) the accounts provided by official sources.

A third factor which favoured the development of mediated scandal was the diffusion of new information and communication technologies. The uses of electricity for the purposes of communication were pioneered in the late nineteenth and early twentieth centuries, resulting in the development of radio broadcasting on a mass scale from the 1920s on, and television broadcasting from the late 1940s on. These new technologies of mediated communication greatly increased the visibility of political leaders and other public figures, as well as creating a whole new category of well-known individuals – film stars, pop stars, radio and TV personalities, etc. – who owed their fame primarily to the fact that they were visible through these media. Moreover, these new technologies, by virtue of the audio and visual richness of the messages they conveyed, helped to create a new kind of intimacy in the public domain, enabling political leaders and others to appear before distant audiences as individuals who could disclose – and increasingly did disclose – aspects of their personal life. The new technologies also provided an ever more sophisticated array of devices for monitoring and recording activities. The more that political leaders and others became visible as individuals in the public domain and the more sophisticated the technologies became, the more likely it was that previously hidden regions of activity would begin to surface. Greater visibility did not necessarily imply greater openness, but it did increase the risk that activities carried out in privacy or semi-secrecy would find their way into the public domain.

3

Scandal as a Mediated Event

We have seen how, with the development of modern societies, a distinctive form of scandal emerged which was interwoven with mediated forms of communication. The term 'scandal' continued to be applied to actions and events which unfolded in the shared locales of everyday life, but increasingly the term was associated with a cluster of phenomena that were shaped by print and other media. What are the characteristics of these mediated scandals? How do they differ from the localized scandals of everyday life? How does the unfolding of scandals in the media alter their character as events?

In this chapter I shall try to answer these questions by examining the features of scandal as a mediated event. My approach in this chapter will be primarily analytical. In the previous chapter I traced the historical emergence of mediated scandals; I tried to show that, as a distinctive type of event, mediated scandals arose in the late eighteenth and nineteenth centuries and, for various reasons, flourished in the twentieth. I now want to focus on this type of event and analyse some of its characteristics. I shall begin by comparing mediated scandals with their localized counterparts. I shall then examine the structure of mediated scandals as events, showing that they have a distinctive temporal and sequential structure which is shaped by the operational practices of media and other organizations. I shall look more carefully at mediated scandals as situated events, examining some of the agents and organizations that are involved in the production of scandal. Finally, I shall consider the ways in which mediated scandals are experienced by individuals, both the individuals whose lives are directly affected by scandals and the individuals who are spectators of them.

Throughout this analysis I shall try to show that mediated scandals are events in their own right, distinct in certain respects from the localized scandals which unfold in the shared contexts of everyday life. Mediated scandals are events which extend well beyond the original actions or transgressions which lie at their heart. We could describe these scandals as 'mediated events', because they are events which are constituted in part by mediated forms of communication. Disclosure through the media, and commentary in the media, are not secondary or incidental features of these forms of scandal: they are partly constitutive of them.

Some Characteristics of Mediated Scandals

In order to clarify the characteristics of mediated scandals, I shall begin by drawing a broad contrast between localized scandals and mediated scandals. Table 3.1 summarizes the main points of comparison.

I have argued that the primary sense of 'scandal' today is the sense

Table 3.1 Localized and mediated scandals

Characteristics	Localized scandals	Mediated scandals
Type of transgression	predominantly first-order	first-order and second-order
Type of publicness	traditional publicness of co-presence	mediated publicness
Mode of disclosure	face-to-face communication	mediated communication
Mode of disapprobation	face-to-face communication	mediated communication
Evidential base	relatively ephemeral	relatively durable
Spatial-temporal framework	localized	delocalized

which refers to actions or events which involve, among other things, the transgression of certain values, norms or moral codes. In respect of this feature, there is no significant difference between localized and mediated scandals: both involve some form and some degree of transgression (actual or alleged). But whereas localized scandals are concerned most often with first-order transgressions (that is, the transgression of values or norms which have some degree of moral force or bindingness), mediated scandals are more likely to involve a mixture of first-order and second-order transgressions. This is partly because, as mediated scandals unfold, the individuals at the centre of them become caught up in a process which is very difficult to control, and in which their attempts to exercise control can easily come unstuck. It is also partly because their earlier actions and utterances may be fixed in ways which limit their options, and which increase the risk that their subsequent statements may be conclusively disproved. While it is not uncommon for localized scandals to involve second-order transgressions, the latter are a more prominent feature of mediated scandals, for the reasons given above.

All forms of scandal necessarily involve some degree of non-participant knowledge, and hence all scandals are necessarily 'public' affairs, but the types of publicness characteristic of localized and mediated scandals are different. Localized scandals are characterized by what I have called the traditional publicness of co-presence: these are events which unfold in the shared locales of everyday life, where individuals interact with one another face to face. The individuals involved are known to one another personally, and they generally come to know about the actions or events either by witnessing directly certain forms of behaviour which give rise to reasonable suspicion or by hearing about the actions or events from others. Localized scandals are thus commonly linked to the kinds of gossip and rumour which are spread by word of mouth.

Mediated scandals, by contrast, are characterized by what I have called mediated publicness: these are events which unfold, at least in part, through mediated forms of communication, and which thus acquire a publicness that is independent of their capacity to be seen or heard directly by a plurality of co-present others. By virtue of their mediated publicness, the actions or events which lie at the heart of mediated scandals are made visible to others who were not present at the time and place of their occurrence, and who may be situated in spatially distant locales. Whereas the publicness of localized scandals is shaped by the dynamics of face-to-face interaction, mediated scandals acquire a kind of publicness which detaches them from face-to-face interaction and which is shaped by the interactional characteristics of mediated communication.

How do the interactional characteristics of mediated communication shape the occurrence and development of scandals? We can begin to answer this question by introducing a further distinction – this time drawn from the work of the sociologist Erving Goffman.[1] Any action or utterance takes place within a particular interactive framework which involves certain assumptions and conventions as well as the physical features of the setting (spatial layout, furniture, dress, etc.). An individual acting within this framework will to some extent adapt his or her behaviour to it, seeking to project a self-image which is more or less compatible with the framework and with the impression that the individual wishes to convey. The action framework, and the features that are accentuated by the individuals acting within it, comprise what Goffman calls the 'front region'.[2] Actions or aspects of self which are felt to be inappropriate, or which might discredit the image that the person is seeking to project, are suppressed and reserved for other settings and encounters – what Goffman describes as 'back regions'. In back regions individuals often act in ways that knowingly contradict the images they seek to project in front regions. In back regions they relax and allow themselves to lower their guard. They may ease the mechanisms of self-control, no longer requiring themselves to monitor their own actions with the same degree of reflexivity generally employed while acting in front regions.

The distinction between front region and back region is typical of many action contexts – in restaurants, for example, the kitchens are generally separated from the dining areas by corridors or swinging doors and are off-limits to customers. But the use of communication media can alter the nature of front regions and back regions, as well as the relations between them. In the case of face-to-face interaction, the participants share a common front region – the dining room of the restaurant, for example – though each participant may have their own back region relative to this common space. But since mediated interaction generally involves a separation of the contexts within which the participants are situated, it creates an interactive framework that consists of two or more front regions which are separated in space and perhaps also in time. Each of these front regions has its own back regions, and each participant in the mediated interaction must seek to manage the boundary between them. Moreover, given the characteristics of mediated communication and the complexity of these interactional frameworks, the boundaries between front

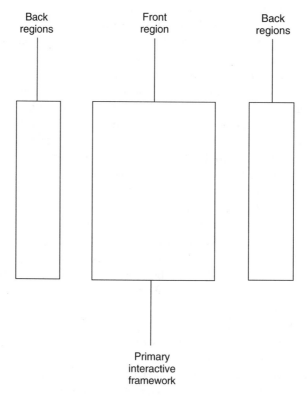

Figure 3.1 The social organization of face-to-face interaction

regions and back regions are relatively porous or 'leaky'. Individuals who wish to project a certain image through the media may find that, despite their best efforts, it is extremely difficult to contain certain forms of behaviour in the back regions where they originally occurred. They may also find that the leakage of this back-region behaviour into the front region renders it visible to others in ways that undermine, or threaten to undermine, the self-image they wish to project.

Figures 3.1 and 3.2 illustrate some of these differences in the social organization of face-to-face interaction and mediated quasi-interaction. In face-to-face interaction, the primary interactive framework is a common front region which is situated in a shared spatial-temporal locale. Each participant in the interaction has his or her own back region of behaviour which can be closed off from the front region, or which he or she can selectively disclose to others. In

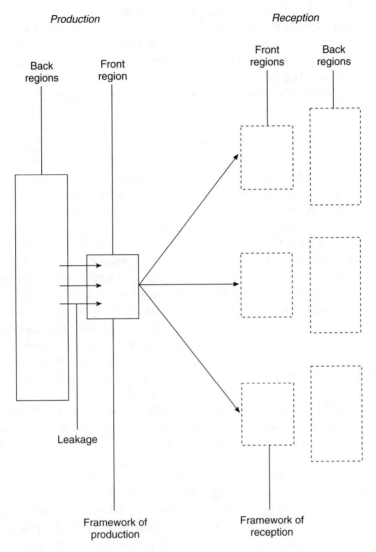

Figure 3.2 The social organization of mediated quasi-interaction

the case of mediated quasi-interaction, by contrast, there is no common front region which serves as the primary interactive framework for all participants. There are production contexts in which there are front regions and back regions, and there is a plurality of spatially dispersed reception contexts, each of which has its own front region and back region. In the case of a television transmission, for example, the front region of the production context might be the area of a studio which is covered by the camera, while the front regions of the contexts of reception will be the various settings (domestic living rooms etc.) in which the programme is watched. Individuals who appear in the front regions of production contexts will generally seek to exclude their back-region behaviour, or to manage carefully which aspects of their back-region behaviour are to appear within the front region. But leakage can easily occur, especially with the ever increasing complexity of communication technologies; and, given the nature of mediated quasi-interaction, the leakage of back-region behaviour into the front region of the production context may quickly become visible to many thousands or millions of recipients.

The leakage of back-region behaviour into front regions occurs in different ways and in different settings – not all leakages constitute scandals. Some leakages constitute no more than fleeting moments of awkwardness or embarrassment – as, for instance, when the former British prime minister John Major, after giving a television interview, allowed himself to relax in the studio and to speak frankly and disparagingly about some members of his party, only to find, much to his embarrassment, that the microphone was still on.[3] But mediated scandals are one set of events which typically involve the leakage of back-region behaviour into front regions in ways which endow the actions lying at the heart of the scandal with a kind of publicness that they would not otherwise have had. Suddenly, actions or events which had hitherto remained largely hidden from view are thrust, via mediated forms of communication, into front regions where they are visible and observable to thousands or millions of others. Part of the controversy associated with mediated scandals, and the shock and outrage to which they sometimes give rise, may on occasion be due less to the character of the transgression as such than to the surprise and discomfort produced by the disclosure of forms of back-region behaviour which are unpalatable or incongruous with the positions held and the images projected by the individuals concerned. The shock experienced by many people on hearing the Watergate tapes, for example, arose not so much from the realization that Nixon may have been involved in a cover-up, since most people had long suspected this, but from the discovery that, behind the carefully managed presentation of Nixon and his administration, there was a back region of behaviour, and associated forms of back-region talk, which seemed altogether inappropriate for the incumbent of the White House.

Both localized and mediated scandals typically involve leaky boundaries between back regions and front regions, but the mode of leakage is different in each case. In localized scandals, the actions or events which lie at the heart of the scandal are typically disclosed to others through face-to-face communication: non-participant knowledge is spread by word of mouth. Of course, various forms of mediated communication may be used to supplement word of mouth, but typically these are relatively closed forms which are oriented to specific others, such as telephone conversations. In the case of mediated scandals, by contrast, the actions or events are typically disclosed by forms of mediated communication which are relatively open-ended, and which transmit knowledge of the events to a plurality of non-participants who are situated in diverse contexts. But here too, the contrast is not absolute. Mediated communication is the principal mode of disclosure in mediated scandals, but this does not mean that face-to-face communication plays no role. In mediated scandals, information is commonly conveyed by word of mouth as well as by the media, and information conveyed by the media is commonly discussed by individuals in the contexts of their day-to-day lives.

Just as localized and mediated scandals can be differentiated in terms of their principal modes of disclosure, so too they can be differentiated in terms of their principal modes of disapprobation. Scandal presupposes, as we have seen, not only the occurrence of acts of transgression which become known to others, but also the expression of disapproval by others. In localized scandals, the expression of disapproval commonly takes the form of oral speech-acts which are uttered in the course of face-to-face communication (or in relatively closed forms of mediated communication). Individuals express their disapproval to others in a variety of communicative settings – in one-to-one conversations, in small gatherings, in public meetings, etc. The repeated articulation of negative speech-acts produces a localized climate of moral censure. In the case of mediated scandals, by contrast, open-ended forms of mediated communication constitute the principal mode of disapprobation. The headlines in newspapers, the articulation of negative judgements in the press, the scathing and sometimes humiliating caricatures of the individuals whose actions (actual or alleged) are the object of reproach: it is the repeated expression of these mediated acts of communication which generates the climate of disapproval characteristic of mediated scandals. Of course, this mediated climate of disapproval does not necessarily correspond to the opinions and attitudes of the individuals who read the newspapers and watch the television programmes.

The articulation of negative judgements in the press can easily become a self-referring discourse, and the extent to which the moral climate generated by it corresponds to the attitudes of recipients is, as we shall see, an open question.

Another respect in which mediated scandals differ from their localized counterparts concerns what I shall describe as their 'evidential base'. Scandals commonly involve knowledge claims by non-participants concerning actions which allegedly occurred in the past, claims that may be contested by the individuals at the centre of the scandal. The trajectory of the scandal may come to depend on the extent to which these claims can be backed up by suitable forms of evidence. At this level of the evidential base, communication media can come to play a crucial role. One of the most important characteristics of communication media is that they 'fix' information or symbolic content in a relatively durable medium. In the temporal flow of face-to-face interaction, the contents of symbolic exchange may have a fleeting existence: words uttered may rapidly fade away, and the preservation of symbolic contents may depend on the fallible and contestable faculty of memory. However, by using certain technical media of communication – paper, photographic film, electromagnetic tape, digital information systems, etc. – the contents of symbolic exchange can be fixed and preserved in a relatively durable fashion. Different media have different degrees of durability, and they vary in the extent to which they allow symbolic contents to be altered or revised. Words written on paper or utterances recorded on tape are more difficult to renounce than words exchanged in face-to-face interaction. Electromagnetic tape can, however, be erased – though erasures may leave traces from which inferences can, in some circumstances, be drawn.

Both localized and mediated scandals may involve the use of communication media of various kinds for the purpose of providing evidence in support of contestable claims, but the fixing of incriminating evidence in relatively durable media is more likely to play an important role in mediated scandals than in their localized counterparts. Localized scandals often involve forms of evidence that are linked to social interaction in particular settings – such as observations of the actions of others, conversations overheard, etc. Hence the evidential base of localized scandals is relatively ephemeral, in the sense that the forms of evidence are likely to rely rather heavily on the faculty of memory (although some fixed symbolic content, such as letters or documents, may also be involved). Mediated scandals, by contrast, are unlikely to rely solely or heavily on relatively ephemeral forms of evidence. Since mediated scandals generally involve the articulation of knowledge claims in the press or other media, and since the making public of such claims may carry risks for media organizations (including the risk of libel), it is common for mediated scandals to involve forms of evidence that are fixed in relatively durable media, from incriminating letters and photographs to tape-recorded conversations.

Nowhere is this more evident than in Watergate. It is quite possible that the investigation of the Watergate break-in would have eventually ground to a halt, and it is at least questionable whether the scandal would have had such dramatic political consequences (culminating in Nixon's resignation in the face of his imminent impeachment), had it not been for the discovery of the secretly recorded tapes which contained incriminating evidence of Nixon's involvement in a cover-up. But the existence of evidence fixed in a relatively durable medium has also played a central role in other mediated scandals. Profumo's hastily scribbled note to Christine Keeler, which began with the epithet 'Darling', would return to haunt him when the scandal began to break. Similarly, in the scandal that destroyed the political career of Jeremy Thorpe – leader of the Liberal Party in Britain from 1967 to 1976 and regarded by many as one of the outstanding politicians of his generation – a crucial role was played by a letter from Thorpe to Norman Scott which contained the infamous line 'Bunnies *can* (and *will*) go to France.' Tape-recordings of telephone conversations allegedly picked up by amateur scanners and purportedly conveying the details of intimate conversations between Prince Charles and Camilla Parker-Bowles (the so-called 'Camillagate' tape) and between Princess Diana and James Gilbey (the 'Squidgygate' tape) played a prominent part in the scandals that surrounded the royal family in the early 1990s. And, of course, the conversations between Monica Lewinsky and Linda Tripp, secretly taped by Tripp and handed over to federal prosecutors, played a crucial role in redirecting Kenneth Starr's flagging investigation of the President and igniting the Clinton–Lewinsky scandal. In these and other cases, fixed symbolic materials provide forms of evidence which may not be entirely conclusive, but which are much more difficult to deny or explain away than unwitnessed events or unrecorded conversations. A contested claim based on unwitnessed events or unrecorded conversations may, in the end, boil down to one person's word against another's, but a message fixed in some medium – an intimate letter, a recorded conversation, a revealing photo, etc. – may provide an incriminating form of evidence.

The importance of evidence fixed in relatively durable media helps to explain why scandals can be fuelled by new technological developments. The development of new technologies – high-powered photographic lenses, concealed cameras, miniature microphones, wire-tapping devices, scanning equipment, etc. – provides an ever more sophisticated array of devices that can be used to record images or conversations (and to do so secretly), and this in turn might provide substantive evidence for the existence of activities which, if disclosed, could form the basis of a scandal. Camillagate highlighted the dangers of using a mobile phone for intimate conversations. The Clinton–Lewinsky scandal highlighted the risks of frank chatting among friends when telephones can easily be tapped and microphones can be hidden on the body; it highlighted the risks of email too, when messages can be recovered from computers after they have been deleted. Of course, new developments in information and communication technology are not the only developments which are relevant here, just as photos, letters and conversations are not the only forms of evidence which can attest to the existence of covert activities. In the case of the Clinton–Lewinsky scandal, for instance, the DNA testing of the infamous semen-stained dress provided a crucial form of evidence which would have been exceedingly difficult to contest. But since the activities which lie at the heart of scandals generally involve social interactions between two or more individuals, it is not surprising that the recording of symbolic exchanges which attest to the existence of these interactions often plays an important role.

The significance of evidence fixed in durable media is heightened by the fact that, as scandals unfold, these forms of evidence may be made available to others by being reproduced in open-ended media like newspapers, magazines and television. When evidence is propelled into the public domain in this way, it may become an acute source of embarrassment for the individuals concerned and make it very difficult for them to sustain their public denials. Moreover, once made available in the media, evidence of this kind is likely to be reproduced on numerous occasions, as material disclosed by one newspaper, for example, is likely to be reported by other newspapers and other media. Through this process of 'extended mediazation',[4] the evidence can be circulated quickly and widely, fuelling the flames of a scandal which, despite attempts to limit the damage, can easily spin out of control.

This brings us to a final point of comparison between localized and mediated scandals. Whereas localized scandals are generally tied to the local communities in which individuals interact with others face to face, mediated scandals unfold within a different spatial-temporal framework. The kinds of interaction made possible by communication media are stretched across space and time. Information and symbolic content can be transmitted to others who are situated in diverse and spatially distant locales; and, by using electronic media, they can be transmitted virtually instantaneously. Moreover, by being fixed in relatively durable media, information and symbolic content can be reread, re-heard and re-viewed on subsequent occasions: the words and images endure. Mediated scandals thus unfold within a spatial-temporal framework which is delocalized in character, where information and communication flow quickly (potentially instantaneously) and where symbolic content can be fixed and reproduced over time. Whereas localized scandals rarely spread beyond the local communities in which they are embedded, mediated scandals are rarely restricted to such communities: their mediated character means that they generally involve individuals who do not share the same locale, and the speed and open-endedness of communication media mean that they can spread quickly and uncontrollably.

Hence mediated scandals can quickly become national events, indeed global events, producing a mixture of alarm and bewilderment among individuals situated in widely dispersed contexts. The development of national and, more recently, global media networks and organizations creates an institutional basis for the delocalization of mediated scandals. Major scandals, such as Profumo, Watergate and the Iran-Contra affair, were widely reported in the international press. The Clinton–Lewinsky scandal became a truly global event, receiving extensive coverage by the press and television throughout the world (including global networks like CNN) and generating much discussion and bemused amazement among individuals in widely dispersed locales. Mediated scandals can also become sedimented aspects of historical memory, preserved in countless media materials (newspaper articles, television broadcasts, books, etc.) and reactivated from time to time – in the way, for example, that the Profumo affair was brought back to life thirty years later by the release of the film *Scandal*, and as Watergate was recalled by films like *All the President's Men* and *Nixon*, by countless books, articles and television programmes which re-examine aspects of the scandal and, indeed, by the very use of the suffix '-gate' to describe events which seem to have the potential to become damaging political scandals.

The Sequential Structure of Mediated Scandals

If we understand mediated scandals as a distinctive type of event which is constituted in part by mediated forms of communication, we can also see that, as events, they have a certain temporal and sequential structure. Mediated scandals typically unfold over a period of time which is punctuated by the rhythms of media organizations, with their distinctive patterns of publication and broadcasting. They also exemplify a certain sequential structure, in the sense that one phase in the unfolding of mediated scandals is typically followed by another. And the unfolding of mediated scandals is interwoven with the constant telling and retelling of stories about the events (or alleged events) which lie at the heart of the scandal. Let us consider each of these points in turn.

Mediated scandals typically extend over a period of time which is always longer than a day and which may last for weeks, months or even years, but which cannot continue indefinitely. They always last longer than a day because the first day that the disclosures and allegations appear in the media can only be the beginning of a potential mediated scandal; whether this develops into a fully fledged scandal depends on the ways that others respond to the initial disclosures and allegations, responses that will emerge in the days, weeks and months that follow. An initial disclosure which is followed by complete silence will not evolve into a scandal. The temporal development of a mediated scandal is shaped by the distinctive rhythms of media organizations and other institutions, such as judicial and political institutions, which play a key role in the disclosure and interpretation of information relevant to the scandal. The intensity of mediated scandals often increases at the time of a trial or an official inquiry, for example, since occasions of this kind provide a focus of attention and a regular flow of information which can be used by media organizations. But while mediated scandals are always stretched over an extended period of time and punctuated by the rhythms of the media and other organizations, they cannot go on forever. A long-running mediated scandal will either reach a point of termination (a confession, a resignation, the outcome of a trial, the result of an official inquiry, etc.) or it will gradually fade out, as public interest wanes and media organizations decide that it no longer merits the attention once devoted to it.

Mediated scandals are not only stretched out in time: they also display a sequential structure in the sense that one phase of the scandal is typically followed by another, although this sequential pattern is by no means rigid or fixed. Indeed, one key feature of mediated scandals is that they are essentially *open-ended*. Retrospectively, we can look back at a mediated scandal and reconstruct the sequential pattern of its development. We can also see retrospectively that some mediated scandals have some common or similar sequential features. But if one is situated in the midst of a mediated scandal and watching (or participating in) its development in real time, it is extremely difficult to predict how it will unfold. Mediated scandals are often very complex events with many sources of uncertainty – what exactly did X do and when did he or she do it? How much did Y know and when exactly did he or she know it? How far is Z willing to go in pressing his or her allegations? One of the reasons why mediated scandals are of interest to readers and viewers is that, for those who are witnessing the unfolding events as they occur, the eventual outcome is intrinsically unclear. Hence they fuel speculation and, like a good novel, they constantly test the capacity of readers and viewers to assess the veracity of the protagonists, to figure out the plot and to predict its resolution.

Nevertheless, with the benefit of hindsight, one can reconstruct the sequential structure of particular scandals. One can also step back from the detail of particular scandals and produce a more general account, provided one recognizes that actual scandals will always differ in their details and unfold in their own distinctive ways. So how might we describe – retrospectively and in a general way – the sequential structure of mediated scandals? We can distinguish four main phases of the mediated scandal: first, there is the pre-scandal phase; second, the phase of the scandal proper; third, the culmination; and fourth, the aftermath.

A breach of norms or moral codes often lies at the origin of a mediated scandal, but transgressions of this kind generally belong to the pre-scandal phase. A mediated scandal does not begin with the transgression itself, but rather with the act of disclosure and/or allegation which turns the original transgression into an object of public knowledge. The pre-scandal phase may involve investigations or inquiries carried out by journalists, the police and others; in some cases they may be carrying out routine investigations which lead unexpectedly to disclosures of a scandalous kind (as, for example, in the Cleveland Street scandal), while on other occasions they may be actively searching for information which would produce (or would be likely to produce) a scandal. The pre-scandal phase may involve the publication of information which subsequently turns out to be relevant to a scandal, although it may not be recognized as such at the time and may not be picked up immediately by others. In some cases, initial disclosures of information may be followed up later when the circumstances are more conducive to the occurrence of scandal, while in other cases, such disclosures may go nowhere. The pre-scandal phase may also be characterized by gossip, rumour and hearsay among individuals who are in a position to know something about the individuals whose actions may become the topic of scandal, but who, for whatever reason, refrain from articulating this knowledge in a public manner. Many political scandals involving sex, for example, are commonly preceded by gossip and the circulation of rumours among political elites, journalists and others, even if, for fear of libel among other things, these rumours remain in the form of private communications. The sexual transgressions of a political figure may be 'common knowledge' in elite circles well before they become public scandals (if they ever do).

The scandal proper begins with the public disclosure of an action or event that sets in motion the process of claim and counter-claim which constitutes the mediated scandal. The precipitating disclosure could be quite discreet – a small item of news on the inside page of a newspaper, for instance. But the public articulation of knowledge may suffice to trigger off a sequence of events which can escalate rapidly, as other media organizations rush to pick up and develop the story. Once the mediated scandal begins to break, its character and subsequent development – and, indeed, whether it develops at all – are shaped by the distinctive pattern of revelations, allegations and denunciations which unfold in the media. The scandal is literally played out in the media, and the activities of media personnel and organizations, with their distinctive practices and rhythms of work, play a crucial role. The media operate as a framing device, focusing attention on an individual or an alleged activity and refusing to let go. Allegations in the media may be met by denials on the part of the individual or individuals whose alleged actions lie at the centre of the scandal. Denials raise the prospect of second-order transgressions, and hence are commonly met by intensified efforts at disclosure by media organizations and others. The individuals at the centre of the scandal, together with their advisers, solicitors and supporters, may become locked in a strategic battle with media organizations and others; each move may be met by a counter-move, allegations may be met by denials, threats of disclosure may be met by threats of libel and so on, in the hope either of flushing out a confession or of forcing one's opponent into silence.

In the midst of this strategic confrontation, it is generally quite unclear to the protagonists just how the battle will unfold. The individuals at the centre of the scandal may believe that if they firmly and repeatedly deny their involvement in the alleged activities and if they can (should it be necessary) plug any leaks and prevent any incriminating evidence from emerging, then the public will eventually grow weary of a story that increasingly seems trumped up. They may seek to close down the lines of inquiry and cut off the flow of information, hoping that the scandal, deprived of fresh disclosures which would fuel speculation, will gradually die out. They might also seek to turn the tables on the press, accusing journalists of muckraking, of adopting unethical practices or of lowering the standards of public debate, thereby hoping to gain the upper hand in the struggle for public opinion. On the other side, journalists and others with access to media channels may be convinced that some kind of transgression or wrongdoing has occurred and may believe that if they can keep up the pressure by disclosing new material, making new connections and expressing opinions and judgements of various kinds, then the scandal will acquire a momentum which will become irreversible, eventually forcing the individuals to admit their culpability and accept the consequences.

The third phase of a mediated scandal is the culmination or dénouement. This is the stage when the scandal is finally brought to a head. Fresh disclosures and renewed speculation may increase the pressure on the individuals at the centre of the scandal. The culminating phase may lead to an admission of guilt, a resignation, a sacking and/or a criminal prosecution, but it can also result in a collapse of the case against the individual(s) concerned and the dissipation of the scandal. In some cases the culminating phase may be a dramatically staged event, such as a trial or a public hearing by a specially convened committee endowed with all the trappings of symbolic power. This staged event may also be a 'media event' in the sense defined by Dayan and Katz – that is, an exceptional occasion which is planned in advance and broadcast live, which interrupts the normal flow of events and which creates an atmosphere of solemnity and high expectation.[5] The televised impeachment debate of the House Judiciary Committee which brought the Watergate scandal to a close and the televised impeachment trial of Clinton were media events in this sense. But on other occasions the culminating phase may be much less dramatic – no trial, no confession, no resignation, just a period of relative calm when the tempo of allegations and denunciations subsides, public interest wanes and the scandal gradually peters out.

The fourth and final phase is the aftermath – that period when the high drama of the scandal and its dénouement have passed, when journalists, politicians and others (including, in many cases, the principals who were involved in the scandal, some of whom have found that there is a profitable market for scandal memoirs) engage in a reflection on the events and their implications. Much of this commentary takes place in the media itself, which, with the kind of self-referentiality which is often characteristic of the media field, tends to devote a good deal of time and attention to events which media organizations have helped to produce. But the aftermath may also be marked by the establishment of a commission of inquiry which may be given the task of carrying out a thorough and wide-ranging review of the circumstances that lay behind a scandal or series of scandals, and of making recommendations that could be implemented by the government or some other body. The Nolan Committee on Standards in Public Life, set up by the former British prime minister John Major in the wake of the cash-for-questions scandal, is a good example of an aftermath inquiry of this kind.

The unfolding of mediated scandals is also interwoven with the telling and retelling of stories about the events (or alleged events) which lie at their heart. Many scandals lend themselves with relative ease to popular forms of story-telling: they are focused on the adventures (or misadventures) of particular individuals – in some cases, powerful, wealthy or well-known individuals – who, driven by greed, desire or the lust for power and success, commit transgressions or crimes which are disgraceful, condemnable or even shocking. Many scandals can readily be moulded into the form of a modern morality tale.[6] Moreover, as a scandal unfolds, the event itself is continuously narrated by a variety of commentators and participants with access to the media, generating a multiplicity of stories which vary in detail and emphasis and which feed off one another while offering their own distinctive twist. Mediated scandals are continuously narrated events, in the sense that they are constituted in part by an array of mediated narratives which are continuously refined and revised as the event unfolds. Readers and viewers find themselves following a distinctive kind of story which has an indeterminate and continuously evolving plot, where each day, following the rhythms of newspaper publications or television broadcasts, one may be confronted by new twists and turns, where old certainties may suddenly crumble and new hypotheses emerge, and where the plot may occasionally become so thick that even the dedicated followers begin to lose their way. But it is to some extent this open-ended narrative structure, combined with the human interest character of scandal as a modern morality tale, which makes the following of scandals a source of pleasure for some and a topic of conversation for many.

Agents and Organizations

So far we have been examining the characteristics of mediated scandals as events – how they differ from localized scandals, how they are structured sequentially and so on. But mediated scandals are also *situated events* which are always embedded in specific social-historical contexts and always involve particular individuals and organizations. Mediated scandals, like all scandals, don't just 'happen': they are brought into existence and sustained over time by the acts and speech-acts of individuals who are situated in specific contexts, often linked to particular organizations and always acting with certain aims and objectives. Every scandal has its *dramatis personae* which include not only the individuals whose actions become the object of scandal but also the individuals who, through their own acts and speech-acts, uncover and disclose these actions and express their disapproval of them.

Who are these individuals whose acts and speech-acts help to create scandal as a mediated event? What kinds of organizations are involved? How should we analyse the social-historical contexts within which mediated scandals, as situated events, occur? I shall address the latter question in the following chapter; here I shall focus on agents and organizations.

There are, of course, many different agents and organizations which may be involved, at some stage, in the creation and development of mediated scandals. The police and other law enforcement agencies often play a crucial role, especially with regard to the investigation of activities which may become the focus of scandal. The legal and judicial systems, with their array of specially qualified officials (lawyers, judges, special prosecutors, etc.) and formal procedures (hearings, trials, etc.) are also key components in the unfolding of many scandals. In some cases, and especially in cases of political scandal, there may also be specific individuals and interest groups which are seeking to use scandal as a means of discrediting their opponents. But there can be no doubt that among the agents and organizations which play a central role in the creation and development of scandals are those which are concerned, directly or indirectly, with the production and diffusion of mediated forms of communication. What is it about media organizations which inclines some individuals working in them to act on occasion as agents in the creation and development of scandal?

Media organizations are complex institutions which vary enormously in terms of their structure and operational practices from one sector to another, and from one national and historical context to another. Nevertheless we can identify several general aspects of media organizations which help us to understand why media personnel may be inclined to orientate themselves towards the creation of scandal. I shall focus on four: (1) financial gain, (2) political objectives, (3) professional self-conceptions, and (4) competitive rivalries. These aspects overlap in complex ways, affecting some media and some media organizations more than others. But together they help to create a climate within the media which facilitates – or even, in some cases, actively encourages – the production of mediated scandals.

(1) Since the development of printing in the late fifteenth century, most media organizations have been established as commercial enterprises operating in market conditions. They have used a variety of media technologies to produce symbolic goods which could be sold in a marketplace or otherwise distributed in ways that generated a positive financial return – in other words, they have been oriented, in differing ways and to varying degrees, towards financial gain. For many media organizations, the capacity to survive and to expand depends (or has depended) on the ability to generate profitable returns on the sale and distribution of symbolic goods.

Given the economic imperatives which shape media organizations as commercial concerns, it is hardly surprising that some media organizations have sought to produce symbolic goods which have a sensationalist, attention-grabbing character. There is nothing new about this tendency: much of the early street literature of the sixteenth and seventeenth centuries, the pamphlets, news sheets and broadsides, were, as we have seen, sensationalist in character and moralistic in tone. But with the transformation of the press from the late eighteenth century on, the nature and scale of this aspect of media organizations changed fundamentally. The rise of the mass circulation press in the nineteenth and twentieth centuries placed greater priority on the need to attract an ever larger number of readers, thus creating a context in which the search for lively, entertaining news became a routinized feature of newspaper production. And in this context, the publication of revelations and allegations which were scandalous (or potentially so) could be seen to have a commercial value: scandals provide vivid, lively stories which could be used to grab the attention of readers and hold it while the plot was unravelled from one day or week to the next.

To say that the economic transformations of the nineteenth century created conditions which were favourable to the production of mediated scandal is not to say that when a particular media organization was involved in disclosing material that was scandalous (or potentially so), it necessarily did so with explicit commercial intent. Journalists and editors may be moved to run stories of this kind without having their eyes fixed on the cash register. The significance of financial gain can easily be exaggerated or misconstrued. There may be some occasions when the motivation to run a scandalous story is largely or exclusively commercial, but this is more likely to be the exception than the rule. The relevance of the orientation to financial gain has less to do with the motivations of media personnel than with the overall structure of media organizations and the constraints which operate on them, a structure which has helped to ensure that a certain genre of news has become a staple feature of newspaper production.

I have emphasized the financial objectives which are built into the structure of media organizations, but of course it is not only these organizations that stand to gain from scandalous stories. The fact that some of these organizations are willing to pay substantial sums of money to acquire relevant information has also helped to create a flourishing secondary market in scandal-related material. A series of quasi-autonomous professions have grown up – self-employed journalists and photographers, agents, publicists, paparazzi, etc. – which draw part of their income from the supply of stories, photos and other material ('dish', as one self-styled media entrepreneur calls it[7]) to newspapers, magazines and other media organizations. Moreover, some of the individuals directly involved in sensitive, clandestine activities can also benefit financially from scandal and they may be tempted to sell their stories, as well as material like letters and photographs, in the secondary market for scandal-related material. From the kiss-and-tell lover to the author of the scandal memoir, participants have found their ways to reap some of scandal's rewards.

(2) The production of mediated scandals is also shaped in some cases by individuals who are using mediated forms of communication to pursue political objectives. Once again, the use of the media

for political purposes has a long history. Many of the pamphlets and broadsides of the sixteenth and seventeenth centuries were intended to be political interventions; and in the early days of the periodical press – in the seventeenth and eighteenth centuries – it was common for newspapers and other periodicals to have an explicit political orientation. We have noted, however, that the rise of mass circulation newspapers in the nineteenth century coincided with a broad depoliticization of the press, as newspapers came to rely less on financial support from political parties and tended increasingly to proclaim their political neutrality. At first sight, the depoliticization of the mass circulation press might seem to weigh against the suggestion that the pursuit of political objectives plays a significant role in the production of mediated scandals. But despite this broad historical trend, there are a number of other factors which have ensured that the pursuit of political objectives through mediated forms of communication has played, and continues to play, an important role in the production of mediated scandal.

In the first place, while many mass circulation newspapers looked to the marketplace for their source of revenue and formally proclaimed their political neutrality, they commonly located themselves in a broad region of the political spectrum and were willing to back particular parties or leaders in a temporary or conditional way. The fact that they did not depend on political parties for their financial support did not prevent them from taking up a position in the political field, albeit one that might be less closely tied to a particular party and might shift over time. Second, while the partisan basis of the press was attenuated in the nineteenth century, it is also clear that some individuals with strong moral and political convictions have held positions of power and influence in the media and have used these positions to pursue their agendas. In late Victorian England, for example, crusading editors like W. T. Stead played an important role in turning a diffuse puritan sentiment into a formidable political force. Stead's relentless determination to expose the moral decadence and hypocrisy of Victorian society was at least partly responsible for numerous scandals, both by virtue of the revelations published in the *Pall Mall Gazette* and by virtue of the moral climate which the puritan lobby helped to produce.

Finally, in more recent decades, the sheer proliferation of mediated forms of communication has helped to ensure that those who wish to use scandal as a political weapon are likely to find some media forum in which revelations and allegations can be turned into public speech. Political or quasi-political organizations and interest groups can produce their own media output in the form of newsletters, leaflets and, increasingly, internet sites; the proliferation of mediated forms of communication enables them to become para-media organizations which are capable of intervening directly in some sector of the public domain. These para-media organizations can also help to shape the contents of mainstream news media by gathering information or making allegations which can be fed into the more established media (or picked up by them). The main inhibiting factor today is not the lack of suitable forums, but rather the threat of libel or other legal sanctions (for instance, in Britain, prosecution under the Official Secrets Act). Hence it is not surprising that the initial revelations or allegations often appear in small or more marginal publications, such as the British satirical magazine *Private Eye*, which live close to the edge in terms of their susceptibility to prosecution for libel, nor is it surprising that the internet, with its relatively anarchic legal structure, has proved to be a popular place for disclosing information or making allegations that are scandalous (or potentially so). If they are not contested legally, revelations or allegations which initially appear in relatively obscure places can be picked up quickly by the mainstream media and turned into a major scandal.

(3) Professional self-conceptions among media personnel also help to shape an orientation towards scandal. The formation of journalism as a profession in the late nineteenth century was accompanied by the emergence of a professional ethos which defined the principles of good journalistic practice. As we noted in the previous chapter, this ethos tended to emphasize two ideals, factuality and entertainment. These ideals, elaborated in various ways, have become part of the professional self-conceptions of journalists and others who work in the media industries. Incorporated into textbooks and courses and reaffirmed by the markers of distinction (prizes etc.) which professions sometimes use to reward achievement within their ranks, these ideals have shaped the ways in which journalists think of themselves and of what they do as journalists. They have shaped, one could say, the practical 'habitus' of journalism.[8]

Of course, not all journalists or all sectors of the media industries gave equal weight to both ideals. Some journalists and some sectors of the press placed more emphasis on entertainment and storytelling, while others oriented themselves primarily towards the ideal of gathering or uncovering facts. The pursuit of either ideal (or a combination of both ideals) could easily give rise to scandal. For journalists and newspapers which emphasized the ideal of entertainment, scandal was wonderful subject matter: it allowed journalists to weave factual content into vivid stories of secret liaisons and misdemeanours involving prominent public figures, while at the same time expressing a strong dose of moral disapproval. But scandal was also closely linked to the aims and practices of journalists and media organizations which sought to emphasize factuality. For investigative journalists came to see themselves not only as reporters who had to probe beneath the surface of things in order to get at the truth, but also as social reformers who sought to shape policy agendas by provoking moral outrage in their readers and viewers. The shaping of policy agendas through the uncovering of hidden activities which shock and surprise, which hit raw nerves in the community and lead policy-makers to respond, became part of the professional self-conception of journalists.[9]

This is not to say, however, that most scandals are the outcome of journalists diligently pursuing their vocation as investigators seeking to uncover unpalatable truths. This may indeed happen on some occasions, but in broad historical terms it is undoubtedly the exception rather than the rule. In many scandals, the main activities of investigation are carried out by individuals other than journalists and by organizations other than the media (such as the police, the courts or official inquiries of various kinds), and the role played by the media is primarily that of selecting and relaying the information produced by others, turning it into engaging stories and providing frameworks of interpretation. The investigative activities of journalists have been a crucial factor in some scandals, but they are seldom the only source of information and in many cases they are secondary to the investigations carried out by others (although journalists themselves may be inclined to exaggerate their own significance, in a way that concurs with their professional self-image[10]). Moreover, the rise of investigative journalism did not by itself imply that all areas of social and political life would be probed with the same degree of critical scrutiny. On the contrary, journalists typically worked within the framework of established conventions which tended to rule out certain spheres of life as legitimate topics of inquiry. Even as recently as the early 1960s, for example, it was common practice for journalists in the United States and elsewhere to refrain from probing and publicizing the private lives of public figures, even when it was well known in political and journalistic circles that a particular figure was involved in extramarital affairs.[11] Why the conventions which govern the activities of journalists should have changed in some contexts since the early 1960s is a question to which we shall return.

(4) A fourth factor that has played an important role in the production of mediated scandal is what we could describe as competitive rivalries. Media organizations do not exist in isolation: they stand in complex relations – often competitive in character – to other media organizations, and their output is shaped to some extent by these interorganizational relations. In producing symbolic goods they are oriented not only to their potential market, but also to the activities of other organizations which are producing for the same (or a similar) market. Like other markets for symbolic goods, the market for news is highly competitive and, as competition intensifies, news-producing organizations must search for new ways to secure competitive advantage. The use of new technologies to reduce costs, the stylization of content and presentation, and the development of new networks of information supply are among the strategies commonly used to secure or improve one's competitive position.

The highly competitive market for news places a premium on speed: news must be *new*, and the latest and most up-to-date news is the most highly valued. In the competitive world of news production, time is of the essence: yesterday's news is no news at all. Hence news organizations struggle against one another to provide the most recent news, or to run a story before any of their competitors (the 'scoop'). Competition also produces a degree of differentiation among news-producing organizations, as they struggle to find a niche which will secure a regular readership or audience. Some organizations seek to establish a reputation as an accurate and reliable source of news, combining detailed coverage of current affairs with authoritative commentary. Other organizations seek to position themselves as providers of entertaining news (and news of entertainment), combining a light coverage of current affairs with a strong emphasis on the lives of prominent personalities.

While the competitive nature of the market for news produces a degree of differentiation among news-producing organizations, it also produces a degree of homogeneity in terms of the material which is regarded as newsworthy. Those who work in news-producing organizations are constantly looking over their shoulders to see what their competitors are doing. A big story for one organization can quickly become a big story for others, since information flows not simply from news-producing organizations to their readers or viewers, but also between the organizations themselves. This 'circular circulation of information', as one critic aptly calls it,[12] has several consequences. First, it produces a degree of *homogeneity* among news-worthy topics, in the sense that a newsworthy topic for one organization is also (or quickly becomes) a newsworthy topic for others. Second, it produces a degree of *media amplification*: the significance of an event is amplified by virtue of the fact that it is picked up by other organizations (and by other media), and thereby given greater prominence and visibility in the public domain. And third, it produces a degree of *self-referentiality*. News-producing organizations report, to some extent, what other news-producing organizations are reporting; they take their cues, at least to some extent, from what their competitors are doing. Hence the same (or similar) stories often appear in different papers or programmes, the same (or similar) photos or film footage are used, and the same (or similar) people are called upon to offer their views. The result is that the world of mediated news tends to become to some extent a world closed in on itself – almost like a hall of mirrors in which each image, and each movement, is reflected in multiple forms.

The competitive rivalry and interconnectedness of media organizations have a bearing on the production of mediated scandal. The pressure to run a story before one's competitors acts as an incentive to disclose information which could spark off a scandal, or which could fuel a scandal which is already underway. The differentiation produced by intensified competition leads to the emergence of organizations which emphasize the entertaining aspects of news, and which in some cases – as with the *News of the World* in Britain and the *National Enquirer* in the United States – regard the production of mediated scandal as a staple component of their output.[13] Competitive rivalry also tends to ensure that once a story with clear scandal potential breaks somewhere in the media, other media organizations will rush to pick it up, report it and develop it further. The first glimmer of scandal tends to produce a scramble for news, as journalists, photographers and others, anxious not to be outdone by their competitors, rush to the scene (what one commentator once described as the 'jackal syndrome'[14]). The scramble for news tends to fuel an incipient scandal and give it ever greater prominence and visibility in the public domain. Ignited by a spark in one medium, a scandal can quickly spread to other media, the flames fanned by the mere fact of being taken up by multiple media organizations which report on the events, reproduce relevant documents, photos or film footage and comment both on the events and on other media organizations' accounts of the events. Once ignited, a mediated scandal can quickly become an uncontrollable blaze.

Experiencing Scandal as a Mediated Event

Just as mediated scandals are events which are played out in the media, so too our ways of experiencing these events are shaped by the distinctive characteristics of mediated forms of communication. For the individuals who find themselves at the centre of an unfolding scandal, the experience is likely to be overwhelming, as events rapidly spin out of control. A great deal of time and energy may be invested in trying to manage a process which is, in some respects, intrinsically unmanageable. Individuals and their families, friends and advisers (and, in some cases, their crisis management teams) may spend a great deal of time elaborating strategies which will, they hope, enable them to outmanoeuvre their opponents, or at least to limit the damage. They may feel anger and indignation at the ways in which their lives have been overturned, and their plans and ambitions called into question, by the actions of journalists and others whose motives may seem malevolent. They may be deeply fearful and anxious about how the scandal will unfold and about how their lives, as well as the lives of those who matter to them, will be affected by it.

In many scandals, the participants are also likely to feel a deep sense of embarrassment, shame and humiliation, as aspects of their private lives (or activities and conversations which were carried out in secrecy and privacy) are suddenly turned into public events, available for thousands or millions of others to see or hear or hear about. Actions or utterances which were originally oriented towards a specific other, and which were produced on the assumption that they would be received only by the person to whom they were addressed, are suddenly removed from their original context and made available to an indefinite range of recipients; private actions and communications, including the intimate and highly personalized exchanges that take place between lovers, are suddenly turned into public goods. One may feel a deep sense of embarrassment and shame on seeing or hearing one's private actions or utterances openly discussed in the public domain. One may also feel deeply humiliated and demeaned by a process which exposes highly personal matters or uncovers hidden aspects of one's character or life, thereby threatening to undermine the image that one would like to project of oneself.

For the individuals who are not participants in mediated scandals but merely observers of them, their experience of these events is shaped by the fact that they derive their knowledge exclusively or very largely from media sources. The scandal is not a 'lived experience' – that is, an experience which they live through in the practical contexts of their daily lives and which impinges directly on them – but rather a 'mediated experience' which is shaped by the distinctive mode of its acquisition.[15] For most people, these scandals are events which afflict distant others, individuals who are remote in space (perhaps also in time) and whom one would probably never encounter in the course of one's daily life. Some are also prominent public figures, and therefore, for many people, remote in terms of their relative status, power and wealth. Through mediated scandals we experience the traumas of these distant others whose lives are laid bare before us. We watch as their personal lives, or hidden aspects of their public lives, are played out in front of us with a vivid, almost uncanny, openness, in an arena where we can be spectators, commentators and critics without ever encountering the individuals whose lives we may come to know so intimately. We may be intrigued by the spectacle that unfolds before us, our curiosity aroused by a series of revelations and explanations which don't quite add up, and at the same time we may feel uneasy about a set of circumstances which enables us to know more about the private lives of public figures than we may ever know about the lives of our own friends and family members. These are circumstances in which intimacy has become detached from familiarity: the intimate knowledge we have of others bears no relation to our closeness to them. It is a kind of non-reciprocal intimacy at a distance.

At the same time, mediated scandals provide us with a new and unsettling view of a world which, in the routine flow of day-to-day life, is generally hidden from view. They are windows on to a world which lies behind the carefully managed self-presentation of political leaders and others who may be in the public eye. As these scandals unfold we experience a world – sometimes shocking, sometimes mildly amusing, often quite absorbing – which is at odds with the images projected of it. Who would have thought, for example, that the President of the United States would discuss policy in the White House in a manner that was indistinguishable from the scheming of a petty gangster? The more elevated the individual (or the institution of which he or she is part), or the more that an individual's success has depended on the projection of a particular self-image, the more interested we are likely to be in revelations which compromise these self-images and show that, despite pretensions to the contrary, these individuals are prone to the same temptations, driven by the same desires and subject to the same weaknesses as ordinary mortals. Compromising revelations of this kind may, on occasion, be a source of amusement and entertainment (as in the case of Hugh Grant and his unbefitting encounter with Divine Brown). But they can also be a source of deep disappointment and dismay, since we may feel that individuals have not lived up to the expectations we have of them and have compromised not only themselves, but also the institutions of which they are part. The revelations of Clinton's sexual encounters with Monica Lewinsky, conveyed in graphic detail by the Starr report and by countless commentators in the media, were felt by many Americans not only to tarnish Clinton's image, but also to devalue and defile the institution of the Presidency.

Since mediated scandals also involve acts of transgression and the expression of moral disapproval, they also provide us with an occasion to reflect on questions of a moral and practical kind. Experiencing mediated events is never just a matter of passively receiving the messages that are presented to us: as recipients, we are always actively involved in making sense of these messages, reflecting on them and discussing them with friends and others with whom we interact in the course of our daily lives. Mediated scandals provide a rich source of conversational subject matter partly because they have, in many cases, a personal focus, a cluster of motives which are relatively easy to understand and an open-ended plot which may change from one day to the next; but they are also good topics of conversation because they often raise ethical questions about which individuals may disagree. Should marital infidelity be condoned? Is homosexuality acceptable? To what extent is the private life of politicians relevant to their public office? Can our politicians be trusted? Are they corrupt? And so on. Mediated scandals provide occasions for individuals to reflect on a range of ethical and political considerations of this kind, to discuss them with others and to think about some of their own convictions. For the most part, this process of thinking about one's convictions is more likely to reaffirm them than to produce a sudden or dramatic change. But we should not rule out the possibility that exposure to an intensifying series of scandals, each involving revelations which seem improper or repugnant in some way, might contribute to a gradual alteration of some people's attitudes over time.

While mediated scandals may at times be absorbing and even shocking or disturbing for some people, and while mediated scandals sometimes provide suitable materials for conversation and reflection in the practical contexts of day-to-day life, this is by no means always the case. Some scandals – especially those involving complicated financial matters or events of labyrinthine complexity – may have a relatively limited capacity to resonate with the lives of ordinary individuals. Partly this may be due to the intrinsic and sometimes baffling complexity of the events themselves, which may be difficult to translate into popular forms of story-telling. In some cases it may also be linked to a certain weariness on the part of recipients who have had their fill of scandalous disclosures, and who are inclined to greet new revelations and allegations with a sigh of resigned indifference (a point to which I shall return). But the limited capacity of some scandals to resonate with the lives of ordinary individuals is also symptomatic of a more general characteristic of mediated experience, what we could call its 'relevance structure'.[16] Individuals do not relate to all experiences equally, but rather prioritize experiences in terms of the extent to which they seem relevant to their lives. The lived experience of day-to-day life has a rather pressing character for most individuals most of the time: it forms the immediate environment in which we live out our lives and interact with others. Mediated experience, by contrast, is more intermittent and detached from the practical contexts of our daily lives, and less likely to impose itself on us with the urgency and immediacy of lived experience.

Hence, however interesting and absorbing the details of a mediated scandal may be, the unfolding of the scandal is likely to be experienced by most individuals as a rather distant event which bears a relatively tenuous connection to the issues which matter most to them in the practical contexts of their daily lives. They may find it hard to see any connection between the actions of these distant individuals whom they have never met (and are never likely to meet) and their own lives and life circumstances; the unfolding events of a mediated scandal may catch their eye from time to time, may even give rise to some discussion and debate with friends and family members, but these events are unlikely to command their undivided attention. The tenuousness of this connection is only exacerbated by the spatial and cultural distances that may be involved when scandals are diffused on an increasingly global scale. For most ordinary individuals in Britain, for example, a scandal involving politicians in Japan or South Korea will seem like an immeasurably remote occurrence: the names will mean little to them, the institutions will be unfamiliar and far removed from their own local and national contexts and any connection with their own lives is likely to seem so tenuous, or to involve so many intermediaries, as to be imperceptible.

The relevance structure of mediated experience thus tends to ensure that, for most people, most mediated scandals will play a relatively peripheral role in their lives (and more peripheral when the scandal is far removed, spatially and culturally, from their own life contexts). Of course, there are exceptions. For any particular individual, the relevance of any experience, whether lived or mediated, is always relative to the set of priorities which form part of his or her life-project and sense of self. Some individuals who have a strong interest in politics, or a strong interest in a certain cultural form like film, sport or popular music, may follow closely the unfolding of a mediated scandal which impinges on their area of interest. They may watch the television and read the papers every day to glean the latest news, eager to keep up with the most recent developments. They may even become a kind of scandal aficionado who, like the dedicated fan, develops networks of social relations with others who share similar interests and concerns, and with whom they can swap the latest stories. (The scandals surrounding Bill Clinton spawned numerous internet newsgroups and networks of this kind, for example.) But these are exceptions. For most people, mediated scandals are events which they experience intermittently and with varying but generally modest levels of interest and attentiveness. They are likely to follow them loosely and episodically (if at all), paying more attention to the headlines and the broad contours than to the fine detail. This does not mean that ordinary individuals have little interest in mediated scandals or attach little significance to them. But it does mean that the ways in which ordinary people view mediated scandals, and the kind of significance they attach to them, may not coincide with the ways in which these events are seen by the individuals – including those working in the media – who, because of the practical circumstances of their lives, have a more direct stake in them.

4

The Nature of Political Scandal

In the previous chapters we considered the phenomenon of scandal in a general way, without reference to any particular kind of scandal. While most of my examples have been drawn from the political sphere, the concepts and arguments that I have developed are applicable not only to political scandals: they would also apply, with suitable refinements and qualifications, to scandals involving film stars, TV celebrities and other prominent figures in public life. But I now want to focus more sharply on political scandal as such: what makes a scandal a *political* scandal? What are its distinctive properties? And why are scandals such a source of concern for political leaders or aspiring leaders? What is it about the nature of politics in modern societies that makes scandal such a serious threat for political leaders?

Once we have considered these questions, I want to turn to an issue of a more substantive kind. If we look back over the long history of political scandal, we can see that the patterns have varied over time: some types of scandal were more prominent at some times and in some places than others. And while there has been considerable variation in the course of the twentieth century, it is difficult to avoid the conclusion that in recent decades and especially since the 1960s, political scandals have become a more significant feature in the political life of many Western states. In Britain, the Profumo affair was a watershed; in the United States, it was Watergate. After Profumo and Watergate, political scandal was never quite the same: it moved from the sidelines of political life into the centre of the field. Why?

How did this happen? How can we explain the fact that scandal has become an increasingly salient feature of modern political life?

Defining Political Scandal

Let us begin by trying to determine the specific features of political scandal: what is it that makes a scandal a *political* scandal, as distinct from a scandal in some other sphere of social life? One seemingly straightforward way of answering this question is to say that a political scandal is any scandal that involves a political leader or figure. It is the fact that the individual at the centre of scandal is a recognized political figure – a leader or aspiring leader, an elected or appointed official, etc. – that the scandal is constituted as a political scandal. But this answer, while seemingly straightforward and intuitively plausible, is not particularly helpful or illuminating. For an individual is a political figure only by virtue of a broader set of social relations and institutions which endows him or her with power. So if we wish to understand the nature of political scandal, we cannot focus on the political figure or leader alone. We have to take account of the social relations and institutions by virtue of which an individual is endowed with political power, or with regard to which an individual seeks to acquire it.

So let us consider a second way of answering the question, one which is more concerned with the character of political institutions. According to Markovits and Silverstein – two political scientists who have written perceptively on political scandal – the defining feature of political scandal stems, not from the status of the individuals involved, but from the nature of the transgression: a political scandal, in their view, necessarily involves a 'violation of due process'.[1] By 'due process' they mean the legally binding rules and procedures which govern the exercise of political power. These rules and procedures are public and inclusive; they define the political game in a way that is open and accessible. The exercise of power, by contrast, tends to be privatizing and exclusive; power is often exercised in a way that is secretive and hidden from view. Political scandals arise at the point where the logic of due process overlaps with the logic of power (see figure 4.1).

On the basis of this account, Markovits and Silverstein draw two rather surprising conclusions. First, they argue that the logic of due process is firmly institutionalized only in the liberal democratic state, and hence it is only in liberal democracies that political scandals

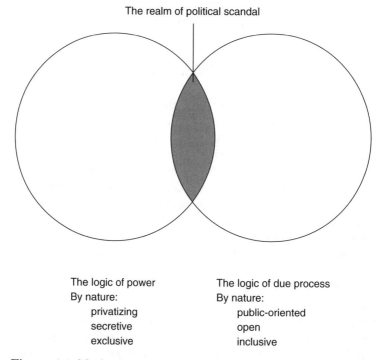

Figure 4.1 Markovits and Silverstein's account of political scandal

can arise. Liberal democracies place great emphasis on due process: by extolling the value of process, they seek to resolve the potential conflict between individualism and personal freedom, on the one hand, and the need for the state to exercise some degree of impersonal power, on the other. The adherence to formal procedures and to the rule of law is valued above all else, for they alone enable liberal democracies to curtail abuses of power. This tension between process and power, which lies at the very heart of the liberal democratic state, is the same tension which underlies the phenomenon of political scandal. 'In our view,' write Markovits and Silverstein, 'the critical feature of any political scandal is not the degree of personal gain involved nor is it the normative merit of the ends sought, but rather it is the presence of any activity that seeks to increase political power at the expense of process and procedure. . . . That, in a nutshell, is why political scandals can only take place in liberal democracies.'[2]

The second conclusion they draw is that many scandals which

involve political figures, and which are commonly regarded as political scandals, are not, in essence, political scandals at all. Markovits and Silverstein do not deny the existence of sex scandals and financial scandals, but they argue that these are not *political* scandals unless they involve a determinate abuse of power at the expense of process and procedure. So, for example, the controversy surrounding Gary Hart's presidential campaign in 1988 was a classic sex scandal and it undoubtedly had damaging consequences for Hart's political career; but this was not, in the view of Markovits and Silverstein, a political scandal, since it did not involve the abuse of power at the expense of process. By contrast, the Profumo affair, while largely remembered and popularly portrayed as a sex scandal, was, on this account, a genuine political scandal, because questions of national security were at stake and because Profumo lied to Parliament, thus violating the procedural conventions of a central democratic institution.

Markovits and Silverstein are quite right to place the phenomenon of political scandal in a broader institutional context. Their arguments help to show that scandal is not a mere ripple on the surface of political life but is linked to and symptomatic of some of the most important structural features of modern societies. However, as an analysis of the distinctive character of political scandal, the account of Markovits and Silverstein is, in my view, too restrictive. It treats one dynamic – the pursuit of power at the expense of process – as the defining feature of political scandal; hence any scandal that does not involve this particular dynamic is, *ipso facto*, non-political. But to exclude from the sphere of political scandal a range of scandalous phenomena in which political figures are centrally involved, and which may have far-reaching consequences in the political field, is, at best, a rather paradoxical conceptual strategy; it is also likely to produce a partial and one-sided account of political scandals. A very complicated and often messy world – where individuals act with a variety of motives and where the consequences of their actions are often unexpected or unforeseen – is viewed through a lens which focuses on one dynamic at the expense of all others, and which obscures the political significance of actions and events which do not concur with this model.

Rather than defining political scandal in terms of the pursuit of power at the expense of process, I shall try to show that it would be best to adopt a more flexible approach. Abuses of power may indeed form the bases for some political scandals, but these are not the only grounds on which political scandals can occur. They are one form of political scandal – what I shall call 'power scandals' – but they are not the only form. There are also political scandals based on the disclosure of sexual transgressions or financial irregularities, and these are quite properly *political* scandals. To rule out the latter as a matter of definition is unduly restrictive.

In a similar vein, one must have reservations about Markovits and Silverstein's claim that political scandals can occur only in liberal democracies. This contention is based, as we have seen, on a particular argument about the link between political scandal and due process, and about the institutionalization of due process in liberal democratic regimes. However, if the link between political scandal and due process is not as close as Markovits and Silverstein suggest, if political scandals can be based on considerations other than the pursuit of power at the expense of process, then we cannot maintain with such confidence that political scandal is a feature of liberal democracies alone. We can allow for the possibility that political scandals will occur (and, indeed, have occurred) in regimes of various kinds, from the absolutist and constitutional monarchies of early modern Europe to the various forms of authoritarian regime which have existed in the twentieth century.

Nevertheless, even if the claim that political scandals can occur only in liberal democracies is too sweeping to be convincing, there is a discernible affinity between political scandal and liberal democracy. Political scandals do appear to be much more common in liberal democracies than in authoritarian regimes or in one-party states. Why? What is the nature of the affinity between political scandal and liberal democracy?

There are several aspects of liberal democracy that render it prone to scandal. In the first place, politics in a liberal democracy is a field of competing forces which are organized and mobilized by means of parties and other interest groups. This creates a tense, sometimes highly charged atmosphere in which conflict and confrontation are the norm; parties and other interest groups are constantly involved in attacking their opponents and seeking to capitalize on their perceived points of weakness. In these circumstances, scandal can be a powerful weapon. To demonstrate or even allege that a political opponent has transgressed a morally binding norm – has been involved in corruption or fraud, for example, or has behaved in a manner involving a substantial degree of deception or hypocrisy – may be an effective way of discrediting him or her. Throw enough mud, the old proverb reminds us, and some of it will stick.

This points to a second consideration that is relevant here: in liberal democracy, reputations matter. The fundamental condition of a liberal democracy is an institutionalized process of election to which political leaders must submit themselves at regular intervals. In the struggle for electoral success, good reputation is a vital resource. Hence the tarnishing of one's reputation through scandal is a risk that political leaders or aspiring leaders must seek energetically to avoid. Scandal plays into the hands of one's opponents who stand only to gain, when the next election comes around, from any damage caused to one's reputation.

A third factor that renders liberal democracy prone to scandal is the relative autonomy of the press. I use the phrase 'relative autonomy' advisedly: in liberal democratic societies, media institutions are not entirely independent of the exercise of political power. Media institutions generally operate within a regulatory framework established by the state; moreover, they may be subjected to various forms of pressure – both direct, through funding arrangements or overt censorship, and indirect – which impinge on their activities. Nevertheless, compared to the position of media institutions in authoritarian and one-party states, the media in liberal democracies have a great deal of political latitude. They are often able to report – subject only to certain legal constraints and journalistic codes of practice – on actions or events which may lead to scandals, and some sectors of the press are particularly well geared to the public articulation of opprobrious discourse. Moreover, given the commercial nature of most media organizations in Western societies and their dependence on revenues generated through the market, these organizations often have a vested interest in producing high-profile stories which will attract the public's attention.

A fourth factor which helps to explain why liberal democracies are prone to scandal stems from the very conditions of political power. In the various forms of authoritarian rule, power is vested ultimately in the person of the ruler or in a party or organization which claims to rule on behalf of the people. In such conditions, the capacity to disclose or allege transgression is heavily skewed in favour of the dominant institutions of political power; scandal may be used as a weapon to discredit rivals or to ostracize opponents (such as 'the enemies of the people'), but it is rarely turned against the current holders of power. The price to be paid for making unauthorized allegations against the holders of power may simply be too high, and may include imprisonment or even death. Many people may suspect or even know that the power-holders are involved in corrupt or illicit activities, but this knowledge may not be articulated in public for fear of reprisal. In liberal democratic regimes, by contrast, the exercise of political power is ultimately governed, at least in principle, by the rule of law. In principle no individual, including the pre-eminent power-holder, stands above the law. Hence allegations concerning transgressions can be made more readily by individuals or media organizations. Such allegations carry risks, of course; an unfounded allegation may result in a libel suit, the payment of substantial damages, and so on. But these are nothing like the risks that may be taken by individuals or organizations which make allegations against power-holders in authoritarian regimes.

So there are a number of factors which help to explain why liberal democracies are more prone to scandal than authoritarian regimes. We can understand the affinity between liberal democracy and political scandal without accepting the sweeping and rather improbable thesis of Markovits and Silverstein. But we are still left with the question of how we should understand the phenomenon of political scandal itself. If we put aside the account of Markovits and Silverstein, what alternatives are there?

Symbolic Power and the Political Field

In the account that I shall develop here, a political scandal is a scandal involving individuals or actions which are situated within a *political field* and which have an impact on relations within the field. It is the political field that constitutes a political scandal as political; it provides the context for the scandal and shapes its pattern of development. So if we wish to understand the nature of political scandal, we must begin by analysing the structure of the political field.

I draw the concept of field from the work of Pierre Bourdieu.[3] Roughly speaking, a field is a structured space of social positions whose properties are defined primarily by the relations between these positions and by the resources attached to them. Individuals act within fields of various kinds; they occupy positions and draw on the resources attached to them in order to pursue their interests and aims. In some cases these positions acquire a certain stability by being incorporated into institutions which have some degree of durability in time and some extension in space. Institutions give shape to fields of interaction and, at the same time, they create new positions within these fields and new life trajectories for the individuals who occupy them.

There are many different fields or spheres of interaction – the fields of art and culture, of work and commercial exchange and so on. What is distinctive about the political field? And how do the properties of the political field shape the kinds of scandals that take place within it? We can provisionally define the political field as the field of action and interaction which bears on the acquisition and exercise of political power. Political power is one form of power; there are other forms, including economic power, coercive power and what I have called 'symbolic power'.[4] Political power is concerned with the coordination of individuals and the regulation of their patterns of interaction. All organizations involve some degree of coordination and regulation, and hence some degree of political power in this sense. But there are a range of institutions which are concerned *primarily* with coordination and regulation, and which pursue these activities in a manner that is relatively centralized within a territory that is more or less circumscribed. These institutions comprise what is generally referred to as the state. When I use the term 'political field', therefore, I am referring primarily to the field of action and interaction which is shaped by the institutions of the state (although the term may be applied, with equal validity and for specific purposes, to fields of interaction which are shaped by institutions situated at lower or higher levels than the state, such as institutions of local government, on the one hand, or transnational institutions like the European Union or the United Nations, on the other).

All states, or state-like institutions, are essentially systems of authority. They involve a complex system of rules and procedures which authorize certain individuals to act in certain ways. A state can exist only if some people are authorized to exercise power and others are obliged to obey. But why do people obey? On what basis does this authority rest? As Max Weber among others has pointed out,[5] the capacity of a state to command authority generally depends on its capacity to exercise two related but distinctive forms of power, which I shall describe as coercive power and symbolic power. Ultimately the state can make recourse to various forms of coercion – that is, to the actual or threatened use of physical force – in order to back up the exercise of political power, both with regard to external conquest or threat and with regard to internal unrest or disobedience. But the use of coercion on a substantial scale can be a risky strategy, and it is generally reserved for exceptional circumstances. In the normal flow of social life, the authority of the state is backed up in a gentler, more pervasive and altogether less transparent fashion: by the diffusion of symbolic forms which are intended to cultivate and sustain a belief in the legitimacy of political power.

In a fundamental sense, therefore, the exercise of political power depends on the use of symbolic power to cultivate and sustain the belief in legitimacy.

What is symbolic power? I use this term to refer to the capacity to intervene in the course of events, to influence the actions and beliefs of others and indeed to create events, by means of the production and transmission of symbolic forms.[6] In exercising symbolic power, individuals draw on various kinds of resources which I shall describe loosely as the 'means of information and communication'. These resources include the technical means of fixation and transmission; the skills, competences and forms of knowledge employed in the production, transmission and reception of information and symbolic content (what Bourdieu refers to as 'cultural capital'[7]); and the accumulated prestige, recognition and respect accorded to certain producers or institutions ('symbolic capital'). Reputation is an aspect of symbolic capital; it is an attribute of an individual or institution but it is also a resource on which individuals can draw in exercising symbolic power. Reputation can be built up over time, either by an individual or by the institution of which he or she is part (or by both). It can also be lost or substantially reduced rather quickly through misconduct, misjudgement or blunders of various kinds.

We are now in a position to give a more precise characterization of the political field: it is the field of action and interaction which bears on the acquisition and exercise of political power through the use of symbolic power among other things. The use of symbolic power is not incidental or secondary to the struggle for political power but is essential to it. Anyone who wishes to acquire political power or to exercise it in a durable and effective fashion must also use symbolic power to cultivate and sustain the belief in legitimacy – unless they are willing to make recourse to coercion, a strategy which is, as we noted earlier, a risky one and which is, in any case, rarely relied on in an exclusive fashion.

This characterization of the political field applies equally well to different forms of state and political regime, from traditional imperial states and classical city-states to the modern form of nation-state, from authoritarian regimes and one-party states to liberal parliamentary democracies. But liberal democracies typically involve a number of institutions which shape the political field in certain ways. First, they involve a parliament – a House of Representatives, House of Commons, etc. – and related institutions which constitute a *political subfield*, that is, a sphere of action and interaction which is occupied by professional or semi-professional politicians and their associated personnel. Second, liberal democracies typically involve a competitive party system which provides a means of formulating policies and mobilizing support both within the political subfield and among the broader population. And third, liberal democracies involve regularized elections through which political representatives are selected (or reselected) according to certain rules of the game.

If we bear in mind these features, we can see that the political field of liberal democracy is characterized by a distinctive double logic.[8] On the one hand, political representatives are members of the political subfield and, in their day-to-day struggles, their conduct and strategies are governed above all by the logic of this subfield, by the demands of party loyalty, the building of coalitions and so on. To the outsider, this subfield can often seem like an esoteric world of internal squabbles, of Byzantine power struggles and impenetrable debates, of distinctions so fine that the differences become imperceptible. But to the insider, these subtle distinctions are part of the very essence of politics, for political conduct within the subfield is inseparable from the activity of distinguishing one's own positions from those of one's opponents and of criticizing or denouncing the latter.

On the other hand, as elected officials, political representatives are also linked to a broader political field of citizens or non-professionals to whom they are accountable in some sense, and on whose support they depend from time to time. The requirement to hold elections at regular intervals ensures that political representatives must, from time to time, present themselves before an electorate and seek, within the framework of a competitive party struggle, to elicit their support. And to elicit support they must seek to persuade; they must cultivate belief, mobilize commitment, establish or renew bonds of trust. An existing or aspiring political representative must strive to mobilize the party faithful and to persuade others that, despite any reservations they may have, they can rely on him or her. As part of this process, existing or aspiring representatives commonly seek to discredit their rivals, to portray them as untrustworthy and unreliable, thereby augmenting their own stature at the expense of their opponents and increasing their chances of electoral success.

So the political field of liberal democracy is characterized by a distinctive double logic, one internal to the subfield of professional or semi-professional politicians and one linking this subfield to a broader field of citizens or non-professionals. Each logic has its own properties; they are not identical or reducible to one another, and politicians who confuse them may do so at their cost. In the practical flow of political life, however, these two logics are woven together in complex ways, and skilful politicians know how to take advantage of their connections without compromising the distinctiveness of each. Moreover, while each logic has its own properties, they both involve fundamentally the use of symbolic power. Whether acting within the political subfield or within the broader political field, representatives must use symbolic power to persuade and confront, to influence actions and beliefs, to cultivate relations of trust and to influence, as best they can, the course of events.

In order to understand the distinctive logic of the political field, we must take account of another factor: the relation between the political field and the media. Within the subfield of professional and semi-professional politicians, individuals interact with one another through face-to-face interaction and through various forms of one-to-one mediated interaction, like letter-writing, telephone conversations, etc. The personalized character of these forms of interaction helps to ensure that the political subfield remains a relatively closed world which is turned in on itself, a world which is governed by its own rules and conventions, where practices may seem arcane to outsiders and where personal connections matter. On the other hand, with the development of the media (newspapers, radio, television, etc.), the relations between politicians and non-professionals become shaped increasingly by these open-ended forms of mediated communication. Of course, politicians still interact with non-professionals through face-to-face interaction (in their local constituencies, in election rallies, etc.) and through correspondence. But with the growing significance of the media, the relations between politicians and non-professionals are increasingly shaped by the kind of mediated quasi-interaction which takes place through the press and television. Increasingly the media become the key arena in which the relations between politicians and non-professionals in the broader political field are created, sustained and, on occasion, destroyed.

The media can itself be conceptualized as a field of interaction with its own distinctive set of interests, positions and career trajectories. In their differing ways, media organizations are all concerned with exercising symbolic power through the use of communication media of various kinds. Some of these organizations bear directly on the political field but they do not coincide with it, since they are generally governed by different principles and oriented towards different aims. The relation between politicians and journalists may on occasion be close and harmonious, as they may be bound together in forms of reciprocal dependency (politicians need the media to present favourable images of themselves and their policies, while journalists rely on politicians and other official sources to provide a regular flow of news). But the relation is also fraught with potential conflict and it can easily become a source of tension, as journalists may pursue agendas or take positions which are opposed to those which politicians or their spokespersons would like them to adopt.

While much of the day-to-day activity of politicians is oriented towards other politicians within the political subfield, they are also aware that their actions and utterances will be scrutinized by journalists and occasionally reported in the media, and that they may become visible thereby to non-professionals in the broader political field. Hence politicians tend to monitor closely the media coverage of their actions and utterances, and increasingly try to shape it by managing the information and images made available and by providing frameworks for the interpretation of events. Occasionally they may use the broadcasting media to appeal directly to non-professionals, bypassing the intermediary levels of reporting and commentary provided by journalists. Non-professionals become the potential witnesses of events which transpire in the political subfield, and on occasion the addressees of messages intended to shape their understanding and to draw them in as potential allies in political struggles. They comprise a kind of 'bystander public'[9] – that is, individuals who, for the most part, do not participate directly in the events that unfold in the political subfield but who can (and often do) form opinions about these events on the basis of the information and images they receive, and whose opinions may in turn influence the actions of individuals within the political subfield.

Both politicians and media personnel seek to monitor the changing opinions of the public on matters of concern within the political subfield, as well as the changing levels of support for particular policies and political figures. Politicians have a long-standing practice of soliciting views from their constituents by means of correspondence and face-to-face discussions in their constituencies. But given the breadth of the political field and the large number of non-professionals, it is difficult for them to obtain reliable indications of public opinion without relying on gauging mechanisms of various kinds. Regular elections and other devices (such as referendums) provide formal gauging mechanisms for assessing the support of members of the public for particular politicians, parties and policies. But since formal mechanisms of this kind are used relatively infrequently, politicians and others come to rely increasingly on a range of informal mechanisms for assessing the range and degree of support. One informal mechanism which has come to play a central role in this regard is the opinion poll. Since dialogue with constituents is necessarily limited and elections are infrequent, opinion polls have become a widely accepted device for assessing support in the broader political field. They are used not only to shape policy but also to assess the impact of policy changes and the popularity of particular leaders or prospective leaders. Frequently reported in the media and commented on by journalists, politicians and others, opinion polls become publicly available and contested indices of the shifting relations between professionals and non-professionals in the broader political field, indices which are monitored closely by politicians and used by them in their struggles with others in the subfield of professional politicians.

We are now in a position to understand why scandal matters within the political field, and why political scandal can be so damaging for actual or aspiring political leaders. Individuals acting within the political field depend crucially, as we have seen, on the use of symbolic power to persuade and influence others and to shape the course of events. While the use of symbolic power is important in many different spheres of social life, it is vital in the political field, since anyone who wishes to acquire political power and exercise it in a durable and effective fashion must use symbolic power to secure the support of others both within the political subfield and within the broader political field. And their capacity to exercise symbolic power depends on, among other things, the symbolic capital at their disposal – that is, on their accumulated prestige, reputation and respect. Hence politicians are particularly vulnerable to anything which threatens to weaken or diminish their stock of symbolic capital, since this may weaken or undermine their capacity to exercise political power. Damage to one's reputation is not merely a personal blow: it can also be a serious political setback, because it can weaken significantly one's capacity to act in the political subfield and to secure the kind of support – both within the subfield and in the broader political field – upon which one's success (and perhaps the success of one's party) ultimately depends. In the political field of liberal democracy, a healthy store of symbolic capital is not merely a useful asset: it is a necessary condition of political effectiveness, just as important as good party organization and substantial financial backing.

Viewed from this perspective, we can see why scandal and the threat of scandal have such significance in the political field: scandal can deplete the symbolic capital upon which the exercise of political power depends. Scandal can erode the foundations of political power precisely because it can destroy (or threaten to destroy) a vital resource upon which politicians must to some extent rely – namely, their reputation and good name, and the respect accorded to them by other politicians and by the public at large. To destroy or damage their reputation is to destroy or damage their credibility, and thereby to weaken or undermine their capacity to persuade and influence others, to secure a bond of trust and to turn their words into deeds. It would therefore be quite mistaken to think of scandal as a superficial phenomenon or as a frivolous distraction from the real substance of politics. For scandal impinges on real sources of power and it can (and often does) have substantial material consequences for the individuals and organizations affected by it.

Most political scandals arise in the region where the political field and subfield overlap with mediated forms of communication. We can illustrate this by the shaded area in figure 4.2. As we can see from this figure, there are two kinds of political scandal. Some political scandals are localized scandals: they arise within the political subfield and remain largely contained within it. This kind of localized political scandal was common in earlier societies (in the court society of early modern Europe, for example) and in those recent (or present-day) societies where the activities of media organizations were (or are) heavily circumscribed. But with the rise of liberal democratic regimes, coupled with the development of media organizations which have a degree of independence from political power, the significance of localized political scandals has been overshadowed by the rise of mediated political scandals. Most political scandals in liberal democratic societies today are mediated political scandals: they arise in the region where the political field and subfield overlap with the media. Even if a scandal first emerges as a localized political scandal, initially restricted to interactions within the political subfield, it is very difficult to contain it at the local level: it is likely to be picked up by the media and turned into a scandal which unfolds in the broader political field. Hence, with the rise of liberal democratic regimes and the development of independent media organizations, the realm of localized political scandals is increasingly drawn into the realm of mediated political scandals, and scandals in the political subfield increasingly spill over into the broader political field.

From this perspective, it is easy to see why political scandals are much more prevalent in liberal democratic societies than in authoritarian regimes. While political scandals do occur within authoritar-

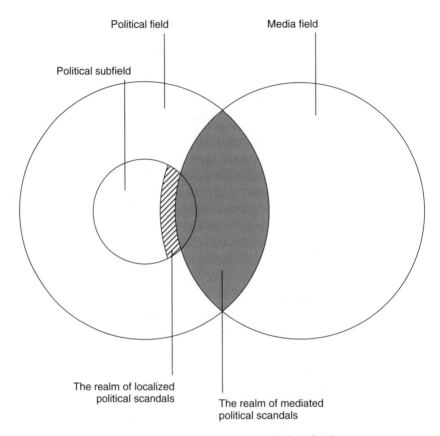

Figure 4.2 Scandal in the political field

ian regimes, they generally remain at the level of localized scandals within the political subfield; if they spread beyond the subfield, they generally do so by word of mouth or by mediated forms of communication which are difficult to control or suppress (such as underground literature). Since authoritarian regimes tend to exercise firm control over the major outlets of mediated communication (newspapers, radio and television broadcasting, etc.), it is generally very difficult for media organizations to play an independent role in the creation or development of political scandal. Moreover, given the different conditions of operation of media organizations in authoritarian societies and the different traditions and conventions which govern the practices of journalists, these organizations are less inclined to act as propagators of scandal than media organizations in liberal democratic societies. Political scandals are not unique to liberal democratic societies; but it is undoubtedly the case that, given the importance of the media in turning scandal into something more than a localized event, political scandals are much more prevalent – and much more significant – within them.

Part of the significance of political scandals in liberal democratic societies is that they are (or become) struggles over the sources of symbolic power. In earlier forms of society and in authoritarian regimes, the symbolic power of political leaders was based primarily on forms of capital that were accumulated within the political sub-field: what was (or is) of prime importance was (or is) the support that a leader (or prospective leader) could elicit from members of the political elite. However, with the development of liberal democratic societies in which political leaders (or prospective leaders) had to elicit support not only from members of the political elite but also from an electorate, they had to build their symbolic power on forms of capital that were accumulated both within the subfield and within the broader political field. They had to build a reputation, a 'good name', both in the eyes of their political peers (members of their party and powerful figures in the political subfield) and in the eyes of ordinary citizens upon whose support they would depend at the time of elections. Political scandals become so significant in liberal democratic societies precisely because they could undermine, or threaten to undermine, the activity – unavoidable for the effective exercise of power in liberal democratic societies – of accumulating the forms of capital upon which symbolic power depends.

We can now understand why political scandals commonly become struggles over symbolic power (and the sources of symbolic power) in the mediated arena of modern politics. The disclosure of trans-gressions (or alleged transgressions) can call into question the repu-tation and good name of the individual (or individuals) concerned, thereby destroying (or threatening to destroy) the symbolic resources they have carefully accumulated, and undermining (or threatening to undermine) their power. The media become the key arena in which this struggle over symbolic power is played out. As the principal medium through which political leaders relate to ordinary citizens, the media become the primary means by which political leaders accumulate symbolic capital in the broader political field. Through the constant management of visibility and the careful presentation of self, political leaders use the media to build up a store of symbolic capital in the eyes of the electorate: and this in turn, by providing them with a popular basis of support, gives them leverage in the political subfield. But political scandal can suddenly undo all of this. Reputations – so important in the political field – can be tarnished or even destroyed. Erstwhile allies within the political subfield can begin to drop away, fearful of being tainted by association. Embattled leaders can use the media to go over the heads of their political peers, addressing ordinary citizens in the broader political field in the hope of swinging public opinion behind them. The fact that political scandal can turn into a struggle for public opinion – as monitored by a continuous stream of opinion poll results reported in the media – is a reflection of the fact that part of what is at stake in scandals is the credibility of leaders, whose reputation and good name have been called into question by the scandal unfolding, or threatening to unfold, around them.

Why is Political Scandal More Prevalent Today?

This account of symbolic power and the political field enables us to understand why scandal matters, why it is more common in liberal democracies than in authoritarian regimes and why it reaches to the very foundations of political power. But it does not explain why scandal has become such a prevalent feature of political life in many liberal democratic societies today. Political scandal has a long history, as we have seen, and there were earlier historical periods (such as the postbellum period in the United States – we shall return to this later) when political scandals flourished. But it seems clear that in recent decades, and especially since the early 1960s, scandals have become an increasingly prevalent feature of political life in many Western societies, including Britain and the United States. Why? How can we explain the growing prevalence of political scandal in some modern liberal democracies?

Let us begin by considering two possible answers to this question, both of which have some *prima facie* plausibility but neither of which provides a convincing explanation. One possible answer is this: it might be argued that the growing prevalence of political scandal is due to a decline in the moral standards of political leaders, both with regard to their personal behaviour and with regard to their general probity in the conduct of office. So it might be argued, for example, that the Profumo scandal was primarily the result of a kind of sexual promiscuity which was characteristic of certain London circles in the 1960s, and that the sex scandals which afflicted Britain's political elites in the 1970s and 1980s were the reflection of a continuing decline in moral standards. Similarly, it might be argued that the corruption scandals which flourished in the United States in the 1970s and 1980s were symptomatic of declining levels of probity among politicians. However, while this may be a popular and seemingly plausible explanation of the growing prevalence of political scandal, there is little evidence to support it. Indeed, it is not at all clear that, in general terms, the moral standards of political leaders today are significantly lower than the standards adhered to by political leaders in the past. (Kennedy's extramarital affairs are only the most obvious example: quite a few earlier American presidents appear to have had liaisons which remained well-kept secrets at the time.)[10] It seems likely that the growing prevalence of political scandal has less to do with a general decline in the moral standards of political leaders than with the changing ways in which, and the extent to which, the activities of leaders are disclosed and scrutinized in the public domain.[11]

There is another way of answering this question which, like the first answer, emphasizes changing moral standards, but which focuses on the standards *applied to* politics rather than the standards of politicians themselves. It could be argued that the growing prevalence of political scandal is due, not so much to a decline in the moral standards of politicians, but rather to a change in the moral codes and conventions that are used to assess the behaviour of politicians and to the growing salience of these codes in the conduct of political life. This line of explanation is more promising. It may be that politicians are more prone to scandal because behaviour that would have been condoned in the past is more likely to be censored today. The acceptance of gifts or personal benefits of various kinds, for example, might have been tolerated in some contexts in the past but is likely to be condemned in many contexts today. But we would still want to know why this change has occurred, and why some kinds of activity which were seemingly tolerated in the past are no longer acceptable today. Moreover, this line of explanation does little to help us understand the recent profusion of sex scandals, since this has taken place in contexts where moral codes and conventions have, if anything, become more varied and contested. If it is the case that the private behaviour of political leaders today is more likely to be assessed in moral terms, we would still want to know why this change (or apparent change) has occurred. So while shifts in moral codes and conventions may have some role to play, we are going to need a more systematic and convincing explanation.

I shall try to show that there are several important changes which underlie the growing prevalence of political scandal. I shall focus on five: (1) the increased visibility of political leaders, (2) the changing technologies of communication and surveillance, (3) the changing culture of journalism, (4) the changing political culture, and (5) the growing legalization of political life. I shall argue that these factors, taken together, enable us to understand why, since the early 1960s, political scandal has become an increasingly prevalent feature of Western liberal democracies such as Britain and the United States.

(1) The increased visibility of political leaders is rooted in the broad social transformations that I outlined in an earlier chapter. The development of communication media created a new kind of visibility which was no longer tied to the sharing of a common locale, a visibility which enabled political leaders – and increasingly *required* them – to appear before others who were situated in contexts that were distant in space (and perhaps also in time). The political field was increasingly constituted as a mediated field – that is, a field in which the mediated visibility of political leaders became increasingly important and in which the relations between political leaders and ordinary citizens were increasingly shaped by mediated forms of communication.

The increasing visibility of political leaders creates conditions which increase the likelihood of political scandal. The more the lives of political leaders are made visible to others (and the more that political leaders accentuate their traits as individuals by disclosing aspects of self through the media), the more likely it is that previously hidden activities which conflict with the images that leaders wish to project will emerge in the public domain, triggering off a series of events which may spin out of control. To some extent, the growing prevalence of political scandal is the other side – the dark side, as it were – of the increasing visibility of political leaders. In this age of mediated visibility, political leaders (and aspiring leaders) know that they must use the media as a way of achieving visibility in the political field – without it, they will go nowhere. But mediated visibility can be a trap. The more visible you are, the more vulnerable you may be, because more visibility will generate more interest from the media and, however much you may wish to manage your self-presentation through the media, you cannot completely control it. As the networks of communication become more ramified and complex, mediated visibility acquires a more unpredictable, uncontrollable character. Political leaders may seek to manage the ways in which they appear through the media, but it becomes increasingly difficult for them to prevent the disclosure of potentially damaging information or images. Mediated visibility can easily slip out of their control and may, on occasion, work against them. Even the spin doctors are vulnerable.[12]

(2) One reason why mediated visibility is so difficult to control is that it depends on technologies of communication and surveillance which are becoming increasingly sophisticated and more widely available. The twentieth century has witnessed a veritable revolution in the technologies available for recording, processing and transmitting information and communication. These new and rapidly changing technologies make it more and more difficult to throw a veil of secrecy around the back-region behaviour of political leaders and other public figures. Increasingly sophisticated technologies – such as those associated with the secret tape-recording of conversations, with long-distance photography, with the covert interception of telecommunications and with the tracking and recovery of digitally codified electronic communication – provide a powerful array of devices which can be used to increase the leakage of back-region behaviour into front regions where, coupled with the activities of media organizations, they can become highly visible. Moreover, as we have seen, these technologies provide new ways of securing and fixing evidence concerning back-region behaviour which allegedly occurred and which, by being disclosed in this way, may precipitate scandal.

It would be too strong to say that these new technologies of communication and surveillance herald 'the end of privacy', as some commentators have suggested.[13] But it is undoubtedly the case that, due in part to the growing availability of these technologies, the social conditions of privacy are changing in fundamental ways. New technologies have created new and more powerful means of 'eavesdropping'. Hence conversations or interactions which individuals believe to be private may, in fact, be picked up and recorded by covert means, and subsequently made available to many thousands or millions of others through the media. Words or actions that were originally produced as private communication or behaviour may unexpectedly acquire a public character, becoming visible in ways that were certainly unanticipated, possibly very embarrassing and perhaps even seriously incriminating.

(3) The existence of new technologies does not by itself explain how and why they are used. The development of new technologies of com-

munication and surveillance has undoubtedly created new opportunities for the leakage of back-region behaviour into front regions, but why have these and other opportunities been exploited? Part of the answer to this question lies in the changing culture of journalism. While the tradition of investigative journalism stretches back to the late nineteenth century, it was given fresh impetus by the tumultuous political events of the 1960s. The sixties were, to some extent, a decade of dissent during which new social movements were willing to challenge the centres of power. In the United States, the civil rights movement and the struggle against the Vietnam War were perhaps the most visible of these movements, but others, such as the women's movement and a questioning of traditional attitudes towards sexuality, were also of major significance. This questioning, critical culture of the 1960s did not by itself transform journalistic practices, but it did help to create a climate which encouraged investigative journalism. A number of newspapers in the United States set up special teams of investigative reporters in the course of the 1960s and early 1970s – *Newsday* established a special team in 1967, the *Chicago Tribune* followed suit in 1968, the *Boston Globe* in 1970.[14] The *New York Times* devoted more resources to investigative reporting throughout the 1960s. In 1967 the Associated Press set up a special team to report on covert government activity: in 1968 this team produced 268 stories, including the disclosure of a secret report on political corruption in Saigon.[15]

While the renewal of investigative reporting goes back to the period before Watergate, it is undoubtedly the case that the events which unfolded between the discovery of the break-in and the resignation of Nixon were a major boost to this trend. Watergate was significant in this context not only because it helped to legitimate the activities of investigative journalists (albeit by virtue of the somewhat romanticized account of Bernstein and Woodward), but also because, for the first time ever, it brought the most hidden regions of the highest office of political power into the public domain, where, suddenly and unexpectedly, they were thrown open to view. And the content that emerged, both in terms of the evidence of criminal wrongdoing and the shockingly crude manoeuvrings of Nixon and his associates, served only to fuel the public's scepticism about the credibility and trustworthiness of their leaders. Watergate helped to foster a climate of scepticism in which no one, not even the President, is above suspicion.

The renewed emphasis on investigative reporting in the 1960s and 1970s helped to alter the culture of journalism and to create a context in which the search for hidden secrets, and the disclosure of these secrets if and when they were found, were increasingly regarded within media circles as an accepted part of journalistic activity. In the context of this broad shift in the culture of journalism, the distinction between different kinds of secrets became blurred and increasingly difficult to draw. Once it was accepted that the curtains which shrouded the upper regions of power could be drawn back, it would be very difficult to maintain a sharp distinction between secrets bearing on the exercise of power and secrets concerning the conduct of private life. Investigative reporting would easily shade into a kind of prurient reporting in which hidden aspects of the exercise of power would be mixed together with hidden aspects of the lives of the powerful.[16] The journalistic codes and conventions which had previously discouraged journalists from reporting on the private lives and affairs of political leaders would be gradually relaxed, and in some quarters abandoned altogether, so that journalists would be less constrained by the ethos of their own profession.

(4) But it is not only changes in the culture of journalism which have contributed to the growing prevalence of political scandal: it is also changes in the broader political culture. These changes are rooted in a series of structural transformations that have shaped the environment in which political activity takes place. Of particular importance in this regard is the gradual decline of class-based party politics, in which parties with sharply opposed belief systems, broadly representing the interests of different social classes, clashed in the political arena. During the second half of the twentieth century, the changing character of work in Western industrial societies – including the decline of traditional industries, like coal and steel, and the rise of the service sector and a range of knowledge-intensive industries – has transformed the social context of politics. Parties could no longer rely on the old social classes which once provided the core of their electoral support. Traditional doctrinal divisions were attenuated, and increasingly parties and their leaders had to struggle to win the support of a growing pool of uncommitted voters – that is, of voters whose political affiliations were less likely to be handed down from one generation to the next and who were more likely to make their decisions on the basis of the options presented to them.

These broad social transformations help us to understand what we could loosely describe as the gradual decline of 'ideological politics' and the growing importance of the 'politics of trust'. The traditional class-based party politics, with its sharply opposed belief systems and its strong contrast between left and right, has not disappeared, but it has been significantly weakened by the social transformations of the postwar period. And in its place has emerged a kind of politics which is based increasingly on the specific policy packages offered by political parties. These policy packages can no longer be backed up by appealing primarily to the class interests of voters, and voters themselves can no longer count on politicians to follow through with their promises by virtue of the long-standing social affiliations of their parties. Moreover, with the decline of the old ideological politics, many people feel increasingly uncertain about how best to tackle the enormously complex problems of the modern world; the world appears increasingly as a bewildering place where there are no simple solutions, and where we have to place more and more faith in our political leaders to make sound judgements and to protect our interests. It is in this context that the question of the credibility and trustworthiness of political leaders becomes an increasingly important issue. People become more concerned with the *character* of the individuals who are (or might become) their leaders and more concerned about their trustworthiness, because increasingly this becomes the principal means of guaranteeing that political promises will be kept and that difficult decisions in the face of complexity and uncertainty will be made on the basis of sound judgement. The politics of trust becomes increasingly important, not because politicians are inherently less trustworthy today than they were in the past, but because the social conditions that had previously underwritten their credibility have been eroded.

This changing political culture has helped to give scandal a greater significance in political life today. Part of the reason why political scandal has become so important today is that it has become a kind of *credibility test* for the politics of trust. The more our political life becomes orientated towards questions of character and trust, the more significance we give to those occasions when the trustworthiness of political leaders is called into question. The more we have to rely on the integrity of politicians to follow through with their promises and on their ability to exercise sound judgement, the more significance we give to those occasions when weaknesses of character and lapses of judgement are brought to the fore. Viewed in this light, we can understand why a scandal concerning the private life of a politician is seen by many people to have broader political significance: it is not so much because they believe that politicians should adhere to strict moral codes in their private life, but because they are worried about what this behaviour tells them about the integrity and credibility of the individual concerned. 'How can we believe a man who lies to his own wife?': the sentiment expressed by this common refrain is not so much a longing for marital fidelity but rather an anxiety about the credibility of a man whose private behaviour does not warrant the trust placed in him.

The gradual decline of ideological politics also means that, within the subfield of professional politicians, fundamental disagreements over matters of principle become less pronounced and political parties search for other means by which they can differentiate themselves from one another. As parties move increasingly towards a common centre ground and compete for a growing pool of uncommitted voters, the character failings of their opponents (actual or alleged) and the infringement of codes of conduct become increasingly potent weapons in the struggle for political advantage. Questions of character become increasingly politicized as parties struggle to differentiate themselves in a context where it is more and more difficult to appeal to fundamental differences of principle, and where, partly in order to compensate for this, parties and their leaders seek more and more to make political capital out of the character failings of others.

Since scandal becomes a credibility test for the politics of trust and since questions of character become increasingly embroiled in partisan struggle, the occurrence of scandal tends to have a cumulative effect: scandal breeds scandal, precisely because each scandal further sharpens the focus on the credibility and trustworthiness of political leaders. The cumulative effect of scandal is incorporated into the electoral cycle, as political parties and prospective leaders use previous failures of the credibility test as a basis on which to build their own election campaigns. Hence, in the aftermath of Watergate, Jimmy Carter built his 1976 presidential campaign on the question of trust and on the promise to ensure that his administration would restore high ethical standards to government – 'I'll never lie to you,' he famously declared during the campaign. Yet no sooner had he taken office than a wave of new scandals began to break. First there was the Lance affair, in which Carter's friend and close adviser was forced to resign as Director of the Office of Management and Budget amid much speculation about financial irregularities in his personal accounts. Then there was 'Billygate', a curiously inflated sequence of events in which Jimmy Carter's brother – an alcoholic with a shaky sense of judgement – found himself at the centre of a scandal-storm concerning his business connections with Libya. And as if that was not enough, there was the strange story of Hamilton Jordan, a White House aide who was accused of snorting cocaine and formally investigated by a special prosecutor, although in the end the charges were dropped. In the wake of Watergate, Jimmy Carter came to power with the pledge to make government honest, decent and clean, but in a political culture focused on questions of character and trust, this was like waving a red flag before the assembled ranks of critics and journalists. The scandals which afflicted Carter's administration did not by themselves destroy his chances of being re-elected in 1980, but doubtless they did not help him either.

(5) There is a further factor which helps to explain the increasing prevalence of political scandal: what we could describe as the growing legalization of political life. This factor is particularly important in the American context, but its relevance is not restricted to the United States. In the American context, the Ethics in Government Act (1978), passed in the aftermath of Watergate, was a landmark in the legal regulation of political life. The Act required high-ranking officials to disclose details of their financial affairs and tightened the rules on conflicts of interest. Perhaps more significantly, it established a new office, the special prosecutor, who could be called upon to investigate cases of possible law-breaking. The special prosecutor would be appointed by a federal court and hence would be independent of the Justice Department. By creating this office, the Act helped to set in motion a new dynamic which would raise the profile of cases of suspected wrongdoing and endow the investigative process with greatly increased powers and resources – a dynamic that was vividly illustrated by the Iran-Contra affair and by the long-running investigations of Bill Clinton that were carried out by Independent Counsel Kenneth Starr. (The office of special prosecutor was renamed independent counsel in 1983.)

While the growing legalization of political life is particularly marked in the American context, a somewhat similar trend can be discerned elsewhere. In British law there is no equivalent of the special prosecutor, but a government official suspected of criminal wrongdoing can be subjected to the normal procedures of criminal investigation. Moreover, prime ministers can set up committees of inquiry to investigate matters of public interest and to make recommendations which can be enacted in law. This practice has been used on numerous occasions since the early 1960s, when a committee of inquiry, headed by Lord Denning, was established by the then prime minister Harold Macmillan to investigate the security implications of

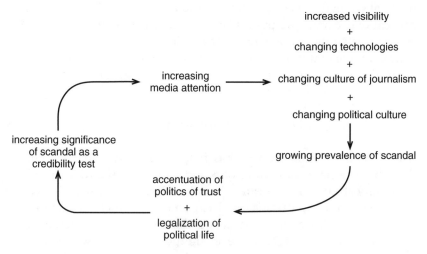

Figure 4.3 The growing prevalence of political scandal

the Profumo affair. More recent committees of inquiry – including those set up in the wake of the Poulson affair in the early 1970s and the cash-for-questions scandal of the early 1990s – have led to a higher degree of regulation of the private financial interests of MPs and to the establishment of explicit codes of conduct.

The various changes that I have described help us to understand the growing prevalence of scandal in the political life of many Western societies since the early 1960s. None of these changes is sufficient by itself to explain this trend, but taken together they form the basis of a plausible explanation. Figure 4.3 summarizes the main elements of this explanation. The increased visibility of political leaders, the changing technologies of communication and surveillance, the changing culture of journalism and the changing political culture have all contributed to the growing prevalence of political scandal. This in turn has led to the accentuation of the politics of trust and to the growing legalization of political life. In these conditions, scandal assumes more and more significance as a credibility test, a factor which fuels media attention and increases still further the like-lihood of scandal. In the context of a political field characterized by a competitive party system and an array of relatively independent media organizations which play a key role in shaping the relations between political professionals and ordinary citizens, and in circum-stances marked by the growing significance of the politics of trust, political scandal is likely to have a cumulative effect. The more political scandals occur, the more likely it is that new scandals will arise and will be amplified by increasing media attention. The dynamic of scandal, media attention and the politics of trust produces a racheting effect which constantly increases the political stakes.

Political Cultures of Scandal

The dynamic outlined above has helped to create what we could describe as a political culture of scandal in many Western societies. By 'political culture' I mean a broad and rather diffuse cluster of rules, conventions, attitudes and expectations which underpin the conduct of political life and shape the forms of interaction and communication that take place in the political field. We have now come to accept, for better or worse, that a subset of these conventions and expectations has come to crystallize around the phenomenon of political scandal. This phenomenon is no longer seen as a rare and exceptional occurrence: rather, it has become an endemic feature of our contemporary political culture and is commonly regarded as such. We may not like it but we know that it is unlikely to go away.

While scandal has become an endemic feature of contemporary political culture, the conditions under which scandals occur and the ways in which they unfold do, of course, vary considerably from one national context to another. The set of conventions and expectations which shapes the occurrence and development of political scandals is not invariant. There is not so much 'a' political culture of scandal but rather a plurality of political cultures of scandal, each characterized by its own distinctive traditions, its own reservoir of precedents and collective memories and its own constantly changing cluster of conventions and expectations. (We shall examine some of these cultures and traditions in the following chapters.) The global expansion of communication media has helped to ensure that these traditions are not wholly distinct; the rapid international diffusion of news and the development of global media organizations like CNN have helped to ensure that some scandals – especially major American scandals like Watergate, Iran-Contra and the Clinton–Lewinsky affair – unfold in an arena that spills well beyond national boundaries. Thanks to the media, some scandals have become part of collective memories in societies far removed from those in which they were primarily situated. But the global diffusion of scandals and the intermingling of traditions have not eradicated the distinctive features which constitute different political cultures of scandal.

What is it like to live in a world where scandal has become an endemic feature of political culture? For those who wish to build a career in the political field, scandal is a risk which they must strive actively and continuously to avoid. Scandal has become an occupational hazard of life in the public domain. Political parties screen their potential candidates to assess their susceptibility to scandal – the 'scandal risk factor'. Parties, governments and political leaders develop strategies to minimize the risk of scandal, and to contain scandals (or limit the damage) in the event that damaging revelations appear. The management of scandal has become an integral part of the strategies used to compete for and exercise power. Parties, governments and leaders know that scandals can be damaging, both to the individuals who find themselves at the centre of them and to the organizations with which they are associated. They know that they must take steps to avoid them or to minimize the damage if they occur – even if they know, at the same time, that the risk of scandal cannot be completely controlled.

For many ordinary people, living in a world where scandal has become an endemic feature of political culture is a deeply ambivalent experience. On the one hand, scandals turn the tables on political leaders and, on occasion, bring to light activities and forms of behaviour which raise serious questions about the propriety and legality of their conduct and about the integrity of their character – in this respect, many people may feel that scandals make a legitimate, if somewhat sensationalized, contribution to political life. On the other hand, many people may also feel that the cycle of scandal has got out of hand. They may watch the seemingly never-ending parade of political scandals with a mixture of bewilderment and despair. They may feel that the media are going too far, that they have become overly preoccupied with scandal and have blown things out of proportion, to such an extent that the cycle of scandal begins to rebound on the media themselves. Many people may grow weary of scandal and sceptical of the media interest. The cycle of scandal gives rise to a kind of weariness, a kind of 'scandal fatigue', on the part of many people. New scandals appear with predictable frequency, but gradually they lose their novelty value and even, in some respects, their capacity to shock and surprise, as readers and viewers become increasingly inured to the spectacle and increasingly familiar with the rules and conventions which produce it.

In describing this distinctive cluster of rules, conventions, attitudes and expectations as 'a political culture of scandal', I do not want to suggest that scandal has come to dominate the political life of Western societies and to overshadow other issues, such as unemployment, poverty, health, environmental destruction, etc. – this is clearly not the case. Nor do I wish to suggest that the dynamic of scandal has become a kind of inexorable machine which is likely to devour any normal, flesh-and-blood human being who has the temerity to present himself or herself for political office today – tempting though this interpretation may be,[17] it is no doubt coloured with an excessive sense of doom. But I do want to maintain that the occurrence of political scandal today is not an isolated event and that the ways in which a political scandal arises and unfolds – and, indeed, the fact that it arises at all – are shaped by the distinctive set of conventions and expectations which comprise this cultural form.

5

Sex Scandals in the Political Field

Not all scandals are political scandals, and not all political scandals are alike. There are a great variety of political scandals, and each has its own particular conditions and characteristics: the more one examines scandals, the more one is struck by the enormous complexity and diversity of the phenomena commonly brought together under this label. Can we take the analysis of political scandal any further? Can we identify some typical forms of political scandal and analyse some of their typical characteristics? Or must we abandon the idea of further analysis and content ourselves with the description of individual cases?

While recognizing that all scandals have an irreducible particularity, we can nevertheless take the analysis a stage further by recalling a point that was made in the first chapter. There we noted that all scandals involve actions or events which transgress certain values or norms and that, while there is a great deal of diversity and variability in the values and norms which are relevant to scandal, nevertheless there are certain types of norm which are more scandal-sensitive than others. Norms and codes governing sexual relations, those governing financial transactions and those governing the pursuit and exercise of political power are particularly scandal-prone.

I shall take this observation as a starting point for my analysis of the forms of political scandal. I shall distinguish between three basic types of political scandal and briefly describe their characteristics. I shall then devote a chapter to each – in this chapter I shall focus on sex scandals in the political field, while in the following chapters

I shall examine financial scandals and what I shall call 'power scandals'.

Three Types of Political Scandal

We can distinguish between three basic types of scandal in the political field: those involving the transgression of sexual codes (sex scandals), those involving the misuse of economic resources (financial scandals) and those involving the abuse of political power (power scandals). Each of these types of political scandal has its key defining features, although in practice any particular scandal is likely to have an array of specific and secondary traits. Each type involves the transgression of norms or conventions and each involves power and resources; but the kinds of norms vary from one type of scandal to another, as do the forms of power and the ways in which they are implicated. Let us briefly consider each of the three types in turn.

The defining feature of sex scandals in the political field is that they involve the public disclosure of activities of political figures which constitute, or which can be portrayed as constituting, a transgression of prevailing norms or codes governing the conduct of sexual relations. Sexual-political scandals involve public revelations and allegations concerning the private life of public figures. They are essentially struggles over symbolic power which can have serious political consequences; money may be involved, but this is a secondary consideration. Sexual-political scandals may involve criminal sex offences, such as offences concerning homosexuality in contexts where homosexual acts are (or were) illegal, sex with a minor, solicitation or prostitution. But many sexual-political scandals (and the vast majority today) do not involve criminal offences of this kind. When legal infringements do occur in sexual-political scandals today, they are often linked to second-order transgressions rather than to the original offence. What is important is not so much that the actions disclosed are illegal, but rather that the norms transgressed have some degree of moral bindingness in the contexts in which they are embedded. The norms do not have to be legally enforced and they do not have to be shared by everyone (indeed, they may be flouted or ignored by many). But they have to have a sufficient degree of moral bindingness to ensure that the public disclosure of actions which transgress them will be accompanied by public expressions of disapproval, and that the actions themselves will be regarded by at least some people as improper or unseemly forms of conduct.

Whereas sexual-political scandals involve the disclosure of aspects of private life which transgress the norms and codes of sexual conduct, financial scandals in the political field are based on the disclosure of activities by political figures which involve an infringement of rules governing the acquisition and allocation of economic resources. Financial-political scandals generally involve hidden linkages between economic and political power which are regarded as improper and which, on being disclosed, precipitate the scandal. Unlike sexual-political scandals, financial scandals in the political field are more likely to involve the breaking of laws – in this case, laws governing financial transactions and the use of financial resources by individuals who hold public office or aspire to it. Hence financial scandals are more likely to result in legal prosecutions.

Both sexual-political scandals and financial-political scandals involve the transgression of norms governing activities which may not be unique to the political field. Power scandals, on the other hand, are based on the disclosure of activities which infringe the rules governing the acquisition or exercise of political power as such. Power scandals are the 'purest' form of political scandal, in the sense that the rules or conventions whose transgression lies at the heart of these scandals are the rules and conventions governing the very form of power – that is, political power – which is constitutive of the political field. Power scandals may involve illicit financial transactions of various kinds, but the financial transgressions are not the source of the scandal: they are secondary to the fact that the activities in question are transgressions of rules governing the exercise of political power. Power scandals reveal covert activities and hidden forms of power which diverge from the norms and procedures which are presumed to regulate the competition for and exercise of political power. These norms and procedures are often incorporated in the constitutional structure of modern states, either explicitly in the form of laws or implicitly in the form of institutionalized practices. Hence, like financial scandals in the political field, power scandals are generally linked to legal prosecution or the threat of it.

Table 5.1 summarizes some of the key features of these three types of political scandal. Sexual-political scandals involve the transgression of sexual norms and codes; they are characterized by struggles over symbolic power and resources, which can in turn have serious consequences for the capacity to exercise political power; whether they involve legal infringements varies from one case to the next.

Table 5.1 Types of political scandal

Characteristics	Types of scandal		
	Sexual-political scandals	Financial-political scandals	Power scandals
Codes transgressed	sexual	financial/political	political
Principal forms of power	symbolic	economic/political	political
Implicated forms of power	political	symbolic	symbolic
Likelihood of legal infringement	variable	moderate to high	high

Financial-political scandals involve the infringement of rules and conventions governing the use of economic resources in relation to the exercise of political power, in ways that can have symbolic and political consequences; in many cases, they give rise to legal prosecution. Power scandals involve the infringement of rules governing the use of political power and are likely to have both political and symbolic consequences; they are also likely to constitute a legal offence.

This typology provides a helpful framework for analysing political scandals and I shall use it in the chapters that follow. In this chapter I shall focus on sex scandals in the political field, while in the next two chapters I shall look at financial-political scandals and power scandals in turn. This way of organizing the material has some clear analytical advantages; it will enable us to examine the characteristics of each type of scandal in more detail and to explore some examples. But it also has some disadvantages. Readers may gain analytical clarity but they will not get a full picture of the many scandals that have characterized the political histories of particular countries, nor will they get a full sense of the ways in which, in any particular national context, different types of scandal can bounce off one another, fuelling the kind of dynamic described in the previous chapter and contributing to the formation of distinctive political cultures of scandal. I shall be using a range of examples drawn primarily from Britain and the United States, and I shall provide some historical background when it is helpful to do so. But my principal aim in this and the next two chapters is to deepen the analysis of the basic forms of political scandal, not to provide a comprehensive narrative history of political scandals in particular national contexts.

Before proceeding any further, I should add a few qualifications about the typology. In the first place, it is important to emphasize that sex scandals and financial scandals are not of course unique to the political field. Sex scandals are common in other spheres of life – among media personalities, for example, or in particular institutions like churches, schools, etc. Financial scandals occur relatively frequently within the economic field (the scandal surrounding the activities of Nick Leeson – a young employee of the London-based Barings Bank who managed, through a series of highly speculative investments on the Singapore stock market, to bring the bank to its knees – being but one recent example). But the fact that sex scandals and financial scandals are not unique to the political field does not mean that they cannot, under certain conditions, constitute political scandals. On those occasions when they are political scandals, what makes them *political* is the fact that they occur within the political field, that they involve individuals who hold or aspire to positions of power within this field and that they have consequences within this field, both in terms of the activities and opportunities of the individuals directly implicated in the scandals and in terms of the actions and responses of others.[1]

A second qualification is that the typology, while certainly wide-ranging, is not exhaustive. It may cover the most important forms of political scandal but it does not purport to cover *every* possible form. I do not wish to rule out the possibility that significant political scandals may occur which do not involve the transgression of sexual codes, financial regulations or rules and conventions governing the exercise of political power. It is perfectly possible, for example, that disclosures concerning the illicit use of drugs by a key political figure might give rise to a major political scandal. But while the typology cannot claim to be exhaustive, it would not be implausible to maintain that, viewed in relation to the historical and empirical record, it covers the vast majority of cases and provides a useful framework for analysis.

Finally, just as the typology is not exhaustive, so too the three main types of political scandal are not mutually exclusive. Each of these types is, to some extent, an 'ideal type' (in Max Weber's terminology) – that is, it is an abstraction which highlights some features of reality at the expense of others. Actual instances of political scandal will exemplify these types in varying ways and to differing degrees – some may exemplify a particular type extremely well, while others may involve a complex mixture of different elements. Moreover, scandals that begin life as one type may be transformed, via a series of second-order transgressions, into a scandal of a different type. Reality is rarely as simple as our theories of it, and the exceedingly murky world of political scandals reflects this maxim well.

Private Life in the Public Domain

Although political scandals can assume different forms and, in particular national contexts, some types of political scandal may be more significant than others, it is undoubtedly the case that political scandals involving sexual transgressions have played, and continue to play, a significant role in many contexts. In certain times and places, a political figure who practised homosexuality, conducted an extramarital affair or frequented prostitutes (among other things) was running the risk of scandal: the public disclosure of these private sexual activities, clandestinely carried out, could have disastrous consequences. In some cases, the risk was heightened by the fact that the activity in question was illegal, and hence the public disclosure could result in criminal prosecution. But the potentially scandalous character of the activity stemmed above all from the fact that the norms and codes of sexual conduct had some degree of moral bindingness in a specific social-historical context, and hence the public disclosure of transgressions had the capacity to stigmatize the individual (or individuals) concerned.

It is not difficult to understand why the disclosure of sexual transgressions might give rise to political scandals in contexts where the norms and codes in question have a relatively high degree of moral bindingness. But it is much less clear why the disclosure of such transgressions should give rise to scandals in contexts where the norms and codes are much more contested, where they are adhered to weakly or rejected by many. One of the paradoxes of sexual-political scandals is that, while they presuppose a degree of moral bindingness of sexual norms and codes, there is not a clear and direct correlation between the seriousness of a sexual-political scandal and the degree of moral bindingness of the relevant norms and codes. How can we explain this paradox?

Part of the explanation – the easiest part – stems from the fact that the stigmatizing potential of illicit sexual activities can be mobilized by particular individuals and organizations which have an interest (personal or political) in exposing sexual misdemeanours, in the knowledge that their public disclosure can cause serious political damage. The stigmatizing potential of illicit sexual activities can also be exploited by the media, some sectors of which have routinized the practice of seeking out sexual transgressions and indiscretions committed by public figures and turning them into the substance of scandal (political and otherwise). Since these activities are carried out by individuals and organizations which have their own agendas and their own interests to pursue, there is no necessary connection between the degree of prominence which a sexual-political scandal receives in the public domain and the degree of opprobrium with which it is condemned, on the one hand, and the extent to which the relevant norms and codes are actually shared or adhered to by ordinary people, on the other. Of course, it is much easier to mobilize the stigmatizing potential of illicit sexual activities when the norms and codes are widely shared, but these activities can have the capacity to stigmatize even when many ordinary people do not adhere to these norms and codes in the practical contexts of their own lives.

Another factor which helps to explain this paradox is that, for reasons outlined in the previous chapter, sexual-political scandals can also serve as credibility tests for actual or aspiring political leaders. In particular social-historical contexts they can be used as, and may be seen as, occasions when the character and trustworthiness of an individual is under scrutiny. And it is perhaps not surprising that when individuals' lives are subjected to intensive scrutiny of this kind, many emerge with some unseemly blemishes on their names.

But the paradox also points to the fact that in many sexual-political scandals there is more at stake than sex. Illicit sexual activity is certainly an important element, but many sexual-political scandals involve other elements as well – elements which may, in some cases, overshadow the significance of the sexual transgression. We can distinguish three such additional elements which feature fairly prominently in sexual-political scandals: (1) hypocrisy, (2) conflicts of interest and (3) second-order transgressions. Let us briefly consider the role of each.

(1) One reason why sex scandals have the potential to damage political figures and their parties, as well as governments, is the hypocrisy factor. The disclosure of illicit sexual activities can be politically dam-

aging if it compromises the policies which are publicly espoused by political figures (or by their parties or governments) – and it can be damaging in this way even in circumstances where the bindingness of the relevant norms and codes is weak. In such cases, the position of a political figure can be undermined by a scandal which stems from illicit sexual activity but which is fuelled by a mixture of mirth and resentment. Many people may not be shocked by the activity which is disclosed, and they may not adhere (or adhere consistently) to the relevant norms and codes in the practical conduct of their own lives. But they may well feel a sense of resentment towards politicians who have the temerity to prescribe forms of behaviour for others to which they themselves do not adhere. A politician whose private behaviour is seen to diverge significantly from his or her publicly stated policies (or those of his or her party or government) may find that his or her position becomes untenable. This was Parkinson's predicament.

Cecil Parkinson was a prominent Conservative politician in Britain during the period of Margaret Thatcher's rise to power. An MP since 1970, he became Secretary of State for Trade and Industry and chairman of the Conservative Party in 1981, organizing Margaret Thatcher's landslide general election victory in 1983. Parkinson had everything going for him – he was charming, successful, good-looking; his career seemed likely to go from strength to strength. But in the summer of 1983 a story began to emerge which would have disastrous consequences. Parkinson had had a long-standing affair with his former secretary, Sara Keays, who had become pregnant and was expecting their child in the autumn. According to Sara Keays, Parkinson had promised to divorce his wife and to marry her instead, but subsequently changed his mind. On 14 September 1983, in the midst of the Conservative Party's annual conference, Parkinson suddenly resigned as party chairman. On 5 October the satirical magazine *Private Eye* broke the news that his secretary was pregnant; the same day Parkinson issued a statement admitting his involvement in the affair. Parkinson remained an MP until 1992, but his career never regained the momentum it had had in the early 1980s. What made the affair particularly damaging for Parkinson's career, and acutely embarrassing for the government, was that it occurred at a time when Thatcher and her associates were attempting to build a political programme around the theme of a return to traditional values, a theme which emphasized the importance of the nuclear family. For Thatcher's erstwhile party chairman to be exposed as the man who made his secretary pregnant, and whose wife and family had to suffer the consequences, could hardly be seen in that context as anything other than hopelessly hypocritical.

The specific details of Parkinson's predicament were of course tied to the circumstances of the time, but the basic structure of his dilemma is one which has featured fairly prominently in sexual-political scandals over the years. This dilemma was at the heart not only of the sex scandal which brought down Margaret Thatcher's chief lieutenant, but also of the numerous sex scandals which afflicted the government of her successor, John Major. Like Thatcher, John Major wanted to reorientate the Conservative Party around certain traditional values – 'back to basics' was the slogan he used at the Conservative Party conference in 1993. But no sooner had he launched his agenda than a new wave of scandals began to break. First there was Steven Norris, the Tory MP and transport minister who, it was alleged in the tabloid press, had five mistresses. Then there was Tim Yeo, the Conservative MP and junior minister for the environment who was forced to resign when the *News of the World* disclosed that he had fathered a child in an extramarital affair. Yeo's position was made particularly difficult by the fact that his mistress was a single mother, at a time when some senior figures in the Con-servative Party were advocating a tough line on single mothers who drew state benefits. (Yeo himself had once remarked that 'it is in everyone's interests to reduce broken families and the number of single parents', a remark that he would come to rue.) And other scan-dals were soon to follow. Driven on by the scandal potential inher-ent in the back-to-basics policy, the press had a field day.

(2) Another reason why sex scandals can be damaging for politi-cians, parties and governments is that they can present conflicts of interest – actual, possible or alleged. On some occasions, illicit sexual activities of politicians may be thought to conflict with their duties and responsibilities as public officials. There may be a risk, actual or perceived, that these activities will compromise their impartiality and colour their judgement; there may also be a risk, actual or perceived, that such activities will compromise the kind of confidentiality required by their post. The dangers associated with disclosure may increase the pressure on them and subject them to extraneous threats, including blackmail. It may be difficult for a politician to con-tinue, and especially to carry a ministerial portfolio, if they appear to be embroiled in conflicts of interest of this kind.

Whether such conflicts of interest are actual or alleged is, in any particular case, likely to be a matter of dispute. In some cases there may be sufficiently strong grounds to suspect a conflict of interests that senior political figures become concerned – as happened, for example, in the Profumo affair, as we shall see. On other occasions, allegations of a conflict of interests may have more to do with a tactical ploy on the part of the media to instigate or inflame a scandal. The possibility of a conflict of interest may serve as an effective pretext to probe the private life of a public figure. And in some circumstances, the mere *appearance* of a conflict of interests may have damaging consequences for a politician. Such was the fate of the hapless David Mellor.

David Mellor was elected as a Conservative MP in 1979, and was made Secretary of State at the new Department of National Heritage created by John Major after the 1992 general election. Mellor's portfolio included responsibility for media, and in July 1992 he commissioned a prominent lawyer, Sir David Calcutt, to carry out a review of issues relating to the freedom of the press. In a climate of concern about the extent of the media's intrusion into the private lives of individuals, Mellor warned newspaper editors that they should show more restraint – they were, he famously declared, 'drinking in the last chance saloon'. On 19 July 1992, the *People* broke the story about his affair with a thirty-one-year-old actress, Antonia de Sancha, whose London flat had been bugged by journalists. The story was quickly picked up by other papers. Lurid accounts proliferated about Mellor's sexual proclivities, including the suggestions (quite possibly fabricated) that the minister liked to make love in a Chelsea strip (the shirt worn by the football team he supported) and that he had a penchant for toe sucking. John Major publicly supported his embattled minister, but by late September Mellor had resigned and his ministerial career was over. 'Toe Job To No Job – Minister finally sunk by scandals' was the merciless headline in the *Sun*. The accumulation of embarrassing revelations and allegations about Mellor's sex life was undoubtedly the centre of the scandal that led to his downfall; he became an object of ridicule and his reputation was battered by the affair. But his position was certainly not helped by the fact that he was the minister in charge of a department which had just initiated a major review of the freedom of the press, and hence it could be reasonably suspected that his judgement might be coloured by his own experiences and by the harsh treatment he himself endured at the hands of the press.

(3) While all sex scandals are based on revelations about illicit sexual activities, many sex scandals in the political field derive their signifi-

cance more from the seriousness of second-order transgressions than from the occurrence of the original offence. Faced with revelations which are embarrassing and which may be very difficult to explain to one's colleagues (let alone to one's family and friends), the most natural response is to deny them. If it came down to a matter of one person's word against another, then surely it would be difficult to sustain allegations of sexual misconduct – denial might well seem like the safest strategy (and the best way to save face). But the strategy of denial can quickly turn into a nightmare. The individual or individuals at the centre of a scandal may find that they become ensnared in an ever more elaborate web of lies which they have to spin in order to maintain the denial. They may find themselves confronted with new forms of evidence which are difficult to explain away. They may find themselves lying in circumstances where they are on their honour to speak the truth (as when they make a personal statement in the House of Commons, for example), or in circumstances when they are under oath. A scandal that began life with the disclosure of a relatively minor sexual transgression may turn into a scandal involving possible criminal offences including perjury, obstruction of justice or even worse.

A Venerable Tradition

While sex scandals in the political field generally involve a good deal more than sex, it is nevertheless the case that sexual transgressions of various kinds lie at their heart. Why should sexual transgressions be a potential source of scandals in some political cultures and not in others? Why do sexual-political scandals feature so prominently in Britain, and less so in some other countries? It would certainly be wrong to suggest that sexual-political scandals are unique to Britain, and misleading to suggest that the only political scandals of any significance in Britain are sexual in character.[2] But it is undoubtedly true that sex plays a major role in the scandals that pepper the political history of Britain. Why?

It is tempting to respond to questions of this kind by suggesting that the British have a traditional squeamishness about sex, and hence are likely to respond censoriously to revelations of sexual transgressions by prominent public figures. There may be a fragment of truth in this suggestion, but it can easily be exaggerated and it is unlikely to provide a compelling explanation of why sex scandals feature so prominently in British political life. A much more important consideration is the fact that there exists a long and venerable tradition of sexual-political scandals in Britain, a tradition which has been nurtured and sustained by the press and which forms part of the political culture. Moreover, whereas in some countries (such as France) there are legally enforceable restrictions on the freedom of the press to report on aspects of private life, no such restrictions exist in Britain. (Today the Press Complaints Commission publishes a code of practice, but adherence to the code is voluntary.) Hence there are relatively few obstacles which lie in the way of editors, journalists and others who are determined to expose clandestine affairs.

The tradition of sexual-political scandals in Britain stretches back to the nineteenth century and before, as we have seen. Throughout this history, sexual-political scandals have been interwoven with changes in moral codes and conventions governing sexuality, with conflicts over these codes and with changing forms of legal regulation; scandals have fed off these codes and conventions and have, in turn, contributed to their transformation. In the late nineteenth century, growing concerns over prostitution and homosexuality created a context in which scandals exposing the horrors of the prostitution trade – the dark underbelly of Victorian society – and scandals based on allegations of homosexuality could flourish. Moreover, the growing emphasis on the importance of the family and on marriage as a gateway to social respectability,[3] coupled with the difficulty of obtaining divorce and the social stigma associated with it, created conditions in which, on the relatively rare occasions when prominent public figures found themselves involved in divorce proceedings, they were likely to become the subject of adverse publicity which could damage or even destroy their careers, as it did with Dilke and Parnell. It was well known that the actual behaviour of individuals did not always live up to ideals of matrimonial fidelity, and widely acknowledged that double standards prevailed with regard to men and women (women, to be respectable, had to be chaste, while men were commonly allowed a greater degree of sexual freedom). But when the details of individuals' private lives were thrust into the public domain, as they were when they became involved in a trial or a criminal investigation, then the pretence of respectability could no longer be maintained and the adverse publicity could have dire consequences.

Since the late nineteenth century, the codes and conventions governing sexual behaviour in Britain have changed in many ways, as have the laws which regulate it. There was a gradual liberalization of the laws governing divorce, culminating in the introduction of no-fault divorce legislation in 1969; with the increase in rates of divorce in the course of the twentieth century (and especially since the 1960s), the stigma associated with marital breakdown has declined. The laws governing male homosexuality were also gradually liberalized, and the Sexual Offences Act of 1967 decriminalized private sexual activity between adult men. Moreover, the rise of the women's movement from the 1960s has contributed to a gradual reconfiguration of social attitudes towards gender and sexuality, and called into question (among other things) the double standards associated with the sexual behaviour of men and women. These and other changes have altered the legal and normative environment of sexual activity in significant ways, and the sex scandals which have featured prominently in British political life since the 1950s have taken place in contexts which are quite different from those that existed in the late nineteenth century.

Despite the changing contexts, certain kinds of sexual transgression have proved to be particularly fertile and durable sources of scandal. These scandal-prone transgressions include adultery and extramarital affairs; sexual involvement with prostitutes and call-girls; and homosexuality. Many of the sexual-political scandals of the nineteenth century involved these kinds of transgressions, and some of the most significant scandals of the twentieth century have shown that such transgressions have not lost their capacity to harm. Britain in the 1960s was certainly very different from the late Victorian period, but the public disclosure of sexual transgressions by public figures, especially when they raised the prospect of conflicts of interest and second-order transgressions, could still have dire consequences for politicians, parties and governments. No single event demonstrates this more clearly than the sequence of revelations and allegations which destroyed the political career of John Profumo.

The Profumo affair had all the ingredients of a classic sex scandal – a clandestine affair, adultery, a potential conflict of interests, second-order transgressions and a stream of revelations about the seamy underside of high society London in the 1960s.[4] It was also interwoven with issues of national security, which helped to ensure that the affair was viewed with concern in senior political circles. John Profumo was a Tory politician from a wealthy, upper-class background. Educated at Harrow and Oxford, he was first elected to Parliament in 1940, and then re-elected in 1950 as MP for Stratford-upon-Avon. In 1954 he married the actress Valerie Hobson. His political career began to take off and in 1960 he was appointed Secretary of State for War in Harold Macmillan's government.

Profumo was rich, clever and well connected, and he seemed destined for higher things.

It was a weekend in July 1961 that marked the beginning of a complex sequence of events which led to Profumo's downfall. Profumo and his wife accepted an invitation from Lord Astor to visit his Cliveden estate in Buckinghamshire. On a warm summer evening Lord Astor and Profumo strolled over to the pool, where an attractive young woman, Christine Keeler, was swimming nude. Keeler was the guest of a man named Stephen Ward, who worked as an osteopath in London and who, in return for treating Lord Astor's back, had been given the use of a cottage at Cliveden. Christine Keeler came from the small Buckinghamshire village of Wraysbury, where she had had an impoverished upbringing. At the age of fifteen she left for London, where she worked as a waitress and then as a topless dancer in a club in Soho. She met Ward at the club, and subsequently moved into his flat in Wimpole Mews.

Shortly after their first encounter at Cliveden, Profumo and Keeler began an affair which was to last for several months. But unknown to Profumo, Keeler was also having an affair with a Soviet naval attaché, Colonel Eugene Ivanov. The British intelligence service MI5 were monitoring Ivanov's movements, since they suspected that he might be tempted to defect. MI5 knew about Ivanov's involvement with Keeler and had contacted Ward for information; they also learned that Profumo was seeing Keeler. MI5 asked the Cabinet Secretary, Sir Norman Brook, to speak to Profumo and alert him to the dangers, which Brook did on 9 August. Following his meeting with Brook, Profumo wrote a hastily scribbled note to Keeler on War Office stationery which would return to haunt him:

> Darling,
>   In great haste & because I can get no reply from your phone – Alas something's blown up tomorrow night & I can't therefore make it. I'm terribly sorry especially as I leave the next day for various trips & then a holiday so won't be able to see you again until some time in September. Blast it. Please take great care of yourself & don't run away.
>   Love J.
>   I'm writing this 'cos I know you're off for the day tomorrow & I want you to know before you go if I still can't reach you by phone.[5]

Profumo's affair with Christine Keeler lasted until December 1961, when it was finally broken off. But the scandal did not erupt until much later, in spring 1963. In the course of 1962 the circumstances of Keeler's life deteriorated, culminating in an incident outside Ward's flat when one of her spurned lovers, Johnny Edge-combe, fired several gunshots at the door of the flat. Ward asked her to leave and Keeler turned to others for help. She began to talk about her earlier affair with Profumo, claiming that Ward had asked her to get information from Profumo about the nuclear arming of Germany. She told this to a former Labour MP, John Lewis, who passed the story on to George Wigg, a Labour MP who had a strong interest in defence issues; Wigg had clashed with Profumo on various occasions and he was not averse to pressing him again when the opportunity arose. She also spoke to a journalist, Paul Mann, who persuaded her to take her story to the press. The *Sunday Pictorial* offered her £1,000 for which she agreed to let them publish her story, and she gave them the 'Darling' letter; but Ward intervened, anxious to stop the story from going any further, and the newspaper eventually backed off.

Westminster and Fleet Street were awash with rumours, though newspapers were afraid to put anything in print for fear of libel. Then, in early March 1963, *Westminster Confidential*, a small-circulation weekly newsletter run by an expatriate American journalist named Andrew Roth, ventured into print with an article which sketched the main themes of the story and alluded to the existence of 'a letter, apparently signed "Jack", on the stationery of the Secretary for W—r'. Shortly after that, on 14 March, the trial of Johnny Edge-combe began at the Old Bailey. Edgecombe was charged with the attempted murder of Christine Keeler, but Keeler disappeared as the trial began, fuelling speculation that pressure was being put on her to keep quiet. Under the protection of parliamentary privilege (which shielded him from the laws of libel) George Wigg raised the issue in the House on 21 March; without mentioning Profumo by name, he referred to the rumours involving 'a member of the Government front bench' and challenged the government to deny them. Stories which had until then remained at the level of rumour and gossip were now turned into public allegations in the House; privately Profumo had always insisted on his innocence, but now he was forced to respond in public. On 22 March he made a personal statement to the House. (By convention, an MP who makes a personal statement in the House is never questioned by others, but it is assumed that he will tell the truth; failure to do so would be a serious breach of trust.) Profumo acknowledged that he had met Miss Keeler on several occasions between July and December 1961 but he explicitly denied that they had had an affair – 'There was no impropriety whatsoever in my acquaintanceship with Miss Keeler' were the fateful words. Profumo threatened to sue for libel if scandalous allegations were made outside the House.

There were many who did not believe Profumo's denial, including George Wigg. A few days after Profumo made his statement, Wigg appeared on the BBC television programme *Panorama* and alleged that Ivanov and Ward were security risks. As the police stepped up their investigations of Ward, his friends and associates began to desert him and his practice began to collapse. Increasingly desperate, Ward wrote to various politicians – including the Home Secretary and the leader of the Labour Party, Harold Wilson – to protest his innocence; he also claimed that Profumo had been lying. Wilson went to see the Prime Minister on 27 May and urged him to take action to ensure that there had been no breach of security; shortly afterwards, the Prime Minister agreed to set up an inquiry under Lord Dilhorne. When Profumo was recalled from holiday to appear before the inquiry, he had decided that the game was up. He spoke to the Chief Whip and the Prime Minister's Private Secretary and told them that he had lied. On 4 June he resigned both as a minister and as an MP. In his letter of resignation, made public the following day, Profumo retracted his earlier denial:

Dear Prime Minister,

You will recollect that on 22 March, following certain allegations made in Parliament, I made a personal statement. At that time rumour had charged me with assisting in the disappearance of a witness and with being involved in some possible breach of security.

So serious were these charges that I allowed myself to think that my personal association with that witness, which had also been the subject of rumour, was, by comparison, of minor importance only. In my statement I said that there had been no impropriety in this association. To my very deep regret I have to admit that this was not true, and that I misled you, my colleagues, and the House.

I ask you to understand that I did this to protect, as I thought, my wife and family, who were equally misled, as were my professional advisers.

I have come to realize that, by this deception, I have been guilty of a grave misdemeanour, and despite the fact that there is no truth whatsoever in the other charges, I cannot remain a member of your Administration, nor of the House of Commons.

I cannot tell you of my deep remorse for the embarrassment I have caused to you, to my colleagues in the Government, to my constituents and to the Party which I have served for the past 25 years.

Yours sincerely,

Jack Profumo[6]

7 John Profumo after his resignation, June 1963. Profumo's admission that he had lied to the House concerning his relationship with Christine Keeler left his reputation in shreds.

Profumo's resignation was headline news in Britain and across the world. With restrictions now removed, the press was filled with stories about the affair and about apparent goings-on in the more decadent regions of London's high society. Plenty of fresh material was provided by the trial of another former boyfriend of Keeler (Lucky Gordon, who was charged with assaulting her), by the arrest and trial of Ward on the charge of having knowingly lived on the earnings of prostitution, and by the serialization of the 'Confessions of Christine' in the *News of the World* (Keeler was paid £23,000 for her story). Although Profumo had already resigned, pressure rapidly mounted on the government to take responsibility for failing to act sooner. Following a debate in the House on 17 June, Macmillan announced that an inquiry would be conducted by Lord Denning to examine the security implications of the affair. The report, published on 26 September, concluded that there were no security leaks and laid

8 Christine Keeler in July 1963. Photos of Keeler adorned the pages of the press in the weeks following Profumo's resignation, and her 'Confessions' were serialized in the *News of the World*.

responsibility for the scandal largely at the feet of Stephen Ward and the press.

Macmillan's government had nevertheless been severely shaken by the affair. For Macmillan himself, the revelation of Profumo's deceit was clearly a deep personal blow ('My spirit is not broken, but my zest has gone,' he told a colleague before the Commons debate); he successfully resisted calls for his resignation over the affair but, suffering from poor health, he stepped down in October. Stephen Ward took a drug overdose before his trial finished and died on 3 August. Christine Keeler was convicted of committing perjury at Gordon's trial and was sentenced to prison for nine months. Her 1989 autobiography, *Scandal!*, formed the basis of the film which re-enacted the events three decades after they occurred. The man at the centre of the scandal, John Profumo, withdrew completely from political life and devoted himself to welfare work in London's East End.

Was Profumo's political career destroyed by the disclosure of his affair with Christine Keeler or by the second-order transgressions and possible conflicts of interest which stemmed from it? It is hard to be sure and there is no way of effectively testing either hypothesis. Given Christine Keeler's shady occupation and dubious friends, the disclosure of the affair would undoubtedly have been damaging for Profumo, even without the additional elements. But the existence of a potential security risk made the situation immeasurably worse, especially in the wake of the Vassall affair.[7] And there can be little doubt that by repeatedly denying the rumours when questioned by his colleagues and publicly denying them when he made a personal statement in the House, Profumo did immense damage to his cause. Had he admitted the affair early on, he would still have had to face allegations that his sexual indiscretions had placed national security at risk, allegations which might have led in any case to his resignation as Secretary of State for War. But the fact that he denied the affair and was forced to admit that he had lied to the House was an offence that sealed his fate: this second-order transgression left his reputation in shreds and made it exceedingly difficult, if not impossible, for him to continue either as a minister or as an MP.

Some of the circumstances that brought down Profumo recurred ten years later in the scandals that surrounded Lord Lambton and Lord Jellicoe, two aristocratic Conservative politicians who resigned from their ministerial posts in 1973 when their links with call-girl networks were disclosed.[8] But the sex scandal which dominated the 1970s in Britain was the strange affair that destroyed the political career of Jeremy Thorpe. Leader of the Liberal Party and a prominent member of the political establishment, Thorpe was regarded by many as one of the most talented politicians of his generation. The son of a Conservative MP, he was converted to liberalism by his godmother, Megan Lloyd George, daughter of the former Liberal leader. After leaving Oxford, he practised law for several years before being elected as MP for North Devon in 1959. In 1967 Thorpe was elected leader of the Liberal Party, a position he held for nearly a decade. By the early 1970s he was a Privy Councillor and a well-known national figure. After his first wife died in a car crash, he married the Countess of Harewood in 1973. His personal life seemed stable and his political future seemed bright. Some regarded him as the most promising Liberal leader since Lloyd George.

The events which unravelled Thorpe's career began back in 1960. One weekend he visited a friend's riding stables near Chipping Norton in Oxfordshire. There he met a young man who was working as a groom at the stables. The young man – he was then known as Norman Josiffe, but later changed his name to Norman Scott – was subsequently to allege that, not long after he met Thorpe, he went to visit the MP at the House of Commons. Scott was now unemployed, having apparently been sacked from the stables after being accused of stealing a horse. According to Scott, Thorpe drove him to the home of Thorpe's mother in Surrey, where they had dinner and retired to separate rooms. Scott maintained that Thorpe then came into his bedroom dressed in pyjamas and a dressing gown, hugged Scott, said that he looked like a frightened rabbit and called him a 'poor bunny', and then forcefully had sex with him. The following day Thorpe apparently drove him back to London and (according to Scott) gave him money to rent a flat. These alleged events remained private at the time.

In the following months and years, Thorpe tried to help out Scott, who was an unstable and unreliable figure. Thorpe tried to find jobs for him, and placed ads in *Country Life* on his behalf. In 1962 Thorpe wrote to Scott in Somerset, where Thorpe had found him a job tending horses. Knowing that he wanted to study dressage in France, Thorpe remarked at the end of the letter 'Bunnies *can* (and *will*) go to France.' Scott kept the letter and it was to re-surface fourteen years later, with unfortunate consequences for its author.

As Thorpe's political career began to take off, Scott's life disintegrated and he made growing demands on Thorpe, who became increasingly concerned about Scott's behaviour and about the possibility that damaging allegations could be made against him. Rumours circulated as Scott, embittered by Thorpe's refusal to meet his demands, began to talk. Then, in October 1975, a bizarre series of events occurred. Scott and his dog – a Great Dane – were picked up in Barnstaple by a man named Andrew Newton and driven to a remote part of Exmoor. Apparently Newton then shot the Great Dane and turned the gun towards Scott. Either the pistol jammed or Newton wanted only to frighten Scott – in any case, Scott was left on Exmoor with his dead dog, while Newton drove away.

The pressure on Thorpe mounted. In January 1976 Scott appeared in court in Barnstaple for an unrelated matter (he was charged with dishonestly obtaining social security benefits) and he used this occasion to state publicly that he felt he was being 'hounded' by people because he had once had a homosexual relationship with Thorpe. Scott's allegations were widely reported in the press but they were flatly denied by Thorpe, whose parliamentary colleagues temporarily rallied around him. Then, in early May, the former Liberal MP Peter Bessell – an old friend and former confidant of Thorpe – poured more fuel on the flames: he confessed to the *Daily Mail* that he had concocted a story in order to conceal payments that had been made to Scott by him and by another of Thorpe's friends (the Manchester banker David Holmes). Bessell had previously claimed that Scott was blackmailing him, but he now admitted that the payments were made to protect Thorpe. Scott was now threatening to make public two letters from Thorpe, including the 'bunnies' letter, so Thorpe decided to pre-empt him by publishing the letters himself – they appeared in the *Sunday Times* on 9 May 1976, together with a brief statement by Thorpe. While the publication of the 'bunnies' letter was undoubtedly awkward and embarrassing for Thorpe, he continued to proclaim his innocence, strenuously denying that he had ever had a homosexual relationship with Scott or that he had anything to do with the payment of hush money and the killing of Scott's dog.

Despite his denials, the adverse publicity made Thorpe's position as leader of the Liberal Party increasingly untenable. As the support of his parliamentary colleagues drained away, Thorpe resigned as leader on 10 May and took a place on the back benches. 'Thorpe bows to the inevitable,' began the editorial in the *Guardian*;[9] what exactly had happened between Thorpe and Scott remained shrouded in uncertainty, but by this stage Thorpe had lost the trust of his colleagues. And Thorpe's troubles were not over. After Andrew Newton was released from prison in April 1977, he sold a story to the *Evening News* in which he said that he was hired to kill Scott. The police began to investigate the allegations of a murder plot; Bessell, in return for immunity from prosecution, gave a statement which implicated Thorpe. In August 1978 Thorpe was charged, together with three others, with conspiracy and incitement to murder. With the prospect of a criminal trial looming, Thorpe lost his seat in the 1979 general election.

Thorpe's trial at the Old Bailey began on 9 May 1979 and the proceedings dominated the news for the following six weeks. Scott's story of their alleged homosexual relationship was reported in full – no details were spared. Bessell told of how Thorpe had wanted to get rid of Scott – it would be 'no worse than shooting a sick dog', Thorpe had apparently said – and of how he, Thorpe and Holmes had plotted to kill him. But the evidence was thin and both Scott and Bessell were effectively discredited under cross-examination. On 22 June the

9 *The Times*, 11 May 1976, announcing the resignation of Jeremy Thorpe, leader of the Liberal Party. The accumulation of tawdry allegations about a homosexual relationship with Norman Scott undermined Thorpe's position as leader and destroyed his political career.

jury delivered a verdict of not guilty. Thorpe was acquitted of all charges but his political career was in ruins. He never returned to public life.

Although Thorpe always denied that he had had a sexual relationship with Scott, the accumulation of tawdry allegations, compromising forms of evidence (including the infamous 'bunnies' letter) and criminal charges proved too much for his reputation to bear. The alleged offence which lay at the origin of the scandal – the homosexual relationship – had the potential to do considerable damage. Homosexuality was still illegal in Britain in the early 1960s, when the relationship between Thorpe and Scott had allegedly occurred. Although the law was liberalized in 1967, the public disclosure of homosexual activity still had the capacity to stigmatize; even allegations of homosexuality, strenuously denied, could cause symbolic damage. In the event, the original transgression (actual or merely alleged) was overshadowed by an escalating series of allegations, bizarre events, unanswered questions and, in the end, criminal charges which gradually undermined Thorpe's credibility and destroyed his political career.

Britain in the 1980s and 1990s has had no shortage of sex scandals, though none quite as dramatic as the scandals that overwhelmed Profumo and Thorpe. An accumulation of sex scandals, beginning with the disclosure of Cecil Parkinson's affair in 1983 and culminating in a small wave of resignations during John Major's administration in the early 1990s, helped to earn the Conservative Party an unsavoury reputation for being the party of sleaze (a reputation to which a series of financial-political scandals also contributed generously, as we shall see). This was a reputation that the Tories would find difficult to shake off, and that would come back to haunt them even when they had long been displaced from the corridors of power.[10] Many of the more recent sex scandals have involved elements of hypocrisy and conflicts of interest (as in the cases of Parkinson and Mellor), as well as second-order transgressions. Today the disclosure of an extramarital affair is unlikely, in and by itself, to prove fatal for the career of a politician in Britain; this kind of transgression no longer elicits the kind of moral reprehension that it once did. But if it is linked to other factors (hypocrisy or conflicts of interest) or if it gives rise to second-order transgressions of sufficient gravity (including repeated public denials), then it can have very damaging consequences.

Given the importance of second-order transgressions in sexual-political scandals, it is hardly surprising that some political leaders have come to appreciate their significance and have tried to avoid the risk of being caught out by them. The most straightforward way of doing this is openly to admit the original offence as soon as it is disclosed (or as soon as it becomes clear that it will be disclosed). Open admission may be awkward and embarrassing in the short term. But in contexts where norms and codes of sexual behaviour have become more lax and contested, and in cases where the original offence was a relatively minor transgression (such as a brief extramarital affair), open admission may be the wisest strategy in the long term, since it may prevent the scandal from escalating into a prolonged struggle over the accuracy or otherwise of public denials, with all the dangers inherent in attempting to conceal evidence and ensure the complicity of others, and all the risks involved in making public statements that turn out to be false. This was the strategy adopted, with some success, by Paddy Ashdown.

Paddy Ashdown was the leader of Britain's Liberal Democratic Party from 1988 until he stepped down in 1999. (The Liberal Democratic Party was formed in 1988 through the merger of the Liberal Party and the Social Democratic Party.) In 1987, while he was MP for Yeovil and a year before he became leader of the Liberal Democrats, Ashdown had an extramarital affair with his secretary, Tricia Howard. The affair was short-lived and remained secret; it did not affect his bid for the leadership of the party. Several years later, while Tricia Howard was going through a divorce, Ashdown consulted his solicitor, fearing that his name might get mentioned; his solicitor made notes of the conversation and put them in the office safe. In January 1992, just before the general election, reporters from the *News of the World* began to pursue Tricia Howard, offering her large sums of money for her story of the affair. She phoned Ashdown, who phoned his solicitor, who discovered that his notes had been stolen from the office safe during a burglary two weeks earlier. Ashdown's solicitor secured an injunction which would prevent the document being published, but Ashdown knew that it was only a matter of time before the news would break. Hearing that a story about the affair would be run in the *Scotsman* (which was not covered by the English injunction), Ashdown held a hastily convened press conference at Westminster on 6 February 1992 in which he openly admitted the affair. He also posed for photographs in front of his home, with his wife standing by him. The event was widely reported in the press, but Ashdown's open admission, while no doubt personally embarrassing for him, prevented the disclosure from escalating into a scandal involving second-order transgressions. Ashdown's popularity did not diminish in the wake of the disclosure (indeed, there were some signs that his popularity actually increased) and his political career as leader of the Liberal Democrats was not significantly or adversely affected.

As a way of coping with an incipient scandal, Ashdown's strategy was remarkably successful. But he had the advantage of knowing that the original affair was brief and took place several years earlier; that the original offence was, so far as sexual transgressions go, relatively minor and carried relatively little stigma in Britain in the 1990s; that his wife and others would stand by him; and that no further revelations were likely to emerge which would fuel the scandal and which could prove damaging. Under these very favourable conditions, open admission was a sensible (even if personally difficult) strategy. Under less favourable conditions, it is understandable that political leaders might hesitate to follow this path. They might well fear, with some justification, that the consequences of open admission would be less benign. Many sexual-political scandals are much murkier than the Ashdown affair, and involve elements other than a relatively minor sexual transgression buried in the past. Moreover, some sexual transgressions, such as those involving homosexuality, prostitution or aberrant sexual practices, still have the capacity to harm, especially if they are disclosed in suspicious circumstances (as Ron Davies, among others, found to his cost[11]). It is understandable that political leaders, fearing the potential damage that could be caused to their reputations and careers by public revelations about their private lives, should respond with public denials. But public denials carry their own risks, and they may have consequences that are more serious than the original transgressions they were meant to conceal.

Changing Times

The existence of a long tradition of sexual-political scandals is not unique to Britain. A long tradition also exists in the United States, although the conditions and consequences of sex scandals in the American political field have changed significantly in recent years. One can trace the history of American sexual-political scandals back to the origins of the republic in the late eighteenth century.[12] Alexander Hamilton, the first Secretary of the Treasury, member of the Continental Congress and Constitutional Convention and co-author of the Federalist Papers, found himself embroiled in a scandal involving an affair with Mrs Maria Reynolds. Information about the affair was passed to the political journalist and pamphleteer James Thomson Callender, who made it public in his *History of the United States for the Year 1796*. Alexander felt obliged to reply to this and other allegations, which he did by publishing a pamphlet of his own in 1797 in which he admitted that he had an 'amorous connection' with Mrs Reynolds but rejected the charge that he had embezzled Treasury Funds.[13] Whether these allegations and Hamilton's partial confession significantly damaged his political career is unclear, but doubtless they did not advance it.

Callender also played a key role in fuelling the scandals that flourished around Thomas Jefferson, who held the Presidency from 1801 to 1809. The most prominent of these concerned Jefferson's affair with a young slave girl, Sally Hemmings.[14] The affair probably began in 1788 in Paris, where Jefferson served for four years as minister to France. Sally was sent to Paris to accompany Jefferson's daughter, Polly; Polly was eight years old at the time, and Sally was fourteen. (Jefferson's wife, Martha, had died in 1782, having given birth to six children.) When Sally returned to Virginia, she was pregnant with a child who was born in late 1789 or early 1790. It appears that she had five children by Jefferson, four of whom survived to adulthood and were formally emancipated. But the affair remained at the level of rumour and gossip for more than a decade and became public knowledge only after Jefferson had become President. One of Jefferson's first acts as President was to pardon Callender, who had been imprisoned for sedition. Despite this generous act, Callender soon fell out with Jefferson and, on 1 September 1802, he published an article in the *Richmond Recorder* which made public Jefferson's long-standing affair with Sally Hemmings. 'It is well known that the man, *whom it delighteth the people to honor*, keeps and for many years has kept, as his concubine, one of his slaves'[15] – so the article began. Other newspapers quickly picked up on the story. Many called on Jefferson to deny the allegations, but he remained silent (wisely, as it happens). Despite the scandal, he was re-elected as President two years later.

Jefferson was not the only American president or presidential candidate to find himself at the centre of rumours and allegations concerning clandestine and illicit sexual affairs. During the presidential election of 1884, the Democratic candidate Grover Cleveland became the focus of a scandal that threatened to derail his campaign. On 21 July 1884, ten days after he had won the Democratic Party's nomination, an article appeared on the front page of the *Buffalo Evening Telegraph* alleging that Cleveland had fathered an illegitimate child ten years earlier. Since Cleveland had partly built his political reputation as a critic of Republican corruption, this untimely allegation was very awkward to say the least. Cleveland chose to be open about the affair, admitting that, as a bachelor, he had had a brief liaison with a young widow named Maria Crofts Halpin, who had given birth to a son in September 1874. Although Cleveland was not sure whether the son was his, he had made arrangements to support him and to secure his adoption. The Republicans tried to exploit the scandal for all it was worth, but Cleveland's candid admission took some of the wind out of their sails and he went on to win the presidential election.

While sex scandals have been a sporadic feature of American political life for some two hundred years, it is also clear that there were many occasions when presidents and other political figures engaged in illicit sexual activities which did not become fully fledged scandals. It seems certain that Warren Harding had two long-term extramarital affairs during his political career, which began with his election to the state senate of Ohio in 1896 and culminated with his election as President in 1920. One of these affairs – with Carrie Phillips, a young woman from Ohio who had married one of Harding's close friends – probably began in 1904 and continued intermittently for fifteen years; it was a topic of local gossip and became a source of concern to Republican Party bosses in the run-up to the 1920 presidential election, but it never erupted into a public scandal. A second affair – with Nan Britton, another young woman from Harding's home town who was thirty years younger than he was – began in the summer of 1917 and continued until shortly before his death in 1923. They regularly met at hotels in New York and Washington, and in October 1919 Nan gave birth to an illegitimate daughter. After Harding's inauguration as President, Nan made several visits to the White House, and on some of these occasions they apparently retreated to a small closet near the Oval Office to make love. Although some security staff at the White House and others probably knew of the affair, it did not become public knowledge until several years after the President's death, when Nan published her account of the affair in *The President's Daughter*. During the affairs Harding wrote many letters to both women, some more than forty pages in length, but these letters remained in the private domain. (Following Carrie Phillips's death, 105 letters from Harding were found in a locked box in her home; the letters were sealed by court order until 2014.)

It is likely that Franklin D. Roosevelt was also involved in two long-term extramarital affairs, one with his wife's former secretary, Lucy Page Mercer, and another with his own secretary of some twenty years, Missy LeHand. FDR's wife, Eleanor, became aware of her husband's affair with Lucy in 1918, but the affair appears to have continued intermittently until FDR's death in 1945; it did not become public knowledge until 1946. It seems likely that Dwight Eisenhower had a long-term amorous relationship with the young Irish woman, Kay Summersby, who was his driver while he was stationed in Europe during the Second World War. This affair was probably never consummated, but it appears to have been intimate and serious. In 1952, just before Eisenhower won the Republican nomination for the Presidency, rumours circulated that he had written to General Marshall shortly after the war ended, asking to be relieved of his duties since he was planning to divorce his wife, Mamie, and marry Kay; whether such a letter was ever written remains unclear, since it was never found. The affair remained secret until after Eisenhower's death in 1969. Kay Summersby's account of the relationship, *Past Forgetting*, was published in 1976, a year after her own death.

While various presidents and other politicians had extramarital affairs that never became scandals, none compare, in terms of the sheer number as well as the brazenness, to the sexual adventures of JFK. It was well known in political circles at the time that Kennedy had numerous extramarital affairs during his political career. Some probably extended over a number of years, such as his affairs with Joan Lundberg, Pam Turnure and Judy Campbell, while others were fleeting and casual affairs. Some of these affairs were conducted with a lack of discretion that, in retrospect, looks positively reckless. Kennedy allegedly invited attractive women to the White House to swim nude in the pool. Judy Campbell seems to have been a frequent visitor to the White House in 1961–2, and often phoned Kennedy at the White House. But none of these affairs erupted into a scandal. They were the subject of rumour and gossip among Washington's political elite and they were a source of concern for some of Kennedy's advisers, who feared what might happen if his numerous affairs became publicly known. Kennedy's private life was rich in scandal potential and, had his sexual liaisons been made public in the run-up to the 1960 presidential election (which Kennedy won by a slim margin), the political consequences could have been serious. But the scandal that might have happened never did.

Three decades later, Bill Clinton was not so fortunate. Nor was Gary Hart, the senator from Colorado whose bid for the Democratic presidential nomination in 1988 was scuppered by the controversy surrounding his alleged affair with the twenty-nine-year-old model Donna Rice.[16] Nor was Bob Packwood, the Republican senator from Oregon, who found himself at the centre of allegations that he had sexually harassed a number of female employees who had worked for him.[17] And there were many other political figures who, in the 1970s, 1980s and 1990s, found themselves at the centre of sex scandals which disrupted, or threatened to disrupt, their careers (including Wilbur Mills, Wayne Hays and Thomas Evans[18]). The political climate in the United States was changing, and aspects of private life that might have remained hidden in earlier decades, or to which journalists might have turned a blind eye, were increasingly subjected to scrutiny in the public domain. How can we understand this change?

Four developments were particularly important in helping to create the conditions in which sex scandals became an increasingly prominent feature of American political life (and here I am drawing on the analysis offered, at a more general level, in the previous chapter). First, the changing culture of journalism gradually eroded the informal norms and conventions which had discouraged journalists and editors from publishing details of the private lives of political figures. From the late 1960s on, the private lives of politicians increasingly became a focus of investigation by journalists and others, who became increasingly assertive and intrusive in their attempts to acquire details about private lives. The tragedy at Chappaquiddick in 1969, which resulted in the death of Mary Jo Kopechne and undoubtedly damaged Edward Kennedy's political career,[19] was a pivotal occasion when the private conduct of a prominent political figure was extensively discussed in the public domain, and hence an occasion which probably contributed to a shift in the norms and conventions governing journalistic practice.

The second development was the changing political culture of the 1960s and 1970s. The decline of class-based politics and the growing significance of the politics of trust placed more emphasis on questions of character, an emphasis that was reinforced by the events that led to Nixon's downfall. The emphasis on questions of character has helped to create conditions in which political parties and other organizations might be tempted to use scandal as a weapon to damage or destroy their opponents: when questions of character are at stake, it is more difficult to maintain that the private conduct of political leaders is irrelevant to their public roles, and hence unwanted disclosures about misbehaviour in the private realm can have damaging consequences. The politics of trust, with its emphasis on questions of character, can slide very easily into a dirty politics in which personal indiscretions are used as weapons in the struggle for political advantage.

A third development concerned the changing norms and expectations of sexual conduct. It is often assumed that the 1960s was a time of sexual liberation and experimentation, and that this was followed by a kind of moral backlash which was less tolerant of illicit forms of sexual behaviour. There may be some substance to this view, but at best it tells only part of the story. Probably more important for the issues that concern us here is the fact that, due largely to the women's movement, there was a growing sensitivity in American society to certain forms of male behaviour which might have been regarded as normal or acceptable in previous decades. In a context where questions of gender inequality have been intensively discussed in the public domain, the double standards associated with promiscuous male behaviour may be viewed with less equanimity, and behaviour which could be interpreted as an unwanted sexual advance is likely to become an increasingly sensitive issue. These forms of behaviour might have been tolerated in the past (and even regarded by some as perfectly normal expressions of male sexuality), but increasingly they have become the focus of critical scrutiny and open conflict. It is significant that in the 1990s several prominent political figures – including Judge Clarence Thomas,[20] Senator Bob Packwood and, of course, Bill Clinton – found themselves involved in highly publicized sexual harassment cases.

A fourth development was the growing legalization of political life. This is exemplified above all by the legislation enacted in the wake of Watergate, which sought to establish new ethical standards in the political sphere and which created the powerful new office of special prosecutor. But also important was the enactment of state and federal laws on sexual harassment and misconduct, as well as the development of rules and formal complaints procedures for dealing with allegations about sexual harassment and misconduct in government offices.

These were the developments that shaped the context within which Clinton's political career was nearly derailed on more than one occasion by surreptitious sexual affairs. Given the changes that had taken place since the late 1960s, his promiscuous personal behaviour was always going to carry some political risks, but what ultimately brought him to the brink of impeachment was a series of second-order transgressions stemming from a sexual harassment case. Clinton learned the hard way that, when sex scandals threaten to engulf a political career, denial is a very dangerous course.

Clinton's difficulties began in the late 1970s and early 1980s, while he was Attorney General and then Governor of Arkansas. Clinton met Gennifer Flowers in the late 1970s when she was working as a reporter for a local television station, and they began a long-term affair. It also seems likely that Clinton had several other affairs and casual sexual encounters while he was Governor. Stories circulated about Clinton's alleged affairs, but throughout the 1980s they remained largely at the level of rumour and gossip. In October 1990 a disgruntled former employee, Larry Nichols, filed a lawsuit for unfair dismissal, accusing Clinton of misconduct in office and alleging that he had misused state resources to facilitate his extramarital affairs with six women. The case was reported in the local press but it did not go much further at the time. However, after Clinton had declared his candidacy for the Presidency in October 1991, the question of his extramarital affairs became a matter of intense interest in some quarters of the national press. On 13 January 1992 a supermarket tabloid, the *Star*, reported the allegations made in the Nichols lawsuit as its lead story. The *Star* also contacted Gennifer Flowers, who agreed to corroborate the story for a substantial sum.

Clinton was in the middle of a closely fought primary campaign and suddenly he found himself staring into the void. He had to cope with damaging allegations about dodging the draft and with the prospect of further damaging revelations about his alleged affair with Gennifer Flowers. Well aware that Hart's campaign for the democratic nomination had been scuppered by damaging revelations of this kind, Clinton went on the offensive. Bill and Hillary Clinton agreed to be interviewed by Steve Kroft on the CBS TV show *60 Minutes*, which was broadcast on 26 January 1992, immediately after the Super Bowl (which ensured a large audience). The strategy of the Clintons was carefully devised. When asked about his alleged affair with Gennifer Flowers, Bill Clinton did not openly admit it, but he was also careful not to deny it:

Kroft: You've been saying all week that you've got to put this issue behind you. Are you prepared tonight to say that you've never had an extramarital affair?

Bill Clinton: I'm not prepared tonight to say that any married couple should ever discuss that with anyone but themselves. . . .

Kroft: . . . That's what you've been saying essentially for the last couple of months.

Bill Clinton: . . . You go back and listen to what I've said. You know, I have acknowledged wrongdoing. I have acknowledged causing pain in my marriage. I have said things to you tonight and to the American people from the beginning that no American politician ever has. I think most Americans who are watching this tonight, they'll know what we're saying . . .

Kroft: . . . I agree with you that everyone wants to put this behind you. And the reason the problem has not gone away is because your answer is not a denial . . .

Bill Clinton: Of course it's not. And let's take it from your point of view, that won't make it go away. I mean if you deny, then you have a whole other horde of people going down there offering more money and trying to prove that you lied. And if you say yes, then you have

just what I have already said by being open and telling you that we
have had problems . . .²¹

Clinton knew very well that a public denial of the affair would only
fuel the flames of a scandal that was threatening to derail his campaign. His strategy was to refuse to deny it and, at the same time, to
avoid openly admitting it by responding only at the general level of
acknowledging that he had caused pain in his marriage. Hillary stood
by her husband and made it clear that she loved and respected him
despite the difficulties they had been through. Both did their best to
turn the tables on the press, accusing them of engaging in a game of
'gotcha' and reminding viewers that it was not only Bill's character,
but also the character of the press, that would be tested by the coming
campaign.

Broadly speaking, the Clintons' strategy worked. Bill Clinton's
opponents could accuse him of philandering and evasiveness, but
they were deprived of the opportunity to demonstrate that his public
denials were false. Further allegations and revelations emerged in
the following months. Gennifer Flowers appeared on television, gave
interviews to magazines and released further extracts from telephone
conversations with Bill Clinton that she had secretly taped in the
early 1990s. These disclosures were undoubtedly awkward
for Clinton and his advisers, who were in the midst of waging a
campaign against an incumbent President, but they did not
prevent Clinton from winning the election in November. The revelations about his alleged affair with Gennifer Flowers had not
done his reputation any good, but he had managed, with Hillary's
help, to deflect their political impact. The worst, however, was still
to come.

Clinton's first term as President was plagued with further allegations about sexual misconduct while he was Governor of Arkansas.
In January 1994 the conservative magazine *The American Spectator*
published an article called 'His cheatin' heart: Living with the
Clintons'; it was written by David Brock, a journalist who had won
many admirers on the right for his unflattering portrayal of Anita
Hill. The article recounted the stories of two Arkansas state troopers
who claimed that, as part of their official duties, they had helped to
facilitate and cover up Clinton's affairs and sexual encounters; two
other troopers corroborated the stories. Among other things, the
troopers described an incident which allegedly occurred at the Excelsior Hotel in Little Rock, Arkansas on 8 May 1991. While attending
the third annual Governor's Quality Management Conference at the

hotel, Clinton had apparently eyed a woman who was working at the reception desk; he asked one of the troopers to approach the woman, whom the trooper remembered only as Paula, tell her that the Governor thought she was attractive and take her to a room in the hotel where he would be waiting. The stories were quickly picked up by the mainstream media, which reported the details, featured further interviews with the troopers and commented copiously on the alleged events: thus 'troopergate' was born.

One woman who had worked at the reception desk that day was Paula Jones. When she heard about the article, she felt it implied that she had had sex with Clinton and she decided to seek legal advice. In February 1994 she appeared at a press conference in Washington and announced that she was suing President Clinton for severe emotional distress, deprivation of civil rights and deformation of character in relation to the incident which had allegedly occurred at the Excelsior Hotel. (She could not formally sue him for sexual harassment because Arkansas state law required this to be done within six months of the incident.) Jones alleged that she had been escorted to Clinton's suite where he had made unwanted sexual advances, including dropping his pants, exposing his erect penis and asking her to 'kiss it'; she claimed she could prove her allegations because there were distinguishing marks in Clinton's genital area. Clinton's lawyers tried to arrange for the trial to be deferred until after Clinton had left office, but on 27 May 1997 the Supreme Court ruled that Jones was entitled to proceed with her case. Jones turned down an out-of-court settlement and, with the help of the Rutherford Institute (a Virginia-based legal organization specializing in civil liberties and religious freedom cases), she filed an amended legal complaint on 5 December 1997. Her lawyers announced that they would subpoena documents and witnesses, including Clinton and at least ten women with whom he had allegedly had affairs or sexual encounters. Jones's lawyers wanted to show that Clinton had repeatedly become involved with government employees under his control. One of the women they would eventually decide to subpoena was Monica Lewinsky.

Clinton first met Monica Lewinsky in August 1995, shortly after she had begun work as an intern at the White House. Their affair began in mid-November, when the White House staff was depleted by a temporary government shutdown. Monica was twenty-one at the time. The affair continued intermittently for eighteen months, with secret meetings in the Oval Office and other private rooms at the White House, affectionate fondling and oral sex, the exchange of gifts and numerous phone calls. Monica became deeply involved

10 The President and the intern, 17 November 1995. This photo was taken in the Chief of Staff's office during the government shutdown, shortly after Monica Lewinsky had begun work as an intern at the White House.

emotionally. But in April 1996 she was transferred to the Pentagon; it was there that she met Linda Tripp. Increasingly Monica confided in Tripp, and eventually told her about her relationship with the President. Unknown to Monica, Tripp had an agenda of her own. A former White House employee who disliked Clinton and his admin-istration, Tripp was toying with the idea of writing a book about life behind the scenes at the White House, a project she had discussed with the New York literary agent and publicist Lucianne Goldberg. Tripp was also in touch with a reporter from *Newsweek*, Michael Isikoff, who was researching the Paula Jones case. In summer 1997 Tripp became concerned that she might be subpoenaed in the Paula Jones case and, apparently at the suggestion of Lucianne Goldberg, decided to tape-record her conversations with Monica, so that she could corroborate her story. She began secretly recording their con-versations in early October. She also persuaded Monica to keep the now legendary navy-blue dress which had been stained with the President's semen during one of their clandestine encounters earlier in the year.

Late in 1997, both Monica and Linda Tripp were subpoenaed in the Paula Jones case. Monica signed an affidavit on 7 January 1998 in which she denied that she had ever had a sexual relationship with the President. The following week she gave Tripp three pages of typed notes, headed 'points to make in an affidavit', which indicated some of the things she might say in her testimony (what became known as the 'talking points memo'). Tripp became increasingly worried about her position and decided to contact the Office of the Independent Counsel (OIC), Kenneth Starr, who had for several years been investigating a separate set of issues stemming from the Clintons' involvement in a failed land deal in Arkansas (the so-called Whitewater scandal – discussed in more detail in the following chapter). Investigators from the OIC arranged for Tripp to wear a body wire when she met Monica for lunch on 12 January, and again when she met her at the Ritz-Carlton Hotel on the morning of 16 January. On the latter occasion Monica was escorted to a room in the hotel where she was confronted by FBI agents and Starr's deputies. They told her that she could face prosecution for perjury, obstruction of justice and witness tampering unless she was willing to cooperate with the OIC's investigation.

The following day, not knowing that Monica had been confronted by the FBI and deputies from the OIC, Clinton gave his testimony under oath at a deposition in the Paula Jones case. He said that he had seen Ms Lewinsky on two or three occasions during the government shutdown in autumn 1995 but could not recall whether he had been alone with her. He had received presents from her on one or two occasions, and may have given her a hat pin. But he stated categorically that he had never had sexual relations with her.[22] The next day, Sunday 18 January, Clinton met with his secretary, Betty Currie, to review his relationship with Monica Lewinsky. He said a number of things to Betty Currie on that occasion, such as 'You were always there when she was there, right?', 'We were never really alone' and 'You could see and hear everything', which might be interpreted as trying to influence her.

Until then, allegations about Clinton's affair with Monica were still not public knowledge. But on 18 January the internet gossip columnist Matt Drudge reported a rumour that *Newsweek* was planning to publish a story about the affair but had decided at the last minute not to (apparently at the request of the OIC);[23] the next day, *The Drudge Report* elaborated the story and mentioned Monica by name. On Wednesday 21 January, the story broke in the national press. Under the headline 'Clinton accused of urging aide to lie', the

11 President Clinton appearing before the television cameras at a press gathering on 26 January 1998. Waving his finger at the audience, Clinton publicly and vehemently denies the allegation that he had 'sexual relations with that woman, Miss Lewinsky'.

Washington Post reported that Starr was investigating whether Clinton and his close friend Vernon Jordan had pressurized the former intern to lie about whether she had had an affair with the President.[24] Later that day Clinton went on national television to deny the allegations. The Clinton–Lewinsky scandal had begun. Day after day the press and television news – not only in the United States but across the world – were dominated by reports about the alleged affair, including details that were allegedly contained on the tapes secretly recorded by Tripp. Senior political figures, advisers and commentators began to speculate about possible impeachment. Faced with this mounting pressure, Clinton appeared with his wife Hillary at a press gathering on 26 January and made a televised statement in which he explicitly and publicly denied that he had had an affair with Monica Lewinsky: 'I want you to listen to me, I'm going to say this again,' asserted Clinton, waving his finger indignantly at the audience, 'I did not have sexual relations with that woman, Miss Lewinsky. I never told anybody to lie, not a single time – never. These allegations are false. And I need to go back to work for the American people.'[25] The following morning Hillary gave a television interview in which she defended her husband and claimed that the allegations were part of a 'vast rightwing conspiracy that has been conspiring against my husband since the day he announced for President.'[26]

But the scandal refused to go away. The Paula Jones case, which had initially triggered the scandal, was thrown out on 1 April by the Arkansas judge who heard the pre-trial evidence, but Starr's investigation into the Monica Lewinsky affair continued throughout the summer. Starr's investigation now centred on whether Clinton had committed perjury in his testimony for the Paula Jones case, had obstructed justice and had tampered with a potential witness. As the evidence of his alleged affair with Monica Lewinsky continued to grow (including indications that the stain on her dress was indeed semen), Clinton eventually accepted that his strategy of outright denial could no longer be plausibly sustained. He agreed to testify to the Grand Jury on 17 August; during this testimony he admitted that he had been alone with Ms Lewinsky on multiple occasions and, on some of these occasions, he had engaged in conduct that was wrong. Later that day he made a televised address in which he publicly acknowledged for the first time that he had had a relationship with Ms Lewinsky that was not appropriate – 'in fact, it was wrong . . . It constituted a critical lapse of judgment and a personal failure on my part for which I am solely and completely responsible. I misled people, including even my wife. I deeply regret that.'[27]

Starr's report to Congress was released on 11 September. In a decision that was itself remarkable, the report and much of the accompanying material was made available on the internet where it could be accessed by internet users anywhere in the world; it was also published in book form and much discussed in the media. In a way that echoed the release of the transcripts of Nixon's private conversations during the Watergate crisis twenty-five years earlier, readers and viewers were presented with a full account of the sexual encounters between Clinton and Lewinsky in secluded parts of the White House – the language was turgid, but no details were spared. The publication of this very personal material was no doubt deeply embarrassing and humiliating for the individuals involved.[28] The Starr Report also listed eleven possible grounds for impeachment, including perjury, witness tampering, obstruction of justice and abuse of power, and maintained that there was substantial evidence to support them. Despite clear signs that the majority of Americans had grown weary of the long, drawn-out affair, the Republican-controlled House voted on 19 December to impeach the President, making Clinton the first elected President ever to be impeached. But, as most commentators expected, Clinton's trial in the Senate resulted in his acquittal on 12 February, with voting on each of the two articles of impeachment (perjury and obstruction of justice) broadly fol-

12 The Clinton family leaving the White House on the way to Martha's Vineyard, Massachusetts, 18 August 1998. The previous day Clinton had admitted in a televised address that he had had an inappropriate relationship with Monica Lewinsky.

lowing partisan lines and falling well short of the two-thirds majority required for conviction.

The Clinton–Lewinsky affair was undoubtedly the most significant sex scandal in American political history. It dominated the news for more than a year and brought Clinton to the edge of being removed from office. But as with most sexual-political scandals, what nearly destroyed Clinton were second-order transgressions rather than his illicit encounters with the former intern: had Clinton not sought to conceal his relationship with Lewinsky around the time of his testimony in the Paula Jones case, it is unlikely that the affair would have provided a sufficiently rich source of material to warrant extended further investigation culminating in impeachment proceedings. The disclosure of the relationship would undoubtedly have been difficult and damaging for Clinton, coming as it would have done in the wake of revelations about other sexual incidents and affairs. But the attempt to conceal it was disastrous, for this is what led to the second-order transgressions committed in relation to the Paula Jones case and gave Kenneth Starr the ammunition he was looking for to press his case against the President.

Much has been made of the fact that Starr is a man of deeply conservative values and beliefs and that Paula Jones's legal fees were being paid by the right-wing Rutherford Institute: it is undoubtedly the case that Clinton, as a liberal reformer who still harboured some of the idealism of the 1960s, had many political enemies. There is undoubtedly some substance to the claim – mooted by Hillary Clinton but developed in much greater detail by others[29] – that the tenacious investigation of the Lewinsky affair was fuelled by the activities of conservative individuals and organizations who were determined to discredit the Clintons, and who were prepared to use their connections to the media as a way of achieving their ends. Moreover, when the Lewinsky scandal erupted in January 1998, it did so within a political field which was highly polarized, and the scandal immediately became a focal point around which the battles between Democrats and Republicans were fought out. But Bill Clinton was in some respects his own worst enemy. In an age of high media visibility, philandering on the scale that Clinton appeared to engage in was politically reckless to say the least. By allowing himself to become involved with a junior White House intern, he had laid himself open to the charge not only that he was a philanderer, but also that he had abused his position of power. Every President will have his enemies, but Clinton did himself no favours by supplying his enemies with generous quantities of ammunition.

In the eyes of many ordinary Americans, the Clinton–Lewinsky scandal was an event that had been blown out of proportion by a combination of partisan interests and media hype. This was a true media scandal, driven on by a dogged investigative team and a multitude of media organizations which were tripping over themselves to publish the latest revelation. For many people, this was a scandal that had become self-perpetuating, fuelled by the activities and commentaries of politicians and media personnel who were in danger of losing a sense of proportion about the seriousness of the offences committed. Many people's opinion of Clinton's character and integrity was significantly lowered by the affair, and many felt that he had devalued the Presidency. But at the same time they felt that he had competently performed his duties as President and that the seriousness of the offences – both the affair that was at the heart of the scandal and the second-order transgressions committed in relation to it – were not of sufficient seriousness to warrant resignation or impeachment. And in this judgement they were probably right.

6

Financial Scandals in the Political Field

Financial scandals in the political field are based on allegations about the misuse of money or other financial irregularities. They generally involve the disclosure of hidden linkages (or allegations about hidden linkages) between economic and political power, linkages which are regarded as improper and which, on being disclosed, precipitate the scandal. The activities which lie at the heart of financial-political scandals are likely to involve the infringement of rules governing the acquisition and allocation of economic resources. In some cases they may also involve the breaking of laws governing financial transactions and the use of resources by individuals who hold public office or aspire to it. Hence financial scandals are more likely than sex scandals to raise legal issues and to result in criminal prosecution.

In this chapter I want to focus on financial-political scandals and examine some of their characteristics. I shall begin by considering the nature of financial-political scandals in a general way, exploring the relation between this type of scandal and broader institutional, legal and cultural factors. I shall then examine the rise of financial-political scandals in Britain and in the United States in turn, highlighting some of the distinctive themes. Finally, I shall look in some detail at the issues involved in a speculative land deal in Arkansas which threatened to derail the Clinton Administration in the early 1990s – the so-called Whitewater affair.

The Interlacing of Money and Power

Financial-political scandals are based on the disclosure of activities by political figures or public officials (or on allegations about activities) which involve the infringement of rules governing the acquisition and use of money and other financial resources. We can distinguish several forms of financial-political scandal, depending on the type of infringement involved. One form involves the improper exchange of economic resources (money, gifts, etc.) for the purposes of influencing political decisions or outcomes – in other words, bribery. A second type involves the misappropriation of public funds, fraud, deception or the misuse of information for personal or private gain. A third form involves the existence of private, undeclared financial interests which might conflict, or be seen to conflict, with a politician's public duties and responsibilities. A fourth type comprises various kinds of electoral corruption and malpractice, including bribing electors, gerrymandering and the misappropriation of campaign funds. In differing ways, these various forms of financial-political scandal highlight an illicit interlacing of money and power, thus raising the prospect that the rules and procedures for the exercise of political power might be compromised by the influence of hidden economic interests.

Many of the infringements which underlie financial-political scandals could be loosely regarded as forms of corruption – although 'corruption' is a broad term, as we have seen, and there are forms of corruption which do not necessarily involve financial misdealing (such as nepotism). Moreover, the existence of bribery or corruption does not by itself give rise to financial-political scandal. Bribery or corruption can (and often does) remain hidden; and in some contexts where it is known about, it may be tolerated, ignored or accepted as a quasi-legitimate practice (what George Washington Plunkitt of Tammany Hall called 'honest graft'). The history of financial-political scandals does not coincide with the history of bribery and corruption, because the occurrence of financial-political scandals presupposes specific social and cultural conditions. A financial-political scandal will occur only if the infringements concerned are publicly disclosed and only if they are regarded in a particular context as sufficiently serious to elicit a disapprobatory public response.

The history of financial-political scandals, and the nature and extent of such scandals today, vary considerably from one national context to another. These differences can be explained by a combination of several factors: (a) historical and institutional differences in the systems of political power and the relations between political and economic power; (b) differences in law and in the codes of practice – both formal and informal – which govern the activities of politicians and civil servants; (c) differences in the extent to which infringements are investigated by journalists and others and reported in the press; and (d) differences in the extent to which publicly disclosed infringements are regarded as morally and politically unacceptable. The history of financial-political scandals is a history which is shaped by the overlapping influence of these institutional, legal and cultural factors, and hence it is a history which reflects the specific and varying characteristics of particular national cultures.

Italy, for instance, is a country in which financial-political scandals have played a prominent role in recent decades. But to understand these scandals, we have to see that they are part and parcel of a long history of institutionalized corruption and clientelistic exchange which underpins the Italian political system.[1] The reestablishment of the party system after the Second World War was partly built on forms of patronage and corruption which had existed in Italy since the early phases of state formation. Given the relative weakness of formal political institutions, a great deal of power was concentrated in the hands of political parties, which entered into complex relations of bargaining and exchange in order to consolidate and expand their power bases. Parties permeated many spheres of social, political and economic life, creating extensive networks of interdependence in which party support was rewarded with influence and benefits of various kinds. Corruption was endemic and systemic; it was also tolerated to some extent, since the networks of mutual dependence were so widespread.

So why did a series of high-profile financial-political scandals suddenly erupt in Italy in the 1980s and 1990s? The occurrence of these scandals was linked to the breakdown of this system of party rule and the forms of patronage and clientelistic exchange on which it was based. In the early 1980s, the Christian Democratic Party, which had dominated postwar coalition governments, lost its monopoly of the premiership; and the metamorphosis of the Communist Party further weakened the old alliances, which had been based partly on the strategy of excluding the Communists from power. As the old alliances began to crumble, the opportunities to expose corruption increased and the levels of tolerance began to decline. A series of financial-political scandals began to unveil the hidden forms of corruption and clientelistic exchange which were deeply ingrained features of Italian political life.

The history of financial-political scandals in Britain is quite different from that of Italy, as is the history of financial-political scandals in the United States and elsewhere. Each of these histories is in itself enormously complex, and a brief analysis can hardly do justice to it. But even a cursory account of the development of financial-political scandals in Britain and the United States will enable us to see that each of these histories displays certain distinctive features, and will enable us to discern some broad similarities and differences. In Britain there was a sustained attempt in the nineteenth century to clamp down on corruption in government. This did not completely eliminate corruption or close down the space for corruption scandals, as we shall see, but it reduced the more blatant forms of corruption, like straightforward bribery, and tended to ensure that financial-political scandals gravitated towards more subtle forms, such as those involving conflicts of interest or the exchange of favours. In the early decades of the twentieth century, the abuse of the honours system was a focal point for scandals of this kind, although in more recent decades the controversies have been concerned predominantly with the extraparliamentary interests of MPs.

In the United States, by contrast, corruption became relatively pervasive and entrenched at different levels of government in the course of the nineteenth century, due in part to certain social and economic developments, such as the rapid growth of cities and the emergence of municipal party machines. In late nineteenth-century America, financial-political scandals were rife; major scandals – most notably, the Teapot Dome scandal – also featured prominently in the early twentieth century. Since the 1950s, financial-political scandals in the United States have centred increasingly on questions concerning conflicts of interest. In a context where political lobbying is a widespread practice, political campaigning is exorbitantly expensive and – especially since Watergate – levels of suspicion and anxiety are high, this has proved to be a fertile ground for scandal.

Private Interests and Public Duties

The history of financial-political scandals in Britain is part of a much longer history, stretching back into the early modern period and before, of political struggles surrounding the uses and alleged abuses of state resources and public funds. The political system of early modern England, like those of other early modern European states, harboured numerous forms of corruption, including patronage, nepotism, bribery, graft, the selling of titles and the misappropriation of public funds. Occasionally these forms of corruption became highly contested political issues – as was the case, for example, during the reign of James I. In 1619 the Star Chamber began proceedings against the Earl of Suffolk for the misuse of the Crown's resources; in 1621 the Lord Chancellor, Francis Bacon, was impeached on grounds of accepting bribes; and three years later the Lord Treasurer, Lionel Cranfield, was also impeached on charges of bribery and corruption.[2] Faced with mounting criticism in the late eighteenth and nineteenth centuries, Parliament made a determined effort to clamp down on bribery and corruption in government. This movement of reform culminated in a series of Acts of Parliament – passed in 1889, 1906 and 1916 and commonly referred to as the Prevention of Corruption Acts – which provided a wide-ranging set of rules to outlaw bribery and corruption in both the public and the private spheres.

With the rise of mediated scandals in the nineteenth and twentieth centuries, allegations of corruption among public officials became a common theme of scandals in the political field. Although the scale of corruption may have been reduced by the reforms set in motion in the nineteenth century, public allegations of corruption flourished in late Victorian and Edwardian Britain. The revelations that emerged from the bankruptcy court following the collapse in 1898 of the business empire of Ernest Hooley – a former Nottingham lace manufacturer who had amassed a small fortune by using dubious methods to promote companies and sell stock – heightened public concern about the abuse of corporate power and the entanglement of business and political interests. (A common practice of Hooley and other company promoters was to pay politicians and titled notables to add their names to boards of directors – 'guinea pig directors' – in order to give an air of authority to precarious business ventures.) During the Boer War, the political atmosphere at Westminster was charged with allegations that military contractors were making exorbitant profits at taxpayers' expense and that the Colonial Secretary, Joseph Chamberlain, had shown favouritism to certain firms (in particular, to the firm of Kynoch and Co. of Birmingham, whose chairman, Arthur Chamberlain, was Joseph's brother, and to the firm of

Hoskins and Sons Ltd, whose managing director, Neville Chamberlain, was Joseph's son). The Liberal daily, the *Morning Leader*, took the initiative in disclosing the financial interests and family connections of the Colonial Secretary, helping to turn the 'contracting scandals' into a major political controversy.[3]

In launching their attacks on Chamberlain and on the Balfour administration more generally, the Liberals were inclined to present themselves as a party which adhered to higher moral standards than its rivals. When the Liberals came to power in 1906, they were anxious to avoid the kinds of corruption scandals which had blighted Balfour's administration. The first measure to reach the statute book was the Prevention of Corruption Act of 1906. But despite their good intentions, the Liberals in power found themselves plagued with corruption scandals of their own. They were the target of attacks by disgruntled Unionists and others who were deeply suspicious of the Liberals' self-righteousness and tireless in their attempts to unearth corruption in the new administration. Allegations proliferated in journals and newspapers like the *Morning Post*, the *National Review* and the *Eye-Witness*. But it was the revelation that ministers had speculated on American Marconi shares which plunged the Liberal government into crisis.

The origins of the Marconi scandal lay in a plan submitted to the Colonial Office in 1910 by the Marconi Wireless Telegraph Company to build a network of wireless stations which would link together different parts of the British Empire.[4] In March 1912 the Post Office signed a tender with the Marconi Company to build the first six stations, but the government was forced to postpone ratification in the face of rumours stemming from the City about secret dealings in Marconi shares. The price of shares rose dramatically in March and April (from £3 6s 3d in December 1911 to £9 in April), and it was common knowledge that some members of Asquith's government had connections with the Marconi Company (the Attorney-General, Rufus Isaacs, was the brother of the managing director of the English Marconi Company, Godfrey Isaacs). It was suspected in some quarters that members of the government had used their positions and influence to help secure a large contract from which they (or members of their family) would benefit personally, and some believed that ministers of the Crown had used their inside knowledge of the negotiations for the contract to speculate on Marconi shares.

Rumours to this effect circulated in Westminster throughout the summer of 1912, and in late July the rumours began to appear in print. On 20 July an article appeared in the weekly journal *Outlook*, and in August a series of articles began to appear in the *Eye-Witness* under the headline 'The Marconi scandal' (a label that would stick). In a Commons debate on 11 October, both Isaacs and Lloyd George, the Chancellor of the Exchequer, dismissed the rumours and denied any wrongdoing. But the government agreed to set up a Commons select committee to investigate the affair. As the inquiry proceeded, a new and unexpected dimension came to light. In March 1912, Godfrey Isaacs had gone to New York to discuss business in relation to the American Marconi Company, of which he was a director. (The English and American Marconi companies were formally distinct, although the English company had a substantial stake in the American company.) When Godfrey Isaacs returned to London, he met with his brothers, Rufus and Harry, and offered them the opportunity to buy shares in the American Marconi Company, which was planning to float a new issue on the London stock exchange. Harry agreed to buy 50,000 shares; Rufus initially declined the offer, but then decided a week later to buy 10,000 shares from his brother Harry. Rufus in turn offered 1,000 shares each to Lloyd George and to the Master of Elibank, who was the government's Chief Whip. Elibank later bought a further 3,000 shares on behalf of the Liberal Party. The ministers had thus acquired shares in the American Marconi Company, at advantageous prices, before they were publicly available on the stock exchange and in the knowledge that the English Marconi Company had signed the tender for the Post Office contract.

The disclosure of the secret share dealings gave fresh impetus to the scandal. The Isaacs brothers and Lloyd George were called before the select committee and their purchase of the shares in the American Marconi Company was probed in detail. But the select committee was divided along partisan lines, and the outcome of the nine-month investigation was inconclusive. The majority report concluded that the American Marconi Company had no interest in the contract between the English company and the British government and it cleared the ministers of any blame, while a minority report rejected this view and accused the ministers of grave impropriety in purchasing the shares. The majority report was regarded by many as a whitewash. Isaacs and Lloyd George had steadfastly refused to admit any wrongdoing, but in the debate in the House of Commons on 18 June 1913 they offered limited and qualified apologies, conceding that, had they enjoyed the benefit of hindsight, they would not have entered into the transactions ('I acted carelessly, I acted

THE MARCONI OCTOPUS.

Liberal Party. "ANOTHER TENTACLE OR TWO AND I'M DONE!"

13 'The Marconi Octopus', from *Punch*, 18 June 1913. The disclosure of secret dealings in Marconi shares threatened to ensnare Asquith's Liberal government.

mistakenly, but I acted innocently,' as Lloyd George put it[5]). The following day the House passed a resolution, with a government majority of 78, which accepted the ministers' regrets but rejected the charge of corruption and acquitted them of acting otherwise than in good faith.

The Liberal government survived the Marconi scandal, and the political careers of Isaacs and Lloyd George were not significantly impeded by it. (Amid some controversy, Asquith promoted Isaacs to Lord Chief Justice in October 1913, and Lloyd George went on to become Prime Minister.) But the Marconi scandal was not an isolated event; it overlapped with allegations of corruption in relation to the purchase of silver bullion by the India Office, and with allegations that the Liberal Party stood to benefit from a government contract with the Mexican Eagle Oil Company to supply the navy with oil. The governments of Asquith and Lloyd George were also plagued with allegations of corruption in relation to the honours system. Titles such as peerages, baronetcies and knighthoods are awarded in principle for distinguished public service, but suspicions were often raised that some individuals were being rewarded more for their contributions to party funds than for their achievements in public life. Allegations of trafficking in honours were relatively common in the early decades of the twentieth century; it was widely believed that political parties, both Conservative and Liberal, had regularly abused the honours system in order to reward generous donors. But discontent with the honours system reached a crisis point in 1922, when Lloyd George's coalition government announced its intention to award a peerage to the South African financier and mineowner Joseph Robinson.

There was cause to be concerned about the award of a peerage to Robinson, since his credentials in the sphere of public service were far from clear. Robinson had been fined £500,000 for fraudulent business practices in South Africa, and the Privy Council had turned down his request for an appeal. When his name appeared on the 1922 Birthday Honours List, critics of the coalition government were quick to denounce this as a flagrant abuse of the system. The *Morning Post* attacked it as another sign of the political corruption which had begun with the Marconi scandal, and launched its own investigation to uncover the sale of honours racket. Lloyd George was forced to concede a debate in the House of Commons on 17 July and to set up a royal commission to examine the honours system. Robinson himself was persuaded to decline his peerage, which he did in a letter read out in the House of Lords on 29 June.

The honours scandal was undoubtedly an awkward moment for Lloyd George and his coalition government. Lloyd George did not remain in power long enough to act on the recommendations of the royal commission (he resigned in October 1922), but his successor, Bonar Law, accepted the need to introduce some modifications to the system. Given the terms of reference of the royal commission (to concentrate on advising the government about the procedures that should be adopted in the future rather than to investigate events in the past), its report did little to appease the critics who believed that Lloyd George had systematically abused the honours system, building up a network of brokers and touts – like Maundy Gregory, thought by some to have been the orchestrator of the sale of honours racket[6] – to fill the coffers of the Liberal Party. But the scandal did focus public debate on the question of political corruption and on the misuse of public honours for private, party-political ends. It also contributed to the growing breach between Lloyd George and the Conservative Party and further weakened an already ailing coalition government.

The issues raised by these scandals of the first two decades of the twentieth century continued to haunt British political life in subsequent decades, manifesting themselves from time to time in fresh scandals involving allegations of corruption in public life. In 1949 John Belcher resigned as Labour MP for Sowerby following revelations that, as a junior trade minister in Clement Attlee's postwar government, he had accepted gifts, holidays and entertainment from a number of businessmen and intermediaries – most notably from Sidney Stanley, a wheeler-dealer who persuaded businessmen that he could fix things in the political sphere and occasionally induced them to hand over substantial sums for the purpose. But one of the most significant financial-political scandals of recent British history was the scandal that unfolded around the activities of the enterprising architect from Yorkshire, John Poulson.

In 1932 Poulson set up a small architectural practice in Pontefract, West Yorkshire. In the course of the next thirty years he expanded this into one of the most successful architectural practices in the north east of England, winning many contracts with local authorities and nationalized industries. In 1964 Poulson set up a new company with the aim of securing more contracts abroad, and he enlisted the Conservative MP Reginald Maudling to serve as chairman. Maudling had entered Parliament in 1950 and had become Chancellor of the Exchequer in Harold Macmillan's government in the early 1960s. When the Conservatives were returned to power in 1970, Maudling became Home Secretary in the government of Edward Heath. But at roughly the same time, Poulson's business empire began to collapse. In 1972 Poulson filed for bankruptcy and, in the hearings that followed, it emerged that he had made a series of substantial payments in cash and gifts to local politicians, MPs and civil servants. Among these payments was a £5,000 annual covenant to the Adeline Genée Theatre Trust, a charity supported by Maudling's wife. On 18 July 1972 Maudling suddenly resigned as Home Secretary. It subsequently emerged not only that Poulson had established the annual covenant, but also that Maudling had acquired substantial shares in Poulson's companies and that his son had become a manager of one. Poulson was found guilty of corruption and sentenced to imprisonment; numerous others, including senior civil servants and prominent local politicians, were also prosecuted. Maudling and two other MPs who had been involved with Poulson – John Cordle and Albert Roberts – were not charged with criminal activity, but the corruption scandal put an end to Maudling's ministerial career.[7]

The Poulson affair renewed debate in Parliament and in the press about the private financial interests of MPs. This matter had been addressed by a parliamentary inquiry in 1969, although little action was taken at the time. In the wake of the Poulson affair, Parliament resolved to establish a Register of Members' Interests in which MPs would be expected to declare relevant financial interests. But this was, in effect, a system of self-regulation which gave a good deal of discretion to individual MPs, since they were left with the responsibility for deciding which financial interests were relevant and should therefore be disclosed. The lack of clarity concerning the rules of disclosure, together with the growth of lobbying and the persistence of a long-standing tradition of tolerance towards the private financial activities of MPs, have helped to ensure that some of the conditions which underpinned financial-political scandals in Britain have by no means disappeared.

This was pointedly demonstrated by a series of scandals which afflicted the Conservative government of John Major in the early 1990s, and which contributed to the Conservatives' growing reputation for sleaze. These scandals centred on the willingness of MPs to act on behalf of outside interests in the conduct of their parliamentary duties. In the early 1990s, rumours were circulating in Westminster that some MPs were secretly accepting cash to ask parliamentary questions. (Tabling parliamentary questions is a means by which MPs can prise information out of the government, since the minister to whom they are addressed is obliged to reply.) But despite the rumours, there was no clear evidence that the practice was occurring – until, that is, reporters working for the *Sunday Times* Insight team set out to prove it. Posing as a businessman, a reporter contacted ten Labour MPs and ten Conservative MPs and offered each £1,000 to table a question. Two of the MPs – both Conservative, Graham Riddick and David Tredinnick – accepted the cash (though Riddick, thinking better of it, subsequently returned the cheque). On 10 July 1994, under the headline 'Revealed: MPs who accept £1,000 to ask a Parliamentary question', the *Sunday Times* ran the story which precipitated the 'cash for questions' scandal. Tredinnick initially denied the allegations, but the reporter had secretly taped his conversations with the MPs and, when the *Sunday Times* released the tapes, Tredinnick's denials collapsed. The matter was referred to the parliamentary Committee of Privileges for investigation. But before the committee could complete its inquiry and make its recommendations, other ministers found themselves caught up in a rapidly unfolding sequence of corruption allegations.

On 20 October 1994, the *Guardian* ran a cash-for-questions story which they had been investigating for several months, alleging that two Conservative MPs, Tim Smith and Neil Hamilton, had been paid by the Egyptian businessman Mohamed Al Fayed to ask questions which would be helpful to him during his bitter struggle to gain control of Harrods.[8] Smith immediately resigned as a Northern Ireland minister, but Hamilton denied the allegations and issued a writ for libel against the *Guardian*. Hamilton's position was weakened by the additional disclosure that he and his wife had once spent six nights (in September 1987) at the Ritz Hotel in Paris as guests of Al Fayed, who owned the hotel; in the course of a week, the Hamiltons had apparently run up a bill in excess of £2,000, which was covered by Al Fayed. Hamilton was forced to resign as a trade minister and his libel case eventually collapsed, as further evidence emerged that he had accepted payments from Al Fayed and from the lobbyist Ian Greer, who worked on Al Fayed's behalf – 'A liar and a cheat' was the bold headline in the *Guardian*, above a large photo of Hamilton, on the day after the case collapsed. Hamilton continued to proclaim his innocence (he later admitted that he had accepted money from Greer but denied taking cash from Al Fayed, whom he sued – unsuccessfully – for libel[9]). But the MP was thoroughly

14 Front page of the *Guardian*, 1 October 1996, the day after Neil Hamilton's libel action against the *Guardian* had collapsed. Hamilton's reputation was destroyed by the cash-for-questions scandal and by his ill-fated libel cases against the *Guardian* and Mohamed Al Fayed.

disgraced by the affair and, in the 1997 general election, he lost his parliamentary seat.

Neil Hamilton was not the only government minister who would come to regret that he had accepted hospitality at the Paris Ritz. In the course of inquiries into the affairs of Tim Smith and Neil Hamilton, the editor of the *Guardian* was informed by Al Fayed that another Conservative MP, Jonathan Aitken, had stayed at the Ritz on a weekend in September 1993. Aitken was Minister of State for Defence Procurement at the time, and it appeared that his bill at the

Paris Ritz – some 8,010 French francs – had been paid by an Arab businessman and arms broker, Said Ayas, who was a close associate of Prince Mohammed of Saudi Arabia. In correspondence with the *Guardian*, Aitken repeatedly denied that his hotel bill had been paid by Ayas, insisting that the weekend in Paris was a family occasion and that the bill was paid by his wife.[10] On 27 October 1994, in a political context dominated by the cash-for-questions scandal and allegations of Tory sleaze, the *Guardian* published a front-page article about the mysterious hotel bill of Jonathan Aitken, who had by now been promoted to Chief Secretary to the Treasury in John Major's government; the following day the *Guardian* published a copy of the bill. The Labour opposition seized the opportunity to raise the issue in the House, where Aitken strongly rejected the suggestion that the bill had been paid by Mr Ayas. The focus of the controversy shifted temporarily to the question of how the *Guardian* had obtained a copy of the bill (a question which led to the resignation of the *Guardian*'s editor[11]), but the issue of who had paid the bill refused to go away. In April 1995 the *Guardian* and a Granada Television *World in Action* programme repeated the allegations and added a few more (including the claim that Aitken had procured prostitutes for Arab clients), to which Aitken responded by suing them for libel. 'If it falls to me to start a fight to cut out the cancer of bent and twisted journalism in our country with the simple sword of truth and the trusty shield of British fair play, so be it. I am ready for the fight'[12] – valiant words, but, as it turned out, the besieged minister's position was a good deal more precarious than he was letting on.

Faced with a court case, Aitken stepped down from the Cabinet in July 1995; he subsequently lost his seat in the 1997 general election, which brought Labour to power. The libel action, which reached the High Court in June 1997, collapsed when a British Airways security officer produced flight coupons which showed that Aitken's wife and daughter had flown to Geneva on the weekend that they were supposed to be at the Paris Ritz. Aitken was subsequently prosecuted for perjury and for perverting the course of justice (he had prevailed upon his daughter to sign a false witness statement) and sentenced to eighteen months' imprisonment. The former Cabinet minister and Privy Councillor was thoroughly disgraced, he was faced with huge debts and his political career was in ruins.

Why had Aitken gone to such lengths to conceal what happened at the Paris Ritz on a weekend in 1993? In a political context dominated by allegations of Tory sleaze, it would undoubtedly have been very awkward for the Chief Secretary to the Treasury to admit that he had accepted hospitality from a wealthy Arab businessman. Accepting hospitality of this kind would probably have been a contravention of ministerial guidelines and, in this charged political context, such an admission may well have led to his resignation or expulsion from the Cabinet. It is very likely that it would have damaged his reputation and career. And once he had embarked on the path of concealment, the methods he used to support his story and to try to silence his critics became ever more elaborate. He was running the risk of compounding the original offence with a series of second-order transgressions: it was a calculated risk in an all-or-nothing struggle, and in the end he lost it all. But it also seems likely that there was more at stake in the weekend at the Paris Ritz than a breach of ministerial guidelines on accepting hospitality. In 1993 Aitken was Minister of Defence Procurement, and there is some evidence to suggest that he had gone to Paris to try to secure a number of major arms deals with British firms which involved the payment of secret commissions into Swiss bank accounts.[13] If so, this would help to explain why Aitken was so concerned to conceal the details of his weekend at the Paris Ritz. It would also link the Aitken affair to the blurred boundary between political power and the arms trade which, as we shall see in the following chapter, has been a rich source of scandals in British political life.

In the political context of the early 1990s, the flood of revelations and allegations about cash-for-questions and ministerial improprieties contributed to a growing climate of unease about the extra-parliamentary interests and activities of MPs. It was in this context, and shortly after the revelations that several MPs had agreed to ask questions for cash, that the then prime minister John Major established a committee, under the chairmanship of Lord Nolan, to examine standards in public life. The first report of the Nolan Committee was published in May 1995 and made a series of recommendations concerning the conduct of MPs. The committee proposed, among other things, that the practice of MPs selling their services to lobbying firms should be banned; that MPs should be required to disclose fully their consultancy agreements and payments; that a new code of conduct for MPs should be drawn up; and that a Parliamentary Commissioner for Standards should be appointed to assume responsibility for maintaining the Register of Members' Interests, for advising on the Code of Conduct and for investigating allegations of misconduct.[14] These and other recommendations were accepted by

Parliament, which implemented a new Code of Conduct for MPs in July 1995, appointed a new Parliamentary Commissioner for Standards and expanded the Register of Members' Interests to indicate the amounts of remuneration received from outside employment relevant to their activities as MPs.

Given the political climate of Westminster in the mid-1990s and the political capital that the Labour Party tried to make out of allegations of Tory sleaze, it is hardly surprising that when Labour was swept to power in the May 1997 general election, they found themselves under close scrutiny for the faintest sign of corruption. The critics did not have to wait long. In early November 1997, Tony Blair's new government found itself in the spotlight when it emerged that the Labour Party had accepted a donation of £1 million from the Formula One impresario Bernie Ecclestone. This revelation came at a very awkward time, since the Labour government had been trying for several months to modify the policy of the European Union on tobacco advertising in a way that would continue to allow the sponsorship of sport, and tobacco companies are major sponsors of Formula One. The potential conflict of interest forced Tony Blair into a public apology and induced the Labour Party to return the donation. In July the following year, the *Observer* ran a story about a number of former Labour Party aides who had become lobbyists and who claimed to be able to provide access to confidential documents and key government officials. No minister was singled out for blame, but the government found itself struggling to shake off the suggestion that its new style of Labour Party politics had created its own kind of sleaze (what the Tory opposition dubbed 'the culture of cronyism'). Faced with the prospect that its attacks on Tory sleaze in the early 1990s would return to haunt the Labour Party in power, Tony Blair sought to defuse the controversy and reassure the public by insisting that his government had to be 'purer than pure' and would take severe action against anyone guilty of impropriety. The lobbying scandal passed without ministerial casualties, but the stakes had been raised still further.

It was in this political climate of heightened sensitivity that, six months later, the man who was in some respects an emblematic figure of New Labour, Peter Mandelson, found his fortunes suddenly turning. Mandelson had played a key role in transforming the Labour Party's public relations strategy in the 1980s and 1990s – so much so that he was regarded by many as New Labour's chief 'spin doctor'. He was elected as MP for Hartlepool in 1992 and helped to fashion the Labour Party's successful election campaign in 1997. He initially served as Minister without Portfolio in Tony Blair's government, assuming responsibility for the coordination and presentation of policy, before being promoted to Secretary of State for Trade and Industry in July 1998. But on 22 December the *Guardian* disclosed that, two years earlier, Mandelson had accepted a loan of £373,000 from a wealthy political colleague, Geoffrey Robinson, in order to buy a house in Notting Hill, a fashionable part of London. Mandelson had not disclosed the loan in the Register of Members' Interests nor, it seemed, had he told his building society about the loan when he submitted his application for a mortgage. While initially protesting against allegations of impropriety and insisting that he had done nothing wrong, Mandelson's protests were short-lived: on 23 December he resigned as Trade and Industry Secretary. Geoffrey Robinson, who had risen to the post of Paymaster General in Tony Blair's government, resigned on the same day. 'I am sorry about this situation,' said Mandelson in his resignation letter. 'But we came to power promising to uphold the highest possible standards in public life. We have not just to do so, but we must be seen to do so.'[15] Even at the moment of his downfall, this man who had built his reputation on his alleged nous for the management of visibility was not about to renounce the importance of the art. Mandelson's offence was not serious enough to destroy his political career (after a brief spell on the back benches, he was brought back into the Cabinet as Minister of State for Northern Ireland), but the disclosure of the loan was undoubtedly a setback and a firm reminder that, in the age of mediated visibility, even the masters of spin are vulnerable to scandal.

The financial scandals which characterized British politics in the 1990s have demonstrated that while corruption may not be as systemic in Britain as it is in some countries (such as Italy) and while financial scandals may not be as prevalent in Britain as they have been in the United States and elsewhere, they nevertheless continue to play a significant role in British political life. The cash-for-questions scandal helped to focus attention on the extraparliamentary interests of MPs, and this has proved to be a rich vein for investigative journalists and others to tap. Newspapers like the *Sunday Times* and the *Guardian* have been assertive in their attempts to uncover and publicize financial improprieties among politicians, but the scandals have also been fuelled by the activities of other individuals who had their own agendas to pursue (most notably, the Egyptian businessman Mohamed Al Fayed). MPs such as Neil Hamilton and Jonathan Aitken were thoroughly disgraced by the scandals which engulfed them (and by their ill-fated libel cases), while others found that their political careers suffered temporary or permanent setbacks. In a political climate where the differences of principle between the major parties were less pronounced than they had been in the past, the question of 'sleaze' – exemplified both by the financial scandals surrounding Hamilton, Aitken and others and by the sex scandals which afflicted the Conservatives in the 1980s and early 1990s – became a key focus of partisan struggle in the political field. Having made the most of the Tories' difficulties, it is hardly surprising that when the Labour Party was returned to power in 1997, it was subjected to intensive scrutiny, nor is it surprising that when evidence of improprieties began to emerge, the Prime Minister would find himself under pressure to act swiftly and decisively to distance his party and his government from the offending individuals (even when they were close and valued colleagues). In a political climate characterized by a heightened sensitivity to scandal, the risks associated with tolerating impropriety within one's ranks, and above all with being *seen* to tolerate impropriety, were judged to be too high.

Politics and Corporate Power

The development of financial-political scandals in the United States was shaped by a different set of historical and institutional considerations. Some of the forms of corruption that characterized the British political system in the seventeenth and eighteenth centuries were carried over to the early colonial government in America, which developed elaborate systems of patronage and nepotism. The attack on corruption became a rallying cry for the American revolutionaries, who aspired to create a republic that would be free from the kinds of political patronage that characterized the ancien régime. This aim seemed to be achieved with some degree of success during the first few decades of the new republic. But in nineteenth-century America, corruption flourished. From the 1820s on and at all levels of government – municipal, state and federal – corruption became a pervasive and increasingly entrenched feature of the American political system.[16]

Among the factors that shaped this development, three were particularly important. First, the rapid growth of cities in the early nineteenth century created new demands for the provision of services which existing political institutions were unable to meet. Party organizations stepped in to fill the vacuum and used their control of municipal governments to build up powerful party machines. The party organizations were able to build up financial resources by collecting kickbacks on municipal contracts and other forms of corruption. The party machines were further strengthened by the influx of immigrants who gave their support to party organizations in return for jobs and other kinds of patronage and support. The best known of these municipal party machines was the Democratic organization at Tammany Hall in New York City, but powerful party organizations also emerged in Philadelphia, Chicago and other major cities.

A second factor which fostered the growth of corruption in the United States was the development of what was commonly known as the 'spoils system'. This was the practice by which individuals elected to key political offices were able to fill a range of administrative posts with appointments of their own choosing. This practice was relatively common at the municipal and state levels of government in the early nineteenth century and contributed further to the power of party organizations, which could reward loyal supporters with government jobs. The extension of the practice to the federal level was facilitated by the passage of the Tenure of Office Act in 1820, which limited the term of office of some federal employees to four years, and by Andrew Jackson's endorsement of the four-year-term rule as a general principle for federal appointments when he assumed the Presidency in 1829. The motivation behind the principle of rotation was to render public office more accountable, but it created new opportunities for political patronage and encouraged the filling of posts on the basis of partisan allegiance rather than fitness for office.

A third factor which underpinned the growth of corruption was the westward expansion of the union and the rapid development of a commercialized market economy. The opening of new lands to settlement was accompanied by a great deal of speculation and intrigue, and many of the land schemes involved favouritism and fraud. The construction of the railroads was also a major source of corruption, since they were dependent on state governments which granted franchises and regulated their operation. The emergence of large and powerful corporations created new opportunities for the intermingling of economic and political power. Some corporations sought to use their financial muscle to secure the cooperation of politicians and party bosses and to influence legislative and other activities which could have a direct bearing on their profitability. Some politicians and party bosses, in turn, saw this as an opportunity to fill the party coffers or to improve their personal lifestyle. By 1850 several lobbies were operating in Congress, giving rise to new forms of commercial influence on the political process and new temptations for congressmen.

The growth of corruption in nineteenth-century America was also accompanied by the development of the press and the emergence of new forms of journalism – developments which, taken together, created the conditions for the wave of financial-political scandals which characterized the postbellum years. By the time of President Grant's administration in the aftermath of the Civil War, the party machines were well established and corruption was widespread at all levels of government. At the same time, political corruption was increasingly becoming a topic of criticism and debate within the political field itself, and increasingly becoming a focus of concern for journalists and editors who were seeking to develop their professional identities and careers. The convergence of these developments spawned a series of scandals which highlighted problems of corruption at municipal, state and federal levels, and which helped to ensure that the period of Grant's Presidency (1869–77) would be remembered as one of the most corrupt in American history.

Among these scandals was the highly charged controversy which eventually culminated in the downfall of the Tweed ring in New York City.[17] From 1866 until 1871, William Marcy Tweed was the boss of the Democratic Party machine which, from its base at Tammany Hall, had effectively gained control of the city. Through a combination of force and graft, Tweed built up a powerful network of patronage and support which extended from the municipal government to the state legislature, which incorporated the police and the courts and which siphoned off substantial sums from kickbacks on municipal contracts, among other things. The ring probably generated between $30 million and $100 million in three years, and probably employed at least 12,000 people through patronage alone. For the most part, the press was supportive of Tweed (it too benefited from the ring, both through regular advertising and through cash payments and gifts), but two papers – *Harper's Weekly* and the *New York Times* – gradually mounted a crusade against the ring. In 1868 *Harper's Weekly* began printing Thomas Nast's brilliant political cartoons, and from autumn 1870 the *Times* began a sustained attack on the ring. But the *Times*'s attack, while full of venom and moral indignation, lacked the kind of hard evidence that would give it real force – until, that is, two disgruntled employees, acting independently, handed

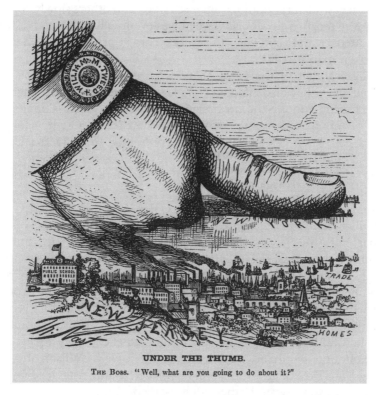

UNDER THE THUMB.

THE BOSS. "Well, what are you going to do about it?"

15 'Under the thumb', from *Harper's Weekly*, 10 June 1871. The corruption of the Tweed ring was a favourite target for Thomas Nast's political cartoons.

over details of the ring's corrupt practices to the paper. On 22 July 1871, under the headline 'The secret accounts: proofs of undoubted frauds brought to light', the *Times* documented case after case of corruption and fraud; a special supplement, published on 29 July in English and German, provided further details. These publications caused a sensation and helped to crystallize a concerted movement of reform. The ring fought back – George Jones, the publisher of the *Times*, was offered a bribe of $500,000, and Mayor Oakey Hall condemned the disclosures of the *Times* as 'a tempest of ciphers and calumny' – but the days of the Tweed ring were now numbered. In the municipal elections in November, Tammany Hall suffered one of the worst defeats in its history up to then. Stripped of power and patronage, many members of the ring fled and were never brought to justice, while prosecutions against Tweed and others slowly worked their way through the courts. Tweed was eventually convicted of fifty-one offences and sentenced to several years in prison, where he died a broken man in 1878.

The scandals of the Gilded Age were not restricted to the municipal level: they also affected state legislatures as well as the federal government. Among the most significant of the congressional scandals of this period was the Crédit Mobilier fraud. Crédit Mobilier was a construction company which contracted to build the Union Pacific railroad. But Crédit Mobilier was itself owned by some of the large shareholders of the Union Pacific, who were reaping exorbitant profits from the deal. To prevent congressional investigation of this cosy arrangement, congressman Oakes Ames distributed Crédit Mobilier shares among some of his colleagues. The stock was offered at par, but Ames gave credit generously and allowed congressmen to purchase the stock out of dividends earned. But on 4 September 1872, under the headline 'The king of frauds: how the Crédit Mobilier bought its way into Congress', the *New York Sun* exposed the arrangement. A congressional investigation into the affair recommended that Ames, another congressman and a senator should be expelled (although they were not in fact expelled, since their terms were about to expire anyway). Vice President Henry Wilson and outgoing Vice President Colfax were implicated and disgraced by the scandal, as were several other congressmen.

The exposure of the Tweed ring and the Crédit Mobilier fraud were prominent scandals at the time but by no means exceptional: the last three decades of the nineteenth century were littered with financial-political scandals of various kinds, including the Sanborn contracts scandal (1874), the Whiskey Ring scandal (1875), the Belknap affair (1876), the Star Route fraud (1881) and the controversy surrounding Senator Nelson Aldrich and his links with the Sugar Trust (1894).[18] These and other scandals provided some stimulus for statutory reform. The Pendleton Civil Service Reform Act of 1883 was the most tangible outcome of this movement of reform, but other legislation of a more specific kind – such as the abolition of the moiety system[19] which was the basis of the Sanborn contracts scandal – was also introduced.[20] These and other reforms helped to reduce the most blatant forms of corruption and fraud. But some of the weaknesses of the administrative traditions of the nineteenth century persisted into the twentieth; the growing role of organized crime networks, which in some cases filled the vacuum left by the decline of municipal party machines, created new sources of corruption; and the more subtle forms of political corruption – such as those involving corporate influence, conflicts of interest, the misappropriation of funds and the misuse of public office for personal gain – found fresh grounds in which to flourish.

During the first half of the twentieth century, the most significant financial-political scandals at the level of the federal government occurred during the Harding and Truman administrations. Harding's brief Presidency (1921–3) was afflicted by numerous scandals, but the most widely publicized of these was the scandal known as Teapot Dome.[21] Some years earlier the federal government had set aside several tracts of land as naval oil reserves – two in California and one, called Teapot Dome, in Wyoming. In July 1921 Albert Fall, the Secretary of the Interior in Harding's administration, granted a lease to Edward Doheny's Pan-American Petroleum and Transport Company to drill offset wells in one of the Californian reserves, and in April 1922 he leased Teapot Dome to Harry Sinclair's Mammoth Oil Company. The exploitation of the reserves was opposed by conservationists and others, who called for a Senate investigation. The committee began its hearings in October 1923 and for several months the investigation appeared to be going nowhere. But then it emerged, rather unexpectedly, that Fall had received $100,000 in autumn 1921, which he had used to expand his ranch holdings in New Mexico; Fall initially claimed that he had borrowed the money from a friend, but it eventually became clear that the money had come from Doheny. Subsequent investigations revealed that Fall had also received bonds worth $233,000 which had been purchased from the profits of a trading company linked to Sinclair, as well as substantial sums in cash. Altogether, Fall had received over $400,000 from the two oil men. Fall had resigned before the Senate investigation began, but his reputation was now thoroughly tarnished and his career was in ruins. He was convicted of bribery in 1929 and served nine months in prison. Teapot Dome claimed other casualties too, including the Secretary of the Navy, Edwin Denby, who resigned in February 1924, and the Attorney General, Harry Daugherty, who resigned in March. The scandal dominated the headlines in early 1924 and became a key issue in the presidential campaign, although the Republican candidate, Calvin Coolidge (who had succeeded Harding following his death in 1923 and went on to win the 1924 election), managed to escape relatively unscathed.

The Truman administration (1945–53) was equally fraught with scandals involving allegations of corruption among government officials. The most serious of these were based on revelations concerning the activities of officials in a number of government agencies, including the Bureau of Internal Revenue and the Reconstruction Finance Corporation.[22] The revelations of widespread corruption among tax officials were the most alarming. In March 1951, following a series of allegations and disclosures, a subcommittee of the House Ways and Means Committee was established under the chairmanship of Cecil King to investigate irregularities in the Internal Revenue Service. The investigations uncovered numerous cases of tax fixing, bribery, tax evasion and other offences; in 1951 alone, 166 internal revenue officials were fired or forced to resign. Theron Lamar Caudle, Assistant Attorney General in charge of the Tax Division, was fired in November 1951 and later tried and convicted on charges of conspiracy. Joseph Nunan, who served as Commissioner of Internal Revenue from 1944 to 1947, was convicted of tax evasion in 1954 and sentenced to five years' imprisonment. Numerous tax collectors were removed from office, and some were prosecuted for the acceptance or extortion of bribes in return for lowering or overlooking tax liability.

At roughly the same time as these damaging revelations were emerging, the Truman administration was also shaken by the disclosure of serious mismanagement and corruption in the Reconstruction Finance Corporation (RFC). The RFC was originally set up in 1932, at a time of deepening depression; its aim was to lend federal money to banks, businesses and other organizations when it judged such loans to be in the public interest. In 1949, amid growing speculation of mismanagement in the RFC, a subcommittee of the Senate Banking and Currency Committee launched an investigation under the chairmanship of Senator J. William Fulbright. In February 1951 the subcommittee published its report, documenting the activities of an influence ring in which power stemmed from the White House itself, via the administrative assistant to the President, Donald Dawson. Truman dismissed the report, labelling it 'asinine', to which Fulbright responded by announcing public hearings. The testimony before the Fulbright subcommittee provided a litany of mismanagement and corruption – loans made to dubious organizations and highly speculative ventures, gifts lavished on key figures (including a mink coat worth $8,540 which was given to the wife of Merl Young, an RFC employee, and which became a symbol of the corruption in the Truman administration) and numerous other instances of influence peddling. Truman himself was not directly implicated in the scandals that surrounded the RFC, the Internal Revenue Service and other organizations, but his reputation was undoubtedly tarnished by the fact that he presided over an administration which was widely perceived as corrupt, and because he failed to act quickly and decisively to clamp down on corruption when the revelations first emerged.

The Republicans made the most of Truman's difficulties in the run-up to the 1952 presidential election, and Eisenhower built his campaign partly on the pledge to end corruption in high places. But financial-political scandals have remained a persistent feature of American politics from the 1950s on, despite Eisenhower's pledge. Indeed, Eisenhower was still on the campaign trail when the first scandal erupted: on 18 September 1952 the *New York Post* alleged in a lead story that a 'millionaires' club' comprising a number of wealthy California businessmen had given vice-presidential candidate Richard Nixon between $16,000 and $17,000 since he was elected to the Senate in 1950, apparently to help with his expenses. Nixon initially brushed off the disclosure and expected it to fade away. But it rapidly escalated into a major crisis, and within a matter of days it was threatening both to derail the Republican campaign and to end his vice-presidential ambitions. In a dramatic and unprecedented bid to save his candidature, Nixon decided to make a television broadcast in which he would speak directly to voters and seek to persuade them of his innocence – the now famous 'Checkers' speech.[23] Nixon's appeal worked; the fund crisis blew over and Nixon was hailed by many as a man of courage who had faced his critics down. But Eisenhower's difficulties were not over. His administration was dogged by a series of financial-political scandals, culminating in the resignation of the Presidential Assistant, Sherman Adams, in 1958.[24] Adams's position was rendered untenable when it emerged that he had accepted various gifts (including an oriental rug and the payment of hotel bills) from a New England textile magnate, Bernard Goldfine, and that he had also interceded on Goldfine's behalf with the chairman of the Federal Trade Commission.

Many of the financial-political scandals in the United States in the post-1950 period have involved conflicts of interest in which the duties and responsibilities of public officials were compromised by their personal interests, or in which individuals used their public positions for personal gain. The occurrence of conflicts of interest may involve explicit forms of corruption, such as bribery, blackmail or kickbacks. But the kind of corruption involved is often less clear-cut and shades into a grey area of activities where it may be less easy to demonstrate impropriety and apportion blame. Politicians themselves may be inclined to tolerate a degree of interest overlap, and may be averse to introducing legislation or clear codes of conduct which would seek to minimize conflicts of interest.

Of course, conflicts of interest are not new, but a number of developments have helped to give them greater significance and salience in recent American politics. In the first place, the growth of the lobbying system has created a complex array of networks and pressure groups where corporate power overlaps with political office. In the United States today, it is estimated that corporations spend more than $1.2 billion to support 14,000 officially registered lobbyists in Washington DC alone – roughly twenty-seven lobbyists for each member of Congress. The presence of a large number of lobbyists with substantial resources at their disposal creates many forms of interaction and reciprocal exchange where the boundaries between private interests and public duties become blurred, where favours can carry hidden obligations, where hospitality can shade into influence and where public officials might find themselves tempted to take advantage of opportunities for personal and political gain.

A second important development is the rising cost of elections and changes in the regulations governing financial contributions to political parties and campaigns. The growing role of television as a principal medium for election campaigning has helped to ensure that running for office in the United States has become an exorbitantly expensive business; according to one estimate, the average cost of winning a seat in the US Senate in 1996 was $4.7 million.[25] More and more effort must be devoted to fund-raising, with the risk that successful candidates may find themselves in hock to large individual or corporate donors. In the early 1970s Congress introduced new legislation to limit individual contributions and strengthen disclosure requirements. But these changes tended to make candidates more dependent on the fund-raising activities of political action committees (or PACs), which gave rise to new forms of financial power and pressure.

A third factor which has helped to give more salience to conflicts of interest is that, thanks partly to the scandals of the postwar period, politicians, journalists and others have become increasingly concerned with the question of what constitutes unethical behaviour in politics and how to prevent it. This question was an important part of political debates in the 1950s and 1960s, and both President Kennedy and President Johnson issued codes to try to reduce conflicts of interest and to establish certain minimum standards of conduct. But since the early 1970s this trend has become much more pronounced.[26] Undoubtedly Watergate was a crucial factor in this regard, helping to create a new climate of anxiety and investigatory zeal which increased the likelihood that conflicts of interest and other forms of corruption would be exposed and condemned. Both houses of Congress passed new ethics codes for their members, and in 1978 Congress passed the Ethics in Government Act which, among other things, tightened rules on conflicts of interest, lobbying and the disclosure of financial information by high-level government officials. Conscious of the need not only to address these issues but also to be seen to be doing so, Congress became more active in enforcing codes of behaviour and investigating alleged infringements. At the same time, the media and other organizations became increasingly aggressive and proactive in disclosing conflicts of interest and other instances of actual or alleged financial wrongdoing.

The cumulative result of these developments was that, not long after Watergate, Congress became the focus of a series of financial-political scandals. Among these was the Gulf Oil scandal, triggered off by the revelation in 1975 that the Gulf Oil Corporation had made illegal campaign contributions over a period of ten years to Nixon and to numerous congressional candidates (although only one congressman, Senate Minority Leader Hugh Scott, pleaded guilty to receiving a large undeclared sum from Gulf). Then there was 'Koreagate', a scandal that stemmed from the activities of a South Korean lobbyist, Tongsun Park, who was indicted in August 1977 on charges of conspiring to bribe public officials. Apparently with the help of the Korean Central Intelligence Agency, Tongsun Park had given campaign contributions and cash gifts to congressmen and provided free trips to Korea, with the aim of influencing congressional attitudes towards South Korea. Tongsun Park was able to fund this activity by virtue of his position as the sole agent for US rice sales to Korea. Brought before a congressional committee in April 1978, Tongsun Park testified that he had presented gifts and made campaign contributions to thirty members of Congress. Former congressman Richard Hanna was convicted of conspiring to defraud the government and spent a year in prison. Three other congressmen were formally reprimanded by the House for failing to report cash gifts from Tongsun Park (although two were subsequently re-elected to the House).

But perhaps the most telling of the congressional scandals of the 1970s and 1980s was the Abscam affair, which highlighted both the increasingly sensitive ethical climate of the post-Watergate period and the increasingly aggressive stance of law enforcement agencies. Abscam was an FBI 'sting' operation in which agents, posing as representatives of two imaginary Arab sheikhs, offered congressmen bribes in return for promises of help in dealing with immigration problems among other things.[27] The operation initially began life in 1977 as part of an FBI crackdown on organized crime, but it took on a new significance when, towards the end of its two-year existence, it netted several prominent politicians. Operating behind a dummy corporation called Abdul Enterprises Ltd (hence the name 'Abscam', short for Abdul scam), the agents laid out their bait: they let it be known that the sheikhs had billions of dollars from oil revenue which they wanted to invest in the US, and that they eventually wanted to obtain permanent residence there. Almost from the beginning, the FBI recorded everything: telephone calls were taped, meetings in hotel rooms and other venues were secretly filmed, etc. Video cameras fitted with special lenses were mounted behind the screens of TV sets, in ceiling light fixtures and behind walls and doors. Towards the end of 1978 a number of politicians began to appear in the net – initially Angelo Errichetti, the shady Mayor of Camden, New Jersey, who became a key intermediary as the operation unfolded, but others too were soon drawn in, including a senator and several congressmen. Errichetti was secretly filmed accepting large bribes for arranging a gambling licence to build a casino in Atlantic City. Senator Harrison Williams agreed to use his influence in Washington to help win government contracts for a titanium mine in return for a $17 million stake in the corporation. Several congressmen were filmed accepting large sums of money in envelopes and briefcases in return for promising to help with immigration problems, among other things.

In early February 1980 the Abscam operation suddenly became public. The FBI decided to wind up the operation and break the cover on 2 February 1980, and the following day it was headline news in the national press. Some of the secret videotapes were subsequently shown on television. Lawyers for the senator and the congressmen argued that the FBI operation was a case of illegal entrapment, but the force of the video evidence against them was overwhelming. In one videotape, shown on national television, viewers could see Congressman Michael Meyers taking a briefcase containing a $50,000 bribe from an undercover agent (Tony Amoroso) and could hear him saying, 'Tony, you're going – let me just say this to you – you're going about this the right way . . . I'm gonna tell you something real simple and short. Money talks in this business and bullshit walks. And it works the same way down in

Washington.'[28] These stark revelations, in which congressmen were caught red-handed engaging in the most blatant forms of corruption, were shocking and offensive to many people. In October 1980 Meyers was expelled from the House (he was the first member to be expelled since 1861). Five of the six congressmen involved in Abscam failed to win re-election in the congressional elections in the fall of 1980; the one who was re-elected, Raymond Lederer of Pennsylvania, subsequently resigned his seat in 1981, following his conviction on charges of bribery. Harrison Williams resigned from the Senate in March 1982 in the face of his imminent expulsion. All seven were convicted of criminal offences and sentenced to terms of imprisonment.

Financial-political scandals claimed other congressional victims in the 1980s and 1990s. In the late 1980s and early 1990s, five senators found themselves caught up in a scandal stemming from the collapse of the Savings and Loan industry, a scandal that became known as the Keating Five.[29] The senators were formally rebuked for accepting large campaign contributions from the owner of a Savings and Loan, Charles Keating, while also intervening on Keating's behalf with state and federal regulators. In 1989 the Speaker of the House, Jim Wright, was forced to resign in the face of numerous charges of financial impropriety including the acceptance of gifts, accepting favours from a Texas businessman named George Mallick (who had hired his wife and allowed him the use of a car and apartment) and violating House rules on outside earnings by selling large quantities of his book, *Reflections of a Public Man*, to campaign contributors and keeping the royalties (which were calculated at a highly inflated rate of 55 per cent). In the ethically charged and highly partisan climate of the post-Watergate Congress, these and other charges were sufficient to undermine Wright's position as Speaker of the House. In 1994, the chairman of the House Ways and Means Committee, Dan Rostenkowski, was indicted on seventeen counts of fraud and embezzlement, including misappropriating public funds, charging Congress for furniture which was given to friends and placing 'ghost' employees on his payroll.

The executive branch of government was also afflicted by a series of financial-political scandals in the post-Watergate period. Bert Lance was forced to resign as Carter's Budget Director in September 1977, amid controversy over his past business practices. Numerous officials in Reagan's administration were investigated on charges of financial impropriety, and there were several high-profile resignations. In 1982 Reagan's National Security Advisor, Richard Allen, was forced to resign amid allegations of financial wrongdoing, including an accusation that he had accepted a gift of $1,000 from a Japanese reporter. Deputy Secretary of Defence Paul Thayer resigned in January 1984 to face charges of insider trading brought against him by the Securities and Exchange Commission. In September 1984 Secretary of Labor Raymond Donovan was indicted on charges of having defrauded the New York City Transit Authority on a subway construction project in 1979–80; he was eventually acquitted, but he resigned in March 1985 and his political career was over. Reagan's first Attorney General, William French Smith, resigned in January 1984 amid allegations of tax dodging. His successor, Edwin Meese, was the subject of two investigations by special prosecutors – one by Jacob Stein in 1984 and a second by James McKay in 1987 – involving allegations of corruption; neither investigation resulted in prosecution, but Meese stepped down after the publication of the McKay Report. These and other scandals helped to give Reagan's administration a reputation for sleaze, although the scandal that would come to dominate Reagan's second term was not a financial scandal but rather a power scandal – the Iran-Contra affair (we shall examine this in the following chapter). While the Bush administration was less troubled by financial-political scandals, Bush's Chief of Staff John Sununu resigned in December 1991 amid charges that he had used government planes and cars for his personal benefit.

Like many presidential hopefuls in the past, Clinton campaigned on the promise to clean up politics, vowing to deliver 'the most ethical administration ever', but he soon found that members of his administration – and, indeed, that he and his wife – were being investigated on grounds of possible financial wrongdoing. An independent counsel was appointed to investigate the business affairs of Secretary of Commerce Ronald Brown. The Secretary of Housing and Urban Development, Henry Cisneros, was investigated by a special prosecutor for allegedly lying to the FBI about payments to a former mistress. Secretary of Transportation Frederico Pena was investigated over allegations of misappropriating federal funds to build Denver's new airport. Secretary of Agriculture Mike Espy was forced to resign in the face of allegations that he had accepted gifts from companies that were regulated by his department. And the Clintons themselves became the subjects of a long-running investigation into their involvement in a speculative land deal in Arkansas and its relation to a failed Savings and Loan – the so-called Whitewater affair.

The Whitewater Imbroglio

The origins of the Whitewater affair date from the late 1970s, when Bill Clinton was Attorney General in Arkansas.[30] Jim McDougal, a friend of the Clintons who had several real estate developments, found 230 acres along the White River in north-central Arkansas and invited the Clintons to join him and his wife in a speculative investment. The plan was to purchase the land with a bank loan of $200,000 and then divide the land into forty-four lots which would be sold individually; the sale of the lots would enable them to pay off the loan as well as the interest. As it turned out, the sale of the lots was disappointingly slow and the Whitewater Development Company did not generate sufficient revenue to cover the interest; the partners eventually had to borrow more and more money to meet the payments. In the meantime, McDougal went into banking and, in 1983, acquired a Savings and Loan which he renamed Madison Guaranty. Taking advantage of the new legislation which deregulated the Savings and Loan Industry, McDougal set up a subsidiary of Madison Guaranty, called Madison Financial Corp., which he used as a vehicle for business investments. He also employed the Rose Law Firm, where Hillary Clinton worked, to do legal work for him and paid them a monthly retainer. But McDougal's business empire became increasingly mired in debt and his financial position became increasingly desperate. In 1986 he was ousted from the failing Savings and Loan, which was placed under government supervision, and in 1989 he was indicted on eleven felony counts, including bank fraud and the misapplication of bank funds. In 1987 Hillary Clinton took over the management of Whitewater.

After Bill Clinton declared his candidacy for the Presidency in October 1991, a reporter from the *New York Times*, Jeff Gerth, began to investigate Clinton's financial affairs in Arkansas. He spoke with McDougal, among others, and began to piece together connections between the failed Savings and Loan, the Rose Law Firm and the unsuccessful real estate investment at Whitewater. On 8 March 1992 the *New York Times* published a front page story under the headline 'Clintons joined S. & L. operator in an Ozark real-estate venture'.[31] The timing of the story was awkward for Clinton: his campaign was in full swing and, in the wake of the Gennifer Flowers affair and the controversy surrounding the draft, it was certainly not helpful to have Clinton linked to a failed S&L and to have questions raised about possible conflicts of interest. The story was reported by other papers and elicited a defensive response from the Clintons, who insisted that

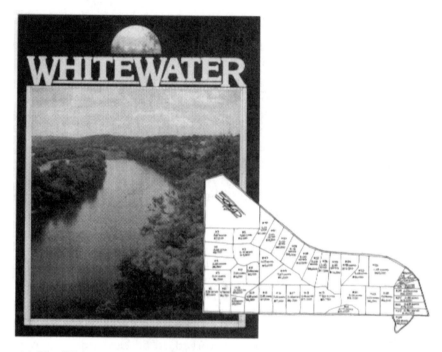

16 The Whitewater sales brochure. The plot of land along the White River in north-central Arkansas was divided into forty-four lots (*inset*) which were to be sold off individually, but the sale of the lots was disappointingly slow.

they had lost money on the venture and denied any wrongdoing. In the absence of fresh disclosures and given the complexity of the Whitewater imbroglio, the story gradually faded from the news. By summer 1992, Whitewater seemed dead as a political issue. After Clinton had been elected and was waiting to be inaugurated, his advisers discreetly arranged for the President-elect and his wife to extricate themselves from Whitewater (the Clintons' stake was handed over to McDougal for a nominal fee of $1,000).

It was the death in suspicious circumstances of the Deputy Counsel to the President, Vincent Foster, which rekindled media interest in Whitewater. Foster was an old friend of the Clintons, and he had worked with Hillary Clinton at the Rose Law Firm in Little Rock. When he joined the Clintons in Washington, he soon found himself having to deal with a scandal stemming from allegations of corruption in the White House travel office – what was quickly dubbed 'Travelgate' by the press.[32] The pressure seemed to take a heavy toll on Foster, and on 20 July 1993 he was found dead in Fort Marcy National Park, having apparently committed suicide. His office was subsequently searched by the Counsel to the President, Bernard Nussbaum, and various documents were removed. Since Foster had taken over responsibility for dealing with Whitewater on the Clintons' behalf in the period since they disposed of their interest, his sudden death and the removal of documents from his office were bound to arouse suspicions. (The White House later admitted that among the documents removed were a number of files relating to Whitewater, an admission that elicited a storm of criticism.) Moreover, shortly after Foster's death, it emerged that the RTC[33] investigation of McDougal's failed Savings and Loan, Madison Guaranty, was likely to result in criminal referrals. These two developments renewed the media's interest in Whitewater; Jeff Gerth from the *New York Times* and Susan Schmidt from the *Washington Post*, in particular, actively pursued the story, anxious not to be out-scooped by the other. On 31 October 1993 the *Washington Post* broke the story with a front-page article reporting that the RTC had asked federal prosecutors in Little Rock to begin criminal investigations of Madison Guaranty, explicitly linking the failed Savings and Loan to Whitewater and to the Clintons. Major stories appeared in the *Post* on subsequent days and other papers soon joined the fray, providing a flurry of fresh revelations and allegations. On 11 November the story was aired on NBC's *Nightly News*, with aerial footage of the rugged track of land along the White River. The NBC correspondent reported allegations that Clinton had used his position as governor to help secure a loan for the McDougals and alluded to a possible link between the investigations in Arkansas and Foster's death. Whitewater was back with a vengeance.

As the media became increasingly preoccupied with Whitewater and with speculation about Foster's death, the White House responded by denying any wrongdoing and stonewalling requests for further information. Some of the media coverage was undoubtedly partisan in character, and some was linked to the activities of right-wing political organizations – such as Citizens United, Accuracy in Media, the Landmark Legal Foundation and the Western Journalism Center – which were deeply hostile to the Clintons and to the Clinton administration.[34] But the uncooperative response of the White House served only to reinforce the suspicion that there must be something to hide. The calls for an independent investigation, both from the media and from Congress, grew louder. Amid growing concern that Whitewater would derail Clinton's legislative programme, the White

House set up a special unit – the Whitewater Response Team, as it was called – to deal with the crisis. On a state visit to Russia, Ukraine and the Baltic States in January 1994, Clinton found himself having to deal with questions about Whitewater. Although opinions in the White House were divided on the issue of whether the President should support an independent investigation, Clinton was swayed in favour of the idea, in the hope that it would take some of the heat out of the crisis and lead to a relatively speedy resolution. While still in the Ukraine, he decided to ask for the appointment of an Independent Counsel.

Robert Fiske, a moderate Republican, was appointed as Independent Counsel to investigate the Whitewater affair. But in August 1994 Fiske was replaced by a more conservative Republican, Kenneth Starr, who had served as solicitor general in the Bush administration. In the mid-term elections in November, the Republicans gained control of both houses of Congress for the first time in several decades. The Whitewater affair was now at the centre of a highly charged political field in which a Democratic President faced a Republican-controlled Congress infused with memories of Watergate and the Iran-Contra affair. In May 1995 the Senate voted to begin hearings into Whitewater and related issues, to be chaired by the Republican senator Alfonse D'Amato. The Senate Special Committee began its hearings in summer 1995 and submitted its report the following year. The committee's report was divided along partisan lines.[35] The majority Republican report was severely critical of the way that the Clintons and a number of White House officials had handled the Whitewater issue, alleging among other things that they had engaged in a process of concealment and obstruction, that the removal of documents from Foster's office had amounted to highly improper conduct, that the Clintons had been actively involved in securing loans for Whitewater (rather than merely passive investors, as they had claimed) and that the Clintons had made a series of erroneous deductions on their tax returns in relation to Whitewater; a minority Democrat report denied most of these charges and rejected what it called 'the superheated and untenable conclusions' of the majority report. Hence the results of the Senate investigations were rather inconclusive and did not produce clear-cut evidence that would show that the Clintons had engaged in illegal activity in relation to the Whitewater investment or had been guilty of serious conflicts of interest.

There were, however, a number of political casualties in the Whitewater affair. One of the most senior was the Counsel to the Presi-

dent, Bernard Nussbaum, who resigned in March 1994 in the face
of allegations that he had had improper contact with officials involved
in the RTC investigation of Madison Guaranty. Several Treasury officials – including Roger Altman, the Deputy Secretary of the Treasury and acting head of the RTC, and Jean Hanson, the General
Counsel at the Treasury – also resigned after being criticized for
improper contact with White House officials on the criminal referrals. The Associate Attorney General Webster Hubbell was forced to
resign from the Justice Department when questions were asked about
his unorthodox billing practices when he had been a partner at the
Rose Law Firm; Hubbell was subsequently indicted for fraud and
imprisoned. The Clintons' business associates in Arkansas, Jim and
Susan McDougal, were both indicted on numerous charges including conspiracy and fraud and sentenced to prison, where Jim
McDougal died in 1998. No action was taken against the Clintons
themselves over Whitewater, but the story was not over for Bill. The
protracted investigation by the Independent Counsel, Kenneth Starr,
eventually shifted its focus to a cluster of issues stemming from the
President's testimony in the Paula Jones sexual harassment case. The
investigative apparatus set up to examine the Whitewater affair then
became the prosecuting organization at the centre of the Clinton–
Lewinsky scandal.

Why did Whitewater turn into such a prolonged political inquisi-
tion, stretching out over a period of more than five years? In retrospect the amount of effort and expense devoted to investigating the
Whitewater affair seems excessive in relation to the seriousness of
any actual or alleged offence (although, of course, when the investigations began there was a great deal of uncertainty about exactly
what offences had occurred and whether any had been committed
by the Clintons). Whitewater was not a scandal precipitated by the
disclosure of an offence, but rather a scandal driven by the search for
an offence. It was a scandal built on the proliferation of hunches,
hypotheses and suspicions, more or less well founded, of possible
wrongdoing, rather than a scandal built (as with Abscam, for
example) on the public disclosure of a clear-cut offence. As it turned
out, there were serious offences committed in relation to Whitewater, but no evidence emerged to demonstrate conclusively that
serious offences were committed by the Clintons. So why did the
investigations continue for so long?

Part of the explanation is provided by the sheer complexity of the
events and the difficulty of establishing what happened several years
earlier in Arkansas. Part of the explanation is also provided by the

way in which the crisis was handled by the White House: the removal of documents from Foster's office and the reluctance to disclose information about Whitewater served only to fuel speculation and to strengthen the resolve of those who were investigating the affair. But there were several other factors of a more general kind which help to explain the tenacity of the Whitewater investigations. In the first place, Whitewater did not occur in isolation: it came on the heels of Travelgate and of the controversies which had threatened to derail Clinton's presidential campaign (most notably the Gennifer Flowers affair), and it was accompanied by ongoing speculation about other aspects of the Clintons' lives in Arkansas (including speculation about Bill Clinton's extramarital affairs while governor, prompted by the publication in January 1994 of the accounts of state troopers who had formerly worked for him). Whitewater erupted in a context where a good deal of suspicion already existed about the Clintons; and given the occurrence of fresh disclosures that were awkward or embarrassing, the White House found itself having to fight its public relations battles on several fronts at once.

A second important factor was the role played by the media and by conservative political organizations and activists with access to the media. It would be too strong to say that the media 'invented Whitewater'[36] – the Clintons were actually involved in a speculative land deal in Arkansas which went badly wrong – but it is undoubtedly the case that the unfolding of the Whitewater affair from 1993 on was profoundly shaped by the activities of media and para-media organizations. Competition within the media field produced a scramble for stories and for the latest piece of news, and once stories had appeared in one sector of the press they were frequently reported in others. Conservative para-media political organizations like Accuracy in Media and Citizens United played an important role in gathering information, seeking out informants and transmitting potentially damaging material to the mainstream media. Numerous internet sites were also devoted to Whitewater, providing a constant stream of news, gossip and speculation about the events that took place in Arkansas and about the circumstances surrounding Vincent Foster's death. (Speculation about Foster's death was (and remains) a particularly popular topic for these sites, and conspiracy theories abound.) The flood of information and speculation about Whitewater, stemming from a variety of media and para-media sources which were in some cases linked to strongly conservative political agendas, tended to produce a media-driven scandal which quickly acquired a momentum of its own and which, given the complexity of the events and the way the White House responded, could not be easily contained or brought to a close.

There are two further factors which help to explain the prolonged nature of the Whitewater affair: the highly partisan character of the political field and the dynamic of an investigation conducted by an Independent Counsel. When the Republicans gained control of both houses of Congress in November 1994, Whitewater became a focus of party-political struggle and the Republicans, with majorities in both houses, were able to set the terms of the congressional inquiries. Moreover, with the appointment of an Independent Counsel with a relatively open remit,[37] there was always the possibility that the investigation could continue for an extended period of time and move on to issues which were only tangentially related to the original allegations. When the question of appointing an Independent Counsel was discussed by White House staff in January 1994, Bernard Nussbaum strongly opposed the idea, arguing that it would become a 'roving searchlight' that would continue to probe until it found something wrong, even if this had nothing to do with Whitewater – 'They will broaden [the investigation] to areas we haven't even contemplated.'[38] As it turned out, Nussbaum's remarks were prescient.

The Whitewater affair stands in a long line of financial-political scandals which have characterized American politics since the early nineteenth century. Whitewater differed in some respects from many earlier scandals – not least because it centred on activities which took place before Clinton became President and because the extent to which the Clintons were guilty of any wrongdoing remained unclear. But Whitewater was also a testimony to a changed political culture of scandal in the United States, a culture in which the media had become more aggressive in their search for possible wrongdoing by political leaders and less restrained in their willingness to report it, in which politicians had become more inclined to launch formal investigations in cases of alleged wrongdoing and in which scandal itself had become a potent weapon in a political field where questions of character and trust were key focal points of debate. These changes have many sources, but the one event above all others which has shaped the political culture of scandal in the United States since the 1970s is Watergate.

Power Scandals

Power scandals are scandals that involve the misuse or abuse of political power as such. They are based on the alleged occurrence of actions or activities which contravene or seek to circumvent the rules, laws and established procedures that govern the exercise of political power. Power scandals are the 'purest' form of political scandal, in the sense that the rules or conventions whose transgression lies at the heart of political scandal are the rules and conventions governing the form of power – that is, political power – which is constitutive of the political field. Power scandals may involve illicit financial transactions of various kinds, but the financial transactions are not the source of the scandal: they are secondary to the fact that the activities in question are transgressions of rules and laws governing the exercise of political power.

It is partly because power scandals are the purest form of political scandal that they have come to assume such significance within the political field. What we see in power scandals is not the illicit intrusion of extraneous factors – sex, money – into the field of political power, but rather the illicit use of political power itself. This phenomenon is particularly troubling in liberal democratic societies, precisely because these are societies in which the exercise of political power is based on the rule of law; hence the flouting of these rules can be seen or portrayed as an activity which undermines the very foundations of legitimate power. This helps to explain why one of the greatest scandals of the modern period – Watergate – has acquired a kind of paradigmatic status, becoming the reference point (exemplified by the widespread use of the suffix '-gate') for many subsequent scandals. Watergate stands out as an emblem of modern political scandals because what was at stake in this affair was whether the highest officer of the state – the President – had secretly flouted the rules, laws and procedures governing the legitimate exercise of power. But Watergate was also significant because it highlighted the fact that, behind the public settings in which political power is visibly exercised, there were hidden forms of power and decision-making which were unaccountable and which could, on occasion, involve illicit or even criminal action.

In this chapter I shall focus on power scandals and examine some of their features. I shall begin by analysing in more detail the nature of power scandals in relation to the political systems in which they occur. Then I shall look at some examples, but in this chapter I shall proceed a little differently from the previous two. Given the significance of Watergate as a power scandal, I shall begin by analysing this event and its aftermath; I shall also examine the most important American power scandal of the post-Watergate age, the Iran-Contra affair. I shall then turn to Britain and retrace the rise of a particular genre of power scandal – what I shall call 'security scandals' – which, for various reasons, have featured prominently in Britain since the late nineteenth century. The final section will focus on one area of the British political system which has proved to be a particularly fertile source of power scandals in recent years: the blurred boundary between the political and military domains.

The Unveiling of Hidden Powers

A key feature of power scandals is that they involve the unveiling of hidden forms of power, and actual or alleged abuses of power, which had hitherto been concealed beneath the public settings in which power is displayed and the publicly acknowledged procedures through which it is exercised. Of course, there is nothing new about the existence of hidden forms of power within the state. In the traditional monarchical states of medieval and early modern Europe, the affairs of state were conducted in the relatively closed circles of the court, in ways that were largely invisible to most of the subject population. When rulers and royalty appeared before their subjects, they did so primarily in order to affirm their power publicly, not to render public (or visible) the grounds on which their decisions and policies were based, nor to try to persuade the population that their decisions and policies were the right ones. The publicness of power was concerned above all with its exaltation.

The development of the modern constitutional state limited the invisibility of power in certain respects. The secret Cabinet was replaced or supplemented by a range of institutions that were more open and accountable in character. Rules and procedures were developed which defined the conditions under which individuals could acquire and exercise power, as well as the conditions under which they could be removed from office. Important political decisions and matters of policy were subjected to debate within parliamentary bodies, the proceedings of which were made public in varying ways. Citizens were provided with certain basic rights, in some cases formally recognized in law, which guaranteed, among other things, their freedom of expression and association. In these and other respects, power was rendered more visible and decision-making processes became more public and accountable, but this process was neither uniform nor unimpeded. Those in positions of power found new ways of concealing some of their activities and new grounds for doing so. New forms of invisible power and hidden government were invented; new networks and alliances were formed which could operate behind closed doors. The traditional doctrine of the *arcana imperii* – which held that the power of the prince was more effective and true to its aim if it was hidden from the gaze of the people and, like divine will, invisible – was gradually transformed into the modern principle of official secrecy and applied to those areas regarded as vital to the security and stability of the state.[1]

The development of new forms of invisible power, combined with the rise of the media, created the conditions for the emergence of power scandals. These are scandals in which hidden forms of power are suddenly disclosed in the public domain, giving rise to the kind of public disapprobation which constitutes the scandal. There are various ways in which these hidden forms of power can transgress accepted rules and procedures. In some cases they might infringe the rules and procedures which regulate the processes – including electoral processes – by which individuals *acquire* power. In other cases they might violate, bypass or subvert (or threaten to subvert) the publicly agreed procedures that govern the ways in which power can be *exercised* by office holders. As with other types of scandal, power scandals also commonly involve second-order transgressions which may give rise to other charges, such as that of obstruction of justice.

Hidden forms of power can develop in different ways and flourish in a variety of contexts. In some cases they may involve elaborate

networks of power and influence which extend across many different sectors of social and political life. In other cases they may involve
small groups of individuals whose activities are covert and oriented
towards particular goals. One area of state activity which lends itself
with particular ease to the emergence of hidden forms of power is
the area of state security – partly because the emphasis on secrecy in
this domain (in some cases backed up by tough legislation) can create
a veil beneath which covert forms of power can flourish. Hence the
development of the security services, whose origins can be traced
back to the late nineteenth century, has also created the conditions
for the emergence of a particular type of power scandal which occurs
when the veil of secrecy breaks down.

As with financial-political scandals, the nature and extent of power
scandals varies considerably from one national context to another,
and the variations are linked to a range of institutional, legal and cultural differences. Again, Italy provides an illuminating point of comparison. The power scandals which shook the political establishment
in Italy in the 1980s were – like the financial-political scandals with
which they were closely linked – deeply rooted in the forms of clientelistic exchange and mutual interdependence which underpin the
Italian political system. These networks of interdependence created
a shadow government, a *sottogoverno*, in which hidden forms of power
and patronage flourished. It was this hidden system of power that
was partially uncovered by the power scandals of the 1980s, and most
notably by the P-2 affair.[2] As the P-2 scandal unfolded, the system
of *sottogoverno* was partially unveiled, exposing forms of power,
patronage, corruption and even subversion which conflicted with the
principles of democratic government. These hidden forms of power
and patronage constituted a kind of secret state within the state – a
network of powerful individuals and organizations which played a key
role in the exercise of political and economic power but which operated outside the normal mechanisms of democratic accountability.
This was not a network that was opposed to the state but rather one
that was integral to it, providing channels through which information, personal contacts and information flowed. Licio Gelli, the
Grand Master of the P-2 masonic lodge, was an intermediary in this
network, coordinating activities, putting individuals into contact with
one another and facilitating the flows of information and resources
through channels which owed their efficacy to the fact that they were
hidden.

The kinds of power scandals that have occurred in Britain and the
United States are different in many ways from those which erupted

in Italy in the 1980s, even if, like P-2, they are also concerned with hidden forms of power. In the United States, the most significant power scandals of recent decades – Watergate and the Iran-Contra affair – were shaped by some of the distinctive characteristics of the American political system. The formal separation of power between the executive, the legislative and the judiciary, and the massive expansion of the executive branch since the Second World War, created space for the development of clandestine and semi-clandestine organizations within the executive sphere. In Britain, by contrast, the office serving the Prime Minister is relatively small; it is not inconceivable that the Prime Minister's office could harbour clandestine organizations, but there is much less scope in the British political system for developments of this kind. British political life does lend itself to power scandals, but they tend to occur primarily in the sphere of intelligence and security, and on the boundary between the political and military domains.

Watergate and the Iran-Contra Affair

When five men were arrested on the night of 16 June 1972, carrying bugging devices and attempting to break into the headquarters of the Democratic National Committee in a hotel and apartment complex known as Watergate in Washington DC, it was by no means clear why they were engaged in this covert activity or who had authorized the operation.[3] Three of the five were born in Cuba, one was a US-born mercenary who had fought in Cuba, and the fifth was James McCord, a former employee of the CIA who had also worked as a 'security coordinator' for a special committee set up in 1971 to work for the re-election of President Nixon (the CRP or Committee to Re-Elect the President – 'CREEP' as it was commonly called in the press). Address books found on two of the burglars contained the name of Howard Hunt, an ex-CIA man who had been employed as a consultant by Nixon's Special Counsel at the White House, Charles Colson. Both Colson and Hunt had been part of a secret organization (the White House Special Investigations Unit, later known as the 'plumbers') which had been created by Nixon in 1971 to investigate and plug unauthorized leaks in the wake of the Pentagon Papers affair.[4]

The five men appeared in court on the following day, Saturday 17 June. Most identified themselves as 'anti-communists'. When McCord was asked his occupation, he said that he was a security

17 Front page of the *Washington Post*, 19 June 1972, reporting the arrest of five men in connection with the bugging of the Democratic National Committee headquarters in Watergate.

consultant who had retired from the CIA – a comment that appears to have made a strong impression on a local reporter from the *Washington Post*, Bob Woodward, who was in the courtroom to cover the case. Press reports quickly identified McCord as a security coordinator of CRP. During the following weeks and months, Woodward, together with another colleague from the *Post*, Carl Bernstein, as well as a few reporters from the *New York Times* and the Long Island paper *Newsday*, pursued various leads and tried to find evidence which would link the burglary to a secret CRP fund used for espionage and other purposes and which would implicate higher-ranking officials in the White House; their reports helped to keep the story in the public eye, but the evidence was inconclusive. While the break-in initially received a flurry of publicity in the mainstream media, it quickly slid down the news agenda and was displaced by other events. From the beginning, the White House publicly dissociated itself from the break-in and tried to play down its significance – it was, in the words of Ron Ziegler, Nixon's press secretary, 'a third-rate burglary attempt' which didn't merit serious attention. Only much later did it become clear that, in the days following the break-in, Nixon and his aides were very concerned about the potential political fallout and immediately began taking steps to control the situation. They destroyed documents that might contain incriminating evidence and held a series of secret meetings in the Oval Office and elsewhere to plan their strategy – including, as subsequently became clear, their strategy to curtail the FBI's investigation of the affair.

The immediate political impact of Watergate was negligible and Nixon won the November 1972 presidential election by a landslide. But in the course of the following year, the incipient scandal gradually escalated into a major crisis. Fresh life was breathed into the story by the trial of the five burglars and two others (Howard Hunt and Gordon Liddy, an officer at CRP who had also been associated with the 'plumbers'), which began on 8 January 1973 before Judge John Sirica. All seven men were found guilty but none had implicated anyone else. Amid speculation that those convicted had been paid off and that higher officials were being protected, the Senate voted on 7 February to establish a select committee, under the chairmanship of Senator Sam Ervin, to investigate the affair. On 23 March Judge Sirica imposed tough sentences on six of the defendants – up to twenty years for Liddy, thirty-five years for Hunt and forty years for the others. At the same time, Sirica read out in court a letter he had received from McCord which claimed that political pressure had been applied to the defendants to plead guilty and remain silent, that perjury had been committed during the trial and that others involved in the Watergate operation had not been identified. McCord's sentencing was postponed (he was eventually granted immunity from further prosecution), but his letter was a bombshell that broke the case wide open. From this point on, events connected with Watergate received extensive coverage in the media – both the print media and television – and the Watergate cover-up slowly began to unravel.

The Senate select committee began its televised hearings on 17

May and continued into the summer. In late June the former White House Counsel who had been fired by Nixon in April, John Dean, appeared before the committee and gave testimony which effectively implicated Nixon in the cover-up. Senator Howard Baker's now famous question to Dean – 'What did the President know and when did he know it?' – became the leitmotif of the ensuing investigations. It was also during the select committee's hearings that the means to answer Baker's question unexpectedly came into view. On 16 July 1973, Alexander Butterfield, a former assistant of Nixon's Chief of Staff, revealed publicly for the first time a little known secret which he had mentioned to investigators in a closed session a few days earlier, and which was to prove decisive for the subsequent course of events: Nixon had installed a secret system for taping conversations in his private offices in the White House.[5] The revelation was sensational news, and both the select committee and the Special Prosecutor Archibald Cox (who had been appointed in May at the request of the Senate) immediately wrote to the President and asked to hear a number of relevant tapes. Nixon refused, citing executive privilege. Both the committee and the Special Prosecutor responded by issuing subpoenas to gain access to the tapes, initiating a protracted struggle which would eventually culminate in Nixon's resignation. On 19 October Nixon indicated that he was willing to make available a 'summary' of the tapes, the authenticity of which would be verified by one senator (Senator John Stennis). When Cox refused to accept the Stennis compromise, Nixon ordered Cox to be dismissed, abolished the office of Watergate Special Prosecutor and sealed the offices of the Watergate Special Prosecution Force; the Attorney General and Deputy Attorney General both refused to fire Cox and resigned, and Nixon's order was carried out by the Solicitor General, Robert Bork. The so-called 'Saturday Night Massacre' caused an immediate uproar, significantly weakening Nixon's position in the opinion polls[6] and triggering the first serious moves towards impeachment. As the House began to consider the case for impeachment on 23 October, Nixon suddenly reversed his decision and agreed to hand over the subpoenaed tapes.

Once Nixon had abandoned his initial refusal to hand over the tapes, the floodgates were open and, through the autumn of 1973 and spring of 1974, he found himself faced with fresh demands for the release of more and more tapes. He stalled, protested and tried to outmanoeuvre the investigators (most brazenly by releasing edited transcripts in April 1974[7]), but in the end he was obliged to hand

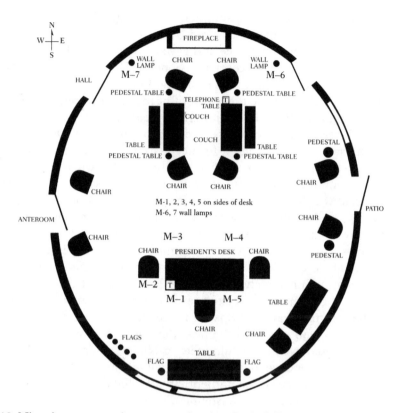

18 Nixon's secret taping system in the Oval Office. Five microphones (M-1 to M-5) were hidden in the President's desk and two (M-6 and M-7) in wall lamps.

over further tapes. The fact that Watergate turned into a struggle over access to the tapes is explained by their perceived significance as forms of evidence which might demonstrate how much the President knew about the break-in, when he knew it and what role he played, if any, in a subsequent cover-up. Nixon had denied absolutely that he had known in advance about the break-in or had participated in any way in a cover-up, so clear evidence to the contrary would put him in an extremely difficult position. In the event, the evidence proved fatal. One of the tapes was found to contain a gap of eighteen and a half minutes, erasing part of a conversation between Nixon and Robert Haldeman, his Chief of Staff, which took place on 20 June 1972 – the day Nixon returned to the White House after the break-in. The unexplained gap, punctuated by a mysterious buzzing noise, served only to fuel distrust and to damage further the President's rapidly waning credibility.

But it was the tape from 23 June 1972, which the Supreme Court ordered Nixon to hand over on 24 July 1974, which finally rendered his position untenable. This was the 'smoking gun' tape in which Nixon and Haldeman could be heard discussing how to curtail the FBI's investigation of the break-in, and Nixon could be heard agreeing with Haldeman's suggestion that the Deputy Director of the CIA, Vernon Walters, should be asked to intervene and tell the FBI to call off their investigation. When Nixon's closest advisers listened to this tape, they doubted whether he could survive the release of the transcript and they urged him to resign. Televised impeachment proceedings were already underway in the House, and some of Nixon's aides felt sure that the release of this transcript would seal his fate. But Nixon decided that he would release the transcript with an accompanying statement and assess the reaction to it, before deciding whether to resign. The transcript was released on Monday 5 August 1974, with a statement in which Nixon admitted that some sections were 'at variance with some of my previous statements'. After a long series of damaging disclosures, this was the last straw. Nixon's remaining support in the House and the Senate rapidly fell away, and some of his most vigorous erstwhile defenders spoke out against him. Impeachment now seemed certain. On 8 August, Nixon announced his resignation in a televised broadcast.

Nixon was never convicted of planning or ordering the break-in which led to his downfall. His offences were second-order transgressions: it was his role in the cover-up, and his repeated denials of any knowledge of a cover-up which subsequently turned out to be untrue, which destroyed his Presidency. The Articles of Impeachment charged him with obstruction of justice and with disobeying subpoenas issued in the course of the congressional inquiry, and his credibility was undermined by the fact that, with the release of the tapes, it became clear that he had misled Congress and the public about the extent of his knowledge of the break-in and about his role in, and knowledge of, the subsequent cover-up.

The release of the tapes also brought into the open a hidden world of power which few ordinary citizens would have imagined. With the publication of the transcripts in April 1974, ordinary people were suddenly able to glimpse a back region of power which had never been visible before, and for many the revelation was shocking. Here was a secret world in which deliberations between the President and

19 The *Washington Post*, 9 August 1974, announces Nixon's final act as President.

his closest advisers seemed hardly distinguishable from the machinations of petty criminals – like 'the back room of a second-rate advertising agency in a suburb of hell', as one commentator unkindly put it.[8] Even though the transcripts were edited by Nixon before being released, the language was crude and the phrase 'expletive deleted' frequently appeared. Time and again, the President and his advisers could be seen discussing how to deal with their enemies, how to contain the Watergate affair and prevent it from harming the White House, and how to secure the silence of those who could make further damaging revelations. The now-infamous conversation between Nixon and John Dean on 21 March 1973, in which Dean explained the seriousness of the situation and warned of 'a cancer within, close to the Presidency, that is growing', is symptomatic; having described the background to the break-in and what he knew about it, Dean continues:

[Dean]—So that is it. That is the extent of the knowledge. So where are the soft spots on this? Well, first of all, there is the problem of the continued blackmail which will not only go on now, but it will go on while these people are in prison, and it will compound the obstruction of justice situation. It will cost money. It is dangerous. People around here are not pros at this sort of thing. This is the sort of thing Mafia people can do: washing money, getting clean money, and things like that. We just don't know about those things, because we are not criminals and not used to dealing in that business.

[President Nixon] – That's right.

D—It is a tough thing to know how to do.

P—Maybe it takes a gang to do that.

D—That's right. There is a real problem as to whether we could even do it. Plus there is a real problem in raising money. Mitchell has been working on raising some money. He is one of the ones with the most to lose. But there is no denying the fact that the White House, in Ehrlichman, Haldeman and Dean are involved in some of the early money decisions.

P—How much money do you need?

D—I would say these people are going to cost a million dollars over the next two years.

P—We could get that. On the money, if you need the money you could get that. You could get a million dollars. You could get it in cash. I know where it could be gotten. It is not easy, but it could be done. But the question is who the hell would handle it? Any ideas on that?

D—That's right. Well, I think that is something that Mitchell ought to be charged with.

P—I would think so too.

D—And get some pros to help him.

P—Let me say there shouldn't be a lot of people running around getting money—[9]

Even in its edited form, this kind of material was deeply disturbing for many readers.[10] With the release of the transcripts, back-region conversations between the President and his closest advisers were suddenly thrust into the public domain, presenting Nixon in a way that was radically at odds with the image of the principled statesman and honest politician that he had tried so hard to cultivate. These were conversations that were never intended for public consumption and, by being made public, they displayed a President with his guard completely down, talking freely and coarsely about activities that were highly questionable in moral, political and legal terms. The reaction in the media and among politicians was overwhelmingly negative. Even the conservative *Chicago Tribune*, a paper which had previously supported Nixon's election and re-election, was now calling for his impeachment: 'We saw the public man in his first administration, and we were impressed. Now in about 300,000 words we have seen the private man, and we are appalled.'[11] Within the broader political field, opinion polls indicated that impeachment sentiment was on the rise, up from 53 per cent before the release of the transcripts to 58 per cent after exposure to their content.[12]

The release of the transcripts was a desperate move by a President under siege. Knowing that his hold on power was becoming increasingly tenuous, Nixon hoped that, by releasing the transcripts to the general public, he would be able to demonstrate that he was innocent of criminal action or intent and would be able thereby to outflank the investigators and his critics in the press and on Capitol Hill (a tactic that had served him well in the fund crisis some twenty years earlier). But the strategy backfired disastrously; it was too late, the level of distrust was too high and Nixon had underestimated the negative impact that the release of the transcripts would have. Although the transcripts did not definitely inculpate Nixon in the cover-up in the way that the 'smoking gun' tape (released four months later) did, they further undermined his rapidly diminishing credibility and support, both on Capitol Hill and in the broader political field.

The release of the transcripts and other disclosures which emerged during the Watergate investigations also opened a window on to a world of clandestine networks and organizations which existed behind the public facade of power. Here was a world of shadow organizations which were created to pursue particular aims, which had their own secret funds and were prepared to use them to finance operations that were on the margins of legality. Groups like the 'plumbers' and 'CREEP' were part of a covert network of surveillance and intelligence-gathering organizations which Nixon built up around himself: they were run by his own people, they bypassed formal institutions (Nixon mistrusted the FBI and did not see eye-to-eye with its Director, J. Edgar Hoover) and they were ultimately accountable to Nixon and his small coterie of advisers and aides. Of course, Nixon did not invent covert organizations in the political sphere (just as he did not invent secret taping systems in the White House). But it was during the Watergate investigations that these covert organizations, with their secret funds and dubious methods, were brought into the full light of day.

Nixon was thoroughly disgraced by the quagmire of Watergate. Although he was formally pardoned by President Ford and never indicted on criminal charges, his political career was abruptly ended and his reputation permanently tarnished by the events which led to his resignation. Many of the individuals involved in the cover-up were convicted on criminal charges and served prison sentences – Gordon Liddy served fifty-two months, Haldeman and Ehrlichman served eighteen months, the former Attorney General John Mitchell served nineteen months, Colson served seven months and John Dean served four. The political careers of these and other individuals also ended with Watergate. Some forged new careers in the business world and in the media; many wrote memoirs and appeared as guest speakers on television and on the lecture circuit, activities that rewarded them handsomely. But their careers in the field of political administration were effectively over.

The broader political consequences of Watergate are less easy to document but were, in all likelihood, both far-reaching and profound. The ordeal of Watergate had a discernible impact on (1) the legislative activity and political climate of Congress, (2) the practical conduct of presidential politics, and (3) the political orientation of the media. Congress passed a number of laws in the late 1970s which had a traceable connection to Watergate – most notably the Ethics in Government Act of 1978, which established the office of Special Prosecutor (subsequently renamed the Independent Counsel) to investigate cases of alleged wrongdoing by senior officials in a presidential administration.[13] Moreover, many commentators have noted how, in the aftermath of Watergate, the conduct of American presidential politics altered in various ways, as actual and aspiring presidents (and their teams of aides and advisers) struggled to avoid the kind of catastrophe that had engulfed the Nixon administration.[14] The experience of Watergate also contributed to a gradual shift in the rules of engagement of the media, as journalists, editors and other individuals with access to mediated forms of communication became more inclined to search for, seize upon and make public information and allegations concerning the private, covert and potentially compromising activities of presidents and other political figures.

The immediate post-Watergate period was marked, as we have seen, by a series of political scandals of varying degrees of significance, most involving allegations of financial irregularities. But the major scandal which preoccupied American politics in the 1980s was, like Watergate, primarily a scandal about power and its misuse. When the Iran-Contra affair began to break in autumn 1986, it revealed a pattern of covert activities that was similar in some ways to that revealed by the Watergate inquiry. For as the story of the Iran-Contra connection began to unfold, it became clear that officials within the Reagan administration were pursuing, in effect, a covert foreign policy, relying on secret funding, shadow organizations and a variety of intermediaries to bypass official channels of government.

The Iran-Contra scandal initially broke when an article appeared in a Beirut magazine, *Al Shiraa*, on 3 November 1986, revealing that Reagan's former National Security Advisor, Robert McFarlane, had been involved in a secret mission to Tehran earlier in that year to discuss the provision of military supplies to Iran in return for the release of American hostages who were being held in Lebanon.[15] The story was confirmed the following day by the Speaker of the Iranian parliament, Ali Akbar Hashemi Rafsanjani. By 6 November the story was front page news in the national press in the United States. The disclosure of the secret mission was potentially extremely embarrassing for President Reagan, since he had publicly declared on numerous occasions that he would not deal with terrorists and since his administration was at the time advocating a worldwide ban on arms sales to Iran. The administration's initial response to the *Al Shiraa* revelation was to say nothing, but the pressure rapidly mounted as the media began to speculate about a Watergate-style cover-up. In an attempt to quell further speculation, Reagan made a televised speech on 13 November in which he firmly denied that his administration had traded weapons for hostages. The pressure, however, refused to die down; inconsistencies in Reagan's statements to the press and divisions within his administration served only to fuel further speculation. By 20 November the administration was in disarray. The following day Reagan's Attorney General, Edwin

Meese, agreed to investigate the affair and to report back to the President on 24 November.

It was during Meese's hurried investigation that another dimension emerged – 'the secret within the secret', as one of the chief protagonists, Oliver North, subsequently described it.[16] While looking through documents in North's office at the National Security Council (where North, a Lieutenant Colonel in the Marine Corps, had been employed since 1981), Meese's investigators came across a memo dated April 1986 which appeared to be from North to the National Security Advisor, Admiral John Poindexter, and which indicated that some of the proceeds from the sale of arms to Iran would be used to purchase weapons for the Contras in Nicaragua, to help them continue their struggle against the left-wing Sandinista government. (It subsequently emerged that North had been shredding documents for several weeks before Meese's investigation, and even continued shredding while the investigation was underway, but this memo he had somehow missed.) The discovery that funds from the sale of arms to Iran had been secretly 'diverted' to the Contras was potentially explosive, since Congress had passed a series of restrictions between 1982 and 1986 (known as the Boland Amendments) which were intended to limit or preclude the involvement of US intelligence agencies in Nicaragua, either directly, or indirectly through the disbursement of funds. Meese quickly saw the political dangers: not only would the administration now be faced with the charge of trading arms for hostages, but it might also be accused of using the proceeds from the arms sales to fund covertly, and in breach of the will of Congress, a paramilitary organization in Nicaragua.

Meese was concerned about the possibility that this new information would leak out and provide Reagan's opponents in Congress with the kind of ammunition that could be very damaging for the President and his administration.[17] Meese met with Reagan and his Chief of Staff, Donald Regan, on Monday 24 November and they decided to convene a televised press conference the following day to make the information public. At noon on the 25th, Reagan and Meese walked out to face the waiting reporters and cameras; Reagan announced that Poindexter had resigned and North had been sacked, and Meese explained that, in the course of his inquiries, he had discovered that funds derived from the sale of arms to Iran had been diverted to the Contras. Meese insisted that no government official apart from North and Poindexter had known anything about this operation, and that the President knew nothing about it until Meese reported it to him. Further investigations were quickly set in motion.

-- The residual funds from this transaction are allocated as
   follows:

   - $2 million will be used to purchase replacement TOWs
     for the original 508 sold by Israel to Iran for the
     release of Benjamin Weir. This is the only way that we
     have found to meet our commitment to replenish these
     stocks.

   - $12 million will be used to purchase critically needed
     supplies for the Nicaraguan Democratic Resistance
     Forces. This materiel is essential to cover shortages
     in resistance inventories resulting from their current
     offensives and Sandinista counter-attacks and to
     "bridge" the period between now and when Congressionally-
     approved lethal assistance (beyond the $25 million in
     "defensive" arms) can be delivered.

The ultimate objective in the trip to Tehran is to commence the
process of improving U.S.-Iranian relations. Both sides are
aware that the Iran-Iraq War is a major factor that must be
discussed. We should not, however, view this meeting as a
session which will result in immediate Iranian agreement to
proceed with a settlement with Iraq. Rather, this meeting, the
first high-level U.S.-Iranian contact in five years, should be
seen as a chance to move in this direction. These discussions,
as well as follow-on talks, should be governed by the Terms of
Reference (TOR) (Tab A) with the recognition that this is,
hopefully, the first of many meetings and that the hostage issue,
once behind us, improves the opportunities for this relationship.

Finally, we should recognize that the Iranians will undoubtedly
want to discuss additional arms and commercial transactions as
"quids" for accommodating ████████████████████, Nicaragua,
and Iraq. Our emphasis on the Soviet military and subversive
threat, a useful mechanism in bringing them to agreement on the
hostage issue, has also served to increase their desire for means
to protect themselves against/deter the Soviets.

RECOMMENDATION

That the President approve the structure depicted above under
"Current Situation" and the Terms of Reference at Tab A.

                Approve _____   Disapprove _____

Attachment
     Tab A - U.S.-Iranian Terms of Reference

20 The final page of a memo from Oliver North *circa* 4 April 1986 and entitled 'Release of American Hostages in Beirut' – the so-called 'diversion memo'. It was the discovery of this memo during the search of North's office in November 1986 which revealed that residual funds from the sale of arms to Iran had been secretly 'diverted' to the Contras. There was no signature or initial at the bottom to indicate that the President had seen and approved the memo.

On 26 November Reagan announced the establishment of a special commission, headed by Senator John Tower, to examine the National Security Council (NSC) and its role in the affair. On 2 December, under pressure from Congress, he agreed to the appointment of an Independent Counsel to investigate the sale of arms to Iran and the diversion of funds to the Contras; on 19 December, a federal court appointed Lawrence Walsh to this post. Congress resolved to carry out its own investigations, which included televised hearings before special committees of the House and Senate between May and August 1987.

In the course of these investigations, the intricate details of the covert operations involved in the Iran-Contra affair gradually emerged into the public arena. It became clear that US involvement in the sale of arms to Iran had begun in July 1985, when Reagan's National Security Advisor at the time, Robert McFarlane, had met with his Israeli counterpart to discuss the idea that US arms might be supplied to Iran, with the prospect that this might lead to the release of American hostages in Lebanon. In August the first shipment of a hundred TOW anti-tank missiles took place, and in September another four hundred were shipped; the missiles were supplied to Iran from Israeli stocks which would be replenished by the Americans, and a complex network of intermediary arms dealers and foreign bank accounts was used to shield the countries concerned. In subsequent deliveries the CIA and NSC became more actively involved. An evolving pattern emerged in which the US Army supplied weapons and military spare parts to the CIA, who sold them to two middlemen named Richard Secord (a retired US Air Force officer) and Albert Hakim (an Iranian-born businessman), who operated a Swiss bank account called Lake Resources; they sold them to an Iranian arms dealer named Manucher Ghorbanifar, who collaborated with a Saudi Arabian financier and arms broker named Adnan Khashoggi; and they sold them on to the Iranian government. The money flowed in the opposite direction through a variety of bank accounts (mainly in Switzerland), with each party taking a cut. Oliver North took on a key role in coordinating the operation. The deals were loosely linked to assurances from the Iranians that they would use their influence among pro-Iranian groups in Lebanon to help secure the release of American hostages. In early 1986 North came up with the idea (prompted, according to North, by a suggestion from Ghorbanifar) of using some of the profits from these sales to purchase supplies for the Contras, with whom he had been working covertly since 1984. Since Congress had cut off the flow of resources to the Contras, North had helped to raise funds through private and third-country sources and to build up a clandestine network – involving ships, warehouses, aircraft and a secret airstrip in Costa Rica – for the supply of military equipment and other provisions. By proposing to channel some of the proceeds from the sale of arms to Iran into the Contra supply network, he forged a connection between two covert operations which had hitherto been carried out relatively independently.

The disclosure of these and other details into the public domain had the potential to be extremely damaging to the Reagan administration, but the Iran-Contra affair never developed into the kind of political catastrophe that Watergate had been. The investigations became a focal point of political commentary in the media throughout 1987, and there were some political casualties – Donald Regan, the White House Chief of Staff, resigned on 27 February 1987, the day after the report of the Tower Commission was published, and North, Poindexter and three other men were indicted on criminal charges. (North was convicted on three relatively minor charges and given a suspended three-year prison sentence, and Poindexter was convicted on five counts and sentenced to six months in prison, but both men successfully appealed against their convictions.) Although there was much speculation at the outset of an impending crisis that might lead to impeachment, Reagan himself emerged relatively unscathed. Why? How was the crisis contained?

Partly it was contained because no incriminating evidence was found that clearly implicated other senior members of the administration. There was no equivalent of the 'smoking gun' tape which had incriminated Nixon, and Oliver North had shredded a great deal of the relevant documentation. It seems likely that Reagan had known about the secret attempts to use the sale of weapons to Iran as a lever to secure the release of hostages as early as December 1985, but his role in the initiative and the extent of his knowledge remained unclear. (McFarlane said that Reagan had orally approved the first shipment, while Donald Regan said that he had done so only retrospectively; Reagan himself told the Tower Commission that he could not recall whether he had approved it or not.) The administration firmly denied that Reagan had known anything about the diversion of funds to the Contras until he was told by Meese in November 1986, at which point Poindexter resigned and North was sacked. North subsequently claimed that Reagan must have known about the diversion, but he had to concede that he had never communicated directly with the President about it. (North said that he had sent numerous memos to Poindexter about the diversion and believed that these memos were passed up the line to the President 'because documents of this type generally were',[18] but copies of most of these memos had been shredded by North and he had no firm evidence that any had been received, read or approved by the President.)

Moreover, it is clear that there was a deliberate strategy on the part of some individuals in the administration to insulate Reagan from the potential consequences of scandal in the event that the covert operations became public. This emerged in the course of Poindexter's testimony before the congressional hearings on 15 July 1987. Washington was awash with rumours that Poindexter would defend himself by saying that he had told the President about the diversion on more than one occasion, but Poindexter went on record saying that he alone had taken the decision to divert the funds and that, while he had assumed that the President would have approved of the operation had he told him about it, he never did explicitly tell him: 'although I was convinced that we could properly do it and that the President would approve if asked, I made a very deliberate decision not to ask the President so that I could insulate him from the decision and provide some future deniability for the President if it ever leaked out.'[19] The concern to ensure future deniability – or 'plausible deniability' as it was also described by Poindexter and others – shaped the ways in which the covert operations were planned and executed and helped to determine the extent to which (or the form in which) knowledge of these operations was passed on to senior government officials, and especially the President. It was a concern for which Reagan would have cause to be grateful. Thanks to Poindexter's discretion and his willingness to accept full responsibility ('the buck stops here with me'[20]), coupled with the dearth of incriminating evidence, the covert operations could be plausibly attributed to the initiative of an overzealous employee in the NSC whose activities were authorized by Poindexter alone. Reagan pleaded ignorance or an inability to recall exactly what he did or did not know or do at earlier points in time – a plea which, given the general frailty of his grasp of detail, did not appear altogether implausible.

As power scandals, both Watergate and the Iran-Contra affair were rooted in the distinctive characteristics of the American political system. Each scandal had its own peculiar features and personnel, but both were shaped by certain broad characteristics of the American political system and their transformation over time – in particular, by the formal separation between the executive, the legislature and the judiciary, and by the growing power of the executive branch.

With the expansion of the American state in the course of the twentieth century and the rise of the United States as a global power, the executive branch has expanded substantially and the White House has assumed an increasingly important role in the formation and implementation of policy. The White House staff was very small throughout the nineteenth century and still numbered only 51 in 1943; by 1971, the President's immediate staff had risen to more than 580 full-time employees.[21] Any incoming President must bring with him a large number of trusted advisers and administrators who will help him to run the executive branch and who will provide him with his own sources of expertise. Moreover, unlike the British Prime Minister who is generally the leader of the largest party in Parliament, the President is elected in a process that is formally independent of congressional elections. Hence it is not uncommon for a President elected with a large majority to find himself facing a Congress in which one or both of the houses are controlled by the opposing party.

In these circumstances one can understand how organizations like the 'plumbers' and 'CREEP' could emerge, and how they could operate in a clandestine or semi-clandestine fashion: these were organizations which were set up to further the aims of executive power, and their activities – in some cases plainly criminal – were shielded by the complexity of the ever expanding White House bureaucracy. It is also quite understandable that shadow organizations of this kind would operate in autonomous or quasi-autonomous ways, with responsibility for operational details being delegated downwards in the chain of command. Even presidents (like Nixon) who had a hands-on approach to the exercise of power might well remain ignorant of the day-to-day activities and detailed plans of the many members of staff, organizations and shadow organizations which operate broadly within the executive sphere. Moreover, given the separation of power between the executive, legislative and judicial spheres, it is not surprising that the unfolding of the Watergate scandal was shaped by the struggle between the different branches of government. Many of the key disclosures emerged during the hearings of the special investigating committee established by the Senate; and, once the existence of the tapes became known, access to them became the pivotal issue in the unfolding of the scandal, an issue which brought the executive branch into direct conflict with Congress and the Supreme Court.

It is clear that the Iran-Contra affair was also rooted in the activities of clandestine or semi-clandestine organizations operating within the executive branch – in this case, under the umbrella of the National Security Council, an agency set up in 1947 to advise the President on matters of national security. The fact that the NSC was given such a significant role in the Reagan administration was part of a broader attempt by the White House to retain control of foreign policy in the face of growing pressure from Congress. In sensitive areas of foreign policy, such as those involving covert operations, the strategy of the Reagan administration was to proceed in ways which circumvented the normal channels, and hence avoided the formal mechanisms of scrutiny and accountability. This strategy involved several different elements.[22] First, decision-making concerning covert operations was concentrated in a small circle of individuals who could be delegated with the authority to devise the *modus operandi* without being obliged to report the details of all operations to higher authorities, thereby implementing the broad policy objectives of the administration while preserving deniability. Second, the resources for covert operations were drawn to a large extent from unofficial sources, such as foreign governments, wealthy individuals and, in the case of the Iran-Contra affair, from the proceeds derived from the secret sale of arms. Third, many of the personnel involved were private individuals – in some cases former employees of the military or the CIA – who could be contracted to provide specific services or support. (In setting up the Iran-Contra operation, for example, Oliver North relied heavily on the services of Richard Secord, a retired military officer with a long experience of covert operations, and on Secord's business partner, Albert Hakim. Secord handled many of the operational duties, hiring specialized staff, setting up shell corporations overseas, purchasing weapons and ammunition, building warehouses, buying and leasing airplanes, hiring pilots, etc.) By relying on private individuals and unofficial sources of finance, covert operations could be planned and carried out in ways that bypassed normal channels of public accountability or congressional review.

The fact that Watergate and the Iran-Contra affair were both rooted in distinctive features of the American political system does not of course mean that power scandals are distinctively or predominantly American – on the contrary, they have flourished (and continue to flourish) elsewhere. It simply means that the power scandals which occur elsewhere are similarly shaped by the characteristics of the political systems in which they are embedded. In Britain, the office of the Prime Minister is relatively small and provides much less scope for the development of clandestine and semi-clandestine organizations. Moreover, since the British Prime Minister is generally the leader of the largest party in Parliament, the potential for conflict between the executive and legislative branches of government is less pronounced. But this does not mean that there are no power scandals in Britain. British political life is also prone to power scandals, but they tend to occur in certain areas and to assume certain forms. Where British political life lends itself to power scandals is above all in the sphere of intelligence and security, and in those sectors of ministerial responsibility which bear upon it.

The Rise of Security Scandals

Why is the sphere of intelligence and state security a potential breeding ground for political scandal? And why has Britain experienced a series of high-profile security scandals in the postwar period? There are several factors that help to explain the propensity for political scandal within the sphere of intelligence and state security. To begin with, the sphere of state security has been characterized by the growth of organizations and networks – such as the Special Branch, MI5 and the SIS (or MI6) in Britain, and the FBI and CIA in the United States – which operate largely covertly. The origins of these organizations can be traced back to the late nineteenth century, when nation-states began to centralize and professionalize the activities of surveillance and intelligence-gathering. In Britain, the Special Branch of the Metropolitan Police emerged in the 1880s, largely as a response to the Fenian bombing campaign of 1881–5.[23] It was explicitly conceived of as a secret network, to be staffed by specially selected police officers, which could monitor the activities of Irish nationalists in Britain, Ireland and America, with the aim of detecting and averting further bombing campaigns. The foundations of the modern British secret service were laid during the first decade of the twentieth century, when fears about the activities of German spies in Britain led to the creation of the Secret Service Bureau in 1909.[24] The Bureau was initially divided into military and naval sections, but these were soon transformed into a home department responsible for counter-espionage (the precursor of MI5) and a foreign department responsible for espionage (the forerunner of the Secret Intelligence Service – SIS, otherwise known as MI6). Both departments expanded rapidly during the First World War, when the systematic gathering of intelligence, and the decoding of enemy messages transmitted by radio signals, became a crucial part of the war effort.

The early security services were based on the twin principles of secrecy and limited accountability.[25] It was assumed that the activities of the security services should remain as secret as possible for as long as possible, and that secret service personnel were accountable in their activities to the heads of their departments and to the Prime Minister but not to Parliament. 'It is the essence of a Secret Service that it must be secret,' remarked Austen Chamberlain, speaking to the Commons as Foreign Secretary in November 1924, 'and if you once begin disclosure it is perfectly obvious to me, as to hon. Gentlemen opposite, that there is no longer any Secret Service and that you must do without it.'[26] The emphasis on secrecy was backed up in Britain by a series of Official Secrets Acts which turned certain types of unauthorized disclosures into criminal offences. The first Official Secrets Act, passed in 1889, was precipitated by the dismissal of a draughtsman in Chatham Dockyard for selling confidential information about warship design; a second Act, passed in 1911, extended the scope of the law to apply to all possessors of official information, whether government employees or not, and eased the conditions of its application.[27] The Official Secrets Acts turned the idea of state secrecy into a legally enforceable condition. In the nineteenth century and before, state secrecy had been a matter of discretion and self-restraint governed by gentlemanly codes of honour; but from the late nineteenth century on, state secrecy became a matter of legal regulation, and unauthorized disclosures were punishable as crimes.

The development of security services based on the principles of secrecy and limited accountability created the conditions under which security scandals could flourish. The veil of secrecy and the lack of accountability provided a cover for activities which could become a source of scandal on those occasions – albeit relatively rare – when the veil of secrecy broke down. The history of the security services from the late nineteenth century to the present day is peppered with scandals of this kind. We can distinguish between two different types of security scandal. One type of security scandal stems from the fact that secrecy and limited accountability can serve as a cover for – and perhaps a temptation to – roguery and wrongdoing on the part of security and intelligence personnel, as well as for an excess of zeal. I shall describe this as the 'dirty tricks' scandal. Individuals are less likely to follow strict codes of behaviour if they think that they are unlikely to be found out; and the temptation to bend the rules may be all the greater when these individuals are confronting opponents who seem prepared to use all the means at their disposal to achieve their ends. Moreover, secrecy is likely to arouse suspicions of roguery and wrongdoing and to fuel speculation, even if it is difficult to determine for certain whether it occurred.

Suspicions of roguery and wrongdoing have been present since the very origins of the modern security services. With the formation of the Special Branch in the 1880s, fears were frequently expressed that police officers, operating beneath the veil of secrecy, would act as *agents provocateurs*, fabricating evidence or provoking criminal action in order to secure a conviction. For the most part, suspicions of this kind remained at the level of speculation and accusation; they were a source of potential scandal, but so long as there was no clear-cut evidence of wrongdoing, the political damage could be contained. Such was the case, for example, with the conviction of John Daly and James Egan for treason and dynamite offences in August 1884.[28] Daly had been arrested at Birkenhead station, carrying parcels which contained parts for grenades. Egan owned a house in Birmingham where Daly had stayed; he was arrested by police who found a canister of nitroglycerine buried in the garden. Daly was sentenced to life imprisonment and Egan to twenty years. But two years later the Chief Constable of Birmingham told a member of his watch committee, Alderman Henry Manton, that the grenades had been planted on Daly; they had, he claimed, been bought in America with money supplied by the Irish police and put in Daly's coat pockets by an agent in their pay. On the basis of information from another source, Manton suspected that the nitroglycerine found in Egan's garden had also been planted. Manton wrote to Gladstone, Home Secretary Matthews and Parnell. On 24 September 1890 the allegations were reported in *The Times*, and the issue was debated in the House of Commons in August 1891 and February 1892. Manton pursued the case for ten years but his efforts were to no avail, since the Home Office never admitted impropriety and Manton could never prove it.

Although the controversy surrounding the convictions of Daly and Egan never erupted into a fully fledged political scandal, many of the essential ingredients were there; what was missing was some clear-cut evidence of wrongdoing and a determined campaign by the media to expose it. But the Daly and Egan affair foreshadowed a set of circumstances which would haunt the security services throughout the twentieth century: the veil of secrecy beneath which they operated would serve as a constant temptation to act in illegal and improper ways, thereby running the risk of being exposed and discredited by bungled operations, unauthorized revelations and unwelcome media attention. Countless incidents attest to the fact that this risk is not merely academic, from the controversial claims of Patrick McIntyre – a disgruntled former officer of the Special Branch who in 1895 published a series of damning allegations in *Reynolds's Newspaper* about the underhand methods used by the service[29] – to a series of high-profile revelations and allegations in the 1980s and 1990s which have pointed an unwanted spotlight on the activities of the security services.

In 1988, for example, the security services found themselves at the centre of a major political controversy precipitated by the killing of three members of the Irish Republican Army (IRA) in Gibraltar. The three IRA members were shot dead by officers of the British security services on 6 March 1988, following intelligence reports that they were allegedly involved in the final preparations for a bomb attack against a changing of the guard ceremony outside the Governor's residence. The three were found to be unarmed. The shootings elicited a strong reaction in the press and in some political quarters. The Irish government expressed serious concern that the three had been shot dead rather than arrested, and a number of politicians in Britain and elsewhere called for a public explanation. At the inquest in Gibraltar, the six members of the security services involved in the operation and a senior MI5 officer (all of whom appeared behind a screen at the inquest) insisted that they had not planned to kill the IRA members but had acted to prevent the detonation of what they believed to be a car bomb. The inquest concluded that the killings had been lawful, but many people remained unconvinced.

Other troubling revelations emerged in the late 1980s when the British government attempted to suppress the publication of *Spycatcher*, the memoirs of a former MI5 agent, Peter Wright.[30] Wright had worked for MI5 from 1955 until he retired from the service in January 1976. Following his retirement, he went to live in Australia, where he wrote his memoirs. It was widely assumed that the memoirs would contain detailed allegations about treachery and irregular activities within MI5 – Wright had already made it clear, in a television interview in 1984, that he believed that the former Director General of MI5, Sir Roger Hollis, had been a double agent working for the Soviet Union (an allegation that had been made several years earlier by the journalist Chapman Pincher[31]) and the press had already leaked allegations of dirty tricks, including the claim that MI5 had drawn up plans to remove Harold Wilson from office as Prime Minister during 1974–6. The British government moved to suppress the publication of *Spycatcher*, obtaining a temporary injunction from the Supreme Court of New South Wales in September 1985 on the grounds that publication would contravene the Official Secrets Act. But the court rejected the British government's application for a permanent injunction and *Spycatcher* was published in Australia in October 1987. Despite the widespread availability of the book in Australia, the United States and elsewhere, the British government tried to prevent the media in the UK from repeating and discussing its allegations, but both the High Court and the Court of Appeal in London rejected the government's application, largely on the grounds that the worldwide dissemination of the book had already undermined any duty of confidence which might apply to newspapers and other third parties.

The *Spycatcher* affair also highlighted a second type of security scandal which has featured prominently in the political history of twentieth-century Britain – the counter-intelligence (or 'spy') scandal. The highly sensitive character of Wright's memoirs stemmed in part from the fact that they stood in a long line of very damaging revelations about duplicity and betrayal at the heart of Britain's security services. The veil of secrecy which surrounded the activities (and even the existence) of these services also helped to create an environment in which further secrets could evolve and remain hidden from insiders as well as outsiders – secrets within secrets. This pattern began to develop in a significant way in the 1930s, when Soviet intelligence successfully recruited a number of long-term penetration agents (subsequently known as 'moles') while they were undergraduates at Cambridge, in the hope that they would eventually move into the upper echelons of the British establishment and work within it. The most notorious of these agents were Guy Burgess and Donald Maclean, but they were not alone. An old Etonian, Guy Burgess went up to Trinity College, Cambridge in 1929 to read history. He entered a world where communist ideas held some attraction for bright, iconoclastic students who, despite their privileged backgrounds, had little sympathy for the established political parties, and who were inclined to see the Soviet Union as a beacon of hope for the future. Like many of his contemporaries, Burgess was drawn to communism and spent a brief spell as a member of the Communist Party. After leaving Cambridge he worked for *The Times* and the BBC, eventually joining a special intelligence unit of the War Office in 1938. He moved to the Foreign Office in 1944 and, in November 1950, he was sent to the British Embassy in Washington DC as Second Secretary. Donald Maclean went up to Trinity Hall, Cambridge in 1931, where he read modern languages. He overlapped with Burgess and, like him, was drawn to communism. In 1934 Maclean joined the Foreign Office and, in 1944, he was posted to the British Embassy in Washington, where he served as First Secretary and then Head of Chancery. As part of his duties Maclean frequently visited the headquarters of the US Atomic Energy Commission, and he served as secretary to the Combined Policy Committee on Atomic Development.

American intelligence services became suspicious of Maclean after monitoring the flow of coded information from the Soviet consulate in New York, from which they inferred that the Soviets had a source inside the British Embassy. Circumstantial evidence pointed to Maclean (the intercepts revealed that the source visited the consulate twice a week, which coincided with Maclean's trips between Washington and New York to visit his wife, who was staying at her mother's home), but the evidence was not conclusive. In 1948 Maclean was recalled to London and then transferred to Cairo, where he took up a post as Head of Chancery at the British Embassy. He drank excessively and his psychological condition deteriorated; after several outbursts of violent behaviour, he was transferred back to London and given psychiatric treatment, before being appointed head of the American Department at the Foreign Office. In May 1951 Burgess was recalled from Washington for bad behaviour; given his eccentric, bohemian lifestyle, this reprimand was not surprising, but the incident which led to his recall was almost certainly engineered. Although it was not realized by the authorities at the time, Burgess returned to London with the knowledge that Maclean was under suspicion. MI5 was due to interrogate Maclean on 28 May 1951, but three days before the planned interrogation, Burgess and Maclean suddenly disappeared. Neither MI5 nor MI6 seemed to know for certain where they had gone. (In fact, they had driven to Southampton in a rented car and caught an overnight ferry to France.) In July 1952 Maclean's wife left London with their three children to live in Paris and then Geneva; on 11 September 1953 she and the children also disappeared, having told her mother (who was staying with her in Geneva) that she was going to visit an old friend – a certain 'Robin Muir', who did not in fact exist – at his villa near Montreux. Burgess and Maclean eventually resurfaced at a press conference in Moscow in February 1956, issuing written statements claiming that they had left England 'to work for peace'. Both died in exile – Burgess in 1963 and Maclean twenty years later.

The sudden disappearance of Burgess and Maclean on 25 May 1951 was kept out of the public eye for a fortnight, but in early June the press was filled with dramatic accounts of their midnight flight.

On 7 June the government officially acknowledged that the two men had disappeared, but refrained from commenting on the widespread speculation that they were spies. The government resisted calls for the establishment of a royal commission to investigate the circumstances of their disappearance and the security implications of the case. But the whereabouts of Burgess and Maclean remained unknown to the public until September 1955, when the Sunday newspaper the *People* published the story of Vladimir Petrov, a high-ranking Soviet diplomat in Australia who worked for Soviet intelligence and who defected in April 1954. Petrov revealed, among other things, that both Burgess and Maclean were spies who had been recruited while they were students at Cambridge, and that they had been in the Soviet Union since their defection in 1951. These revelations prompted the government to issue a White Paper which documented some of the details of the case.

The White Paper answered some questions but left others unresolved. One question it left unresolved was whether Burgess and Maclean had been tipped off by a high-ranking official who was in a position to know that the net was beginning to close around them – the so-called 'third man'. The man who had fallen under suspicion was Harold 'Kim' Philby. Philby had known Burgess and Maclean since their undergraduate days together at Cambridge. He worked as a foreign correspondent for *The Times* in the 1930s, and joined MI6 in 1941, eventually assuming responsibility for Soviet counter-intelligence. In October 1949 he was appointed First Secretary at the British Embassy in Washington, where he was responsible for security liaison with the CIA and the FBI. Philby's assignment to Washington overlapped with that of Burgess, and Burgess stayed with Philby and his family at their Washington home. Following the defection of Burgess and Maclean, it was suspected by many that Philby had passed on sensitive CIA information to Burgess, who used his recall to London as the occasion to warn Maclean and orchestrate their escape. In a statement to the House of Commons on 7 November 1955, the then Foreign Secretary Harold Macmillan explained that Philby had been asked to resign from the Foreign Service in July 1951, on the grounds that investigations carried out after the disappearance of Burgess and Maclean had revealed that he had had communist associates during and after his university days, but that no evidence had been found to show that he was responsible for warning Burgess and Maclean. Philby was subsequently re-employed by MI6 as an agent in the Middle East, based in Beirut and using his position as a foreign correspondent for the *Observer* and *The Economist* as a cover. But further suspicion was cast on him in 1962, following the defection to the West of Anatoli Golitsyn, a KGB officer, who informed the CIA that Philby was a Soviet spy. Philby was questioned again in January 1963, when he finally confessed that he had been a Soviet agent since 1934; he also admitted that he had warned Maclean in 1951. On the night of 23 January 1963, Philby disappeared from Beirut, eventually turning up in Moscow where he remained until his death in 1988.

But all was not over. On 15 November 1979, the then Prime Minister Margaret Thatcher made a statement to the House of Commons in which she revealed that Sir Anthony Blunt – a prominent art historian who had held various appointments in the Royal Household from 1945 to 1978 – had passed secret information to the Soviet Union while he was a member of the security services during the war. The statement followed a great deal of speculation in the press, precipitated by the publication in 1979 of Andrew Boyle's *The Climate of Treason* which suggested that an individual holding a high public office – unnamed by Boyle – had been the 'fourth man' in the network involving Philby, Burgess and Maclean.[32] Anthony Blunt had gone up to Trinity College, Cambridge in 1926, and remained for several years as a Fellow after he finished his undergraduate studies. He became a close friend of Guy Burgess, both of whom were members of the exclusive Cambridge club known as The Apostles. Blunt joined MI5 in 1940 and worked for the service throughout the war. In 1945 he resigned from MI5 and resumed his career as an art historian, rising quickly to a senior and respected position within the field. He was appointed Surveyor of the King's Pictures in 1945, and Surveyor of the Queen's Pictures in 1952; appointed Director of the Courtauld Institute and Professor of History of Art in 1947; awarded a knighthood in 1956; and appointed Adviser for the Queen's Pictures and Drawings in 1972. Soon after the disappearance of Burgess and Maclean, however, Blunt had come under suspicion as a possible collaborator. He was interviewed on numerous occasions, but there was not sufficient evidence to convict him. In 1964 the then Attorney General, Sir John Hobson, decided that it would be in the public interest to try to obtain a confession from Blunt, and he authorized the offer of immunity from prosecution if he were to confess. Blunt then admitted that he had been an agent for Soviet intelligence, that he had 'talent-spotted' for them at Cambridge during the 1930s, that he had passed on sensitive information to the Russians while he was working for MI5, and that he had used his previous contacts to help Burgess and Maclean to defect in 1951. Blunt's confession (and the details of it) remained a closely guarded secret; the Queen's private secretary was informed, but Blunt was allowed to retain his appointment in the Royal Household. It was only after the details became public in 1979 that Blunt was stripped of his knighthood.

The activities of Burgess, Maclean, Philby and Blunt are a vivid illustration of how, beneath the veil of secrecy which shrouds the security services, counter-intelligence networks and cells can develop and remain hidden for years. They are a vivid illustration but by no means an isolated case – many other names could be added to the list, from the physicist Alan Nunn May, convicted in 1946 for supplying atomic secrets to the Russians, to Michael Bettaney, an MI5 officer with ten years of service who was arrested in 1983 after delivering classified documents to the KGB. But what is it about the revelation of these counter-intelligence activities that constitutes a scandal? And in what sense are these scandals political?

There are two aspects of these activities that are capable of eliciting the type of response – one of public outrage, condemnation or reproach – which is constitutive of scandal. One aspect is the sheer treachery involved in activity of this kind: serving as a double agent can readily be seen and portrayed as an act of treason of the highest order, a betrayal of the trust that has been vested in someone as a public servant charged with the task of ensuring the security of the state and protecting the lives of its citizens. That the disclosure of such acts should elicit expressions of outrage and fervent condemnation in the press is hardly surprising. But there is another aspect of counter-intelligence activity which can fuel the kind of reproachful response characteristic of scandal: the disclosure of such activities calls into question the competence of the security services themselves and can readily escalate into a scandal involving an array of second-order transgressions, actual or alleged. How could a double agent remain undetected for so long, unless the vetting procedures and security mechanisms were woefully inadequate? How could double agents escape just as the net was closing around them, unless there was collusion at higher levels? (This, of course, was the suspicion that fuelled the most recent episode of this long-running saga, as Peter Wright's *Spycatcher* alleged that the highest ranking double agent in MI5 during the period 1956–65 was none other than its Director General, Sir Roger Hollis.)

These disclosures, allegations and rebukes may have all the characteristics of a mediated scandal, but are they *political* scandals? The individuals at the centre of these scandals – Burgess, Maclean, etc. –

were employees of the state but they were not, of course, significant political actors: does this not suggest that these scandals, however prominently they have featured in the political history of postwar Britain, are something other than political scandals? This would be an understandable reservation, but the arguments in favour of treating counter-intelligence scandals as political scandals are, in my view, more compelling. In the first place, these are scandals which take place in the political field, broadly conceived, and which can have significant repercussions on governments and on individuals who occupy key political positions. Second, they are scandals which impinge on one of the most sensitive political issues – namely, the security of the state, and the arrangements that political authorities make to gather and control information which is regarded as vital to the state's security and stability. Part of the significance of counter-intelligence scandals is that they bring into sharp relief a realm of activity which is normally hidden from view, and which has become an intrinsic part of the invisible infrastructure of modern states. Moreover, in exposing this normally invisible infrastructure, counter-intelligence scandals also tend to display it in an unfavourable light, highlighting the failures, both personal and institutional, which allowed counter-intelligence activities and networks to develop. Hence this infrastructure is called into question at the very moment when it is exposed to public view, contributing to a sense of distrust and fuelling calls for greater openness and accountability on the part of the security services.

Why have security scandals featured so prominently in the recent political history of Britain? Part of the answer to this question is circumstantial. The counter-intelligence scandals involving Burgess, Maclean, Philby and Blunt were rooted in the peculiar circumstances of their recruitment in the intellectual milieu of Cambridge in the 1930s, in the laxity of the procedures used by the security services to guard against treachery and in the political culture of the Cold War. But there is another factor of a more structural kind which helps to explain the salience of security scandals in British political history. Britain has a long tradition of secrecy in politics which stretches back to the nineteenth century and before. We noted earlier how the old gentlemanly codes of honour, which based state secrecy on the discretion and self-restraint of those who held power, were replaced by a series of Official Secrets Acts which placed tough legal restrictions on the unauthorized disclosure of information by employees of the state. This legal apparatus helped to create a culture of secrecy within which hidden powers could flourish. Within this culture of secrecy, protected from external scrutiny by tough legal strictures, the traditional codes and conventions of British public school life became effective operating principles. Recruitment to the security services relied on old boy networks, supported by mutual trust between colleagues who shared the same privileged backgrounds. Double agents could pursue their activities in the knowledge that conventions of honour and mutual trust would inhibit others from suspecting their duplicity. The tough legal restrictions on disclosure also meant that any attempt to unmask the activities of hidden powers within the security services, either by former employees or by investigative writers, was likely to be subject to criminal prosecution. The risk of prosecution inhibited investigation and discouraged the publication of information and allegations concerning covert activities; but it also ensured that, on those occasions when allegations were made in public (as with *Spycatcher*), they would become the focus of legal confrontation and would acquire thereby an added degree of public visibility. In the wake of the scandals surrounding Burgess, Maclean and their associates, a number of measures have been taken to tighten up the vetting procedures within the security services. But a series of recent, high-profile cases involving disgruntled former employees of MI5 and MI6 has served only to confirm the point that, for reasons which are rooted in their history and culture, the British security services are chronically vulnerable to scandal.[33]

Of course, security scandals are not unique to Britain. During the period of the Cold War, counter-intelligence scandals were relatively common in the United States, fuelled by the fervent anti-communism which characterized American political life from the late 1940s on. Scandals involving dirty tricks on the part of the security services have also featured prominently in the political histories of many Western countries. The CIA has frequently found itself at the centre of allegations of dirty tricks and illegal practices in pursuing covert foreign policy objectives,[34] and the security services of other countries have sometimes attracted unwanted publicity of this kind (as did the French security service, for example, over the *Rainbow Warrior* affair[35]). British political life may be prone to security scandals, but certainly it does not have a monopoly on them.

Blurred Boundaries

While scandals stemming from the activities of the security and intelligence services have been conspicuous in Britain and elsewhere, security scandals are not the only kind of power scandal which has marked British politics in recent years. British political life has not been racked by power scandals on the scale of Watergate or the Iran-Contra affair, but it has not been free of such scandals either. And there is one area of the British political system which has proved to be a particularly fertile source of power scandals: the blurred boundary between the political and military domains. This boundary is a potential source of conflict between the moral and political considerations that may inform the publicly stated foreign policy of governments, on the one hand, and the interests of the arms (or arms-related) industry, on the other. If conflicts of this kind arise, government officials may seek for various reasons to conceal them or to turn a blind eye, drawing them behind the veil of secrecy associated with security-related issues. The conditions are created for a scandal based on revelations which strongly suggest that government officials are conducting a covert foreign policy, or are secretly colluding with individuals and organizations in the private sector that are contravening the publicly stated policy of the government.

Perhaps the most significant example of this kind of scandal in recent British politics is the Matrix Churchill affair. Matrix Churchill was a machine tool company based in Coventry whose directors were arrested in October 1990 and charged with breaking sanctions which banned the export of defence equipment to Iraq.[36] The sanctions were drawn up in December 1984 by the then Foreign Secretary, Sir Geoffrey Howe, and publicly announced in Parliament in October 1985. They prohibited the supply of defence equipment to both Iran and Iraq, which were engaged in a prolonged and very costly war. After eight years of conflict with no clear outcome, a ceasefire between Iran and Iraq was finally declared in August 1988, but officially the ban on exports of defence equipment remained unaltered until 19 July 1990, when a more liberal export policy towards Iraq was approved by a cabinet committee. But on three occasions between February 1988 and November 1989, government ministers approved requests to issue licences for the export of machine tools to Iraq from Matrix Churchill, which had been bought in 1987 by an Iraqi-controlled company, TDG. Export licences had also been granted to other firms involved in manufacturing machine tools. The ministers apparently believed that the equipment was destined for civil use, despite the fact that intelligence reports warned that they could be used in the munitions industry. In June 1990, officials from Customs and Excise began investigating Matrix Churchill, looking for evidence of violations of the export ban. On 16 October they raided the plant and arrested the three directors – Paul Henderson, Peter Allen and Trevor Abraham – for the illegal export of machine tools to Iraq.

Henderson, Allen and Abraham were committed for trial at the Old Bailey, but stories soon began to appear in the press alleging that government ministers had known that Matrix Churchill machine tools were destined for military use and had turned a blind eye. On 2 December 1990 the *Sunday Times* splashed a story on its front page with the headline 'How minister helped arm Saddam's soldiers'. The article referred to a meeting in January 1988 at the Department of Trade and Industry when representatives of the British machine tool industry met junior trade minister Alan Clark to discuss fears that export licences would be revoked, and quoted an unnamed managing director who had attended the meeting as saying that Clark had given 'a nod and a wink' to the sale of machine tools to Iraq. The following day the Minister for Trade at the DTI, Tim Sainsbury, made a statement in the House explaining that Clark strongly denied the views imputed to him and maintaining that the government's restrictions on the sale of defence equipment to Iraq had been scrupulously followed.

The trial was scheduled to begin on 12 October 1992, but preparations were complicated by the fact that some of the evidence sought by the defence included secret government documents. Although it was not publicly known at the time, one of the defendants, Paul Henderson, and one of his associates at Matrix Churchill, Mark Gutteridge, had worked for many years as informants for the security services. As businessmen who frequently travelled to Eastern Europe and elsewhere, they were contacted by MI5 and MI6 and asked to provide information that might be helpful for the security services. Both Henderson and Gutteridge had spoken to officers from MI6 about the military uses of machine tools in Iraq, and they were convinced that this information had been conveyed to the DTI and to government ministers. Lawyers acting for the defence requested the release of documents which might support this view, including the records of conversations with MI6 officers, but this request was initially blocked by the issuing of six Public Interest Immunity (PII) certificates, signed by four different ministers – Kenneth Clarke, the Home Secretary, Malcolm Rifkind, the Defence Secretary, Michael Heseltine, the new President of the Board of Trade, and Tristan Garel-Jones, a minister at the Foreign Office. The certificates were issued on the grounds that disclosure of the documents would damage national security and threaten the operations of the security services. But the issuing of the certificates also meant that potentially vital evidence was unavailable to the defence, and the judge eventually ruled that the documents should be released in order to ensure a fair trial.

The trial continued until the first week of November, when Alan Clark was called to testify. Questioned about the meeting in January 1988 with representatives of the machine tool industry, Clark admitted that when he had said at the meeting that 'The Iraqis will be using the current order for general engineering purposes', he was being 'economical' with the '*actualité*'.[37] Clark explained that it would not have been appropriate at a meeting of that kind to have said that the tools would be used for making munitions, even though he knew at the time that current orders were likely to be used in this way. It was, he added, a matter of 'Whitehall cosmetics' to keep the records ambiguous by emphasizing 'general engineering purposes'. Following these candid admissions, the case against the three defendants collapsed and the trial was abandoned.

The collapse of the Matrix Churchill trial was a serious embarrassment for the government and fuelled allegations that the use of PIIs had been part of a cover-up on the part of ministers who did not want the complicity and duplicity of the government to be exposed. Not only, it seemed, had ministers known that the machine tools for which they had granted export licences would be used for military purposes, but they were also willing to use PII certificates to withhold information which could materially affect the outcome of a criminal trial. Faced with a barrage of criticism and serious allegations of government misconduct, the Prime Minister John Major set up an inquiry under Lord Justice Scott to examine a range of issues relating to the export of equipment to Iraq and the prosecution of the Matrix Churchill directors and others.[38] When the Scott Inquiry published its report in February 1996, the government claimed that it had been exonerated, since the inquiry had found no evidence of a conspiracy or a cover-up. But the report largely substantiated claims that ministers had misled Parliament concerning government policy on exports to Iraq, and that the government had mishandled the prosecution in the Matrix Churchill case. Despite calls for the resignation of William Waldegrave, a former minister at the Foreign Office, and the Attorney General Sir Nicholas Lyell, no heads rolled, and the government survived a vote of confidence by a margin of one. But the report raised serious questions about ministerial responsibility and called for a comprehensive review of the system for monitoring and controlling arms exports. It also highlighted the dangers of the culture of secrecy that tended to prevail in Whitehall. 'The report goes beyond the career of individual Ministers or the reputation of some officials,' remarked Robin Cook from the opposition benches. 'It reveals the price that Britain pays for a culture of secrecy in government.'[39]

It was against the backcloth of the arms-to-Iraq scandals and the Scott Inquiry that Robin Cook announced, when he became Foreign Secretary in the Labour government that came to power in 1997, that he would introduce an 'ethical dimension' to Britain's foreign policy. It was not long, however, before this new ethical foreign policy was coming under pressure from sources very similar to those that had caused such embarrassment to the Conservatives. Shortly after assuming power, the Labour government faced political pressure to revoke licences granted by the previous administration for the export of Hawk fighter jets to Indonesia; it chose not to revoke the licences, claiming that it would not be practical or feasible to do so. In October 1999, following a military coup in Pakistan, the British government announced that it was halting development aid to Pakistan, but it made no formal change of policy on arms exports. Then, on 20 January 2000, under the headline 'Britain's ethical foreign policy: keeping the Hawk jets in action', an article appeared on the front page of the *Guardian* revealing that the government had decided to allow spare parts for Hawk jets to be supplied to Zimbabwe, despite the fact that Zimbabwe was engaged in a bloody civil war in Congo; the *Guardian* claimed that the decision had been taken by the Prime Minister himself, overruling the reservations of his Foreign Secretary. These and other incidents called into question the extent to which the Labour government had managed in practice to produce a significant shift in policy towards the export of arms, despite the wish of some senior ministers to do so.[40] They also provided further testimony to the fact that, in a context where the arms industry is a powerful sector of the economy and is heavily oriented towards the export trade (the UK is the world's second largest exporter of defence equipment and secures around a quarter of the world market), there is a constant pressure for government ministers to act in ways which will not disadvantage the arms industry in the lucrative global marketplace for defence equipment, even at the risk of compromising the moral and political considerations that allegedly inform their foreign policy and giving rise to the kind of arms-related power scandals that have afflicted both Conservative and Labour governments in recent years.

The Consequences of Scandal

Scandals may have become a prominent feature of the political landscape, but do they really matter? Are they largely a form of entertainment drummed up by a media industry eager to exploit our prurient interest in the affairs of others? Or are they events which raise serious issues about the use and abuse of power, about the importance of reputation and about the changing nature of public life? Undoubtedly these are among the most important questions to ask about the phenomenon of scandal, but they are also among the most difficult to answer in a clear and convincing fashion. The difficulty stems in part from the sheer diversity and complexity of the events that we commonly bring together under the label 'scandal'. Each event is rooted in circumstances which make it unique, and each involves individuals whose lives are shaped by their own peculiar motivations, ambitions, opportunities and faults. Sometimes a scandal has ruinous consequences for an individual, effectively terminating his or her career, whereas in other circumstances a person may survive largely unscathed. Moreover, there are, as we have seen, different types of scandal, involving the transgression of different kinds of codes or the misuse of different forms of power, and we cannot assume that the consequences of these different types of scandal will be the same.

Given this diversity and complexity, any attempt to generalize about the nature of scandal and its consequences is likely to be a hazardous undertaking. I intend nevertheless to take a few steps in this direction. I shall begin by considering what seem to me to be some mistaken ways of thinking about this issue. Although there is not an elaborate body of literature on which we can draw, we can distinguish a number of different ways in which the question of the nature of scandal and its consequences could be addressed. I shall consider four such approaches, and try to show that each is unsatisfactory. I shall then outline an alternative view which might form the basis for a more compelling account.

Four Theories of Scandal and its Consequences

(1) One way of thinking about scandal is to see it as an ephemeral event, largely fabricated by the media, which has little or no bearing on the material factors and processes which shape social and political life – let us call this the 'no-consequence theory'. According to this theory, scandals in general, and political scandals in particular, are inconsequential distractions produced by a media culture which has become preoccupied with personalities and celebrities, and which has turned the sensationalized disclosure of the private lives of public figures into a self-perpetuating form of journalism. These disclosures may be titillating or entertaining for readers or viewers, and occasionally awkward or embarrassing for public figures. But beyond the entertainment value and the temporary inconvenience they may cause, scandals have no lasting significance and tell us nothing of any enduring value about social and political life.

There is, undoubtedly, a good deal of *prima facie* evidence to support the no-consequence theory. For all the pages of newsprint devoted to scandals of various kinds, for all the revelations concerning the private lives of public figures, for all the agonized debate about Watergate or the Iran-Contra affair (to mention only two), what difference has it made, at the end of the day, to the institutional organization and practical conduct of social and political life? The careers of some individuals may have been affected (some detrimentally, while others, such as Oliver North, found themselves suddenly and unexpectedly basking in a new-found fame); but apart from these personal and largely unpredictable consequences, scandals have – or so it could be argued – no significant and determinate impact on social and political life.

Although the no-consequence theory has some plausibility, it does not offer, I think, a compelling account of the social and political significance of scandal. Even if one were to accept the limited terms of reference of this theory, it would be difficult to maintain that scandals have had no significant and determinate impact. Take Watergate: although this scandal was no doubt rather exceptional, it did have a discernible impact on the legislative activity of Congress and on the practical conduct of American presidential politics, as we have seen. In Britain, the impact of scandal on the legal and regulatory framework of politics may have been less profound, but there are many instances where scandals have precipitated significant changes – the Register of Members' Interests, for example, was established in the wake of the Poulson affair, and the codes of conduct for MPs were subsequently strengthened following the report of the Nolan Committee.

So even if one takes a narrow view of what would count as 'significant and determinate impact', it is difficult to defend the no-consequences theory. And if we take a broader view, we can see that this theory is also rather misleading. For it obscures the fact that in a world where symbolic capital is a scarce and valuable resource, reputation really does matter. Damage to one's reputation can (and often does) result in a damaged career and even a damaged life; and damage of this kind can (and sometimes does) have consequences which spread beyond the lives of the individuals concerned, weakening or even undermining the institutions or policies with which they are or have been linked.

(2) There is a second way of thinking about scandal which acknowledges that scandals can have important consequences but maintains that these consequences are essentially conservative, in the sense that scandals involve a reaffirmation and consolidation of the status quo. Scandals are rituals of collective absolution: moments when a society confronts the shortcomings and transgressions of its members and, by working through the sometimes painful process of disclosure, denunciation and retribution, ultimately reinforces the norms, conventions and institutions which constitute the social order. This 'functionalist theory of scandal', as I shall call it, is indebted to Durkheim's account of religion.[1] Just as religious practices serve to reaffirm the collective sentiments and ideas which give unity to social groups, so too scandals serve to reinforce the norms and conventions which were transgressed by the activities in question. In our modern, mediated world, scandal is a secularized form of sin.

Once again, this theory is not altogether implausible. Many scandals seem to involve a temporary disruption of the social or political order, in which the individuals responsible for the disturbance are punished and the status quo is restored more or less unchanged;

belief in the social order is reaffirmed by the public demonstration of its capacity to expose and condemn – and perhaps eventually to forgive and pardon – the transgressor. Sex scandals lend themselves readily to this kind of interpretation: think of Profumo's fall from grace, where the adulterous transgressions of a cabinet minister were exacerbated by the unconscionable sin of lying in Parliament, and where the resignation and public humiliation of the transgressor served – or so one could argue – both to reaffirm the codes of honour which underpin parliamentary debate and to fire a warning shot across the bows of any politician who might be tempted to transgress sexual mores. There but for the grace of God . . . It would not be difficult to construct a similar line of argument with regard to the numerous other scandals in which acts of sexual transgression played an important role.

But what about financial scandals and political scandals: can they be coherently interpreted as rituals of collective absolution which reaffirm the social order? At first glance this might seem less likely, but the American sociologist Jeffrey Alexander has argued that Watergate can be plausibly interpreted along these lines.[2] Watergate, argues Alexander, was no ordinary political event; although initially it seemed to many people to be a rather trivial affair, it soon became the focus of a fundamental social crisis in which the most sacred values of the American social and political order were at stake. This transformation occurred because 'Watergate' was turned into a symbol of pollution which was threatening to contaminate the very centre of American society, thereby eliciting deep fears and anxieties which were addressed by instigating a ritualized process of sacralization and purification. The televised hearings of the Senate select committee became a civic ritual which recreated and reaffirmed the sacred, generalized morality upon which the more mundane aspects of American political life are based. They constituted a 'liminal' experience which unfolded in its own time and space, divorced from the mundane issues and conflicts of everyday politics, and which 'revivified the civic religion upon which democratic conceptions of "office" have depended throughout American history'.[3] Through their questions, comments and statements, the senators constantly invoked the fundamental ideas and founding myths of the American republic; they spoke in the name of law and justice, striving to rise above personal or party-political concerns. The release of the transcripts of the White House tapes only served to confirm the extent of the pollution that had invaded the sacred centre of the American political system. And the impeachment hearings were the final cleansing ceremony of this political ritual, 'a rite of expulsion in which the body politic rid itself of the last and most menacing source of sacred impurity.'[4]

Watergate was followed by a period of intense soul-searching, involving a heightened sensitivity to any behaviour on the part of politicians which might be perceived as sinful. The result was a series of mini-scandals which, by being labelled with the suffix '-gate', continued to mobilize some of the sacred values that had been articulated during the Watergate crisis. But as Watergate receded further into the past, the more mundane problems of politics – economic difficulties, foreign crises, party-political conflicts – returned to the centre of political life. This resumption of the routine did not mean, however, that Watergate had no effect. For the 'codes that regulate political authority in America had been sharply renewed',[5] and the values that underpin the social and political order had been articulated and reaffirmed through a sacred ritual in which the American people, via their television sets, had participated.

This interpretation of Watergate is illuminating in some respects. It helps to make sense of the reverential tone which characterized many of the proceedings, among other things. But in other respects, this account is rather misleading. A series of contingent events involving mundane political conflicts, contested allegations and unexpected disclosures of various kinds, and in which the outcome remained unclear to participants and observers until very late in the day, is interpreted by Alexander as a ritualized process of purification; the contingency, unpredictability and conflict-ridden character of these events is largely eclipsed by an interpretation which emphasizes the rituals through which society, conceived as a kind of collective social body, condemns and expels a polluting agent. Moreover, while the use of religious concepts may be illuminating in some respects, it is misleading in others, since the legal and judicial processes which led to the resignation of Nixon have little substantive connection to the ceremonies of institutionalized religions; there may be certain formal similarities in terms of the solemnity of the occasion, etc., but the principles which underlie these processes are very different.

Another difficulty with Alexander's account concerns his emphasis on the renewal and reaffirmation of fundamental values. The removal of Nixon from office may have led to a renewal of values and a strengthening of belief in the political system among some individuals and groups, but it would be quite misleading to emphasize this aspect in a way which neglects the significance of a contrary trend. For it is also very likely that the highly visible sequence of events which culminated in Nixon's resignation contributed to a growing cynicism and distrust among large sectors of the population towards politicians in general, towards government and towards politics as an arena of action – a cynicism and distrust that did not begin with Watergate but to which Watergate contributed signifi-cantly.[6] For many people, Watergate was a window on to a hidden world of politics which they had never seen before, and the public disclosure of the murky, mundane reality of this world, so far from renewing their belief in the system, was enough to confirm their deepest fears.

Finally, whatever the merits of Alexander's interpretation of Watergate, it is unlikely that this account would provide a suitable model for analysing political scandals more generally. Alexander is interested in Watergate primarily because it seems to illustrate the general thesis, derived from his reading of Durkheim, that social and political crises set in motion a process of ritualization through which fundamental values are renewed. His interpretation of Watergate is part of a broader theory of social order and social reproduction; it is not a contribution to a theory of scandal (or a theory of political scandal) as such. Hence Alexander's account tells us relatively little about the distinctive characteristics and consequences of scandal – from the 'big' scandals like Watergate to the many smaller scandals which have become such a common feature of social and political life.

(3) There is a third way of thinking about scandal which emphasizes its potentially deleterious impact on the sphere of public discourse and debate – I shall call this the 'trivialization theory'. This is a theory that reflects the way in which many people think about scandal and its impact, although it can be filled out by drawing on some of the ideas associated with critical theories of the media and of the public sphere. According to this theory, the media's preoccupation with scandal tends to undermine the quality of public discourse and debate, focusing people's attention on relatively trivial matters while the important issues are pushed to the margins of the public sphere. Lurid stories about the personal indiscretions of public figures domi-nate the news, while the substantive problems which affect people's lives (poverty, unemployment, inflation, crime, etc.), and serious dis-cussion of the policies that might be adopted to address them, are increasingly eclipsed. This trend may have begun in the tabloids and the popular press, but the growing competition within the media field has ensured that the broadsheets and the electronic media have been drawn into the fray. The result has been a 'tabloidization' of the media

and a 'privatization' of the public sphere; the public space created by the media has been filled with a kind of generalized chat show about the private lives of politicians, and politics itself has become increasingly indistinguishable from entertainment.

There are different ways in which this theory could be elaborated. One way would be to draw on Habermas's account of the decline of the public sphere and to maintain that the proliferation of mediated scandals is both symptomatic of and contributes to this process. Habermas argued that the rise of the periodical press in eighteenth-century Europe helped to stimulate the formation of a new kind of public sphere in early modern societies – a 'bourgeois public sphere' – which consisted of private individuals who came together, in salons and coffee houses, to debate issues of public concern.[7] The distinctive feature of this new sphere of debate, according to Habermas, is that it involved the public use of reason. Individuals used the new opportunities created by the periodical press to argue openly and critically about questions of power and authority; the periodical press was not merely a mouthpiece for governments but also a forum, relatively independent of the state, in which the activities of those in power could be subjected to critical scrutiny. However, with the decline of coffee-house culture in the late eighteenth century and the growing commercialization of the press in the nineteenth century, the bourgeois public sphere was largely undermined. The press – once an exemplary forum of rational-critical debate – was transformed into another domain of cultural consumption, and the values of leisure and entertainment increasingly displaced the concern with reasoned argument and debate.

Habermas did not explicitly address the theme of scandal, but it would not be difficult to develop an argument about the rise of mediated scandals and their impact on the basis of his account. The rise of mediated scandals testifies, one could argue, to the decline of the public sphere; it represents the colonization of public space by personal and private issues, and the triumph of entertainment values over the concern with reasoned argument and debate.[8] The press and other media become a forum for a kind of generalized gossip in which lurid disclosures about the private indiscretions of public figures increasingly displace serious debate about the key issues of social and political life. Sex scandals, with their personalized and highly moralistic character, provide ready-made stories for those sectors of the press which are orientated towards maximum sales and popular taste. But given the competition between media organizations and the scramble for 'hot stories' among journalists, other sectors of the press are quickly pulled in the same direction. The logic of competition erodes the boundaries between those forms of journalism orientated towards advocacy or objectivity, on the one hand, and the kind of journalism orientated towards entertainment, on the other, as more and more news organizations become concerned with providing commercially viable forms of 'info-tainment'. The growing importance of television, one could argue, tends to exacerbate this trend. The 'live' and highly visual character of television accentuates the personal qualities of public figures, who appear increasingly like media celebrities on our screens, and thereby also raises the stakes associated with revelations and allegations which cast doubt on these qualities. The distinction between politics and entertainment becomes increasingly blurred; celebrities from the entertainment industry intermingle with figures from public life, and in the eyes of ordinary people these worlds begin to merge. By becoming preoccupied with scandal, by devoting more and more pages of newsprint and more and more hours of airtime to the personal indiscretions and misadventures of politicians/celebrities, the media have cut themselves adrift from the idea of the press as a critical watchdog. They have become a testimony – or so one could argue – to the historical decline of the public sphere.

This argument has considerable force. It offers a sharp critical perspective on the profusion of mediated scandals in recent decades: what these scandals allegedly produce is an overall deterioration of the quality of public life in our societies, as those institutions which provide some of the most important bases of public life – both newspapers and television – become increasingly absorbed by the relentless search for scandal. Public debate is impoverished and politics itself is trivialized by the self-perpetuating cycle of scandalous disclosures. But while this argument has some force, it is also misleading in certain respects; and it fails to see that, while scandals often involve an element of entertainment, there is a good deal more at stake.

The argument is misleading in at least two respects. First, in historical terms, the argument tends to view the past through rose-tinted glasses, contrasting the present with an earlier historical period in which the public sphere allegedly provided a more vibrant forum for reasoned argument and debate. But whether the public culture of earlier historical periods – such as the print and coffee-house culture of eighteenth-century Europe – actually amounted to a more vibrant public sphere, facilitating and promoting reasoned debate to a greater extent than today, is a moot point.[9] Access to media products was more restricted in earlier historical periods and dependent on resources and skills (such as literacy) which were very unevenly distributed. Moreover, arguments of this kind tend to underestimate the extent to which media products in earlier historical periods were sensationalist in character and moralistic in tone. Modern mediated scandals may have some distinctive properties which differentiate them from earlier forms of scandal, but the use of the printed word to sensationalize and moralize, to expose and condemn, has a long history.

A second respect in which the argument is misleading is that it tends to emphasize one type of scandal at the expense of others. This line of argument has particular force when it is developed in relation to scandals which involve illicit sex – the lurid and endless stories of politicians, celebrities and other public figures who have allegedly transgressed some sexual norm. But the argument is much less persuasive when it is considered in relation to other types of political scandal which feature prominently in the media. While it could be plausibly argued that the preoccupation with sex scandals produces a degree of trivialization of public debate, it would be much more difficult to maintain that disclosures concerning the abuse of power or the misappropriation of public funds should be viewed in the same way.

The trivialization theory also fails to see that there is more at stake in scandal than entertainment. It is too quick to dismiss scandal as a prime example of tabloidization, an illustration of how the media are increasingly driven by commercial imperatives and have succumbed to the logic of the marketplace, relinquishing their autonomy as a cultural institution and orientating themselves increasingly towards the maximization of sales in a highly competitive field. This may be part of what is involved in the profusion of mediated scandals, but it is not everything. For scandals also raise serious questions about power, reputation and trust, and about the ways in which those who have power are rendered visible and accountable to others. The main weakness of the trivialization theory is that, by taking the emphasis on lurid stories about the private lives of public figures as its main point of reference, it fails to see that there is more at stake in scandal than the commercial exploitation of relatively trivial pursuits.

(4) There is a fourth way of thinking about scandal which turns the trivialization theory on its head. This fourth approach argues that scandal, so far from debasing the quality of public debate, enriches it by calling into question the dominant norms of journalism and by

turning the tables on the powerful and the privileged. I shall describe this as the 'subversion theory of scandal'. Again, this is not a theory which can be found explicitly formulated in the literature, but it is a theory which could be developed on the basis of some of the assumptions associated with a more playful, 'postmodern' approach to popular culture. The postmodern approach tends to eschew an overly judgemental attitude towards the texts of popular culture. Rather than analysing these texts in terms of evaluative categories derived from a reflection on works of 'high culture', the postmodern approach tends to see popular texts as cultural forms involving their own distinctive kinds of symbolic richness and playful insubordination. These texts, with their emphasis on sensationalism and excess, on offensiveness and bad taste, are like rebellious children who refuse to play by the rules. They entertain their readers and viewers precisely because they reject dominant norms and conventions and, by flouting them in an overt and even exaggerated fashion, subject them to a kind of subversive laughter. Like the carnival in earlier historical periods, many texts of popular culture today are characterized by parody and ribaldry, by inversions, humiliations, travesties and transgressions which, by their very vulgarity and excessiveness, turn the world upside down.

As developed by John Fiske and others, this broad line of argument offers a certain way of thinking about the significance of scandals in the popular press.[10] Fiske distinguishes between two main types of news: what he calls 'official news', which is the news of the 'quality' press and network television, and what he calls 'popular news' (which is pejoratively referred to by its critics as the tabloid press).[11] The organs of official news tend to operate within certain norms about objectivity, 'truth' and good reporting. They adopt a serious, impersonal tone, investigating public issues on grounds largely chosen by public officials, and they seek to produce understanding and belief in their readers and viewers. Popular news, by contrast, tends to reject a clear-cut distinction between fact and fiction. It focuses on the boundaries between public and private life, frequently confronting public figures with issues they would prefer to bury. Its style is irreverent and sensationalist. Popular news seeks to provoke and disrupt; it calls into question the power of official news to define what is real and newsworthy, and calls into question the kind of belief that official news seeks to produce. Popular news cultivates scepticism and disbelief; it invites readers and viewers to laugh at individuals whose power and influence depend on being taken seriously by others. Hence scandalous stories in the popular press can be seen as a subversion of power and privilege. 'What these stories do', claims one commentator, 'is bash the "power-bloc" – or those representatives of it whose attributes and actions can be most meaningfully represented for their readers.'[12] They offer a popular form of political criticism, nourishing scepticism towards structures of power and enabling those without power to express their anger and frustration through subversive laughter at the foibles and misfortunes of the powerful.

The merit of this approach is that it urges us to think about cultural works in a differentiated fashion and to recognize that certain genres of popular culture, including the tabloid press, may operate according to their own distinctive norms, conventions and aesthetic criteria. But as a way of thinking about the political content of popular culture in general, and the political significance of scandal in particular, this approach is quite inadequate. In the first place, it would be rash to assume that laughter at the misfortunes of the powerful is, in and by itself, a subversive act. One might laugh at the sight of a government minister who, like the hapless David Mellor or the reckless Gary Hart, is caught in a compromising situation, but it is by no means clear that there is anything subversive about laughter of this kind – no norms may be challenged, no values may be questioned, no relations of power may be undermined. Like laughter at a sexist or racist joke, those who enjoy themselves at the expense of others may remain deeply conservative in their attitudes and beliefs.

Second, and equally unsatisfactory, is the broad opposition between 'the people' and 'the power-bloc' which characterizes this approach. Fiske draws this opposition from Stuart Hall and adapts it to his own ends, arguing that cultural forms in late capitalist societies are structured around a fundamental opposition between an alliance of forces of domination ('the power-bloc') and a shifting set of allegiances among subordinate groups ('the people').[13] Popular culture, explains Fiske, is culture created by the people out of the products of the mass media: they may take up cultural forms produced by the power-bloc, but they turn them into popular culture by transforming them to suit their own interests and tastes, which are generally opposed to those of the power-bloc. But this broad opposition between 'the people' and 'the power-bloc' is a breathtakingly simple way of viewing the nature and organization of power in contemporary societies. The multiple forms of power and the complex ways in which they are used by individuals and groups in particular contexts are subsumed by this account under a single, sweeping, binary opposition. The use of a binary opposition between the people and the power-bloc may be limited to certain currents of cultural studies, and perhaps even to certain contexts of analysis. But this is not an intellectual strategy that anyone with a sober sense of the complexity of social and political life would want to embrace.

A third difficulty with this approach is that, in emphasizing the broad opposition between the people and the power-bloc, it both overestimates the complicity of the 'official news' and exaggerates the radical character of the tabloid press. The world of official news, on this account, is firmly in the grip of the power-bloc; by adhering to the journalistic norms of objectivity and truth, official news presents the world as a domain of facts, marginalizes arguments and alternative points of view and thereby serves the interests of the powerful. Popular news, by contrast, undermines the power-bloc by rejecting the norms of objectivity and truth, provoking scepticism and disbelief and fuelling the popular imagination with visions of alternative realities. But once again, this account greatly oversimplifies things. There may indeed be a degree of complicity between the media of 'official news' and the key institutions of political and economic power, but it is nowhere near as seamless and total as Fiske suggests. Journalists working for the 'quality' press have on many occasions produced stories which are just as uncomfortable as (and in some cases a good deal more consequential than) the stories which appear in the popular press. On the other hand, to maintain that popular news is intrinsically more radical and subversive than official news, and that it aligns itself more readily with the interests of the people by virtue of its transgressive and excessive qualities, is to turn a blind eye to the more conservative aspects of the popular press and to treat as relatively insignificant the fact that the popular press, no less than the 'official news', is part of a large, commercialized industry.

Of course, Fiske is well aware that the popular press is part of a commercialized media industry, but he wants to maintain nonetheless that it is more subversive than official news and more closely tied to the interests of the people. This is because, first, it is opposed to the 'normal' and the 'official', and hence intrinsically aligned with subordinate groups ('it is a popular knowledge and a repressed knowledge, just as the people are repressed social formations'[14]); and second, it is an open and engaging form of discourse which invites readers to interpret it in their own way, to fabricate creatively their own readings and interpretations rather than simply accepting the 'truth' of what is said. But neither of these arguments demonstrates with any degree of conviction that the popular press, by virtue of its stylistic and rhetorical strategies, is an intrinsically radical and subversive cultural form.

Finally, whatever the merits of this approach as a way of understanding popular culture more generally, it is unlikely to provide a satisfactory framework for analysing scandal and its consequences. For while scandals do feature prominently in the popular press, they are by no means restricted to it. The 'quality' press has also played an important role in the creation of mediated scandals – especially scandals involving financial irregularities and abuses of power, but sex scandals too. Moreover, while the carnivalesque mocking of the powerful and the privileged may be evident in some scandals (*à la* Mellor and Hart), this is hardly the most striking or significant feature of all. It would be difficult to develop a satisfactory account of scandal and its consequences on the basis of an argument which is concerned primarily with the characteristics of popular culture, since mediated scandal cannot be understood as a genre specific to the popular press.

Power, Reputation and Trust: Towards a Social Theory of Scandal

Is there a way of thinking about scandal and its consequences which is more promising than the accounts we have considered so far? Is it possible to develop an alternative approach which will shed more light on the significance of scandal and its impact on social and political life? In this final section I shall outline an approach which I shall describe, rather broadly, as a 'social theory of scandal' and which will, I hope, provide the basis for a more plausible account. The essence of this approach can be succinctly stated: *scandals are struggles over symbolic power in which reputation and trust are at stake.* Scandals do not necessarily destroy reputation and undermine trust, but they have the *capacity* to do so. And it is because of this capacity, this potential for damaging reputation and corroding relations of trust, that scandals are of such significance in the political field.

In characterizing scandals in this way, I do not want to suggest that scandals are *only* struggles over symbolic power, and that the *only* things at stake in scandal are reputation and trust. Clearly this is not so, and many scandals involve other forms of power and other issues. Some scandals are concerned above all with political power, with the infringement of rules and procedures for exercising it and with the development of covert networks which bypass formal mechanisms of accountability, as we have seen; other scandals are concerned with hidden linkages between political and economic power, calling attention to forms of corruption and conflicts of interest which are incompatible with the standards of conduct that might be expected of public officials. But even scandals focused on political and economic power are *also* concerned with symbolic power; *all* scandals involve struggles over symbolic power and the sources of symbolic power, even if *some* scandals also involve other forms of power and other issues. Scandals are social struggles which are fought out in the public domain and which are constituted by the acts and speech-acts of individuals and organizations which expose, allege and condemn, as well as by the acts and speech-acts of those who are at the centre of the allegations and find themselves caught up in the unfolding drama.

In emphasizing the importance of symbolic power, reputation and trust, I do not wish to underestimate the significance of other forms of power, nor do I wish to play down the role of other issues (such as corruption, conflicts of interest and the accountability of power) which are involved in many scandals. In previous chapters I have examined the role of these other issues and forms of power in some detail. But if we were to focus on political or economic power alone, we would never understand the nature of scandal and its consequences. We must also see that scandals are struggles over symbolic power in which reputation and trust, among other things, are at stake.

Symbolic power, I argued earlier, is one of four basic forms of power; it refers to the capacity to intervene in the course of events and shape their outcome, as well as the capacity to influence the actions and beliefs of others, by means of the production and transmission of symbolic forms. The exercise of symbolic power depends on resources of various kinds, including what I have called 'symbolic capital'. Reputation is an aspect of symbolic capital; it is the relative estimation or esteem accorded to an individual or institution by others. The higher the estimation and the greater the range of individuals who hold it, the higher is one's reputation.

We can distinguish between two types of reputation – what I shall call 'skill-specific reputation' and 'character reputation'. Skill-specific reputation is the kind of reputation one acquires for the deployment of particular skills. One might acquire a high reputation as a pianist or a cellist by virtue of the fact that, in the eyes of others, one has attained a high level of proficiency in playing this instrument. Character reputation, by contrast, is the kind of reputation one acquires for being a reliable and trustworthy individual, a person of probity and integrity. You do not have to display any specific skills in order to acquire a reputation for good character, but you do have to display a pattern of behaviour over time which others can judge to be worthy of their esteem.

Both types of reputation constitute a resource that individuals can draw on and use in order to pursue their interests and aims. A pianist who has earned a high reputation as an outstanding musician can use this to his or her advantage in negotiating the terms of a contract. A second-hand car dealer who has a reputation for honesty and reliability may find that his reputation is his most valuable asset. But reputation is also an unusual kind of resource which has some peculiar characteristics – let me highlight four. In the first place, reputation can take a long time to accumulate. It is possible to 'get rich quickly', as when a first-time author launches his or her writing career with a book that is widely acclaimed. But for most individuals and institutions, the process of building a reputation is a long and arduous task. They must invest a great deal of effort over an extended period of time, and avail themselves of networks within which they can gain the recognition of others,[15] in order to build a good and relatively stable reputation.

A second feature of reputation is that it is intrinsically contestable (and quite often contested). Given that reputation depends on the estimations of others, it is intrinsically open to the possibility of disagreement and dispute, since others will not necessarily concur in their estimations. Character reputation is particularly prone to differential assessments, since the criteria on which it is based are not clear-cut and individuals may have widely differing beliefs about someone's character traits. But even in the case of skill-specific reputation there may be plenty of room for disagreement about the extent to which an individual possesses the skills and attributes on which his or her reputation is allegedly based – about whether, in other words, his or her reputation is well founded.

Third, unlike money or other types of economic capital, reputation is a resource which is not depleted through use.[16] When you spend money you deplete the amount available for future use, but using your reputation to pursue your aims and interests does not necessarily diminish the resource. A second-hand car dealer who incorporates his reputation for honesty and reliability into an advertisement for his current range of cars does not necessarily diminish his reputation by using it in this way; on the contrary, he may consolidate and even augment his reputation by calling it to the attention of others. But while reputation is not necessarily depleted through use, it can be very rapidly and conclusively depleted through misuse. Reputation is, in this respect, a very fragile resource which can be quickly and comprehensively undermined. It is vulnerable to what I shall call 'reputation depleters' which can very rapidly unravel the web of judgements and estimations which form the basis of a reputation.

Finally, reputation is a kind of resource which, if seriously and substantially depleted, may be very difficult to restore. In other words, reputation may, in some circumstances, be a non-renewable resource. A reputation that has taken years to build up may be quickly and permanently destroyed. In this respect, struggles over the sources of symbolic power can be more consequential for individuals (and the organizations of which they are part) than struggles over the sources of economic power: the loss of a substantial sum of money can often be recouped, but a tarnished reputation can last forever. The second-hand car dealer who sells a series of 'lemons' may find that his reputation for honesty and reliability has been dealt a fatal blow. Character reputation is particularly vulnerable to this kind of rapid and permanent depletion, but skill-specific reputation is by no means immune. A highly regarded scientist who is shown to have fabricated the results of an experiment may find that his or her reputation is in ruins.

These characteristics of reputation help us to understand some aspects of scandals and their consequences. Scandals are potential reputation depleters: they have the capacity to deplete reputation very quickly and very thoroughly, and once it is depleted it may be very difficult – in some respects, perhaps impossible – to restore. Moreover, scandals can come to *define* an individual's reputation in ways that overshadow other reputational traits. Who remembers John Profumo for his achievements as a minister of war? Who remembers Richard Nixon without thinking first and foremost of Watergate? The scandals that engulfed these individuals have survived as indelible marks against their reputations. Try as they might (and Nixon tried very hard indeed[17]), these individuals were never able to erase the marks left by the scandals that terminated their political careers.

Of course, the reputational impact of scandals is not always detrimental and not always permanent. Reputation is one of the issues at stake in scandals, but whether an individual's reputation is actually damaged by a scandal, and if so whether the damage is permanent or only temporary, depends on a range of specific circumstances. Scandals are struggles over symbolic power in which the individuals involved are actively and sometimes doggedly seeking to shape the impact of the unfolding events on their reputations and their careers, and the outcome of these struggles will vary from one case to the next. In some cases, as with Profumo and Nixon, an individual's reputation may be permanently damaged or even destroyed; in other cases, as with Reagan and Oliver North in the Iran-Contra affair, individuals may emerge from a scandal with their reputations largely intact (or even enhanced, if they play their cards well and some sectors of the media come to their aid). More commonly, an individual's reputation will be damaged significantly but not permanently or irredeemably. A scandal may culminate in a resignation, prosecution or some other form of career-diminishing and life-demeaning outcome, followed by a period of exile or relative marginalization during which an individual can begin the long and rather arduous process of rebuilding a damaged reputation. An individual may never be able to undo the damage completely, and his or her career may be irreversibly altered (as in the case of Edward Kennedy or Cecil Parkinson, for example). But with determined effort and with the gradual erosion of memory that accompanies the passage of time, individuals may succeed in rebuilding their reputations to some extent and in achieving some degree of political rehabilitation.

The reputational impact of scandal depends not only on a range of specific circumstances, but also on the properties of the fields within which scandals take place. Good reputation is more important in some fields than in others, and hence more vulnerable to the kind of damage that can be inflicted by scandals. In the second-hand car business, a good character reputation is vital, and hence a scandal that exposes a serious scam could be fatal. But in the field of popular entertainment, such as film or pop music, reputation plays a different role. What matters here is not so much one's reputation for honesty and reliability (few, apart from one's agents, employers and friends, may care about this), but rather one's track record in the field coupled with one's notoriety or 'well-knownness'.[18] Scandals involving film stars or pop stars can be deeply embarrassing for the individuals who find themselves at the centre of unwanted publicity, and they can damage or disrupt their careers in various ways. But scandals can also contribute significantly to an individual's well-knownness, and hence, despite the personal discomfort that may be associated with them, they do not necessarily lead to a deterioration of an individual's position in the field. Hugh Grant's image as the coy and endearing Englishman was undoubtedly dented by his reck-less encounter with Divine Brown, but the added well-knownness which accrued from the enormous publicity surrounding this event may have compensated generously for any damage done.

In the field of politics, good reputation is important because it is a vital source of symbolic power. Actual and aspiring political leaders must be able to count on the support of others, both within the restricted field of professional politicians and within the broader political field, and a good reputation is both an effective means and, in some respects, an essential condition for securing and sus-taining this support. A skill-specific reputation for political compe-tence and astuteness is a valuable asset for an actual or aspiring political leader, but so too – and increasingly, if my analysis in chapter 4 is correct – is an undented reputation for honesty, integrity and good character. Political scandals can damage an individual's reputation for political competence and astuteness by exposing a series of misjudgements, miscalculations or bungled decisions – in the way, for example, that the reputation of William Waldegrave was damaged by the Matrix Churchill affair. But it is an individual's char-acter reputation which is most at risk in political scandals. For what many political scandals threaten to expose is a form of dishonesty, hypocrisy or deceit which can only damage the character reputation of an actual or aspiring leader, and hence can weaken or undermine their capacity to mobilize support both within the restricted field of professional politicians and in the broader political field. Political scandals are potential reputation depleters in a field where reputa-tion is a vital source of power.

Reputation is a resource which accrues not only to individuals, but also to institutions. An institution or organization can acquire a repu-tation for quality and efficiency, or for honesty and integrity, just as an individual can, and a good reputation can be a valuable asset for an institution or organization seeking to pursue its aims. Many orga-nizations work very hard to build up and consolidate their reputa-tions in their respective fields, and they actively seek to protect these reputations against threats or incursions of various kinds. Hence reputation depleters can be damaging not only for individuals, but also for the institutions and organizations of which they are part. In the political field, political parties are particularly vulnerable to repu-tation depleters, since they must struggle for electoral support in a highly competitive system; but governments and administrations are also vulnerable, and they may find that damage to their reputation hinders their capacity to pursue their aims and objectives. A party or government which acquires a reputation for sleaze may find it very difficult to shake it off (as the Conservative Party in Britain found in the 1990s), and undoubtedly they will find that it is not an electoral asset. In a political climate characterized by a heightened sensitivity to scandal, leaders of parties and governments may act quickly to dissociate themselves from members who have clearly committed transgressions which precipitate (or threaten to precipitate) scandals, for fear that the latter may damage not only the reputation of individuals but also, by association, the reputation of the party or government. And the more that leaders feel that their parties or governments are vulnerable to reputation depleters, the more likely they are to distance themselves swiftly and unambiguously from their errant members.

But scandals can affect institutions in other ways too: they can have long-term consequences for the character of social relations and institutions and the forms of trust which underpin them. Most social relations and institutions in modern societies are based to some extent on forms of trust – that is, on presumptions concerning the competence, reliability and good intentions of other agents or systems of action. Trust is a way of coping with the freedom of others in circumstances of uncertainty or risk where your actions and decisions depend on the actions of others.[19] If you buy a second-hand car, you are taking a risk; but if you buy the car from a dealer you trust, then you are seeking to reduce the risk by basing your decision on the presumption that the dealer is competent, reliable and honest and will not sell you a lemon. Trust presupposes the possibility of disappointment, and presupposes the knowledge that disappointment is possible. If you knew that a second-hand car was as good as the dealer claimed and there was no possibility that your knowledge was mistaken, then there would be no need to place your trust in the dealer.

Most forms of social interaction and cooperation depend on some level of trust, although the ways in which trust is built up and incorporated in social relationships vary from one context to another. In contexts of face-to-face interaction, trust is often based on personal knowledge of particular individuals with whom one interacts in the course of one's day-to-day life; face-to-face interaction is a practical testing ground where one can monitor the behaviour of others over time and test their words against their deeds. This 'thick' trust is often characteristic of localized settings and small-scale communities; it is also relatively robust, since it is based on personal knowledge that may have been tested over an extended period of time. In more complex organizations, however, and in the context of social inter-actions and relationships which are stretched across space and time, trust tends to be based on factors other than the personal knowledge of particular individuals. Here reputation can play an important role: although we may have no personal knowledge of particular individ-uals, we may be inclined to trust them if they have a reputation for trustworthiness. But other factors can also play a role in creating 'thinner' forms of social trust. For example, the existence of norms of reciprocity and cooperative networks of interaction which are extended in space and time, and which have a significant degree of historical depth, can help to create social trust and facilitate cooperation.[20]

Like reputation, these forms of trust can be viewed as resources that individuals are able to draw on and employ in conducting and extending their social interactions and relationships with others. Trust has been described by Putnam, Coleman and others as an aspect of 'social capital', by which they mean those features of social organization, such as trust, norms and networks, which facilitate the coordination of action.[21] Here I shall not examine the concept of social capital. But trust, like reputation, has some distinctive charac-teristics, and I want to analyse these briefly. In the first place, trust, like reputation, is a resource which is not depleted through use. On the contrary, the more that it is used, the greater the stock of trust there may be: like learning to speak a foreign language, the resource expands through use.[22] Moreover, not only does the resource expand through use, but it also tends to decline if it is *not* used. The more one engages in trusting interactions with others, the more likely it is that the reservoir of trust will grow; on the other hand, the less one engages in trusting interactions, the more likely it is that the resource will atrophy and decline. Hence trust tends to be cumulative and self-reinforcing.[23] The more one engages in trusting interactions with others, the more trust there is, and hence the more likely it is that this resource will be used to facilitate further interaction.

A second characteristic of trust is that, like reputation, it is a relatively fragile resource which is vulnerable to the effects of what I shall call 'trust depleters'. Trust can be depleted not only through lack of use, but also through *breaches of trust* which can call into ques-tion the presumptions underpinning the conduct of trusting interac-tions with others. The presumptions underpinning trust are always to some extent conjectural, in the sense that they are based both on evidence and on the lack of contrary evidence. Hence the emergence of contrary evidence – exemplified above all by those breaches of trust when an individual discovers that his or her presumptions have been betrayed – can have serious and long-term consequences for the conduct of trusting interactions. Moreover, if trust is radically depleted and replaced by deep distrust, the latter can be very difficult to overcome.[24] Just as trust tends to be cumulative and self-reinforcing, so, too, deep distrust tends to be self-reinforcing and may be impervious to evidence and experience which might show it to be unwarranted.

A third characteristic of trust is that it can be supplemented by various devices which reduce the room to manoeuvre of the individuals engaged in trusting interactions, and thereby provide individuals with some assurance that their presumptions will not be betrayed. These devices enable individuals to *economize on trust*, in the sense that they provide a framework within which individuals can engage in cooperative relations while reducing to some extent their dependence on trust. Contracts, letters of agreement and formalized procedures are devices that are commonly used in this way: they commit individuals to following through with a course of action that has been agreed in advance, and hence reduce the need for the parties to rely exclusively on their presumptions. These devices can be used to support and consolidate relations of trust, and can become an integral part of a virtuous circle of trust, reciprocity and cooperation. But they can also be introduced as repair mechanisms, or even as alternatives to trust, in circumstances where trust is lacking or has been seriously depleted.

Trust is an important component of social relations and interaction in many spheres of social life, from personal relationships in the localized settings of everyday life to the many forms of economic transaction and cooperation in an increasingly globalized world. Trust plays an important role in the political field too, both in terms of facilitating the forms of interaction and cooperation that must be developed and sustained among political representatives within the restricted field of professional politicians, and also in terms of underpinning the forms of participation and support which characterize the broader political field. As professional politicians, leaders and ministers must be able to count on a degree of cooperation from other representatives within their own party and, in some circumstances or on some occasions, beyond it. Leaders and ministers may be able to deploy a range of trust-economizing devices to help secure this cooperation (such as the party whip); but it is unlikely that they could continue for long, and succeed in securing the kind of cooperation necessary to govern effectively, unless they were able to draw on some element of trust among those whose cooperation they require. In a context of deep and pervasive distrust, cooperative political action is likely to fail.

Political leaders and representatives are also dependent on some degree of participation and support from ordinary citizens within the broader political field. In liberal democratic regimes, the relation between political representatives and ordinary citizens is in principle a relation of trust in which, through the electoral process, representatives are granted the power and discretion to act and legislate on behalf of the people who put them in office.[25] In practice, of course, the relation between rulers and ruled has commonly been infused with varying degrees of suspicion and distrust, as ordinary citizens have been inclined to believe that many professional politicians will be tempted to put their own interests above those of the people they are supposed to represent. Some degree of suspicion and distrust is not necessarily counter-productive in a liberal democratic regime: on the contrary, it can help to ensure that the activities of political representatives are regularly scrutinized and rendered more accountable to the electorate.[26] But there are circumstances in which a pervasive and deepening distrust can have counter-productive consequences. Let us consider three.

First, a pervasive and deepening distrust can give rise to the intensified development of trust-economizing devices which can have counter-productive consequences. Viewed historically, the introduction of trust-economizing devices was an essential component of the development of modern democratic institutions. Given the scale and complexity of modern societies, democratic institutions could not rely on the kind of thick trust characteristic of small-scale communities and localized interaction. The development of modern democratic institutions involved the establishment of formal procedures which laid down the rules according to which political power could be contested and exercised, and which could in principle support and nourish thinner forms of social trust. But in conditions of pervasive and deepening distrust, legislators may be inclined to introduce more and more formal procedures in the hope of restoring depleted stocks of trust. Some of these procedures may indeed help, and may create greater openness and accountability in government. But there is the risk that these new procedures will only create further levels of bureaucracy and inefficiency. There is also the risk that they will set in motion a process that may exacerbate rather than alleviate the problems they were intended to address, and hence contribute further to a culture of deepening distrust.

A second counter-productive consequence of pervasive and deepening distrust is that it can incline individuals to place more emphasis on the *character* of leaders or potential leaders rather than on their *competence* as political agents. Trust may involve presumptions both about the character of others – their honesty, reliability and good intentions – and about their technical competence.[27] To trust one's doctor is to trust his or her character, of course, but it is also and above all to trust his or her technical competence as an expert who possesses specialized knowledge and skills. Trust in the political field can also involve presumptions about both the character and the competence of leaders or potential leaders. But in a context of pervasive and deepening distrust, and where one of the factors that has contributed to distrust is the well-publicized character failings of one or more political leaders, there may be a strong tendency, both within the media and in the political deliberations of many ordinary people, to focus on the character traits of leaders or potential leaders, in the hope that an individual of more robust moral fibre might help to rebuild damaged relations of trust. But the preoccupation with character can have counter-productive consequences. For the intensive scrutiny of individuals and their biographies is likely to expose blemishes that might otherwise remain hidden, thereby casting some doubt on the character credentials of many leaders or potential leaders. And more importantly, the preoccupation with character can overshadow questions of competence. We may find ourselves faced with the prospect of being governed by leaders and ministers whose character credentials may be impeccable but whose competence as political agents and whose intellectual grasp of the complex problems confronting modern societies might fall well short of what we could reasonably and legitimately expect.

A third counter-productive consequence stems from the fact that deep distrust tends to be self-reinforcing and, once it sets in, it can be very difficult to overcome. Repeated breaches of trust can generate an attitude of deep distrust among some sectors of the population; individuals may be inclined to distrust, not just particular leaders or potential leaders, but politicians *per se*. They may come to feel that the *government* cannot be trusted, regardless of the particular individuals who happen to be occupying positions of power at a specific point in time, on the grounds that repeated breaches of trust have tipped the balance of probability in favour of the view that particular individuals who hold or aspire to political power are more likely than not to be untrustworthy. This attitude of deep distrust, coupled with the belief that politicians and political institutions are remote from the practical realities of one's life and unlikely to make any significant and positive difference, can lead to a withdrawal from the political process, which may be expressed by a lack of interest in political issues and a disinclination to vote. This kind of deep distrust, and the forms of non-participation to which it may contribute, can be very difficult to overcome. They are unlikely to be assuaged by the introduction of further trust-economizing devices, since these devices can supplement and support relations of trust but are unlikely to be effective in contexts where trust is completely lacking.

These considerations on the role of trust in politics provide the backcloth against which we can explore further the consequences of scandal. Political scandals are not only potential reputation depleters: they are also potential trust depleters in a field where cooperative political action and vibrant democratic government depends on some degree of social trust. Political scandals can fuel suspicion and distrust, and hence they can have a corrosive impact on the relations of social trust that underpin and facilitate cooperative forms of political action. In the United States, Britain and many other Western countries, there has been a marked decline of public trust in government since the early 1960s. In surveys carried out in the United States, roughly three-quarters of respondents in 1964 said that they trusted the federal government to do the right thing most of the time; by 1994, less than a quarter of respondents were prepared to acknowledge such trust.[28] The reasons for this declining trust in government are no doubt varied and complex, but it seems likely that the revelations and allegations associated with political scandals have played a significant role. Recent surveys in the United States tend to support this view: the principal reason given by respondents in 1995 for not trusting the government is the lack of honesty and integrity of public officials; the second reason, not far behind, is that politicians serve their own interests rather than the public's.[29] So there are reasonable grounds for supposing that political scandals can have a corrosive impact on relations of trust.[30]

To say that political scandals can have a corrosive impact on relations of trust is not to say, of course, that they will always have this impact, nor is it to say that this impact, when it does occur, will necessarily weaken democratic institutions. But a major political scandal, or a series of lesser but cumulatively significant scandals, can help to create a culture of deepening distrust which can have the kind of counter-productive consequences outlined above. It can give rise to the intensified development of trust-economizing devices which, in some cases, may serve to exacerbate rather than alleviate the problems they were intended to address, and which may therefore have the unintended consequence of contributing to a culture of deepening distrust. Following the Watergate scandal, the creation of the office of the special prosecutor (or independent counsel) was a way of economizing on trust, since it provided a set of formal and purportedly impartial procedures which could be followed to investigate cases of alleged wrongdoing, and hence which could in principle allay public concern about abuses of power and privilege in high office. But in practice the existence of these procedures has created a machinery of investigation which has tended to increase the extent to which previously hidden aspects of government, and the hidden activities of government officials, are made visible in the public domain, and hence it has probably tended over time to reinforce public concern rather than to allay it.

Political scandals can also help to create a climate in which political leaders or potential leaders are valued more for their character than their competence. A climate of political scandal and of pervasive and deepening distrust can lend support to aspiring leaders whose claim to credibility stems less from their proven capacity to govern effectively than from their claim to stand above the scandals and murky dealings that have tainted their contemporaries. Once again, the post-Watergate period provides some evidence to support this suggestion: the question of character was a central issue in the 1976 presidential race, and Jimmy Carter built his campaign strategy on the promise that he would bring a new level of honesty and moral integrity to the White House. The question of character was also brought into sharp relief by the scandals surrounding Bill Clinton, even if there were some signs that, in the wake of the Lewinsky affair, many ordinary people were prepared to give Clinton credit for his competent performance as president despite his evident character failings. Scandals do not necessarily produce a political climate in which questions of competence are eclipsed by those of character, but they do tend to produce a climate in which questions of character are given ever greater salience. Of course, one should not complain about honesty and moral integrity in politics: it is a good deal better to be governed by virtuous leaders than by rogues. But it would be worrying if the question of character was elevated to such a level of significance that issues of competence were marginalized or eclipsed. To be governed by virtuous but utterly incompetent leaders is unlikely to improve the collective well-being.

Finally, by contributing to a pervasive and deepening distrust, political scandals can produce weakened forms of government. Within the restricted field of professional politicians, major political scandals can help to produce a kind of political paralysis, as leaders and other representatives find themselves obliged to devote a great deal of time and political energy to shoring up an administration under siege. Major scandals, like Watergate or the Iran-Contra affair, can become such a preponderate focus of attention that they crowd out other issues, both from the media and from the agendas of politicians themselves. Repeated allegations of sleaze and corruption, such as those that afflicted John Major's administration in the early 1990s, can have a similar effect. Political leaders may find that their capacity to formulate and implement policies, and more generally to bring about the kind of cooperative political action which the process of governing requires, is compromised by the loss of respect and the corrosion of trust. Presidents and prime ministers may become lame ducks.

But political scandals can also produce weakened forms of government in another sense. A strong democracy is not only a political regime in which elected officials are able to act effectively: it is also a form of government in which the vast majority of ordinary citizens has an active stake in the process by which they are governed. This is not to say that strong democracy requires citizens to be actively and directly involved in all of the decision-making processes that affect their lives: this model of direct participatory democracy is undoubtedly of limited value for understanding the nature of and potential for democratic politics in modern, complex societies. But strong democracy does presuppose that ordinary citizens have some stake in the political processes of government, that they have some interest in and knowledge about the issues that affect their lives and that they have some ability and inclination to participate in political processes, whether this consists in electing representatives to legislate on their behalf or in participating more directly in other forms of political organization.

One of the dangers of political scandals is that they can help to produce an attitude of deep distrust among some sectors of the population, leading to diminishing levels of interest and participation. Some degree of suspicion and distrust can be invigorating for a democratic society, creating a culture of criticism and debate and producing a constant pressure for greater openness and accountability on the part of those who govern. But a pervasive attitude of cynicism and deep distrust can have the opposite effect, leading some sectors of the population to withdraw altogether from the political process. And a society in which significant sectors of the population have effectively given up their stake in the political process, turning their backs on a political system they judge to be irredeemably flawed or corrupt, is not a society with a strong and vibrant democracy. Rather, it is a society with a weakened form of democratic government in which the interest and participation of ordinary citizens has been attenuated by cynicism and deep distrust. Whether this weakened form of democratic government is a condition that can be alleviated or overcome, whether it is possible to create renewed interest and participation in circumstances where the stocks of social trust have been so thoroughly depleted, is a question whose answer remains unclear. But it is difficult to avoid the conclusion that the political culture of scandal is unlikely to make the task of creating a stronger and more inclusive form of democracy any easier.

Conclusion

One may be dismayed but one should not be surprised that, in this modern age of mediated visibility, scandal has become a pervasive feature of social and political life. Scandal is deeply rooted in our historical traditions and closely interwoven with the development of mediated forms of communication, a development which has changed the nature of the public domain and transformed the boundaries between the public and private spheres. Today, those who hold or aspire to positions of prominence in public life, including positions of power and responsibility in the political sphere, find themselves acting within an informational environment which is very different from that which existed several centuries – and even several decades – ago. Thanks to the development of multiple forms of mediated communication and the rise of numerous media organizations which are relatively independent of state power, political actors today must operate in an information environment which is more intensive, more extensive and less controllable than it was in the past. It is *more intensive* in the sense that the sheer quantity of information flow is much greater than before, as more and more organizations and communication networks make available an ever increasing volume of symbolic material. It is *more extensive* in the sense that the range of individuals who are drawn into these networks of communication and capable of receiving the output of media organizations is much greater than it was a century (or even several decades) ago, and in the sense that the geographical spread of these recipients is much wider: today, information flows very quickly through networks which are not only national but increasingly global in scope. And the information environment is *less controllable* in the sense that, given the proliferation of mediated forms of communication, it is much more difficult for political actors to throw a veil of secrecy around their activities and much harder to predict the consequences of unintended and unwanted disclosures. Whether they like it or not, political leaders today are more visible to more people and more closely scrutinized than they ever were in the past, and at the same time they are more exposed to the risk that actions or utterances which were performed or made covertly or in private will be disclosed in the public domain.

The rise of political scandal as a mediated event was closely interwoven with the changing information environment of political action. The kind of political scandal with which we are so familiar today – with its characteristic forms of disclosure and denunciation and its characteristic patterns of development – arose in the late eighteenth and nineteenth centuries, as part of a broader set of changes taking place in the media industries and in the structure of the political field. While the concept of scandal can be traced back to the ancient world and while depictions and allegations regarded as scandalous were relatively common in the print culture of early modern Europe, the rise of political scandal as a mediated event is a more recent historical development. It is a development that was shaped by the social and economic transformations which affected media organizations in the late eighteenth and early nineteenth centuries, and which helped to constitute journalistic practice as a relatively autonomous field of action with its own codes and conventions, its own body of practitioners and its own professional ethos. It is a development that was also shaped by the process of democratization within the political sphere, a process which was accompanied by the demand for more openness and accountability on the part of public officials and which required prospective political leaders to canvass for support within a competitive party system. Political scandal as a mediated event emerged in a social and historical context where the power of media organizations to intervene in and influence the course of events was being significantly enhanced, and where the capacity of political leaders to acquire and exercise power was becoming increasingly dependent on the resources – including symbolic resources like reputation and trust – which would enable them to mobilize support.

While the rise of political scandal was shaped by these broad transformations in the cultural and political spheres, the specific ways in which political scandals have occurred and developed since the late eighteenth century have varied considerably from one national context to another. The occurrence of a political scandal is always a contextualized event: it is part of a specific set of circumstances involving particular agents and organizations embedded in relations of power, presupposing certain norms and conventions which have a degree of moral bindingness and drawing on certain journalistic codes and practices which become sedimented into a kind of tradition. I have distinguished between three main types of political scandal and used this analytical framework to reconstruct the development of political scandals in Britain and the United States from the late eighteenth century to the present day. But I have also tried to show that, despite the historical specificity of political scandals and the differences that exist from one national context to another, a number of changes have occurred since the early 1960s which have helped to give political scandal a new significance in many societies today. These changes include the decline of ideological politics, with its class-based loyalties to political parties and its emphasis on ideological differences and conflicts; the rise of what I have called the politics of trust, with its emphasis on character and on the credibility and trustworthiness of actual or aspiring leaders; the changing culture of journalism; and the growing legalization of political life. Thanks to these developments (to which scandals have themselves contributed), scandals have taken on fresh significance as credibility tests in the context of struggles between political parties which could no longer count on traditional class loyalties and which were no longer divided by strong ideological differences.

Given these changes and given that, with the development of new technologies, the information environment of political action will only become more open and complex, it seems likely that scandal will remain a prominent feature of political life. Political scandal as a mediated event has been with us for two centuries and, energized by recent developments, it is unlikely to disappear in the near future. We shall have to learn to live in a world where the power to reveal and disclose, and the power to turn private activities into public events, is likely to outstrip any attempts that are made to restrict and control it. Political leaders and parties will undoubtedly devote more and more resources to the management of visibility; equipped with their media consultants and spin doctors, they will seek to control the agenda and shape the processes through which political leaders and their actions and policies are presented to distant others. But however much they may seek to manage their visibility in the mediated arena of modern politics, they cannot completely control it; even spin doctors may find themselves unspun, as Peter Mandelson discovered to his cost. The relations between political leaders, parties and governments, on the one hand, and the many media organizations and communication networks, on the other, are simply too complex and too fraught with conflicting aims and expectations to ensure that the wishes of politicians and their advisers will be dutifully reported and accepted without question by those working in the media. Moreover, with the development of new technologies capable of ever more sophisticated forms of detection and recording, and with the proliferation of new networks of communication and information flow which lie outside traditional media channels but which are capable of feeding material into them, the ability of politicians and their advisers to control the agenda and manage their self-presentation is likely to be attenuated even further. There are simply too many sources of information available today, and too many individuals and organizations that have an interest – economic, political or even personal – in obtaining and disclosing material which may not concur happily with the images that politicians would like to present of themselves.

Is this necessarily a politically pernicious state of affairs? Is political scandal a phenomenon to be unequivocally condemned by anyone who is seriously concerned about the political well-being of our societies today? Throughout this book I have tried to resist a blanket condemnation of this kind and have tried to develop a more discriminating way of thinking about political scandal and its consequences. Now, by way of a conclusion, I want to address some issues of a more normative kind about how we should assess the contribution that scandals have made, and are likely to make, to the quality of our public life.

We should not be too quick to assume that scandals will always have a baleful impact on public life, trivializing public debate and distracting people from the issues that really matter. On the contrary, in many cases scandals have highlighted hidden activities which were of questionable propriety, and have helped to stimulate important debates about the conduct and accountability of those who exercise power. Financial scandals in the political field have called attention to forms of corruption and conflicts of interest that might otherwise have gone unnoticed, and the public controversies sparked off by these scandals have, on some occasions, helped to produce significant reforms (as in the case of the civil service reforms in the United States in the late nineteenth century, or, to take a more recent example, the reforms implemented by the House of Commons in the wake of the Nolan Committee's report). Power scandals have called attention to hidden, invisible forms of power which were concealed behind the publicly agreed procedures for exercising power and the publicly declared positions of those who exercise it; in some cases, they have highlighted serious abuses of power and lapses of judgement, and helped to produce more accountable mechanisms for monitoring the activities of power-holders. If we bear in mind considerations of this kind, then we can see that in many cases our critical concern might be directed more effectively towards the activities disclosed by political scandals than towards the phenomenon of political scandal as such. Of course, to emphasize the positive contribution of political scandals is not to suggest that all scandals have salutary political consequences – patently this is not so. Nor do I wish to downplay the importance of thinking critically about political scandals and the potentially deleterious impact that they can have on public life. But the critical assessment of political scandal would be unduly one-sided if it ignored the very important role that scandals have played, both historically and in recent years, in stimulating public debate about the ways in which political power is acquired and exercised in our societies, about the standards of conduct in public life and about the ways in which those who exercise power are rendered accountable in the public domain.

So why should we be worried about political scandal? Should the profusion of political scandal in recent decades be a source of concern to us? And if so, what can we do about it? There are, in my view, a number of reasons why we should be concerned – here I shall focus on three. In the first place, while it is clear that financial scandals and power scandals can make a valuable contribution to public debate about the exercise and accountability of power, it is less clear that sex scandals do, and yet in some national contexts and in some sectors of the press, sex scandals are a predominant form of political scandal. Once again, we should not be too quick to dismiss sex scandals as mere titillation which devalues the quality of public life by focusing attention on the personal indiscretions of political leaders: sex scandals in the political field very often involve, as we have seen, a good deal more than sex. Clandestine sexual activities or liaisons may lie at the origin of sexual-political scandals, but they very often involve other factors too, such as actual or potential conflicts of interest (Profumo), hypocrisy (Parkinson's predicament) and second-order transgressions which may on occasion involve actual or potential infringements of the law (Thorpe, Clinton and many others). Nevertheless, it is undoubtedly the case that some sex scandals do hinge solely or overwhelmingly on revelations or allegations about the private lives of public figures in ways that do not have any demonstrable connection to broader issues of legitimate public interest or concern. And it is also the case that some sectors of the press, and some of the agents and organizations which operate in the media and political fields, have perfected the art of exploiting personal indiscretions and have sought systematically to mobilize symbolic power against political leaders whose private lives may not concur with certain conventional norms and expectations. For anyone concerned with the quality of our public life, these aspects of sexual-political scandals are bound to be troubling.

A second source of concern is what we could describe as the scandal syndrome – that is, the distinctive combination of factors which tends to produce an ever escalating preoccupation with scandal. There are isolated political scandals, but more often than not scandals tend to come in waves, as each scandal raises the political stakes still further and increases the symbolic and political value that might be derived – both for political opponents and for media organizations and personnel – from further revelations. I have tried to reconstruct the logic of this kind of scandal syndrome for the period from the 1960s to the present day, as exemplified by the cultures of political scandal which have developed in Britain and the United States in the post-Profumo, post-Watergate age. For those concerned with the quality of our public life today, the worry – an understandable worry – is that this kind of scandal syndrome tends to become a self-reproducing and self-reinforcing process, driven on by competitive and combative struggles in the media and political fields and giving rise to more and more scandals which increasingly become the focus of mediated forms of public debate, marginalizing or displacing other issues and producing on occasion a climate of political crisis which can debilitate or even paralyse a government. Whatever one might think about the significance of particular scandals, it seems clear that this kind of scandal syndrome does not substantially enhance the quality of our public life.

A third reason to be concerned about political scandal has to do with the possible impact of scandals on the forms and relations of trust which are a vital component of social and political life. As I argued in the previous chapter, the fluid conduct of social interaction depends to some extent on relations of trust which are built up over time. Trust is a kind of resource which can be slowly and gradually accumulated, and which can facilitate cooperative forms of action and interaction. But it is also a fragile resource which can be very rapidly depleted and which, once depleted, can be very difficult to restore. Social relations characterized by deep and pervasive distrust tend to be conflictual, uncooperative and non-participatory: individuals are not inclined to cooperate with those whom they do not trust. And one of the most serious dangers of political scandal, as I tried to show, is that it can contribute to a gradual corrosion of the forms and relations of trust upon which cooperative political action depends. A culture of political scandal which is characterized by recurrent and escalating cycles is likely to produce a culture of growing cynicism and distrust. And while some degree of cynicism and distrust is not necessarily damaging in a democratic society, deep distrust can have pernicious effects. It can fuel the demand for the introduction of more and more trust-economizing devices to try to compensate for the draining away of social trust and it can lead some individuals increasingly to withdraw from any participation in the political sphere.

So there are reasons – good reasons, in my view – to be concerned about political scandal and its consequences for the quality of our public life. Are there ways in which we can act in order to counter the more troubling aspects of political scandal and to minimize the negative consequences? Is there anything that can and should be done? If we accept the basic principles of a democratic society – including the principle of a representative political system in which candidates and their parties regularly compete for power, as well as the principle of free and pluralistic media which are formally independent of the state – then we shall have to accept that there are limits on what can and should be done in this regard. The possibility of political scandal is inherent in the organizing principles of a democratic society, and however much we might wish to criticize particular scandals or forms of scandal, it would not be wise to try to suppress or substantially curtail political scandal as such. The political cost of trying to alter the basic conditions which give rise to scandals would greatly exceed the benefits gained. But there are things of a more limited kind that could be done. In some cases these are things that could be backed up by new legislation or by modifications of existing legislation, but in other cases it is almost certainly best to think in terms of informal conventions and codes of practice, even if these are often rather loose and difficult to enforce. I shall focus on five areas where some modest interventions and alterations could be made.

At the most general level, the best way to respond to political scandals is to create more openness and accountability in government. All bureaucracies, as Max Weber noted, tend to increase the power of bureaucrats and to protect their position by keeping their knowledge and intentions secret.[1] Secrecy has clear advantages for administrative officials: it allows them to pursue their goals without having to explain and justify their actions, it enables them to correct mistakes without having to provide detailed and possibly embarrassing explanations and it protects them from hostile criticism. But secrecy also creates a veil for the abuse of power, as we have seen, and it tends to nurture a climate of suspicion and betrayal. Some insiders may leak information and some outsiders may pry and probe, convinced that there are important secrets to be uncovered. Hence secrecy tends to fuel scandals, which in turn tend to deepen the sense of suspicion: in a culture riven by scandal, inscrutability breeds mistrust. One way to counter this process is to introduce more openness and accountability in bureaucracies and administrative systems, including those of government. More openness leaves less room for suspicion: outsiders have fewer grounds to worry when they can see that there is nothing to hide. It also reduces the risk of leaks and unwanted disclosures – a risk which, given the changing information environment of political action, is likely only to increase unless administrative systems adapt. One could argue, moreover, that greater openness and accountability in our systems of government is an intrinsically desirable feature of a democratic order and an essential means of combating abuses of power.[2] Of course, there will always be areas of government where a degree of secrecy and confidentiality is essential and justifiable – in relation, for instance, to certain matters of defence, or certain stages in the process of policy formation.[3] But it would not be implausible to maintain that an important and desirable feature of a democratic society is that there should be relatively few areas where secrecy and confidentiality are allowed to prevail, that these areas should be clearly defined and agreed in advance, and that there should be effective and accountable mechanisms for monitoring the activities which take place within these realms.

A second way in which we can respond constructively to political scandals is to establish clear standards of conduct for public officials. This is particularly important with regard to financial matters. In many political contexts, the rules governing the financial activities and private financial interests of politicians were traditionally very loose and vague. It was generally assumed that many politicians were individuals of independent means, and generally recognized that many had close connections with (and in some cases financial interests in) private business concerns and other extraparliamentary organizations. The actual or potential conflicts of interest created by these connections have been a rich source of political scandals since the late nineteenth century, although it is only relatively recently that clear and explicit guidelines for politicians have been introduced in some contexts and politicians have been strongly encouraged (if not required) to declare their private financial interests in a public register. Some of the early attempts to develop codes of conduct for public officials in order to minimize conflicts of interest were rather partial and half-hearted, in many cases amounting to voluntary systems of self-regulation with limited inducement to conform. More recent innovations – such as the codes and practices adopted by the House of Commons in the wake of the Nolan Committee's report – represent a clear step forward. The adoption of explicit codes of conduct and public registers in which politicians are required to declare their private interests helps to reduce the realm of vagueness and ambiguity where private interests overlap with public duties and responsibilities. They give politicians clear guidelines or sources of advice with reference to which they can make decisions about their own commitments and activities, and they make the private affiliations of politicians a matter of public record. Of course, such codes and registers will not eliminate all ambiguities, and their adoption will not prevent some individuals from behaving in reprehensible ways. But even a modest reduction of ambiguity is likely to remove some of the sources of actual or potential conflict of interest which can precipitate political scandals and to allay some of the doubts which can drive them forward.

A third measure has to do with the mechanisms for investigating alleged cases of wrongdoing. In order to protect political systems from abuses of power and other misuses of public office, and in order to restore public confidence in the wake of damaging disclosures and allegations, it is essential to ensure that there are robust and effective mechanisms for investigating allegations and for implementing recommendations. This was, of course, one of the principal motivations behind one of the most important pieces of post-Watergate legislation in the United States, the Ethics in Government Act of 1978, which, in addition to tightening the rules on conflicts of interest and public disclosure, created a powerful new office for investigating cases of alleged wrongdoing – the office of the special prosecutor (or independent counsel). But it is clear from recent American political history that there are also dangers with this system: despite the intention of ensuring that the special prosecutor is impartial and independent, such investigations can easily play into party-political conflicts and interests; and a determined prosecutor with ample resources and a relatively open remit may find that the investigation turns into a wide-ranging inquiry which moves well beyond the original focus of concern (the 'roving searchlight' feared by Bernard Nussbaum). While a robust and effective system of investigation is essential, it is also important to ensure that, so far as possible, this system is insulated from partisan interests. In most if not all cases it would also be wise to ensure that any particular investigation has a clear remit and a well-defined focus.

The fourth and fifth measures have to do with the media. For it is clear that while journalists and media organizations have played an important role in calling attention to questionable and corrupt activities by politicians and other public officials, they also bear a good deal of responsibility for some of the excesses. On many occasions they have been overly eager to publish information and allegations about the private lives of public figures when such material has no discernible connection with issues of legitimate public interest. A strong case can be made in favour of some form of protection for the personal privacy of individuals against unwanted intrusion by the media. The freedom of the press is a fundamental principle which should be safeguarded in a democratic society, but it is not a principle which gives the media an untrammelled right to publish any information or allegation about an individual's private life. In the case of political leaders and other public officials, it is not easy to draw a clear dividing line between those aspects of an individual's private life which the media can legitimately investigate and publicize, and those aspects which ought properly to remain off limits. Moreover, it is also clear that journalists cannot always take (and should not be obliged to take) a politician's claims to privacy at face value, since privacy can also be used as a mask to cover up abuses, corrupt practices or conflicts of interest which might be of genuine public concern. But however difficult it is to draw a line between those aspects of private life which are of legitimate public interest, on the one hand, and those which are not, on the other, it is a line which those working in the media should endeavour to draw. This is part of the responsibility that properly belongs to media organizations and media personnel as wielders of symbolic power in the public domain. But if they fail to exercise this responsibility of their own accord, they may well find that the task of drawing the line will increasingly become a matter of law.

While we may legitimately expect and, if necessary, require media organizations to exercise a degree of discretion in the investigation and publication of details and allegations about the private lives of individuals, we must also recognize that, in this age of proliferating networks of communication and information flow, it will be increasingly difficult to control the circulation of information and allegations about the private lives of prominent public figures. Even if mainstream media channels exercised a greater degree of discretion about aspects of private life, it would be extremely difficult – indeed impossible – to prevent such matters from being reported or discussed in the many quasi-public forums that exist on the internet and elsewhere. Moreover, as we have seen, in recent years a number of quasi-political organizations have emerged, especially in the United States, which have access to the media and which have sought to shape the agenda of public debate. In this rapidly changing information environment, the more traditional media organizations and mainstream media channels have an even greater responsibility – and this is my fifth point – to exercise caution and professional judgement in deciding what information and allegations to report. If the circular circulation of information that characterizes the media is not to become the circular circulation of gossip, innuendo, misinformation and unfounded speculation, then media organizations and personnel must be particularly careful to check the accuracy of information and the reliability of sources. It may well be the case that the logic of the media field – with its grinding competition, its relentless search for new stories and its tendency to produce the bandwagon effect – does little to help maintain high standards of accuracy and reliability in the media. But in such circumstances it is all the more important for those who work in the media to be aware of the responsibilities which go along with their power to shape public debate.

And in this new information environment, political leaders should be aware that their actions and utterances, past and present, will be scrutinized as never before. While political leaders are entitled to a degree of personal privacy like any other individual, they should be aware that, given the elasticity of the boundary between personal privacy and legitimate public interest, the changing culture of journalism and the growing emphasis on questions of character and trust in contemporary politics, their actions and utterances are likely to be routinely interrogated in the media with a kind of intensity and censoriousness that was rarely if ever known in the past. Significant lapses of judgement in the private lives of politicians run a higher risk today of becoming serious political liabilities, and the denial of allegations is more likely to be met by scepticism and by a dogged determination to dig deeper. In these circumstances political leaders may find that however much they might wish to protect their privacy, discretion in the conduct of their private lives and honesty in the face of allegations are their best guides. For they may find that, when it comes to matters of sexuality and personal conduct, many people today are less judgemental and a good deal more understanding (if not indifferent) than some of the self-appointed moralists who express their views in the media, and political leaders only inflict more damage on themselves by publicly denying allegations which subsequently turn out to be true. In this modern age of mediated visibility, those who hold or aspire to positions of power will be subjected to a degree of public scrutiny which greatly exceeds what many of their predecessors were obliged to endure, and we should not underestimate the personal anguish and political damage that this can cause. But if it helps to produce more openness and accountability in government, if it stimulates more effective debate about standards of conduct both in public life and in the media and if it encourages our political leaders to handle with greater circumspection and humility the trust that is vested in them as holders of public office, then the gains would not be insignificant.

Notes

Introduction

1 *The Times*, 18 Nov. 1890, p. 9.

2 *Pall Mall Gazette*, 24 May 1886, p. 8.

3 *The Times*, 17 Nov. 1890, p. 4.

4 For a full account of the circumstances surrounding this affair and its aftermath, see F. S. L. Lyons, *The Fall of Parnell, 1890–91* (London: Routledge and Kegan Paul, 1960); F. S. L. Lyons, *Charles Stewart Parnell* (London: Collins, 1977); Trevor Fisher, *Scandal: The Sexual Politics of Late Victorian Britain* (Stroud: Alan Sutton, 1995), ch. 7.

5 For a selection of anthologies and general surveys of scandal, see Colin Wilson and Donald Seaman, *Scandal! An Encyclopaedia* (London: Weidenfeld and Nicolson, 1986); H. Montgomery Hyde, *A Tangled Web: Sex Scandals in British Politics and Society* (London: Constable, 1986); Sean Callery, *Scandals: Gripping Accounts of the Exposed and Deposed* (London: Apple Press, 1992); Bruce Palling (ed.), *The Book of Modern Scandal: From Byron to the Present Day* (London: Weidenfeld and Nicolson, 1995); Matthew Parris, *Great Parliamentary Scandals: Four Centuries of Calumny, Smear and Innuendo* (London: Robson Books, 1995); *Political Scandals and Causes Célèbres since 1945: An International Reference Compendium* (Harlow: Longman, n.d.). I occasionally draw on these various anthologies, and especially on the helpful books by Matthew Parris and H. Montgomery Hyde and the very informative Longman volume.

6 Among the more serious and systematic studies of scandal are the following: Eric de Dampierre, 'Thèmes pour l'étude du scandale', *Annales*, 9.3 (1954), pp. 328–36; Maxime Rodinson, 'De l'histoire de l'anti-

sémitisme à la sociologie du scandale', *Cahiers Internationaux de Sociologie*, 49 (1970), pp. 143–50; Manfred Schmitz, *Theorie und Praxis des politischen Skandals* (Frankfurt: Campus Verlag, 1981); Dirk Käsler et al., *Der politische Skandal: zur symbolischen und dramaturgischen Qualität von Politik* (Opladen: Westdeutscher Verlag, 1991); Anthony King, 'Sex, Money, and Power', in Richard Hodder-Williams and James Ceaser (eds), *Politics in Britain and the United States: Comparative Perspectives* (Durham, N.C.: Duke University Press, 1986), pp. 173–222; Andrei S. Markovits and Mark Silverstein (eds), *The Politics of Scandal: Power and Process in Liberal Democracies* (New York: Holmes and Meier, 1988); Suzanne Garment, *Scandal: The Culture of Mistrust in American Politics* (New York: Doubleday, 1992); James Lull and Stephen Hinerman (eds), *Media Scandals: Morality and Desire in the Popular Culture Marketplace* (Cambridge: Polity Press, 1997); Robert Williams, *Political Scandals in the USA* (Edinburgh: Keele University Press, 1998).

7 For a discussion of political scandals in France, see Philip M. Williams, *Wars, Plots and Scandals in Post-war France* (Cambridge: Cambridge University Press, 1970). For a perceptive analysis of recent political scandals in Italy, see Judith Chubb and Maurizio Vannicelli, 'Italy: A Web of Scandals in a Flawed Democracy', in Markovits and Silverstein, *The Politics of Scandal*, pp. 122–50. Although I shall draw my examples primarily from the Anglo-American world, I shall occasionally use Italy as a point of comparison.

Chapter 1 What is Scandal?

1 *Oxford English Dictionary* (*OED*), 2nd edn (Oxford: Clarendon Press, 1989), vol. 14, p. 573.
2 See Maxime Rodinson, 'De l'histoire de l'antisémitisme à la sociologie du scandale', *Cahiers Internationaux de Sociologie*, 49 (1970), pp. 143–50.
3 See *OED*, vol. 14, pp. 573–4.
4 See Eric de Dampierre, 'Thèmes pour l'étude du scandale', *Annales*, 9.3 (1954), p. 330: 'scandal, in its current sense, is no longer a relation between two people, between someone who scandalizes and someone who is scandalized, but rather an event which breaks out at the heart of a collectivity of people.'
5 As in, for example, 'the scandal of particularity', a phrase used by some theologians to describe the difficulty of seeing the particular man, Jesus, as the universal Saviour (*OED*, vol. 14, p. 573).
6 Anthony King, 'Sex, Money, and Power', in Richard Hodder-Williams and James Ceaser (eds), *Politics in Britain and the United States: Comparative Perspectives* (Durham, N.C.: Duke University Press, 1986), p. 175.

7 This point is made very forcefully by Andrei S. Markovits and Mark Silverstein in their introduction to Markovits and Silverstein (eds), *The Politics of Scandal: Power and Process in Liberal Democracies* (New York: Holmes and Meier, 1988); I shall examine their views in more detail in chapter 4.

8 King draws a somewhat similar distinction between three types of political scandal ('Sex, Money, and Power', p. 179), although, like many commentators, he tends to treat sex scandals as something other than true political scandals. I shall return to these issues in chapter 5.

9 Parkinson's predicament is discussed in more detail in chapter 5.

10 Whether Profumo would have survived the scandal and retained his ministerial position in the absence of this second-order transgression is a moot point. This issue, and other aspects of the Profumo affair, are examined further in chapter 5.

11 See J. L. Austin, *How To Do Things with Words*, 2nd edn, ed. J. O. Urmson and Marina Sbisà (Oxford: Oxford University Press, 1976).

12 This example is discussed in chapter 5.

13 I regard symbolic power as one of four basic forms of power; see John B. Thompson, *The Media and Modernity: A Social Theory of the Media* (Cambridge: Polity Press, 1995), pp. 12–18.

14 *OED*, vol. 6, pp. 699–700.

15 Sally Engle Merry, 'Rethinking Gossip and Scandal', in Donald Block (ed.), *Toward a General Theory of Social Control*, vol. 1: *Fundamentals* (Orlando: Academic Press, 1984), p. 276: 'Gossip is a form of private information that symbolizes intimacy.'

16 The uses of gossip have been discussed by anthropologists, and more recently by historians and others. In addition to the essay by Sally Engle Merry cited above, see especially Max Gluckman, 'Gossip and Scandal', *Current Anthropology*, 4.3 (1963), pp. 307–16; Robert Paine, 'What is Gossip About? An Alternative Hypothesis', *Man*, 2 (1967), pp. 278–85; Ulf Hannerz, 'Gossip, Networks, and Culture in a Black American Ghetto', *Ethnos*, 32 (1967), pp. 35–60; P. M. Spacks, *Gossip* (New York: Knopf, 1985); C. J. Wickham, 'Gossip and Resistance among the Medieval Peasantry', Inaugural Lecture, University of Birmingham, Birmingham, 1995.

17 See Thompson, *The Media and Modernity*, pp. 219–25.

18 *OED*, vol. 14, pp. 241–2.

19 See Ralph L. Rosnow and Gary Alan Fine, *Rumour and Gossip: The Social Psychology of Hearsay* (New York: Elsevier, 1976), pp. 11ff.

20 *OED*, vol. 3, pp. 972–4.

21 For more detailed discussions of the concept of corruption and of the nature and extent of corrupt practices in contemporary societies, see James C. Scott, *Comparative Political Corruption* (Englewood Cliffs, N.J.: Prentice Hall, 1972); Arnold J. Heidenheimer, Michael Johnston and Victor T. Levine (eds), *Political Corruption: A Handbook* (New Brunswick,

N.J.: Transaction, 1989); Syed Hussein Alatas, *Corruption: Its Nature, Causes and Functions* (Aldershot: Gower, 1990).

22 On bribery, see John T. Noonan, Jr, *Bribes* (New York: Macmillan, 1984).

Chapter 2 The Rise of Mediated Scandal

1 For a more detailed account of these transformations, see John B. Thompson, *The Media and Modernity: A Social Theory of the Media* (Cambridge: Polity Press, 1995), ch. 2.

2 See Immanuel Wallerstein, *The Modern World-System I: Capitalist Agriculture and the Origins of the European World-Economy in the Sixteenth Century* (New York: Academic Press, 1974) and *The Modern World-System II: Mercantilism and the Consolidation of the European World-Economy, 1600–1750* (New York: Academic Press, 1980); Michael Mann, *The Sources of Social Power*, vol. 1: *A History of Power from the Beginning to AD 1760* (Cambridge: Cambridge University Press, 1986), chs 12–15.

3 See Charles Tilly (ed.), *The Formation of National States in Western Europe* (Princeton: Princeton University Press, 1975); Charles Tilly, *Coercion, Capital, and European States, AD 990–1990* (Oxford: Blackwell, 1990); Mann, *The Sources of Social Power*, vol. 1, chs 12–16; Michael Mann, *The Sources of Social Power*, vol. 2: *The Rise of Classes and Nation-States, 1760–1914* (Cambridge: Cambridge University Press, 1993).

4 A more detailed discussion of the public–private distinction, and of the changing nature of publicness and visibility, can be found in Thompson, *The Media and Modernity*, ch. 4.

5 See Clifford Geertz, 'Centers, Kings, and Charisma: Reflections on the Symbolics of Power', in his *Local Knowledge: Further Essays in Interpretive Anthropology* (New York: Basic Books, 1983), pp. 121–46; S. R. F. Price, *Rituals and Power: The Roman Imperial Cult in Asia Minor* (Cambridge: Cambridge University Press, 1984).

6 See Peter Burke, *The Fabrication of Louis XIV* (New Haven and London: Yale University Press, 1992); J. H. Elliott, 'Power and Propaganda in the Spain of Philip IV', in Sean Wilentz (ed.), *Rites of Power: Symbolism, Ritual, and Politics since the Middle Ages* (Philadelphia: University of Pennsylvania Press, 1985), pp. 145–73.

7 Burke, *The Fabrication of Louis XIV*, p. 17.

8 This theme is perceptively explored by Kathleen Hall Jamieson in her *Eloquence in an Electronic Age: The Transformation of Political Speechmaking* (New York and Oxford: Oxford University Press, 1988), esp. ch. 3.

9 This point is made very effectively by Joshua Meyrowitz; see his *No Sense of Place: The Impact of Electronic Media on Social Behavior* (New York and Oxford: Oxford University Press, 1985), pp. 270ff.

10 *Remarques sur le gouvernement du royaume,* anonymous pamphlet cited in Burke, *The Fabrication of Louis XIV,* p. 139.

11 Burke, *The Fabrication of Louis XIV,* pp. 135ff.

12 See Robert Darnton, *The Forbidden Best-Sellers of Pre-revolutionary France* (London: HarperCollins, 1976), esp. pp. 76–82. Darnton argues that this literature gradually eroded the legitimacy of the Old Regime: 'like the drip, drip of water on a stone, the denunciations of dissolute kings and wicked ministers wore away the layer of sacredness that made the monarchy legitimate in the eyes of its subjects' (p. 216).

13 See especially Sandra Clark, *The Elizabethan Pamphleteers: Popular Moralistic Pamphlets 1580–1640* (London: Athlone Press, 1983). See also Leslie Shepard, *The History of Street Literature* (Newton Abbott: David and Charles, 1973); Margaret Spufford, *Small Books and Pleasant Histories: Popular Fiction and its Readership in Seventeenth-Century England* (London: Methuen, 1981).

14 See Joseph Frank, *The Beginnings of the English Newspaper, 1620–1660* (Cambridge, Mass.: Harvard University Press, 1961); Joad Raymond, *The Invention of the Newspaper: English Newsbooks 1641–1649* (Oxford: Oxford University Press, 1996).

15 *Mercurius Britanicus,* 92 (4 Aug. 1645), pp. 825–6.

16 *Journals of the House of Lords,* vol. 7 (1644–5), p. 525.

17 See Raymond, *The Invention of the Newspaper,* pp. 42–3, for a fuller account of this episode.

18 Frank, *The Beginnings of the English Newspaper,* pp. 135ff.; Raymond, *The Invention of the Newspaper,* pp. 54ff.

19 See F. S. Siebert, *Freedom of the Press in England, 1476–1776* (Urbana: University of Illinois Press, 1952).

20 For more detailed accounts of Wilkes's political and publishing activities, see Robert Rea, *The English Press in Politics 1760–1774* (Lincoln: University of Nebraska Press, 1963), chs 2–5; John Brewer, *Party Ideology and Popular Politics at the Accession of George III* (Cambridge: Cambridge University Press, 1976), esp. ch. 9.

21 *North Briton,* 45 (23 Apr. 1763).

22 *The Parliamentary History of England, from the Earliest Period to the Year 1803,* vol. 15 (1753–65), cols 1347, 1359–60.

23 See Lucyle Werkmeister, *The London Daily Press 1772–1792* (Lincoln: University of Nebraska Press, 1963).

24 See Alan J. Lee, *The Origins of the Popular Press in England 1855–1914* (London: Croom Helm, 1976).

25 Michael Schudson, *Discovering the News: A Social History of American Newspapers* (New York: Basic Books, 1978), ch. 1.

26 Ibid., ch. 2. 'As news was more or less "invented" in the 1830s, the reporter was a social invention of the 1880s and 1890s' (p. 65).

27 For a more detailed discussion of the moral climate of late nineteenth-century Britain, see Jeffrey Weeks, *Sex, Politics and Society: The Regulation*

of Sexuality since 1800, 2nd edn (London: Longman, 1989), chs 2–6; Trevor Fisher, *Scandal: The Sexual Politics of Late Victorian Britain* (Stroud: Alan Sutton, 1995).

28 See J. W. Robertson Scott, *The Life and Death of a Newspaper* (London: Methuen, 1952).

29 In the spring of 1885, the Chamberlain of the City of London called on Stead and implored him to help rouse public opinion in support of the Bill which, although it had been twice passed through the House of Lords, was being held up in the Commons. ' "All our work," said the Chamberlain, "will be wasted unless you can rouse public opinion and compel the new Government to take up the Bill and pass it into law." ' Stead then visited the head of Scotland Yard and asked whether the violation of young girls was being perpetrated in London. ' "Certainly," replied the chief of the department, "there is no doubt of it". "Why", exclaimed Stead, "the very thought of it is enough to raise hell". "It is true," said the officer, "and although it ought to raise hell it does not even rouse the neighbours." "Then *I* will raise hell," said Stead, and set himself to arouse the nation.' (The quotes are from Robertson Scott, *The Life and Death of a Newspaper*, pp. 125–6.)

30 *Pall Mall Gazette*, 4 July 1885, p. 1. The articles began on 6 July 1885 and ran for five days. For more detailed discussion of the articles and the political response, see Robertson Scott, *The Life and Death of a Newspaper*, chs 13–14; Fisher, *Scandal*, ch. 4; Judith R. Walkowitz, *City of Dreadful Delight: Narratives of Sexual Danger in Late-Victorian London* (Chicago: University of Chicago Press, 1992), chs 3–4.

31 Certainly this is how Stead understood his own role on this occasion: 'With the aid of a few friends', wrote Stead, 'I went disguised into the lowest haunts of criminal vice and obtained only too ample proof of the reality and extent of the evils complained of . . . I was an investigator exposing a vast system of organised crime.' (Quoted in Robertson Scott, *The Life and Death of a Newspaper*, pp. 127–8.)

32 See H. Montgomery Hyde, *The Cleveland Street Scandal* (London: W. H. Allen, 1976).

33 *North London Press*, 16 Nov. 1889, p. 5.

34 See Louis Filler, *The Muckrakers: Crusaders for American Liberalism* (Chicago: Henry Regnery, 1968).

35 See Schudson, *Discovering the News*, ch. 5.

Chapter 3 Scandal as a Mediated Event

1 Erving Goffman, *The Presentation of Self in Everyday Life* (Harmondsworth: Penguin, 1969).

2 Ibid., pp. 100ff.

3 In July 1993 John Major gave an interview to ITN's political editor, Michael Brunson. They were waiting in the studio to shoot 'cutaways' (silent shots used to fill gaps in an edited interview) and neither was aware that the microphone was still on – the conversation was being monitored by BBC staff, who were waiting to record their own interview with the Prime Minister. Major spoke openly and frankly to Brunson about the difficulties he faced at a sensitive stage of the political debate in Britain about European integration. He was trying to secure ratification of the Maastricht Treaty but was facing determined opposition from three Eurosceptic members of his own Cabinet. Why don't you simply sack them, asked Brunson, and replace them with three new Cabinet members? 'I could bring in other people,' replied Major. 'But where do you think most of this poison is coming from? – from the dispossessed and the never-possessed. You can think of ex-ministers who are going around causing all sorts of trouble. We don't want another three more of the bastards out there' (quoted in the *Observer*, 25 July 1993, p. 1). At this point in the conversation someone realized what was happening and turned off the microphone, but the damage was already done. Major's off-the-record remarks were widely reported in the press, with much attention given to his unflattering characterization of his Cabinet colleagues. 'Major hits at Cabinet "bastards"' was the headline on the front page of the relatively restrained *Observer*.

4 See John B. Thompson, *The Media and Modernity: A Social Theory of the Media* (Cambridge: Polity Press, 1995), pp. 110–11.

5 Daniel Dayan and Elihu Katz, *Media Events: The Live Broadcasting of History* (Cambridge, Mass.: Harvard University Press, 1992). It would be a mistake, however, to regard mediated scandals more generally as 'media events' in the sense of Dayan and Katz. For mediated scandals are very rarely events which are carefully orchestrated and planned in advance (although some aspects of some scandals may be).

6 See S. Elizabeth Bird, 'What a Story! Understanding the Audience for Scandal', in James Lull and Stephen Hinerman (eds), *Media Scandals: Morality and Desire in the Popular Culture Marketplace* (Cambridge: Polity Press, 1997), pp. 99–121.

7 'I love dish, I live for dish,' explains Lucianne Goldberg, the self-styled New York agent and publicist who advised Linda Tripp during the Clinton–Lewinsky affair. (It was Goldberg who urged Tripp to tape-record her conversations with Monica Lewinsky.) 'Dish is what you do with dirt, tittle-tattle, intrigue, scandal . . . inside dope.' (Quoted in John Cornwell, 'Kiss of the Spider Woman', *Sunday Times Magazine*, 27 June 1999, p. 17.)

8 The term 'habitus' is borrowed from Bourdieu. He uses this notion to describe a set of durable and generative dispositions which incline agents to act in certain ways. See especially Pierre Bourdieu, *The Logic of Practice*, trans. Richard Nice (Cambridge: Polity Press, 1990), pp. 52ff.

9 The attempt to shape policy agendas by provoking moral outrage was a prominent feature of the work of crusading editors in late nineteenth-century Britain and the United States, and of muckraking journalists like Lincoln Steffens and Ida Tarbell. But it has also become an integral part of the self-understanding of investigative journalists today. This is brought out well by David Protess and his associates in their study of investigative reporting in the United States in the 1980s. 'Investigative journalists *intend* to provoke outrage in their reports of malfeasance,' observe Protess et al. 'Investigative reporters find personal satisfaction in doing stories that lead to civic betterment' (David L. Protess, Fay Lomax Cook, Jack C. Doppelt, James S. Ettema, Margaret T. Gordon, Donna R. Leff and Peter Miller, *The Journalism of Outrage: Investigative Reporting and Agenda Building in America* (New York: Guilford Press, 1991), p. 5). Protess and his associates also show, however, that the policy impact of investigative reporting is much more complicated than the linear mobilization model would suggest. Investigative journalists may seek to shape policy agendas by provoking outrage in readers and viewers, but in practice these agendas are often shaped by the formation of coalitions between journalists and policy-makers which begin to produce outcomes before the results of the investigations are made public.

10 The most obvious example of this is Watergate. In their award-winning account of the role they played in the Watergate scandal, *Washington Post* reporters Bob Woodward and Carl Bernstein presented themselves as detectives who had to struggle against secrecy, lies, false leads and intense political pressure in order to piece together the puzzle that eventually led to Nixon's downfall. (See Bob Woodward and Carl Bernstein, *All the President's Men* (New York: Simon and Schuster, 1974); see also the 1976 film based on the book.) But the account of Woodward and Bernstein tends to exaggerate their own role in the unfolding sequence of events and to downplay the significance of FBI investigations, judicial proceedings and congressional inquiries, during which many of the most important revelations emerged. For an account of the mythification of the role of journalism in Watergate, see Michael Schudson, *Watergate in American Memory: How We Remember, Forget, and Reconstruct the Past* (New York: Basic Books, 1992), pp. 104ff., and 'Watergate and the Press', in his *The Power of News* (Cambridge, Mass.: Harvard University Press, 1995), pp. 142–65.

11 Here John F. Kennedy is the most striking example. Many journalists knew about Kennedy's affairs but simply turned a blind eye. 'There used to be a gentleman's agreement about reporting such things,' observed one former reporter (Raymond Strother, quoted in 'Sex and the Presidency', *Life*, Aug. 1987, p. 71).

12 See Pierre Bourdieu, *On Television*, trans. Priscilla Parkhurst Ferguson (New York: New Press, 1998), pp. 23ff.

13 For a candid, insider's account of the journalistic practices of the tabloid press and their techniques for producing scandal, see Gerry Brown, *Exposed! Sensational True Story of a Fleet Street Reporter* (London: Virgin, 1995). 'The number one priority of a good tabloid editor', remarks Brown, 'is to get the dirt on a major TV celebrity. Number two is to target any middle-ranking celebrity. Number three is scandal about a minor TV celebrity' (p. 146). Brown worked for both the *News of the World* and the *National Enquirer*, so unfortunately he knows what he's talking about.

14 'This syndrome appears after one adventurous member of the mass media reports a certain "fact." In this context, it is irrelevant whether the "fact" is true; the other members of the media adopt it as gospel and spread it across the face of the land. Jackals tend to lurk in the brush until the lion has made his kill; after he has departed, the jackals rush forward to share in the feast. To be a jackal requires neither enterprise nor thought' (J. Herbert Altschull, 'The Journalist and Instant History: An Example of the Jackal Syndrome', *Journalism Quarterly*, 50 (1973), pp. 489–90).

15 On the distinction between lived experience and mediated experience, see Thompson, *The Media and Modernity*, pp. 227–34.

16 Ibid., pp. 229–31.

Chapter 4 The Nature of Political Scandal

1 Andrei S. Markovits and Mark Silverstein, 'Introduction: Power and Process in Liberal Democracies', in Markovits and Silverstein (eds), *The Politics of Scandal: Power and Process in Liberal Democracies* (New York: Holmes and Meier, 1988), p. 6.

2 Ibid.

3 See especially Pierre Bourdieu, *Distinction: A Social Critique of the Judgement of Taste*, trans. Richard Nice (Cambridge, Mass.: Harvard University Press, 1984), pp. 226–56; *The Logic of Practice*, trans. Richard Nice (Cambridge: Polity Press, 1990), pp. 66–8; 'Some Properties of Fields', in his *Sociology in Question*, trans. Richard Nice (London and Thousand Oaks, Calif.: Sage, 1993), pp. 72–7. I also draw on Bourdieu's account of the political field which he develops in 'Political Representation: Elements for a Theory of the Political Field', in his *Language and Symbolic Power*, ed. John B. Thompson, trans. Gino Raymond and Matthew Adamson (Cambridge: Polity Press, 1991), pp. 171–202.

4 For a more detailed discussion of these four forms of power, see John B. Thompson, *The Media and Modernity: A Social Theory of the Media* (Cambridge: Polity Press, 1995), pp. 13–18. See also Michael Mann,

The Sources of Social Power, vol. 1: *A History of Power from the Beginning to AD 1760* (Cambridge: Cambridge University Press, 1986), ch. 1.

5 See Max Weber, 'Politics as a Vocation', in H. H. Gerth and C. Wright Mills (eds), *From Max Weber: Essays in Sociology* (London: Routledge and Kegan Paul, 1948), pp. 77–128.

6 See Thompson, *The Media and Modernity*, pp. 16–17. The term 'symbolic power' is borrowed from Bourdieu, although my use of the term differs in various ways from his; see especially Bourdieu, *Language and Symbolic Power*, pp. 163ff.

7 See Pierre Bourdieu, 'The Forms of Capital', trans. Richard Nice, in J. G. Richardson (ed.), *Handbook of Theory and Research for the Sociology of Education* (Westport, Conn.: Greenwood Press, 1986), pp. 241–58; and *Distinction*, pp. 114ff.

8 See Bourdieu, 'Political Representation', pp. 180ff.

9 On the notion of the 'bystander public', see Gladys Engel Lang and Kurt Lang, *The Battle for Public Opinion: The President, the Press, and the Polls during Watergate* (New York: Columbia University Press, 1983), pp. 21–4.

10 See Wesley O. Hagood, *Presidential Sex: From the Founding Fathers to Bill Clinton* (Secaucus, N.J.: Citadel Press, 1998). This issue is explored in more detail in chapter 5.

11 This point is made very forcefully by Suzanne Garment: 'There is simply no persuasive evidence that the increase in scandal has taken place because of a corresponding rise in corrupt official behavior. Today's myriad scandals come in much larger part from the increased enthusiasm with which the political system now hunts evil in politics and the ever-growing efficiency with which our modern scandal production machine operates' (*Scandal: The Culture of Mistrust in American Politics* (New York: Doubleday, 1992), p. 6). Garment's use of the phrase 'modern scandal production machine' may obscure more than it illuminates, but her general argument in this passage is undoubtedly sound.

12 A point illustrated all too well by the experience of Peter Mandelson, regarded by many as the key media strategist behind Tony Blair's modernizing 'New Labour' Party and its electoral success in the 1997 general election. The scandal that forced him to resign from the Cabinet in December 1998 is discussed in chapter 6.

13 See Reg Whitaker, *The End of Privacy: How Total Surveillance is Becoming a Reality* (New York: New Press, 1999).

14 See Michael Schudson, *Discovering the News: A Social History of American Newspapers* (New York: Basic Books, 1978), pp. 189–90; *Watergate in American Memory: How We Remember, Forget, and Reconstruct the Past* (New York: Basic Books, 1992), pp. 118–19.

15 Schudson, *Discovering the News*, p. 190.

16 On the rise of prurient reporting, see Schudson, *Watergate in American Memory*, pp. 117–18.

17 This is the conclusion towards which Suzanne Garment, in her otherwise thoughtful and insightful study, tends to lean. See her *Scandal*, ch. 11.

Chapter 5 Sex Scandals in the Political Field

1 In treating sex scandals in the political field as a proper form of political scandal (a sexual-political scandal, to be precise), my account differs from much of the academic literature on this topic. Most academic commentators tend to assume that sex scandals in the political field are not truly political scandals. We have already examined the views of Markovits and Silverstein on this issue (see ch. 4 above). Anthony King tends to take a similar view, suggesting that sexual scandals 'are political scandals by accident, not in essence' (Anthony King, 'Sex, Money, and Power', in Richard Hodder-Williams and James Ceaser (eds), *Politics in Britain and the United States: Comparative Perspectives* (Durham, N.C.: Duke University Press, 1986), p. 187). Robert Williams excludes sex scandals from his survey of political scandals in the United States on the grounds that 'they are not politically motivated' (*Political Scandals in the USA* (Edinburgh: Keele University Press, 1998), p. 7). I have argued, by contrast, that sex scandals in the political field can be and should be conceptualized as a type of political scandal.

2 This somewhat misleading impression is conveyed by Anthony King's account: 'The widespread perception that British scandals are peculiarly sexual scandals is true, but not because Britain has more sex scandals than the United States – it does not – but rather because Britain has almost no scandals of any other kind' (King, 'Sex, Money, and Power', p. 183). King's analysis is insightful in many ways, but this judgement is undoubtedly overstated.

3 For further discussion of these aspects of Victorian morality, see Jeffrey Weeks, *Sex, Politics and Society: The Regulation of Sexuality since 1800*, 2nd edn (London: Longman, 1989), ch. 2.

4 For more detailed accounts of the Profumo affair and its aftermath, see Clive Irving, Ron Hall and Jeremy Wallington, *Scandal '63: A Study of the Profumo Affair* (London: Heinemann, 1963); Wayland Young, *The Profumo Affair: Aspects of Conservatism* (Harmondsworth: Penguin, 1963); Phillip Knightley and Caroline Kennedy, *An Affair of State: The Profumo Case and the Framing of Stephen Ward* (London: Jonathan Cape, 1987).

5 The letter was subsequently published on the front page of the *Sunday Mirror* (formerly the *Sunday Pictorial*) on 9 June 1963, the weekend after Profumo had resigned.

6 The letter was published in *The Times* and other newspapers on 6 June 1963.

7 The Vassall affair was one of the many security-related scandals which have featured prominently in Britain in the postwar period (see ch. 7). John Vassall worked on the staff of the naval attaché at the British Embassy in Moscow from 1954 to 1956; in 1956 he returned to London and held various jobs in the Admiralty. Vassall was homosexual, and while he was working in Moscow, he was photographed in compromising situations and blackmailed into spying. For several years he passed sensitive documents over to his Soviet contacts. He was eventually detected in 1962 and sentenced to eighteen years in prison. Macmillan set up a tribunal of inquiry to look into the case, which had become a source of embarrassment to the government. The tribunal published its report on 25 April 1963, at a time when the rumours about Profumo were rife.

8 Lord Lambton was a wealthy landowner, a Conservative MP and Parliamentary Under-Secretary of State at the Ministry of Defence in Edward Heath's government. In 1973 his political career came to an abrupt end. Sometime in 1972 he secured the services of Norma Levy, a young Irish woman who worked for a high-class call-girl ring in London. Rather unwisely, he occasionally paid her with cheques signed in his own name. Norma Levy's husband – an unemployed minicab driver named Colin Levy – recognized Lambton's name and saw an opportunity to make money by selling the story to the press. Colin Levy tried to take some photographs of Lambton in compromising circumstances, and then contacted the *News of the World* with the photos and the cheques signed by Lambton. The *News of the World* was not happy with the quality of the photos, so staff from the paper installed a tape recorder and a camera which would enable them to take photos through a hole in the wall. But the *News of the World* eventually decided not to publish the story and gave the material back to Levy. Levy then approached the *Sunday People*, which took the material and handed it over to the police. The tape-recorded conversations included several references to drugs which, together with the compromising photos, put Lambton in a perilous position. With memories of the Profumo affair still fresh, the government was anxious to avoid a major scandal. Lambton resigned both from his government office and from his parliamentary seat, never to return to public life.

Lord Jellicoe was caught up in the events surrounding Lord Lambton. Like Lambton, Jellicoe was a wealthy aristocrat who had achieved a position of prominence in public life. He held various ministerial offices in the Home Office and in Defence, before becoming a member of the Cabinet in 1970 as Lord Privy Seal, the Minister in charge of the Civil Service and Leader of the House of Lords. On several occasions in late 1972 and early 1973, he hired girls from two escort agencies which advertised in the *Evening Standard*. He did not disclose his name, but he nevertheless became the subject of gossip in the vice underworld of

London. The police, who were investigating high-class vice rings at the time, picked up the information and passed it on to the government. The Prime Minister decided to ask Jellicoe if he knew anything about Lambton's case, which was being discussed by the Cabinet at the time, or anything about Norma Levy. Jellicoe said that he had no knowledge of the Lambton affair but admitted that he himself had used escort agencies. Recognizing that this could have damaging consequences if it became public, Jellicoe resigned. Gradually he returned to public life, sitting on various committees and commissions, but he never returned to the centre of politics.

9 *Guardian*, 11 May 1976, p. 12.

10 This was vividly illustrated by the scandal which erupted around Jeffrey Archer in November 1999. A well-known Conservative politician and best-selling novelist, Archer was a close associate of Margaret Thatcher and served as deputy chairman of the Conservative Party in the 1980s. But he resigned from the party office in 1986, following a series of allegations concerning his relationship with a prostitute, Monica Coghlan. The *News of the World* claimed that Archer had offered her £2,000 to enable her to go abroad, and the *Daily Star* alleged that Archer had paid to have sex with her in a London hotel. Archer admitted that he had offered her money to go abroad but denied that he had slept with her. He sued Express Newspapers (owners of the *Daily Star*) for libel and won: the jury awarded him a record £500,000 damages, and Express Newspapers faced an additional bill of around £700,000 in costs. Archer had lost his position as deputy chairman but he emerged victorious from the trial, ready to begin rebuilding his political career. But twelve years later, the scandal returned to haunt both him and the Conservative Party.

In October 1999 Archer was selected as the Tory candidate for Mayor of London (an office that was created by the Labour Party several years after the Greater London Council had been abolished by Margaret Thatcher). Then, on 21 November 1999, in a classic tabloid scoop, the *News of the World* revealed that Archer had made up a false alibi in the libel trial and had persuaded a friend, Ted Francis, to lie for him. Shortly before the trial, Archer had contacted Francis and invited him to a restaurant, where he asked him to cover for him for the night of 9 September 1986; Francis agreed to write to Archer's lawyer, Lord Mishcon, saying that they had been together in a restaurant that evening. As it happened, the alibi was never used in court, because the *Daily Star* subsequently claimed that Archer had been with the prostitute on the 8th rather than the 9th of September. When Francis decided twelve years later to disclose the false alibi, he contacted the publicist Max Clifford, who brokered a deal with the *News of the World*. A plan was devised which would enable them to obtain further evidence to prove Archer's guilt. They tape-recorded a series of telephone conversations between Francis and Archer in which Archer went over the details of the alibi, explaining why he had concocted it and why it was never used. When extracts from these conversations were published in the *News of the World* on 21 November 1999, Archer's position became untenable and he was forced to step down as the Tory candidate for Mayor of London. Fearful that these revelations would rekindle public perceptions of the Tories as the party of sleaze, senior Conservative Party figures were quick to denounce Archer. 'This is the end of politics for Jeffrey Archer. Let me make it clear – I will not tolerate behaviour like this in my party,' proclaimed William Hague, the leader of the Conservative Party, on the day after the story broke (quoted in the *Guardian*, 23 Nov. 1999, p. 1). Following an internal investigation by the Tory ethics committee, Archer was expelled from the party for five years. The sex scandal and libel trial of 1986–7 were undoubtedly a setback for Archer's political career, but it was a second-order transgression committed in relation to this trial which, twelve years later, was likely to be his nemesis.

The Conservative Party's struggle with the legacy of sleaze was not over, however. As if by some quirk of fate, Jeffrey Archer's main rival for the party's nomination had been none other than Steven Norris, the former transport minister who had gained prominence in the early 1990s when the tabloid press alleged that he had five mistresses; now that Archer was out of the contest, Norris re-emerged as a candidate, much to the chagrin of the Tory leadership. At roughly the same time, a simmering feud between the wealthy Tory Party treasurer and benefactor Michael Ashcroft and *The Times*, which in a series of articles had cast doubt on his business dealings in Belize, found its way to the High Court, although the impending libel action was settled out of court, with each side agreeing to pay its share of the legal costs. But the libel action brought by the former Tory MP Neil Hamilton against Mohamed Al Fayed in relation to the cash-for-questions scandal (discussed in chapter 6) did go to trial in November 1999, thus bringing one of the more discreditable episodes in the party's recent history back into the headlines. Sleaze was an epithet that the Conservatives would find hard to shrug off.

11   Ron Davies was Secretary of State for Wales in Tony Blair's government until 27 October 1998, when he suddenly resigned following a bizarre incident on Clapham Common in South London. According to Davies, he had taken a walk on the common on the night of 26 October and had struck up a conversation with a stranger, who invited the Welsh Secretary to join him and a couple of friends for a drink. They drove off in Davies' car, but the strangers then pulled a knife on him, robbed him and stole his car. He ended up in Brixton police station. Davies said that his decision to go with the stranger was 'a moment of madness' but denied that sex or drugs were involved. However, Clapham Common is well known as a gay cruising area and the press was rife with speculation and allegations about Davies' sexuality.

12   See Michael Schudson, 'Sex Scandals', in Sally Banes, Sheldon Frank and Tem Horwitz (eds), *Our National Passion: Two Hundred Years of Sex in America* (Chicago: Follett, 1976), pp. 41–57; Wesley O. Hagood,

Presidential Sex: From the Founding Fathers to Bill Clinton (Secaucus, N.J.: Citadel Press, 1998). I have drawn on both of these informative studies in the paragraphs that follow.

13 Alexander Hamilton, *Observations on Certain Documents Contained in No. V & VI of 'The History of the United States for the Year 1796,' in which the Charge of Speculation Against Alexander Hamilton, Late Secretary of the Treasury, is Fully Refuted* (Philadelphia, 1979), p. 9.

14 For a fuller account of this affair, see Fawn M. Brodie, *Thomas Jefferson: An Intimate History* (New York: Norton, 1974), chs 16, 17, 25, 26.

15 *Richmond Recorder*, 1 Sept. 1802, quoted in ibid., p. 349.

16 Gary Hart emerged as the early frontrunner in the race for the Democratic presidential nomination in 1988. But he was plagued by rumours that he was a 'womanizer' and that he had had various extra-marital affairs, including an alleged affair with Donna Rice, which was reported as front page news in the *Miami Herald* on 3 May 1987. Hart denied the affair and, in an interview published in the *New York Times Magazine*, he threw down the gauntlet to the press: 'Follow me around, I don't care,' he said, 'I'm serious. If anybody wants to put a tail on me, go ahead. They'd be very bored' (*New York Times Magazine*, 3 May 1987, p. 38). As it happens, that's exactly what reporters from the *Miami Herald* had done. They had staked out his Washington town house on the night of 1–2 May and concluded that he had spent the night with a woman other than his wife. They also claimed that he had accompanied Rice on a cruise to Bimini (off the Florida coast) on a yacht with the unfortunate name *Monkey Business*. The allegations sparked off a fierce controversy, during which Hart became increasingly entangled in evasions about his relationship with Rice. On 8 May, amid rumours that the *Washington Post* was about to publish details of other affairs, Hart withdrew from the race for the Democratic nomination. His four-year drive for the Presidency was ended by five days of controversy about his private life. 'The unmaking of Gary Hart is one of the most startling stories of American politics,' commented the *New York Times*. 'A man who has devoted at least four years of his life to the pursuit of the Presidency is undone by a dalliance' (*New York Times*, 9 May 1987, p. 1). Hart re-entered the race in December but, after a series of disastrous results in the primaries, withdrew again in March 1988 and abandoned his presidential ambitions.

17 A senior Republican from Oregon who served for many years in the Senate, Bob Packwood was a leading advocate of women's rights and was widely respected for his practices of hiring and promoting women. But rumours had circulated for years that there was another side to Packwood's behaviour towards women. These became public in November 1992, when the *Washington Post* published an article reporting that, since his earliest days on Capitol Hill, he had made unwanted sexual advances to a number of women who worked for him. The *Post* said ten

women had, independently of one another, given accounts of Packwood's behaviour towards them; several said that he had grabbed them abruptly, kissed them forcefully and persisted until he had been pushed away. None of the women complained formally, but several decided to leave their jobs within months.

18 Wilbur Mills lost his position as chairman of the House Ways and Means Committee following a scandal in 1974 which erupted when he was stopped in a car that was speeding past Washington's Tidal Basin with no headlights on; he was found to be with Anabella Battistella, better known as Fanne Foxe which she used as her stage name in a Washington strip club. Wayne Hays, chairman of the House Administration Committee and the Democratic Congressional Campaign Committee, resigned after it was disclosed that he had kept a mistress on the congressional payroll. Thomas Evans lost his campaign for re-election to the House in 1982, following revelations of his affair with a lobbyist, Paula Parkinson.

19 On the night of 18 July 1969 Senator Edward Kennedy, then aged thirty-seven, drove off a narrow bridge after leaving a party on Chappaquiddick Island, off the Massachusetts coast. Kennedy managed to free himself from the car but his passenger, Mary Jo Kopechne – a twenty-eight-year-old woman who had previously worked on the campaign staff of Robert Kennedy – was trapped inside and died. Kennedy claimed that he repeatedly dived into the water to try to rescue Kopechne but failed. He then returned to the party and arranged for someone to drive him to the ferry crossing; when they found the ferry closed for the night, he dived in and swam to shore, returning to his hotel in Edgartown. He did not report the accident to the police until the following morning, by which time the car and the body had already been found. In the extensive media coverage that followed, there was much speculation about why Kennedy had not raised the alarm earlier, about whether he had been drunk at the time and whether he was trying to conceal a relationship. Kennedy denied that he was under the influence of alcohol or that he had had an affair with Kopechne, explaining his behaviour by saying that he had been in a state of confusion, grief, exhaustion and shock. He pleaded guilty to a minor charge of leaving the scene of an accident and failing to report it, for which he was given a two-month suspended jail sentence. Kennedy has remained a senator and an influential figure in the Democratic Party, but the Chappaquiddick incident has haunted his political career and permanently dented his presidential prospects.

20 Clarence Thomas was nominated by George Bush in 1991 to fill a vacant position as Supreme Court Judge. During Senate hearings to confirm his appointment, he was accused by Anita Hill – a former employee – of having sexually harassed her when he was chairman of the Equal Employment Opportunity Commission (a position he held from 1982

to 1990). Hill accused him of making sexually offensive remarks to her. On one occasion when they were working in the same office, he allegedly picked up a can of Coca-Cola and, claiming to have found pubic hair on it, asked who put it there. On other occasions, according to Hill, he spoke of the pleasures he had given to women with oral sex and described his penis as being larger than normal, comparing himself to Long Dong Silver, a black porn star. Thomas rejected the allegations and denied that he had had conversations of a sexual nature with Anita Hill, or had in any way harassed her. The allegations were made in televised Senate hearings which lasted for 107 days, during which the issues were extensively discussed in the media. Thomas's nomination was eventually confirmed by a narrow margin (52 votes to 48).

21 *Washington Post*, 27 Jan. 1992, p. 6.

22 When Clinton was subsequently accused of committing perjury in the Jones case, much of his defence turned on a now infamously legalistic definition of 'sexual relations'. Clinton and Monica had oral sex but not intercourse, and Clinton maintained that he did not commit perjury because he did not think that the definition of 'sexual relations' used by the Jones lawyers included oral sex.

23 According to *Newsweek*, the weekly magazine had to make a decision on the night of Saturday 17 January whether to publish the story. Prosecutors from the OIC urged them not to publish on the grounds that the publicity could undermine their attempts to secure a deal with Monica Lewinsky. (*Newsweek*, 2 Feb. 1998, p. 29.)

24 *Washington Post*, 21 Jan. 1998, pp. 1, 6.

25 *Washington Post*, 27 Jan. 1998, p. 1.

26 *Washington Post*, 28 Jan. 1998, p. 21.

27 *Washington Post*, 18 Aug. 1998, p. 5.

28 In her autobiography, published the following year, Lewinsky describes her feelings when the report was published: 'I felt very violated. I really felt raped and physically ill with myself, as if anybody who looked at me would only think about me performing oral sex. I just felt that the whole world looked at me as a whore' (Andrew Morton, *Monica's Story* (London: Michael O'Mara Books, 1999), p. 260).

29 See, for instance, James D. Retter, *Anatomy of a Scandal: An Investigation into the Campaign to Undermine the Clinton Presidency* (Los Angeles: General Publishing Group, 1998); Joe Conason and Gene Lyons, *The Hunting of the President: The Ten-Year Campaign to Destroy Bill and Hillary Clinton* (New York: St Martin's Press, 1999).

Chapter 6   Financial Scandals in the Political Field

1 See Judith Chubb and Maurizio Vannicelli, 'Italy: A Web of Scandals in a Flawed Democracy', in Andrei S. Markovits and Mark Silverstein

(eds), *The Politics of Scandal: Power and Process in Liberal Democracies* (New York: Holmes and Meier, 1988), pp. 122–50.

2 See Alan Doig, *Corruption and Misconduct in Contemporary British Politics* (Harmondsworth: Penguin, 1984), pp. 40–2; Robert Zaller, *The Parliament of 1621: A Study in Constitutional Conflict* (Berkeley: University of California Press, 1971), pp. 75–90; Robert E. Ruigh, *The Parliament of 1624: Politics and Foreign Policy* (Cambridge, Mass.: Harvard University Press, 1971), pp. 316–44.

3 For a more detailed discussion of the contracting scandals, see G. R. Searle, *Corruption in British Politics 1859–1930* (Oxford: Oxford University Press, 1987), ch. 3.

4 See Frances Donaldson, *The Marconi Scandal* (London: Rupert Hart-Davis, 1962); Searle, *Corruption in British Politics*, ch. 8.

5 Quoted in Donaldson, *The Marconi Scandal*, p. 215.

6 See Tom Cullen, *Maundy Gregory: Purveyor of Honours* (London: Bodley Head, 1974).

7 For a more detailed account of the Poulson affair, see Doig, *Corruption and Misconduct*, ch. 5.

8 For an account of the Hamilton affair written by two journalists, see David Leigh and Ed Vulliamy, *Sleaze: The Corruption of Parliament* (London: Fourth Estate, 1997).

9 Hamilton sued Al Fayed for allegations he made on a Channel 4 *Dispatches* documentary which was broadcast in January 1997, and in which Al Fayed claimed that Hamilton had demanded and received thousands of pounds in cash, gift vouchers from Harrods and hospitality at the Paris Ritz, in return for asking parliamentary questions. The case came to trial at the High Court in London in November 1999, five years after the original allegations about Hamilton had appeared in the *Guardian*. On 21 December the jury found in favour of Al Fayed, concluding unanimously that he had established, on 'highly convincing evidence', that Hamilton had acted corruptly in his capacity as an MP. 'A greedy, corrupt liar' was the headline in the *Guardian* on the following day; 'Libel verdict destroys Hamilton' was the headline in *The Times*; 'Fayed demolishes Hamilton in the sleaze trial of the century' read the *Independent*. Hamilton's last-ditch attempt to salvage his reputation had ended in dismal failure. Any hopes he might have harboured of making a political comeback were shattered by the verdict, as the Conservative Party chairman Michael Ancram promptly distanced the party from the former MP ('I trust that the personalities involved will now retire from the scene. They certainly can expect little understanding from this party if they do not', commented Ancram, quoted in the *Guardian*, 22 Dec. 1999, p. 1). Hamilton also faced financial ruin, as he was ordered to pay legal costs estimated at more than £2 million.

10 This correspondence is reproduced in Luke Harding, David Leigh and David Pallister, *The Liar: The Fall of Jonathan Aitken* (The Guardian, 1999).

11 In order to obtain a copy of Aitken's bill, journalists from the *Guardian* had faxed a letter to the Ritz Hotel purporting to come from Aitken himself and using his House of Commons stationery – the 'cod fax'. Shortly after the *Guardian* published the 27 October article, the *Daily Telegraph* revealed the existence of the cod fax, which led many MPs and others to denounce the *Guardian* vociferously for improper and unethical practices. The *Guardian*'s editor, Peter Preston, was obliged to resign from the Press Complaints Commission and subsequently stepped down as editor.

12 Jonathan Aitken, statement made to the press at Conservative Central Office on 10 April 1995, quoted in the *Guardian*, 11 Apr. 1995, p. 2.

13 This suggestion, which was based on Said Ayas's account of the circumstances surrounding the meeting at the Paris Ritz, was put forward by the *Guardian* in its lead article on 5 March 1999.

14 *Standards in Public Life*, First Report of the Committee on Standards in Public Life, Chairman Lord Nolan (London: HMSO, 1995), pp. 3–9.

15 Peter Mandelson's resignation letter to the Prime Minister, reprinted in the *Guardian*, 24 Dec. 1998, p. 1.

16 For more detailed discussions of the history of corruption in the United States, see George C. S. Benson, *Political Corruption in America* (Lexington, Mass.: D. C. Heath, 1978); Abraham S. Eisenstadt, Ari Hoogenboom and Hans L. Trefousse (eds), *Before Watergate: Problems of Corruption in American Society* (Brooklyn, N.Y.: Brooklyn College Press, 1978).

17 For an account of the rise and fall of the Tweed ring, see Alexander B. Callow, Jr, *The Tweed Ring* (New York: Oxford University Press, 1966).

18 For a discussion of these and other Gilded Age scandals, see Eisenstadt, Hoogenboom and Trefousse, *Before Watergate*, esp. pp. 125–64.

19 The moiety system was originally designed to clamp down on smuggling by providing incentives to customs officials and informers. The first Congress in 1789 provided that confiscated smuggled goods would be divided between the government (50%), the informer (25%) and the local customs officials (25%); the proceeds from these forfeitures were known as moieties. The system was clearly open to abuse by local customs officials who were looking for ways to augment their salaries. The shortcomings of the moiety system were highlighted by two well-publicized cases in the early 1870s, one involving the undervaluing of imported goods by Phelps, Dodge and Company and another involving moieties paid to an agent, John Sanborn, to collect unpaid taxes from railroads, distillers and others.

20 See Ari Hoogenboom, *Outlawing the Spoils: A History of the Civil Service Reform Movement, 1865–1883* (Urbana: University of Illinois Press, 1961).

21 For a detailed account of the Teapot Dome scandal, see Burl Noggle,

Teapot Dome: Oil and Politics in the 1920s (Baton Rouge: Louisiana State University Press, 1962).

22 See Jules Abels, *The Truman Scandals* (Chicago, Ill.: Henry Regnery, 1956); Harold F. Gosnell, *Truman's Crises: A Political Biography of Harry S. Truman* (Westport, Conn.: Greenwood Press, 1980), ch. 38; Benson, *Political Corruption in America*, pp. 151–4.

23 Nixon's Checkers speech was in some respects a decisive moment in the history of political scandal (and, more generally, in the history of mediated visibility), since it demonstrated that television could be used as a powerful weapon in the struggle for reputation. Faced with damaging allegations and a mounting chorus of calls for his resignation as vice-presidential candidate, Nixon made the bold decision to do a live broadcast on nationwide television in which, speaking directly to the electorate, he would lay bare the details of his personal finances and present himself as an ordinary American of modest means who had been falsely accused. 'So what I am going to do now,' Nixon explained to the many millions who were watching and listening, 'and this is unprecedented in the history of American politics, is to give this television and radio audience a complete financial history: everything I've earned, everything I've spent, everything I owe.' What followed was an inventory of all of the Nixon family's major assets and liabilities: their house in Washington, 'which cost $41,000 and on which we owe $20,000', a 1950 Oldsmobile car, a $4,500 bank overdraft, a $3,000 loan from his parents, and so on. 'Well, that's about it,' he concluded, 'that's what we have and that's what we owe. It isn't very much but Pat and I have the satisfaction that every dime that we've got is honestly ours.' And then Nixon added, in an emotional tone that would disarm his detractors, that he had in fact received one gift from 'a man down in Texas' who had heard that their two children would like to have a dog: this man sent them a little black-and-white spotted cocker spaniel. 'And our little girl – Tricia, the six year old – named it Checkers. And you know, the kids love that dog and I just want to say right now that, regardless of what "they" say about it, we're going to keep it.'

The Checkers broadcast was a *tour de force* of calculated self-disclosure through the medium of television. Nixon knew exactly what he was doing: going over the heads of the journalists and the professional power-brokers who were clamouring for his resignation, appealing directly to the electorate and presenting himself as an ordinary family man who had worked hard to get where he was and whose personal integrity was above reproach. Approximately 60 million people saw or heard the speech, making it the largest television audience up to that time. Nixon urged people to express their views on whether he should stay on Eisenhower's ticket or resign by wiring or writing to the Republican National Committee. The response was overwhelming. Republican offices throughout the country were flooded with messages of support;

the Washington headquarters alone received more than 160,000 telegrams and 250,000 letters, backing Nixon by a margin of 350 to 1. The gamble paid off handsomely and Nixon's candidacy was saved. But at the same time, Nixon staked his political career on a claim to honesty, openness and personal integrity, a claim which, while it served him well in the fund crisis of 1952, would eventually work against him when the crisis of Watergate began to unfold. Having staked his political career on honesty and integrity, Nixon would eventually be hoisted with his own petard. (For more detailed accounts of the events surrounding the fund crisis and the Checkers speech, see Richard M. Nixon, *Six Crises* (London: W. H. Allen, 1962), pp. 73–129; Richard Nixon, *RN: The Memoirs of Richard Nixon* (London: Sidgwick and Jackson, 1978), pp. 92–110; Jonathan Aitken, *Nixon: A Life* (London: Weidenfeld and Nicolson, 1993), pp. 208–20. The quotes from the Checkers speech are taken from *Nixon*, p. 216.)

24 For a full discussion of financial-political scandals during the Eisenhower period, see David A. Frier, *Conflict of Interest in the Eisenhower Administration* (Ames: Iowa State University Press, 1969).

25 Charles Lewis, *The Buying of Congress: How Special Interests have Stolen your Right to Life, Liberty and the Pursuit of Happiness* (New York: Avon Books, 1998).

26 See Dennis F. Thomson, *Ethics in Congress: From Individual to Institutional Corruption* (Washington, DC: Brookings Institution, 1995).

27 For a more detailed account of the background to and operation of Abscam, see Robert W. Greene, *The Sting Man: Inside Abscam* (New York: E. P. Dutton, 1981).

28 Quoted in ibid., p. 194.

29 The collapse of the Savings and Loan industry was precipitated to a large extent by the deregulation of the industry in the early 1980s. The Savings and Loans were originally established in the early 1930s to promote the construction of new homes through the provision of residential mortgages and to protect financial institutions against the kind of devastation that occurred following the crash of 1929. Savings and Loan deposits were federally insured, and in return for this protection the S&Ls were tightly regulated in terms of the kinds of loans they could make. But economic changes in the 1970s created growing difficulties for the S&L industry; with high inflation and increased competition from high-yield investments, many S&Ls found it difficult to attract new funds. In the early 1980s Congress deregulated the S&L industry, partly with a view to enabling S&Ls to compete more effectively with other financial institutions. The new legislation raised interest rate ceilings, relaxed the rules on the ownership of S&Ls and expanded the range of investments they could make with their federally insured deposits. With the relaxation of the rules on ownership and investment, S&Ls became attractive acquisitions for real estate developers and entrepreneurs, who bought up

S&Ls and used them as sources of capital to finance their own ventures. The fluctuations of the US economy in the 1980s, combined with the high-risk investments and irregular practices of many of the deregulated S&Ls, resulted in one of the worst financial disasters of the twentieth century. Hundreds of S&Ls went bankrupt and the total cost to the taxpayer – excluding interest payments on government bonds sold to bail out the industry – is likely to be between $150 and $175 billion; taking account of interest payments, the figure could be as high as $500 billion. (For a more detailed discussion of the S&L crisis, see James Ring Adams, *The Big Fix: Inside the S&L Scandal* (New York: John Wiley, 1990); Kitty Calavita, Henry N. Pontell and Robert H. Tillman, *Big Money Crime: Fraud and Politics in the Savings and Loan Crisis* (Berkeley: University of California Press, 1999.)

Much of the blame for the S&L crisis lies with Congress for the way in which it deregulated the industry in the early 1980s. But the crisis also became the source of a number of specific scandals, which were fuelled by public anger and resentment about the S&L mess. By focusing on these specific scandals, often involving particular individuals whose activities were excessively greedy and clearly fraudulent, the media found a way of translating the complex issues involved in the S&L crisis into popular forms of story-telling, in many cases at the expense of a thorough analysis of the issues.

The Keating Five scandal was one of the scandals that was linked to the S&L crisis. Charles Keating started out as a real estate developer and in 1984 he bought Lincoln Savings and Loan in Irvine, California. He quickly transformed it from a traditional S&L with the bulk of its assets in home mortgage loans to a financial institution specializing in commercial real estate ventures and other speculative investments. He used his political connections to lobby for further deregulation and to discourage investigation of Lincoln's activities by state and federal regulators. Five senators became involved in acting on Keating's behalf; they also received a total of $1.3 million in campaign contributions from Keating. In 1989 Lincoln Savings and Loan collapsed, and Keating was subsequently convicted on charges of fraud and racketeering. The Senate Ethics Committee carried out a nine-month investigation; it rebuked four senators for displaying insensitivity and poor judgement, and reprimanded the fifth – Senator Alan Cranston from California – for violating established norms of behaviour in the Senate.

30 My account of the Whitewater affair is based primarily on the very detailed reconstruction of events provided by James B. Stewart in *Blood Sport: The President and his Adversaries* (New York: Simon and Schuster, 1996). See also the informative discussion in Robert Williams, *Political Scandals in the USA* (Edinburgh: Keele University Press, 1998), ch. 4.

31 *New York Times*, 8 Mar. 1992, pp. 1, 24.

32 In early May 1993 Catherine Cornelius – a distant relative of Bill Clinton

who had helped with travel arrangements during the campaign – told Vincent Foster and a few other associates that she had discovered major corruption in the White House travel office. She claimed that money was being spent on vacation homes, racehorses and trips to Europe. The allegations were discussed with Bill and Hillary Clinton, and Foster asked an Associate White House Counsel, William Kennedy – another former partner of the Rose Law Firm – to investigate the matter. It was decided to ask an outside consulting firm, Peat Marwick, to carry out an audit. Kennedy also raised the issue with the FBI, which agreed to carry out its own investigation. The preliminary audit from Peat Marwick concluded that there was evidence of mismanagement, and the White House responded by summarily firing seven employees in the travel office. But shortly after that, the *Washington Post* obtained copies of internal memos which indicated that Cornelius wanted to head the travel office and that World Wide Travel – the Little Rock agency that had made most of the campaign's travel arrangements – was being lined up to handle White House travel. In the light of these revelations, the action taken by the White House in shaking up the travel office appeared to be incompetent and self-serving, and the involvement of the FBI raised questions about whether the White House was improperly using the FBI for political purposes. Following a wave of bad press, five of the seven fired employees were reinstated, American Express was contracted to run the travel operation and the Justice Department, the FBI, the Treasury and the Internal Revenue Service announced that they would carry out their own investigations of the affair. William Kennedy was reprimanded and subsequently left the White House.

33 The Resolution Trust Corporation (RTC) was the federal agency created to oversee the crisis in the Savings and Loan industry.

34 Many of these organizations were staffed by very conservative individuals and drew their funding from a variety of conservative groups and foundations. Citizens United, for example, was founded in 1988 by a conservative political activist named Floyd Brown. Armed with an annual budget of around $3 million, Brown's organization became almost exclusively concerned with attacking Clinton, which he did on his daily radio show, *Talk Back to Washington*, on his internet site, citizensunited.org, in his monthly newsletter, *Clinton Watch*, and in his book, '*Slick Willie*': *Why America Cannot Trust Bill Clinton*.

35 See US Senate, *Final Report of the Special Committee to Investigate Whitewater Development Corporation and Related Matters* (Washington: Government Printing Office, 1996).

36 This charge was made by Gene Lyons, a writer and columnist for the *Arkansas Democrat Gazette*, who published an article in *Harper's Magazine* in October 1994 called 'Fool for Scandal: How the *Times* Got Whitewater Wrong'. The article was subsequently expanded into a book: Gene Lyons and the Editors of Harper's Magazine, *Fools for*

Scandal: How the Media Invented Whitewater (New York: Franklin Square Press, 1996).

37 Although the independent counsel legislation had formally lapsed in January 1994, when Robert Fiske was appointed, the Attorney General Janet Reno drew up a charter which set the terms for the investigation. In addition to authorizing the Independent Counsel to investigate whether the President or the First Lady had committed any offences in relation to Whitewater, the charter also authorized the Independent Counsel to investigate 'other allegations or evidence of violation of any federal criminal or civil law by any person or entity developed during the independent counsel's investigation . . .' (quoted in Stewart, *Blood Sport*, p. 399). This provision gave the Independent Counsel leeway to pursue his investigations beyond matters specifically related to Whitewater.

38 Quoted in Stewart, *Blood Sport*, p. 374.

Chapter 7   Power Scandals

1 On the doctrine of the *arcana imperii* and its transformation into the modern principle of state secrecy, see Norberto Bobbio, *Democracy and Dictatorship: The Nature and Limits of State Power*, trans. Peter Kennealy (Cambridge: Polity Press, 1989), pp. 19–21, and his *The Future of Democracy: A Defence of the Rules of the Game*, trans. Roger Griffin (Cambridge: Polity Press, 1987), pp. 79–97.

2 The existence of the secret masonic lodge known as Propaganda Two (or P-2 for short) was discovered almost by accident. In March 1981, two magistrates investigating the activities of the bankrupt financier Michele Sindona went to Palermo to question a man who was known to have helped Sindona, and in the course of the questioning they were led to suspect the involvement of Licio Gelli, a wealthy businessman who had built a large personal fortune in the textile industry. They ordered a search of Gelli's villa and office in Arezzo (Gelli was away at the time); in the office they found a briefcase containing a list of 962 members of P-2 and files about its activities. The list included the names of senior political figures (including two Cabinet ministers), high-ranking officers in the military, police and intelligence services (including the heads of military intelligence and the customs police), members of the judiciary, powerful individuals in the media and numerous businessmen. Gelli – the Grand Master – went into hiding.

Following speculation in the press, the list was published on 21 May 1981: it caused an uproar and precipitated calls for further investigations. It became clear that P-2 was linked to a number of serious events in Italy's recent history, including the collapse of Michele Sindona's financial empire (Sindona was a P-2 member), major scandals involving the Bank of Italy and a state-owned oil company ENI, and the activities of extreme right-wing groups. (Gelli was eventually charged with financing right-wing terrorism and was linked to the Bologna railway station bombings.) The Prime Minister, Arnaldo Forlani, set up a commission to investigate the Lodge, but the Forlani government was seriously compromised by the fact that two ministers from Forlani's party, the Christian Democrats, appeared on the list of P-2 members. Forlani's government collapsed on 26 May when the Socialists refused to cooperate with the other three parties in the coalition to discuss the affair. This marked the end of the Christian Democrats' monopoly on the premiership. In late June a new coalition government was formed under the leadership of Giovanni Spadolini from the Republican Party (PRI). P-2 was outlawed and numerous public officials – including senior civil servants, military officers, chiefs of police and intelligence personnel – were suspended or dismissed. Gelli remained in hiding until he was arrested by Swiss police on 13 September 1982 while trying to withdraw US$55 million from a bank account. The Italian government requested his extradition but he escaped from prison before the final hearing of the extradition case (apparently with the help of his warder). Gelli remained in hiding for four years. Suffering from ill health, he eventually surrendered himself to the Swiss authorities in September 1987. He was extradited to Italy the following February, where he was tried on charges of political conspiracy, criminal association, extortion and fraud. (For further discussion of the P-2 affair and its significance, see Judith Chubb and Maurizio Vannicelli, 'Italy: A Web of Scandals in a Flawed Democracy', in Andrei S. Markovits and Mark Silverstein (eds), *The Politics of Scandal: Power and Process in Liberal Democracies* (New York: Holmes and Meier, 1988), pp. 122–50.)

3 For a more detailed account of the circumstances surrounding Watergate and the unfolding of the affair, see especially Fred Emery, *Watergate: The Corruption of American Politics and the Fall of Richard Nixon* (New York: Simon and Schuster, 1994). For a judicious assessment of the impact of Watergate on American politics and society, see Michael Schudson, *Watergate in American Memory: How We Remember, Forget, and Reconstruct the Past* (New York: Basic Books, 1992).

4 In June 1971 the *New York Times* began publishing extracts from a secret Defence Department document on the war in Vietnam; the document became known as the Pentagon Papers. The document had been leaked by Daniel Ellsberg, a former Pentagon analyst who had worked on the study. Nixon regarded the leaking of the papers as a damaging blow to national security and, in the political controversy which followed the publication of extracts, Nixon and his associates sought to discredit Ellsberg. The office of Ellsberg's psychiatrist, Lewis Fielding, was burgled in an attempt to get Ellsberg's file; it subsequently emerged that this

eaders to p. 203 297

break-in was supervised by Howard Hunt and Gordon Liddy, two figures who were to play a key role in the Watergate affair. It also emerged that Hunt and Liddy had been acting as part of a secret organization – the so-called 'plumbers' – which had been set up, at Nixon's request, to investigate and 'plug' potential leaks. Nixon's Assistant for Domestic Affairs, John Ehrlichman, took primary responsibility for setting up the plumbers unit, and Ehrlichman's assistant, Egil Krogh, was involved in operational issues. Both Ehrlichman and Krogh were eventually tried and convicted for their roles in the Fielding break-in, as were Liddy and Charles Colson (Nixon's Special Counsel).

5 Nixon was not the first president to install secret tape-recording equipment in the White House. The first concealed recording equipment was installed in 1940 during the Presidency of Franklin Roosevelt. Subsequent presidents also used concealed recording equipment in the Oval Office and other rooms; the existence and use of this equipment was a closely guarded secret. In the summer of 1962, for example, Kennedy installed an elaborate recording network, involving a series of concealed switches, microphones and tape recorders and extending from the Oval Office and Cabinet Room into the White House mansion. From July 1962 until his death, he secretly recorded 260 hours of meetings and telephone conversations. Only four people knew about the system, and they all kept it secret. The existence of Kennedy's system only became public in July 1973, following the revelation that Nixon had secretly recorded conversations in the White House. For a full account see William Doyle, *Inside the Oval Office: The White House Tapes from FDR to Clinton* (London: London House, 1999).

6 The firing of Cox appears to have caused lasting damage to Nixon in the opinion polls. Just before the Saturday Night Massacre, a Harris survey asked 'Do you tend to agree or disagree that President Nixon has lost so much credibility that it will be hard for him to be accepted as President again?'; 60 per cent agreed. When the same question was asked a month later, 73 per cent agreed. Support for resignation also increased from 28 per cent in August 1973 to 43 per cent in November. For full details, see Gladys Engel Lang and Kurt Lang, *The Battle for Public Opinion: The President, the Press, and the Polls during Watergate* (New York: Columbia University Press, 1983), pp. 114–17.

7 The publication of the transcripts in April 1974 was Nixon's response to further requests by investigators to hand over more tapes. On 11 April 1974 the House Judiciary Committee, which was considering the case for impeachment, issued a subpoena for forty-two additional tapes of conversations. Rather than handing over the tapes, Nixon decided to produce edited transcripts of certain Watergate-related conversations, which were made public on 30 April 1974 (the deadline set by the House Judiciary Committee for his response to its subpoena). In a television broadcast on the evening of 29 April, Nixon told his audience that the

transcripts 'will at last once and for all show that what I knew and what I did with regard to the Watergate break-in and cover-up were just as I have described them to you from the beginning' (quoted in *The White House Transcripts* (London: Macmillan, 1974), p. 9). Nixon claimed that the purpose of the editing was to delete expletives and remove material which was not relevant to Watergate, but it is clear from subsequent transcriptions that his editorial interventions went further than that.

The White House transcripts were initially released in the form of a large blue book sold by the US Printing Office. Paperback editions were subsequently released by the *New York Times* and the *Washington Post*, and it quickly became a bestseller. Many pages of the transcripts were excerpted in newspapers, and passages were read by professional actors on prime-time television.

8 Joseph Alsop, quoted in R. W. Apple, Jr, 'Introduction', in *The White House Transcripts*, p. 3.

9 *The White House Transcripts*, pp. 146–7.

10 The unexpurgated versions would have been even worse. Nixon removed many of the cruder formulations and massaged the text in a way that played down some of the more alarming aspects of the private conversations with his associates. The actual tenor of the conversations is conveyed more fully by the new transcriptions produced by Stanley I. Kutler and published in his *Abuse of Power: The New Nixon Tapes* (New York: Free Press, 1997). Here is an extract from Kutler's version of the meeting between the President, Dean and Haldeman on 15 September 1972, the day that seven men arrested in connection with the break-in were indicted by a federal grand jury (a heavily edited version of this conversation was the first transcript to appear in the volume released by Nixon in April 1974):

PRESIDENT NIXON: . . . The Grand Jury is dismissed now?

DEAN: That is correct. They'll, they will have completed and they will let them go, so there will be no continued investigation prompted by the Grand Jury's inquiry. The, uh, GAO [General Accounting Office] report that was referred over to Justice is on a shelf right now because they have hundreds of violations. They've got violations of McGovern's; they've got violations of Humphrey's; they've got Jackson violations, and several hundred congressional violations. They don't want to start prosecuting one any more than they want the other. So that's, uh—

PRESIDENT NIXON: They damn well not prosecute us unless they prosecute all the others . . .

What about, uh, uh, watching the McGovern contributors and all that sort of thing?

DEAN: We've got a, we've got a hawk's eye on that.

PRESIDENT NIXON: Yeah.

DEAN: And, uh, he is, he is not in full compliance.

PRESIDENT NIXON: He isn't?

DEAN: No. . . .

PRESIDENT NIXON: They should just, behave and, and, recognize this—this is, again, this is war. We're getting a few short and it'll be over, and we'll give them a few shots and it'll be over. Don't worry. I wouldn't want to be on the other side right now. Would you? I wouldn't want to be in Edward Bennett Williams's position [lawyer for Democratic Party and the *Washington Post*] after this election.

DEAN: No. No.

PRESIDENT NIXON: None of these bastards—

DEAN: He, uh, he's done some rather unethical things that have come to light already, which in—again [Judge] Richey has brought to our attention.

PRESIDENT NIXON: Yeah.

DEAN: He went down—

HALDEMAN: Keep a log on all that.

DEAN: Oh, we are, indeed. Yeah. . . .

HALDEMAN: Because afterwards that's the guy,

PRESIDENT NIXON: We're going after him.

HALDEMAN: That's the guy we've got to ruin. . . .

PRESIDENT NIXON: You want to remember, too, he's an attorney for the *Washington Post*.

DEAN: I'm well aware of that.

PRESIDENT NIXON: I think we are going to fix the sonofabitch. Believe me. We are going to. We've got to, because he's a bad man.

DEAN: Absolutely

PRESIDENT NIXON: He misbehaved very badly in the Hoffa matter. Our—some pretty bad conduct, there, too, but go ahead.

DEAN: Well, that's, uh, along that line, uh, one of the things I've tried to do, is just keep notes on a lot of the people who are emerging as—

PRESIDENT NIXON: That's right.

DEAN: —as less than our friends.

PRESIDENT NIXON: Great.

DEAN: Because this is going to be over some day and they're—we shouldn't forget the way that some of them (unintelligible)—

PRESIDENT NIXON: I want the most, I want the most comprehensive notes on all of those that have tried to do us in. Because they didn't have to do it.

DEAN: That's right.

PRESIDENT NIXON: They didn't have to do it. I mean, if . . . they had a very close election everybody on the other side would understand this game. But now [they] are doing this quite deliberately and they are asking for it and they are going to get it. And this, this—we have not used the power in this first four years as you know.

DEAN: That's true.

PRESIDENT NIXON: We have never used it. We haven't used the Bureau
and we haven't used the Justice Department, but things are going to
change now. And they're going to change, and, they're going to get it
right—

DEAN: That's an exciting prospect.

PRESIDENT NIXON: It's got to be done. It's the only thing to do.

HALDEMAN: We've got to.

PRESIDENT NIXON: Oh, oh, well, we've been just Goddamn fools. For
us to come into this election campaign and not do anything with regard
to the Democratic Senators who are running, and so forth. They're,
they're crooks, they've been stealing, they've been taking (unintelligible).
That's ridiculous. Absolutely ridiculous. It's not going, going to be that
way any more. . . . (*Abuse of Power*, 148–50)

11 *Chicago Tribune*, 9 May 1974, p. 22. The editorial continues: 'What
manner of man is the Richard Nixon who emerges from the transcripts
of the White House tapes? We see a man who, in the words of his old
friend and defender, Sen. Hugh Scott, took a principal role in a "shabby,
immoral and disgusting performance." The key word here is immoral. It
is a lack of concern for morality, a lack of concern for high principles, a
lack of commitment to the high ideals of public office that make the transcripts a sickening exposure of the man and his advisors.'

12 Lang and Lang, *The Battle for Public Opinion*, p. 126.

13 See Schudson, *Watergate in American Memory*, pp. 18ff.; Suzanne
Garment, *Scandal: The Culture of Mistrust in American Politics* (New York:
Doubleday, 1991), pp. 38ff.

14 See, for example, Mark Hertsgaard, *On Bended Knee: The Press and the
Reagan Presidency* (New York: Farrar Straus Giroux, 1988); John Anthony
Maltese, *Spin Control: The White House Office of Communications and the
Management of Presidential News*, 2nd edn (Chapel Hill: University of
North Carolina Press, 1994); Bob Woodward, *Shadow: Five Presidents
and the Legacy of Watergate* (New York: Simon and Schuster, 1999).

15 For a detailed account of the Iran-Contra affair, see Theodore Draper,
A Very Thin Line: The Iran-Contra Affairs (New York: Hill and Wang,
1991). See also Jonathan Marshall, Peter Dale Scott and Jane Hunter,
*The Iran-Contra Connection: Secret Teams and Covert Operations in the
Reagan Era* (Boston: South End Press, 1987); Robert Williams, *Political
Scandals in the USA* (Edinburgh: Keele University Press, 1998), ch. 3.

16 Oliver L. North with William Novak, *Under Fire: An American Story* (New
York: HarperCollins, 1991), p. 19.

17 Draper argues that, following Meese's interview with North on Sunday
23 November, in which North confirmed that funds had been diverted
to the Contras, a kind of 'panic' had gripped Meese and his closest associates: 'They were haunted by former President Nixon's debacle as a
result of his attempted cover-up in the Watergate case and were determined at all costs to avoid a repetition. Nixon had been forced to resign,

but impeachment now seemed to threaten President Reagan unless he did what Nixon had not done – come out publicly with the information at hand' (*A Very Thin Line*, p. 522).

18 North, *Under Fire*, p. 12.

19 John Poindexter, Testimony before the House and Senate Select Iran-Contra Committees on 15 July 1987, reproduced in *The Iran-Contra Puzzle* (Washington, DC: Congressional Quarterly Inc., 1987), p. C-100.

20 Ibid.

21 Mark Silverstein, 'Watergate and the American Political System', in Markovits and Silverstein, *The Politics of Scandal*, p. 26. See also Thomas Cronin, 'The Swelling of the Presidency', in Ronald E. Pynn (ed.), *Watergate and the American Political Process* (New York: Praeger, 1975); Richard P. Nathan, *The Administrative Presidency* (New York: John Wiley, 1983).

22 See Marshall, Scott and Hunter, *The Iran-Contra Connection*, esp. pp. 7ff.

23 See Bernard Porter, *The Origins of the Vigilant State: The London Metropolitan Police Special Branch before the First World War* (Woodbridge: Boydell Press, 1987).

24 See Christopher Andrew, *Secret Service: The Making of the British Intelligence Community* (London: Heinemann, 1985), ch. 2.

25 Ibid., pp. 500ff.

26 Austen Chamberlain, in *Parliamentary Debates (Commons)*, 5th series, vol. 179 (15 Dec. 1924), col. 674.

27 See David Vincent, *The Culture of Secrecy: Britain, 1832–1998* (Oxford: Oxford University Press, 1998), ch. 3. See also David Hooper, *Official Secrets: The Use and Abuse of the Act* (London: Secker and Warburg, 1987).

28 Porter, *The Origins of the Vigilant State*, pp. 73ff.

29 Ibid., pp. 136ff.

30 Peter Wright with Paul Greengrass, *Spycatcher* (Richmond: Heinemann Australia, 1987).

31 Chapman Pincher, *Their Trade is Treachery* (London: Sidgwick and Jackson, 1981).

32 Andrew Boyle, *The Climate of Treason: Five Who Spied for Russia* (London: Hutchinson, 1979). Boyle used the code-name 'Maurice' to disguise the identity of Anthony Blunt in the first edition of his book.

33 In August 1998 a former MI5 officer, David Shayler, was arrested in France after making allegations in the press about MI5 and MI6 activities, including allegations about British involvement in a plot to assassinate the Libyan leader, Colonel Gaddafi. But in November Shayler was released by a French court, which rejected the British government's attempt to extradite him. In May 1999 the intelligence service was thrown into disarray when the names of 117 individuals, many of whom were active agents in MI6, were made available on the internet. Richard Tomlinson, a disgruntled former MI6 officer who had been sacked from the security services, had threatened to disclose the names of MI6 officers on the internet, but he denied that he had been responsible for making this list public.

34 Concern about dirty tricks by the CIA became particularly marked in the 1970s, following revelations that the CIA had been involved in domestic surveillance (contravening its charter, which restricted the CIA to foreign operations) and allegations that it had been involved in plots to assassinate a number of foreign leaders, including Fidel Castro. In 1975 President Ford, conscious of the need to avoid the appearance of a cover-up in the post-Watergate climate, set up the Rockefeller Commission to investigate these and other allegations. The Senate and the House also established select committees to examine the CIA and other intelligence agencies. In the wake of these inquiries, both the House and the Senate set up new intelligence oversight committees to monitor the CIA. As became clear in the Iran-Contra affair, however, the new restrictions did not prevent the CIA from becoming involved in covert operations which circumvented Congress. For an account of CIA activities in the 1980s, see Bob Woodward, *Veil: The Secret Wars of the CIA, 1981–1987* (London: Simon and Schuster, 1987).

35 The *Rainbow Warrior* was a small boat owned by the environmental organization Greenpeace. In 1985 the boat set off for Mururoa atoll, a French dependency in the South Pacific, to protest against French nuclear weapons tests. On the night of 10 July 1985, while the vessel was moored in the harbour in Auckland, New Zealand, two explosions ripped open the hull and sunk it, killing one member of the crew. Several days later the New Zealand police arrested two people who claimed to be Swiss tourists, but who turned out to be agents of the French security service, the DGSE. As further revelations emerged, it seemed increasingly probable that the sinking of the *Rainbow Warrior* was part of a clandestine military operation which had been authorized at a high level of the French government. The ensuing controversy eventually resulted in the resignation of the French Minister of Defence, Charles Hernu, and the dismissal of the Director General of the DGSE, Admiral Pierre Lacoste. But exactly who knew what in the military and political establishment, and how far the responsibility for this operation could be traced up the chain of command, remained shrouded in uncertainty. Despite allegations to the contrary, President Mitterrand denied that he had known about the operation in advance and rejected suggestions of a cover-up, emerging from the scandal largely unscathed. For a more detailed discussion of the *Rainbow Warrior* affair, see Stephen E. Bornstein, 'The Greenpeace Affair and the Peculiarities of French Politics', in Markovits and Silverstein, *The Politics of Scandal*, pp. 91–121.

36 See Paul Henderson, *The Unlikely Spy: An Autobiography* (London: Bloomsbury, 1993); Richard Norton-Taylor, Mark Lloyd and Stephen Cook, *Knee Deep in Dishonour: The Scott Report and its Aftermath* (London: Victor Gollancz, 1996).

37 Alan Clark, evidence given in the Matrix Churchill trial, reproduced in Sir Richard Scott, *Report of the Inquiry into the Export of Defence and Dual-*

Use Goods to Iraq and Related Prosecutions (London: HMSO, 1996), vol. 3, pp. 1459–61.

38 Henderson and his co-directors were not the only individuals who faced prosecution for alleged infringements of the restrictions on exports to Iraq. Perhaps the best known of the other cases concerned the provision of materials which could be used by the Iraqis to build a long-range artillery piece – what became known as the 'supergun'. In 1990 Christopher Cowley, a Bristol-based engineer who worked for the Space Research Corporation, and Peter Mitchell, the managing director of Walter Somers, a foundry in the West Midlands, were arrested in connection with the supergun affair, but the charges against them were eventually dropped and the case never went to trial.

39 Robin Cook, in *Parliamentary Debates (Commons)*, 6th series, vol. 271 (15 Feb. 1996), col. 1146.

40 A joint report from the cross-party defence, foreign affairs, international development and trade and industry committees, published in February 2000, concluded that there had been no radical shift of policy under Labour on the sale of arms to Indonesia and expressed serious concerns about the supply of defence equipment to Pakistan and Zimbabwe. It also criticized the continuing secrecy surrounding arms sales and expressed dismay that the government had not brought forward legislation to implement the recommendations of the Scott Report. See Defence Committee, Foreign Affairs Committee, International Development Committee, Trade and Industry Committee, *Annual Reports for 1997 and 1998 on Strategic Export Controls* (London: Stationery Office, 2000).

Chapter 8 The Consequences of Scandal

1 See Émile Durkheim, *The Elementary Forms of Religious Life*, trans. Joseph Ward Swain (New York: Free Press, 1965). Elements of a functionalist theory of scandal can be found in the work of the anthropologist Max Gluckman, although Gluckman's analysis is concerned primarily with the functions of scandal (and gossip) in small-scale communities; see Max Gluckman, 'Gossip and Scandal', *Current Anthropology*, 4.3 (1963), pp. 307–16.

2 See Jeffrey C. Alexander, 'Culture and Political Crisis: "Watergate" and Durkheimian Sociology', in Jeffrey C. Alexander (ed.), *Durkheimian Sociology: Cultural Studies* (Cambridge: Cambridge University Press, 1988), pp. 187–224; Jeffrey C. Alexander, 'Three Models of Culture and Society Relations: Toward an Analysis of Watergate', in his *Action and its Environments: Toward a New Synthesis* (New York: Columbia University Press, 1988), pp. 153–74.

3 Alexander, 'Culture and Political Crisis', p. 200.

4 Ibid., p. 208.

5 Ibid., p. 216.

6 Alexander appears to discount this possibility, or at least fails to give it adequate consideration. He maintains that, while Watergate may have undermined public confidence in particular individuals and authorities, the 'ritual effervescence' associated with it 'increased faith in the political "system"' (ibid., p. 213). But this claim is not entirely convincing. One of the difficulties here is that the term 'political system' is ambiguous: it could mean *either* representative democracy as a form of government *or* the institutions (Congress, the Presidency, etc.) that comprise the political system of the United States. Individuals may believe at an abstract level that representative democracy is the best available form of government, and at the same time believe that the institutions which make up their political system are deeply flawed and the individuals who hold office cannot in general be trusted; they may believe in democracy as a form of government and at the same time distrust their government.

7 See Jürgen Habermas, *The Structural Transformation of the Public Sphere: An Inquiry into a Category of Bourgeois Society*, trans. Thomas Burger with the assistance of Frederick Lawrence (Cambridge: Polity Press, 1989).

8 Here I am inventing a line of argument which builds on Habermas's account but which is not actually developed by Habermas himself. One can, however, find many variations on these themes in the literature.

9 For a more detailed historical critique of Habermas's argument, see John B. Thompson, *The Media and Modernity: A Social Theory of the Media* (Cambridge: Polity Press, 1995), pp. 71–5.

10 See John Fiske, *Understanding Popular Culture* (Boston: Unwin Hyman, 1989); *Reading the Popular* (London: Routledge, 1989); and 'Popularity and the Politics of Information', in Peter Dahlgren and Colin Sparks (eds), *Journalism and Popular Culture* (London: Sage, 1992), pp. 45–63.

11 Fiske, 'Popularity and the Politics of Information', pp. 47ff. Fiske distinguishes a third type of news, what he calls 'alternative news', but this is less relevant to the issues which concern us here.

12 Ian Connell, 'Personalities in the Popular Media', in Dahlgren and Sparks, *Journalism and Popular Culture*, p. 74.

13 Fiske, 'Popularity and the Politics of Information', pp. 43ff. The distinction is drawn from Stuart Hall, 'Notes on Deconstructing "The Popular"', in Raphael Samuel (ed.), *People's History and Socialist Theory* (London: Routledge and Kegan Paul, 1981), pp. 227–40.

14 Fiske, 'Popularity and the Politics of Information', p. 54.

15 The importance of networks is highlighted by Lang and Lang in their fine study of the building of artistic reputation by etchers; see Gladys

Engel Lang and Kurt Lang, *Etched in Memory: The Building and Survival of Artistic Reputation* (Chapel Hill: University of North Carolina Press, 1990), esp. pp. 233–47.

16 As Hirschman says of resources like love, trust and civic spirit, 'these are resources whose supply may well increase rather than decrease through use.' See Albert O. Hirschman, 'Against Parsimony: Three Easy Ways of Complicating Some Categories of Economic Discourse', *American Economic Review*, Papers and Proceedings, 74.2 (May 1984), pp. 89–96; the above quote is on p. 93.

17 See Michael Schudson, *Watergate in American Memory: How We Remember, Forget, and Reconstruct the Past* (New York: Basic Books, 1992), pp. 188–202.

18 'The celebrity', remarked Daniel Boorstin, 'is a person who is known for his well-knownness' (Daniel J. Boorstin, *The Image: A Guide to Pseudo-Events in America* (New York: Vintage, 1992), p. 57).

19 See Niklas Luhmann, 'Familiarity, Confidence, Trust: Problems and Alternatives', in Diego Gambetta (ed.), *Trust: Making and Breaking Cooperative Relations* (Oxford: Blackwell, 1988), pp. 94–107; Niklas Luhmann, *Trust and Power* (Chichester: Wiley, 1979).

20 See Robert D. Putnam, *Making Democracy Work: Civic Traditions in Modern Italy* (Princeton: Princeton University Press, 1993), esp. ch. 6.

21 Ibid., pp. 167ff.; James S. Coleman, *Foundations of Social Theory* (Cambridge, Mass.: Harvard University Press, 1990), ch. 12.

22 See Hirschman, 'Against Parsimony', p. 93.

23 See Putnam, *Making Democracy Work*, p. 177.

24 See Diego Gambetta, 'Can We Trust Trust?', in Gambetta, *Trust*, pp. 213–37.

25 See John Dunn, 'Trust and Political Agency', in Gambetta, *Trust*, pp. 73–93.

26 See James D. Wright, *The Dissent of the Governed: Alienation and Democracy in America* (New York: Academic Press, 1976); Vivien Hart, *Distrust and Democracy: Political Distrust in Britain and America* (Cambridge: Cambridge University Press, 1978).

27 See Bernard Barber, *The Logic and Limits of Trust* (New Brunswick, N.J.: Rutgers University Press, 1983), ch. 2. Barber distinguishes two main senses of trust: (1) expectations of technically competent role performance, and (2) expectations of fiduciary obligation and responsibility.

28 See Joseph S. Nye, Jr, Philip D. Zelikow and David C. King (eds), *Why People Don't Trust Government* (Cambridge, Mass.: Harvard University Press, 1997). The decline of trust in government has not been a continuous process; there were modest upswings in the early 1980s and mid-1990s. But the overall pattern of decline is clear from the following graph (taken from *Why People Don't Trust Government*, p. 81). Respondents were asked, 'How much of the time do you think you can trust

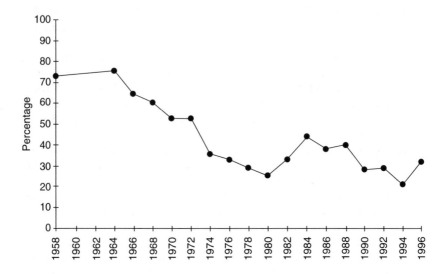

the government in Washington to do what is right – just about always, most of the time, or only some of the time?' The figure traces the percentage who said that they trust the government 'always' or 'most of the time'.

29 See Gary Orren, 'Fall from Grace: The Public's Loss of Faith in Government', in Nye, Zelikow and King, *Why People Don't Trust Government*, pp. 77–107; the survey mentioned is discussed on p. 92. As Orren observes, 'Trust in political and other institutions is closely correlated with the public's perception of the ethics and morality of those institutions' leaders. On both scales, government officials rank low. Americans rate their representatives and senators near the bottom of professions on honesty and ethics – above used-car salesmen but below lawyers' (p. 92).

30 This potential impact of political scandals is recognized by political leaders, who are well aware that relations of trust can be damaged by unwanted disclosures. It is one of the reasons why political leaders may be inclined to respond to major scandals, or to a series of connected but relatively minor scandals, by setting up an official inquiry, like a congressional investigation or a royal commission. Of course, most inquiries of this kind are attempts to discover what really happened, and some may be concerned to ascertain whether there is a case for legal prosecution. But official inquiries are also repair mechanisms which are concerned with trying to restore credibility, to mend and strengthen the fabric of trust which has been torn by a series of damaging revelations.

Conclusion

1 Max Weber, 'Bureaucracy', in H. H. Gerth and C. Wright Mills (eds), *From Max Weber: Essays in Sociology* (London: Routledge and Kegan Paul, 1948), esp. pp. 233–5.

2 For an early and eloquent version of this argument, see Jeremy Bentham, 'Of Publicity', chapter 2 of his *Essay on Political Tactics*, in *The Works of Jeremy Bentham*, vol. 2, ed. John Bowring (Edinburgh: William Tait, 1843), pp. 310–17. 'The greater the number of temptations to which the exercise of political power is exposed,' writes Bentham, 'the more necessary is it to give to those who possess it, the most powerful reasons for resisting them. But there is no reason more constant and more universal than the superintendence of the public' (p. 310).

3 See Sissela Bok, *Secrets: On the Ethics of Concealment and Revelation* (New York: Random House, 1983).

Index